Professional CSS

Cascading Style Sheets for Web Design

Christopher Schmitt
Mark Trammell
Ethan Marcotte
Dunstan Orchard
Todd Dominey

WILEY

Wiley Publishing, Inc.

Professional CSS: Cascading Style Sheets for Web Design

Published by
Wiley Publishing, Inc.
10475 Crosspoint Boulevard
Indianapolis, IN 46256
www.wiley.com

ISBN-13: 978-0-7645-8833-4
ISBN-10: 0-7645-8833-8

Manufactured in the United States of America

10 9 8 7 6 5 4 3 2

1B/RT/QX/QV/IN

For general information on our other products and services or to obtain technical support, please contact our Customer Care Department within the U.S. at (800) 762-2974, outside the U.S. at (317) 572-3993 or fax (317) 572-4002.

Wiley also publishes its books in a variety of electronic formats. Some content that appears in print may not be available in electronic books.

Library of Congress Cataloging-in-Publication Data

Professional CSS : cascading style sheets for Web design / Christopher Schmitt ... [et al.].
      p. cm.
   Includes index.
   ISBN-13: 978-0-7645-8833-4 (paper/website)
   ISBN-10: 0-7645-8833-8 (paper/website)
   1. Web sites—Design. 2. Cascading style sheets. I. Schmitt, Christopher.
   TK5105.888.P674 2005
   006.7—dc22
                              2005012281

About the Authors

Christopher Schmitt is the principal of Heatvision.com, Inc., a new media publishing and design firm based in Tallahassee, Florida. An award-winning Web designer who has been working with the Web since 1993, he interned for both David Siegel and Lynda Weinman in the mid-1990s while an undergraduate at Florida State University pursuing a Fine Arts degree with emphasis on graphic design. He is the author of *The CSS Cookbook* (O'Reilly, 2004) and *Designing CSS Web Pages* (New Riders Press, 2002). He is also the co-author (with Micah Laaker) of *Photoshop CS in 10 Simple Steps or Less* (Wiley, 2004) and contributed four chapters to *XML, HTML, & XHTML Magic* by Molly Holzschlag (New Riders Press, 2001). Christopher has also written for *New Architect* magazine, *A List Apart*, *Digital Web*, and *Web Reference*. In 2000, he led a team to victory in the "Cool Site in a Day" competition, wherein he and five other talented developers built a fully functional, well-designed Web site for a non-profit organization in eight hours. Speaking at conferences such as The Other Dreamweaver Conference and SXSW, he has given talks demonstrating the use and benefits of practical CSS-enabled designs. Also helping to spread the word about Web design, he is the list mom for Babble (`www.babblelist.com`), a mailing list community devoted to advanced Web design and development topics. On his personal Web site, `www.christopherschmitt.com`, he shows his true colors and most recent activities. He is 6'7" tall and does not play professional basketball, but he wouldn't mind a good game of chess.

For Dee. My muse and inspiration for many years and, with hope, many more to come. I would be lost without your wisdom, laughter, empathy, and captivating smiles.

Mark Trammell of Gainesville, Florida, directs the Web presence at the University of Florida.

To Kaye. Your love and abiding support make me who I am. Your joy paints my life with vibrant swaths of color that give memories meaning and our future hope. You are called many things: doctor, lieutenant, professor, wife, but most important, I call you friend.

Ethan Marcotte of Boston co-founded Vertua Studios (`vertua.com`), a Web design shop focused on creating beautiful, user-focused sites. A steering committee member of the Web Standards Project, he is a leading industry voice on standards-based Web design. Ethan is also the curator of `sidesh0w.com`, a popular Web log that is equal parts design, coding, and blather.

Dunstan Orchard of Dorset, UK, and San Francisco is Senior UI Engineer at Apple's online store. He is a member of The Web Standards Project, a silent developer for the popular open source blogging platform Wordpress, and an occasional contributor to his own site at `http://1976design.com/`.

I dedicate my meager portion of this book to my parents and to my girlfriend, Nicole.

Todd Dominey of Atlanta founded Dominey Design (`domineydesign.com`), an interactive Web development and design studio that has produced original work for Budweiser, The Washington Post, Google, Winterfresh Gum, and others. He is also a Senior Interactive Designer at Turner Sports Interactive, designing and developing Web destinations for major PGA tournaments (including the PGA Championship and The Ryder Cup).

Credits

Acquisitions Editor
Debra Williams Cauley

Development Editor
Kevin Shafer

Technical Editor
Molly Holzschlag

Copy Editor
Nancy Rapoport

Editorial Manager
Mary Beth Wakefield

Vice President and Executive Group Publisher
Richard Swadley

Vice President and Publisher
Joseph B. Wikert

Project Coordinator
Michael Kruzil

Graphics and Production Specialists
Lynsey Osborn
Amanda Spagnuolo

Quality Control Technician
Leeann Harney
Carl William Pierce

Proofreading and Indexing
TECHBOOKS Production Services

Foreword

When I met Christopher Schmitt in 1998, he was running *High Five,* the first online magazine dedicated to the art of aesthetic, visually pleasing Web design. To good design, he soon added a commitment to responsible code stewardship. Christopher was an early supporter of The Web Standards Project; in the aftermath of the Browser Wars, he became a tireless and well-learned advocate of CSS design.

Books about CSS-based design are only as good as the CSS and the design they contain. *Professional CSS* boasts the best of both. For this volume, Christopher Schmitt has assembled some of the most talented and influential visual stylists and thinkers designing Web sites today. To make the cut, the designers in this book had to know as much about semantic markup and cascading style sheets as they did about branding, graphic design, and the softer user sciences. (If they also knew from JavaScript and your popular plug-ins, so much the better.) Oh, and they had to be lucid, passionate, entertaining writers — and original thinkers — to boot.

Meeting these tough requirements was a short list of masters: Todd Dominey, Ethan Marcotte, Dunstan Orchard, and Mark Trammell. Each has done incredible things on and for the Web, earning peer respect, winning fame, and above all, satisfying demanding clients while delivering standards-based designs that know everything about the user and nothing of compromise.

As you read this book, you will learn their secrets (including how to include Flash in a standards-based layout without breaking document validity) and discover principles of CSS layout and semantic markup you can put to work on your most challenging professional projects. Please enjoy responsibly.

Jeffrey Zeldman
Founder, Happy Cog Studios
Author, *Designing with Web Standards* (New Riders Press, 2003)

Acknowledgments

Christopher Schmitt: I thank Debra Williams Cauley and the Wiley team for helping me to shepherd the book you are now reading.

Also, special thanks to David Fugate at Waterside for his guidance and support on this project.

With the support of my co-authors Todd, Ethan, Dunstan, and Mark as well as the incomparable Molly as the Technical Editor, the book became better and bolder than my original vision. I thank you all for your hard work.

Special thanks to my family and friends. Their continued support while I was busy managing and writing another book was immeasurable, even those who nodded politely while I ranted about Internet Explorer for Windows.

Mark Trammell: Many thanks to Al, Daniel, Taylor, Joe, Malik, Chuck, Gail, Steve, and Christian for their trust and sage advice. I am truly blessed to serve alongside people who love what they do and why they do it.

Christopher, Dunstan, Ethan, and Todd are among the Web's most talented developers and thoughtful commentators today. I feel privileged and humbled to have worked on this project with them.

Ethan Marcotte: There is a short list of people who need to be thanked when one has written a book such as this, and mine is no different. While Jeffrey Zeldman, Doug Bowman, Dave Shea, and Dan Cederholm are all recognized CSS pioneers, I don't think they receive enough acknowledgment as the talented, inspiring writers they are. I'd like to do so now.

Knowing that Molly Holzschlag was the Technical Editor for this book helped me sleep at night.

I'd like to thank my parents, for talking me down from several ledges during this whole writing business. Richard Ohlsten did the same, and deserves tons of high fives as a result. And while I've not spoken to her in some time, Marion Wells renewed my faith in my writing when I needed it most.

Were it not for Garret Keizer, I wouldn't have the words.

And finally, as I worked through this process, there was one person who was infinitely patient, supportive, and kind. She knows who She is, and there isn't ink enough to thank her properly.

Dunstan Orchard: I acknowledge the help of Douglas Bowman, Mike Davidson, Molly Holzschlag, and my fellow authors.

Todd Dominey: First and foremost, my thanks to everyone at Turner Sports Interactive in Atlanta — notably Phil Sharpe, Michael Adamson, and John Buzzell — for giving me the opportunity to work not just on the 2004 PGA Championship but also The Ryder Cup and numerous other PGA online projects. My participation in this book would not have been possible without their trust and support.

Acknowledgments

Additional thanks to those in the Web development community who early in my professional career provided an immeasurable amount of inspiration and instruction: people like Jeffrey Zeldman, whose tireless promotion of Web standards and well-formed code changed my approach to Web design, and CSS gurus Douglas Bowman, Dan Cederholm, and Dave Shea for not only their continued exploration and experimentation with CSS, but for freely offering their knowledge and code for the rest of the world to benefit from.

Last but certainly not least, my wife, Heather, and our entire family for their support.

Introduction

Designers are traditionally creative types, tending to favor the right brain, while programmers examine the details of a system more clearly, preferring a left-brain mode of thinking. So, when faced with the challenge of designing for the Web, designers are faced with what on the surface appears to be an oxymoron, a *design technology* named cascading style sheets (CSS).

CSS is a Web markup standard set by the Worldwide Web Consortium (W3C) that enables Web designers and developers to define consistent styles in Web pages, and to apply the template to multiple pages. CSS is a valuable tool for streamlining and speeding up Web development, although browser compatibility issues are a major pitfall.

While WYSIWYG Web page editors are getting closer and closer to a complete visual authoring experience, those software applications aren't truly professional CSS design tools. CSS by its nature is a technology that, for the most part, must be written out manually to create compelling work. The problem with that is that most designers have a hard time committing to writing lines of code to get their work done.

Designers who express sheer joy in writing PostScript by hand are hard to find. Designers let Adobe Illustrator (or any similar program) provide a visual authoring environment and hide the coding in the background. All the designer sees is the imagery, while the computer handles the workload.

Another hindrance to using CSS doesn't have anything to do with CSS itself, but rather the implementation of CSS in Web browsers. Browser vendors incorporated the technology into their browsers slowly over time. While CSS support is nearly 100 percent as of now, designers still run into problems when trying to shore up their designs in older or outdated browsers. That means diving into the guts of CSS and coding hacks and workarounds. The bottom line translates into more time writing and revising code, and less time working in WYSIWYG tools.

Does this mean that CSS is this out-of-control or untamable technology? Not in the least, but it does take some concerted effort to wrangle professional-looking designs.

Even if you know the basics of CSS (the properties, the acceptable values, the selectors, and so on), putting the technology to effective use can be difficult to downright frustrating. CSS stymies the best of us — even those who actually understand the W3C specifications as opposed to those who can only skim them in awe in their browsers.

In the right hands, however, CSS is *the* tool.

Once designers have mastered the basics of the technology, the understanding of its purpose, and have obtained a certain amount of experience with the technology, almost any design idea sketched on a cocktail napkin or doctored in Adobe Photoshop becomes possible.

To help you get to that point, keep *Professional CSS* nearby.

Professional CSS is one of the few books on the market today that address designing standards-based CSS on large, multi-page, well-designed, real-world sites using CSS in an integrated fashion. Focusing on the best-practices aspect of Web development, and using examples from real-world Web sites, this book uniquely offers applied, CSS-enabled solutions to design problems.

Whom This Book Is For

Those designers who understand CSS at an intermediate to advanced level, but who are not clear on how to effectively develop CSS-enabled designs at a professional level, will benefit tremendously from the information in this book. In particular, the following readers will find this book most useful:

- ❑ **Intermediate to experienced HTML users new to CSS.** Any professional Web developer who has been exposed to CSS, but needs a better understanding of how to put the pieces together to create professional-level Web sites.

- ❑ **Professional designers.** Professional Web developers learning CSS (without any knowledge of traditional, 1990s-era design practices) and want to understand the best practices for utilizing the technology.

How This Book Is Structured

Core chapters of this book focus on one designer and a Web site that designer worked on. Each chapter provides easily digestible demonstrations of CSS tips and techniques used for the site. Additionally, designers provide greater insight into their process by talking about what they would have done differently.

Following is a brief overview of how this book is organized and which co-authors have contributed their insights:

- ❑ **Chapter 1, "The Planning and Development of Your Site."** To get things rolling, you must be familiar with all the preliminaries that proven professionals iron out before they begin working on their sites. This chapter helps you avoid problems later in the development of your site by properly planning what must be done.

- ❑ **Chapter 2, "Best Practices for XHTML and CSS."** Ethan Marcotte, a steering committee member of the Web Standards Project and a recognized leader of the standards-based Web design movement, shares some insights on using Extended HTML (XHTML) with CSS.

❏ **Chapter 3, "Blogger: Rollovers and Design Improvements."** Dunstan Orchard, also a member of the Web Standards Project, delves into the behind-the-scenes development of a new look and feel for blogger.com (a Google Web log site). Orchard's interview with one of the principals in the project, Douglas Bowman (an influential designer whose highly publicized and hugely successful redesigns of several Web sites have pushed him to the forefront of standards-compliant Web design), provides some extremely valuable insight. This chapter also addresses key issues such as bounding boxes and rollovers.

❏ **Chapter 4, "The PGA Championship."** As a Senior Interactive Designer at Turner Sports Interactive, Todd Dominey has been designing and developing Web destinations for major Professional Golf Association (PGA) tournaments, including the PGA Championship and The Ryder Cup. In this chapter, Dominey provides a first-hand perspective on the ins and outs of designing a site relied upon by millions of sports fans all over the world. Key issues addressed in this chapter include drop shadows, drop-down menus, and embedding Flash content into a Web site.

❏ **Chapter 5, "The University of Florida."** Mark Trammell, who is in charge of directing the Web presence at one of the country's leading universities, discusses how the University of Florida developed a Web site to benefit both students and faculty. Key issues addressed in this chapter include tackling browser compatibility issues, as well as developing functional navigational structures.

❏ **Chapter 6, "ESPN.com: Powerful Layout Changes."** Dunstan Orchard talks with Mike Davidson, Senior Associate Art Directory and Manager of Media Product Development at the Walt Disney Internet Group, about an extremely effective makeover for ESPN.com. Orchard discusses how designers were able to develop a site that provides the flexibility required by an organization feeding its readers up-to-date sports information.

❏ **Chapter 7, "FastCompany.com: Building a Flexible Three-Column Layout."** Ethan Marcotte sat down with Dan Cederholm to discuss the extreme makeover of the Web site for Fast Company, publisher of a popular magazine by the same name. In addition to this provocative interview, Marcotte presents tips on CSS positioning and, in particular, details surrounding effective three-column layouts.

❏ **Chapter 8, "Stuff and Nonsense: Strategies for CSS Switching."** In addition to an interview with Andy Clarke (Creative Director for Stuff and Nonsense), Ethan Marcotte explores how to improve Web site accessibility for all users to further ensure universal access. In this chapter, Marcotte delves into CSS switching and ways to overcome pesky browser compatibility problems. The innovations displayed at the Stuff and Nonsense site provide excellent examples of these techniques.

❏ **Chapter 9, "Bringing It All Together."** Lead author Christopher Schmitt uses his own successful Web site development to show how all the tips and techniques presented in the book can be put to practical use.

Additionally, the appendixes in this book provide handy reference material for HTML 4.01 elements, rules for HTML-to-XHTML conversions, properties of CSS 2.1, and even a troubleshooting guide to help with common problems.

Conventions

To help you get the most from the text and keep track of what's happening, we've used a number of conventions throughout the book.

> **Boxes like this one hold important, not-to-be-forgotten information that is directly relevant to the surrounding text.**

Tips, hints, tricks, and asides to the current discussion are offset and placed in italics like this.

As for styles in the text:

- ❏ We *highlight* important words when we introduce them.
- ❏ We show keyboard strokes like this: Ctrl+A.
- ❏ We show filenames, URLs, and code within the text like so: `persistence.properties`.
- ❏ We present code in two different ways:

```
In code examples we highlight new and important code with a gray background.
```

```
The gray highlighting is not used for code that's less important in the present
context, or has been shown before.
```

Errata

We make every effort to ensure that there are no errors in the text or in the code. However, no one is perfect, and mistakes do occur. If you find an error in one of our books, such as a spelling mistake or faulty piece of code, we would be very grateful for your feedback. By sending in errata you may save another reader hours of frustration and at the same time you will be helping us provide even higher quality information.

To find the errata page for this book, go to `www.wrox.com` and locate the title using the Search box or one of the title lists. Then, on the book details page, click the Book Errata link. On this page you can view all errata that has been submitted for this book and posted by Wrox editors. A complete book list including links to each book's errata is also available at `www.wrox.com/misc-pages/booklist.shtml`.

If you don't spot "your" error on the Book Errata page, go to `www.wrox.com/contact/ techsupport.shtml` and complete the form there to send us the error you have found. We'll check the information and, if appropriate, post a message to the book's errata page and fix the problem in subsequent editions of the book.

p2p.wrox.com

For author and peer discussion, join the P2P forums at p2p.wrox.com. The forums are a Web-based system for you to post messages relating to Wrox books and related technologies and interact with other readers and technology users. The forums offer a subscription feature to e-mail you topics of interest of your choosing when new posts are made to the forums. Wrox authors, editors, other industry experts, and your fellow readers are present on these forums.

At http://p2p.wrox.com you will find a number of different forums that will help you not only as you read this book, but also as you develop your own applications. To join the forums, just follow these steps:

1. Go to p2p.wrox.com and click the Register link.
2. Read the terms of use and click Agree.
3. Complete the required information to join as well as any optional information you wish to provide and click Submit.
4. You will receive an e-mail with information describing how to verify your account and complete the joining process.

You can read messages in the forums without joining P2P, but in order to post your own messages you must join.

Once you join, you can post new messages and respond to messages other users post. You can read messages at any time on the Web. If you would like to have new messages from a particular forum e-mailed to you, click the Subscribe to this Forum icon by the forum name in the forum listing.

For more information about how to use the Wrox P2P, be sure to read the P2P FAQs for answers to questions about how the forum software works as well as many common questions specific to P2P and Wrox books. To read the FAQs, click the FAQ link on any P2P page.

Contents

Contents

Contents

Contents

1

The Planning and Development of Your Site

In the past few years, the design community has seen an explosion of sites powered by cascading style sheets (CSS). Highly visible brands such as Fast Company, ESPN.com, PGA, and Blogger have all adopted CSS for the layout of their sites, delivering their compelling content through this excellent Web technology. Their pages have become lighter and more accessible, while a few style sheet files provide them with global control over the user interface of their entire site. The potential of CSS has been well established by these mainstream sites, and the technology (which languished since its introduction in 1996) is quickly becoming the *de facto* means by which a site's design is built.

However, while CSS has been elevated to near-buzzword status, it's important to remember that style sheets are simply a tool to be used in the overall design and development of your Web site. Granted, that tool is an incredibly powerful one, but it can only *facilitate* high-powered, professional-looking Web sites. Although using style sheets can afford you an unprecedented level of control over your site's design, no technology is a silver bullet. Despite what technology evangelists might tell you, adopting CSS won't inherently make your site more usable, your design more compelling, or your breath more wintergreen-fresh.

So, if we put aside the buzz for a moment, we can see that although CSS is an incredibly important aspect of a Web site's development, it should be viewed in the context of that site's entire lifecycle. In this chapter, we'll discuss the following topics:

- ❑ Understanding your project's scope
- ❑ Establishing the goals for your project
- ❑ The fundamentals of information architecture
- ❑ How to begin your site's design

Establish the Scope

If we were asked to build a house, there are a few questions we'd want answered before agreeing to do the work. How large will the house be? How many rooms? What kind of budget is allocated for this project? All of these questions are meant to establish the *scope* of the construction project. It's a means of gathering information about the project, so that you can more intelligently assess its needs. By establishing the scope of the project, we can better understand exactly how involved the project is, how long it will take to complete, and how much it will cost — all items that are integral to any formal contract.

If you can't tell by now, our construction metaphors aren't exactly our strongest point. But while we might have been snoozing through those episodes of *This Old House*, the parallels to the start of a Web project are uncanny. Before firing up Photoshop or slinging one line of code, you and your client should work together to produce a well-reasoned *scope statement*. This aptly named document not only determines what work will be performed throughout the duration of the project, but also implicitly defines what work is *outside* the scope of the project. This is an incredibly important point. When the deadlines are tight and the expectations high, knowing exactly what is expected of you throughout the course of the project will keep your budget in check, and both you and your client focused.

Most frequently, the scope statement contains the following information:

❑ **Strategy.** This contains some information about the goals and business needs behind the project. Is the site you're designing supposed to increase advertising revenue, or shore up readership numbers? Is the project supposed to increase a site's accessibility, or its search engine ranking?

❑ **Deliverables.** These are the products that will be created over the course of the project. If your project involves some level of site planning, will you be building a site map, or providing wireframes? When the project is finished, will you provide the client with all the Photoshop files used in your designs?

❑ **Assumptions.** This is all of the conditions and constraints that were used to establish the scope and upon which all other timelines and goals are founded. Should any of these initial assumptions change, the scope of the project should be revised accordingly. For example, if initial client meetings uncover only 30 pages on the site that need to be built, then the landscape (and your estimated budget) can change rather drastically when the client informs you two weeks into the project that it has another 300 pages it would like you to redesign.

❑ **Scope management.** No matter how extensively you document your assumptions and timelines, someone will invariably request changes during the course of your project. Whether it's Murphy's Law or bad karma, it doesn't matter — you and your client need to acknowledge that this change will likely occur and mutually agree upon some process for handling it. Some developers will write a separate document detailing how these changes are managed, and how the client approves the resulting changes in schedule and budget.

This isn't an exhaustive list, nor should it be seen as definitive. As we'll no doubt harp at you throughout the remainder of this book, each project has its own needs, its own goals. Because of this, each scope statement should be tailored to reflect this.

However, it is important to remember that it is the project scope that forms the basis for whatever contract you and your client establish. Because of this, the gathering of the requirements should be a highly collaborative process. You and your client should work closely together to flesh out exactly what information should go into the scope statement. Otherwise, if you and your client have differing expectations as to what work falls under the auspices of the project scope, then problems may arise as deadlines approach.

Determining Roles and Responsibilities

No person is an island, and the same is especially true of Web contractors. Every project requires some level of coordination with additional people, whether they are members of your team, or stakeholders from the client's company. As such, a successful project becomes less about providing a set of deliverables at a specific time, and more about managing the different members of the project team. Clearly communicating the expectations placed on every member of the project will help ensure that deadlines are met on time, on budget, and above the client's expectations.

At some point in your professional career, you'll be staffed on a project where its requirements exceed your abilities as an individual. This isn't something to dread, however. Rather, discuss with your client that their project's scope requires additional resources to meet the deadlines, so that you can plan your budget accordingly.

In either scenario, it might be helpful to sketch out a table that outlines not only the various roles distributed throughout your team, but their responsibilities as well. In the following table, we've banged out a rough sketch of what the average project team might look like. Even if you're the sole resource working on a project, this exercise can be quite helpful. Acting in multiple roles can be quite a juggling act throughout the duration of a contract, and a table such as this can help you identify exactly what is required of you, and with whom you'll need to interact.

Role	Responsibilities	Deliverables
Project manager	The overall traffic manager, overseeing the project's progress from gathering requirements to delivery. Works with the client sponsor to define the scope and requirements of the project.	Scope statement (co-author); timelines.
Project sponsor	This primary point-of-contact at the client company defines business requirements, and provides sign-off at various stages of the project.	Scope statement (co-author); creative brief; any additional materials deemed necessary for gathering of requirements.
Information architect	Develops the site's infrastructure and establishes interface guidelines that are both intuitive and scalable.	Site map; wireframes.
Web designer	Establishes the site's visual design, or "look-and-feel."	Graphic mockups; static HTML templates (as well as necessary CSS/image assets); style guide.
Web developer	Responsible for any server-side programming when building a dynamic, database-driven Web site.	Functional specification; application server installation/configuration.
Database developer	Builds the database that will house the Web site's content, and drive other dynamic aspects of the site.	Data model; database installation/configuration.

3

In the first column, we've identified the different roles that are distributed throughout our project team. From there, we've outlined a brief overview of the expectations that will be placed upon them over the course of the project lifecycle. While it's nearly impossible to accurately capture everything that a Web designer is responsible for in fewer than 12 words, this brief synopsis should at least convey the most important aspects of the role. Additionally, we've outlined the specific items each member will deliver over the course of the project. These deliverables should be drawn directly from the scope of the project and matched up to the individual best equipped to deliver them.

Also, you may notice that we've included a "project sponsor" on this table, which is a member of the client organization that shepherds the project from inception to completion. While perhaps not as integrated into the day-to-day execution of project goals and requirements as the rest of your team, this person exercises veto power in critical decisions, defines the business needs that drive the project's goals, and ultimately facilitates communication between your team and other stakeholders from the client company. As a result, this person is integral to the success of your project. Any additional information for which they are responsible should be tracked closely, as though they were a part of your project team.

Budgeting Time and Expectations

After you've assessed the different needs of your project, you will be in a better position to determine how long it will take, and exactly how much it will cost. "Time is money," of course, but that's rarely more true than within the bounds of a consulting engagement. Granted, it's a fine thing to discuss strategy, scope, and staffing, but it's your project's budget that will determine whether or not any of those things actually come to fruition. With a properly established budget, you can begin to add people and technical resources to your project plan, as well as any other expenses that your project might require.

Furthermore, the amount of money allocated to a given project can limit the size of your team. Perhaps our project plan requires two developers and one designer but funds exist only for two full-time resources. As a result, something must go: either reduce the number of staff on our project, or reduce the scope of the project to the point at which two people can easily handle it.

Conversely, the budget could affect the quality of our team: if the funds are not available to hire an experienced application developer, then we might need to hire a less-expensive (and perhaps less-seasoned) resource instead. Or, if the budget is especially tight, *we* just might need to pick up that Perl book and start skimming. Therefore, a solid understanding of any budgetary constraints will help us understand the extent to which we'll need to bootstrap our own skills or those of our team members, and how that preparation will affect timelines.

Managing Change

Let's say that we're nervously eyeing the clock two hours from site launch. We're looking at the last few items on our to-do list and are feeling a bit pressed for time before the site's go-live. Just then, our client sponsor strolls up to say that *his* boss wants some holiday e-cards designed, and that they should go live with the newly rebranded site (this has never happened to us, we swear). Just like that, our priorities have been told to shift, but the project's timelines haven't budged an inch.

This is what is known as "scope creep" and is a part of almost every project. At some point, the requirements outlined at the beginning of the contract may need to be updated to reflect some new or updated business requirement. If our project can't adapt to our client's needs, then we're likely working on the best product they'll never be able to use. So, while this kind of change is expected, it is very important to know how to manage it effectively. No designer wants his or her timelines in a constant state of flux, especially when the budget isn't. How, then, do we manage scope creep within a project? There is no easy answer to this question, but there are a few strategies that might be useful to keep in mind.

Introducing Sign-Off

Once a particular deliverable has been finished and presented to a client, it is usually a good idea to ask the client to formally "sign off" on the work. This sign-off can take the form of an e-mail from the client, minutes from meeting notes, or preferably a physical signed document. No matter the form it takes, it should formally document the client's approval of what has just been delivered. By securing the client's sign-off on a given deliverable, the client confirms that our work meets the requirements that the client set before us. In effect, the client is telling us, "Yes, this is what we asked you to provide for us—let's move on."

Some designers might call this "blazing a paper trail." The rationale frequently is one of offloading accountability onto our client's shoulders: that if any future changes must occur, the fault—and incurred cost—lies not with us as consultants, but upon the client's revised requirements. And, on the face of it, this thinking has a lot of appeal. Whenever possible, we should toe a hard line with the established scope, and ensure that the agreed-upon requirements change as little as possible before the project's completion. Sign-off is one way to help ensure this, enabling us to point to completed work should we ever be asked to undertake time-consuming revisions.

Viewed in a more positive (and somewhat less mercenary) note, sign-off can be a valuable means to increase the level of collaboration between consultant and client. Sign-off provides a scheduled touchpoint for our clients, allowing them to check in on progress made to date. In this, the client almost becomes another member of the project team. Formalizing the approval process integrates the client's decisions into the project lifecycle, and increases the level of interest the client has vested in maintaining the project's momentum.

And on the subject of momentum, sign-off is in itself a valuable device for maintaining a sense of progress from project inception to final delivery. Over the course of a given project, you may find that most deliverables cannot be built unless another has been completed. For example, it isn't possible to begin building HTML templates of our designs if the mockups haven't been finalized—or rather, the template process becomes extremely lengthy and expensive if the design is still undergoing revision. By requiring sign-off on a particular phase of work before the next phase can begin, you can help ensure that your work is delivered on-time and on-budget. That should make parties on both sides of the negotiating table quite happy.

Refer Frequently to the Project Scope

While the scope statement enables us to define the requirements for our project, it also implicitly establishes what is *not* in the agreed-upon scope—a critical point when deadlines are tight and client expectations high. It's important to have established this baseline with your client.

This is where the collaboratively authored aspect of the scope document becomes most important. By working closely with the client at the outset of the project to define its scope, the client has a more concrete understanding of how that scope (and any changes to it) will affect both pricing and timelines. That's not to say that this will mitigate any and all potential scope changes. Rather, it will help facilitate any later reviews of the original proposal and allow both sides of the contract to more intelligently and openly discuss how the new changes will affect schedule and pricing.

Frame the Work Within Your Budget

From this, it's important to remember that the project's budget can be a valuable tool in mitigating scope creep. Just as our scope statement helps us understand what is out of our project's jurisdiction, so, too, can our budget help us mitigate unnecessary changes. If there are insufficient funds for a requested change, then the issue is quickly rendered moot.

Failing that, it's worth discussing with our client just exactly how this change will impact the budget and the project timelines. Frequently, the relationship between additional work and additional time or cost is forgotten in the heat of a fast-paced project. By demonstrating that X amount of work will require Y additional dollars at Z billable hours, we can work with our client to assess exactly how much of a priority the scope change actually is. (We were never especially good at algebra, but please bear with us.)

This might sound as though we're trying to get out of additional work—quite the opposite, in fact (after all, we must pay for those plane tickets to Bali). Rather, it's our responsibility as contractors to help our clients attach a quantitative measure of importance to that work; namely, does the amount of additional time and funds justify the importance of this new project? Weighed in this manner, this latest work can be assessed by our clients against the other parts of the project scope. If the scope change is ultimately decided to be a must-have, then we can work with our client to decide how to proceed—should the timeline and budget for the project be revised, or should some other aspect of the project be foregone to usher in this new task.

Moving Forward

Of course, if the client is willing to alter the scope and the budget to accommodate a vital change, then we need to be equally flexible. Much as we did before beginning the project, we need to establish the scope for the requested change. What kind of work will it entail? How long will it take? How many resources will it require? Once these questions have been answered, we can more accurately estimate exactly *how* this scope creep will affect the project as a whole. If designing those holiday cards will require three days of design and review, then that needs to be communicated to our client. While we might not be able to produce what they're asking for in the requested time, an open and frank discussion about how long this request will take—and how it will therefore impact the larger project—will often follow.

While discussions of pricing and process are no doubt difficult ones to have with your clients, it is extremely important to remain firm on these issues. If it helps, try not to see these discussions as a means to protect the bottom line. Rather, every client will try to test the limits of the project's scope; the more you capitulate to out-of-scope requests on short notice, the more they will anticipate and expect this behavior. This can quickly lead to projects that fly wildly off of the original specification and schedule, which will in turn push back delivery dates. Neither the designer nor the client will be pleased with this result. Therefore, maintaining a firm (but fair) line on these issues will help you meet the project goals—and your client's expectations—successfully.

Constant Communication

Not to sound too much like a greeting card, but communication is quite possibly *the* element that determines a project's success. Conversely, the lack of effective communication can run an otherwise well-planned project aground. As the project manager, you must remain in constant touch with your clients about the status of the project, potential shifts in scope, upcoming delivery dates, and milestones. In short, the more touchpoints you can maintain with your client about how the project is progressing, the better. We've never been on a project that ran off-track because of too much communication. However, we've definitely seen instances where insufficient contact met with disaster.

Designer, Know Thy Goals

There's an implied "All of Them" at the end of this section's heading because any project carries with it a small army of distinct (and, at times, competing) goals. The Rational Unified Process, a software project management methodology (`http://ibm.com/software/awdtools/rup/`), establishes the goals for a project by defining the *Critical Success Factors*, often referred to as CSFs. These factors are something like a laundry list that will help you determine when the project has completed. Some sample CSFs might include:

- ❑ Build for-pay subscription newsletter service into site.
- ❑ Increase traffic by 40 percent over 6 months.
- ❑ Redesign home page to allow for rotation of 728×60 banner ads above the company logo.

There's nothing especially surprising here, and it is, in fact, a rather modest list of business requirements that are key to the success of the project.

Of course, things become complicated when we try to establish *whose* factors define a successful site. In other words, who are the project's "stakeholders"? Who can benefit from the project's successful completion? Conversely, who would be affected by a less-than-successful Web site?

While a client might undertake a redesign to gain more space for advertising on a site (and therefore shore up the company's advertising revenue), this requirement could conflict with users that are just trying to find a particular article buried beneath the banner ads. So, while your redesign might meet the established business goals with flying colors, the site's users might consider the project an unmitigated failure.

So, if business and user needs are in competition, exactly to *whom* are we supposed to listen? As much as we'd like to, we can't give you an easy answer to that question. Obviously, we can't treat business and user needs as an "either/or" scenario. Rather, it is our responsibility to perform a rather delicate balancing act between business and user goals, and ensure (somehow) that both are represented in the work we ultimately produce.

Your Client's Goals

If your project is to be of any value to the client, it must advance the client's business objectives. Frequently, our clients are outside of our own industry. Whether the client comes from the print industry, the automotive industry, or has a small business looking to establish an online presence, they often have little experience with the *how* of Web design. After all, that's why they're talking to us. We have been tasked to take their particular business requirements and goals and realize them online. Of course, the lack of industry understanding works both ways. We often have as little experience with our clients' industries as they do with ours.

Therefore, it's important that both sides of the equation get to know each other. When gathering requirements for your project, find out everything you can about the client, and the context in which the client company operates. It's not possible for us to know too much about the client's industry, business, and goals (both short- and long-term). No question is too basic. We must find out as much as we can about the client's industry, potential sales markets, marketing strategies, and competitors. This knowledge will only help us as we plan and execute a project that will meet the client's needs.

Of course, as we're gathering this information, we should explain our own work as thoroughly and clearly as possible. We should tell our client a story about what this Web project might look like, from beginning to end. We can explain what we'll be building, and what kinds of deliverables we will produce at different stages of the project. But more than explaining *what* we produce, we should explain *why* our projects are structured as they are — we can describe why a site map is important, or why design mockups must be finalized before any HTML can be coded. In doing so, we can demystify the project lifecycle for our clients, and help them better understand the sequence of events that lead them to a successful project end.

Your Audience's Needs

If you were building a house for yourself, you could immediately dive into the planning without taking anyone else's goals into account. Because you're the only person who will be living in your little shack *de résistance*, you can take wild liberties with the structure, layout, and aesthetic of your house. Go on, put the bathroom in the middle of the kitchen — we won't tell anyone, honest. Of course, if you ever have any guests over for dinner, you can bet that you'll get some puzzled glances, and more than a couple questions about what you were thinking.

However, when designing a Web site, our own needs and preferences are the last that we should consider. Rather, we design for others, for our users. If we build a site supplied with world-class content, but the user can't figure out how to navigate beyond the home page, then we've failed not only our users, but in our design as well. A successful, user-centered design can yield high traffic, a flourishing community of satisfied users; an unusable site nets you a high degree of dissatisfaction, the size of which will likely be inversely proportionate to the size of your audience.

Of course, unlike the guests at that ill-fated dinner party, it's a bit more difficult to figure out what your users want. As a result, it's far too easy to leave them out of the equation entirely when we make plans for our sites. Instead, we discuss our pages as a collection of features, areas of functionality, or disparate areas of content. That can easily be a rather cold way of assessing your site — and you can bet that your users will give you the cold shoulder, hurrying off to find a site that helps them achieve their goals, rather than hindering them.

Creating Personas: Putting a Face to Your Audience

So, how do we make a site more usable when we've never met a single one of our users? Given just how virtual our little medium is, our users are often invisible to us. So, instead of thinking of them as a faceless mass of surfers clicking through page after page of our site, we can create *personas* (or user profiles) that give our users a face. Personas are model users who can help you better understand the needs, behavior, and goals of your users. In creating these fictitious profiles, you can better understand and anticipate the behavior patterns of the people who will actually use your site.

Figure 1-1 shows a sample persona.

While Frank is a fabricated user, his usefulness derives from the fact that he is *strategically* fictitious: his biography, aspirations, and professional goals are all drawn from trends sampled from your site's users. By doing so, a persona becomes a valuable guide through the planning, design, and development process. It allows you to put a face to the otherwise faceless people who will be visiting your site, and allows you to avoid the pitfall of basing design decisions on technical or personal biases. Rather than asking yourself how *you* might navigate a certain page, you can ask yourself how your persona might do so. It's a tactic meant to humanize the design process, yes — but ultimately, the quality of your site will improve, as will your users' satisfaction with it.

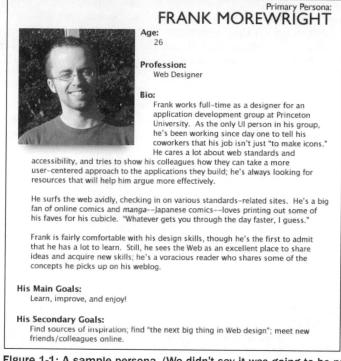

Figure 1-1: A sample persona. (We didn't say it was going to be pretty.)

So, how do we actually create a persona? There are a number of ways to begin this process. The one you pick will ultimately depend on the scope of the project, and the amount of energy you're able to commit to it.

The first (and least "time-expensive") option is to assess what you know of your audience from various internal sources. Examining your site's server logs isn't a bad place to start. These files can give you valuable technical information about your users. At the base of it, this research will yield some important technical demographics: you'll be able to assess what kind of browser landscape exists in your audience and on what operating systems they view the Web. As you'll see in later chapters, each browser has a number of CSS bugs and rendering idiosyncrasies. Knowing what browsers you must support will play a critical role in the development and testing of your site.

Furthermore, you might be able to glean some valuable geographic data as well. As they troll through your site's pages, each visitor will leave their IP address in their wake. From this bit of information, various log analysis tools can tell you from what parts of the world your users originate. Why is this important? If you're building a site for an international audience, your design should be able to speak to people of multiple languages and cultures. For example, will your site's icons convey the same meaning to an American audience as they would to a German one, or even to a user from Singapore? Knowing from *where* your site's audience comes is as important as knowing *what* your audience wants.

> There are a number of log analysis tools available to you in conducting this research. AW Stats (`http://awstats.sourceforge.net`) is a freely available log analyzer that can analyze log formats for such popular Web servers as Apache's httpd and Microsoft's IIS. Webalizer

(www.mrunix.net/webalizer/) is a similar package, but works only with Apache log formats. ShortStat (www.shauninman.com/mentary/past/shortstat_maintenance.php) is a PHP application that can track various kinds of user data. These are only three such packages, and there are dozens, if not hundreds, of alternatives available. Each has its own strengths and weaknesses, which should be assessed according to your needs and technical requirements.

In addition to analyzing server logs, you should interview the site's stakeholders. These are the decision makers, the people who drive the direction of not only the site, but also the business behind it. These people will have a strong bead on the site's audience, and ideally have had close contact with them. As such, they can provide valuable insight into your users' needs, and into which areas of the site would be most relevant to them.

Of course, the best method of creating effective personas is setting aside internal statistics and assumptions, and actually *meeting* some of your users—after all, facts and figures can go only so far in identifying just what it is that your users value. At some point, you need to set aside quantitative data for qualitative interviews; there is no substitute for sitting down with people who will (or currently do) use the pages you're designing. Talking with them about their needs and goals not only creates a vital feedback loop for you as the site's designer, but also helps you put real-life anecdotes and experiences behind the design decisions you'll be making. For example, you might poll your users on any of the following points:

❑ **Technical information.** What kind of browser do they use, and on what kind of computer? How do they use the Web? *Why* do they use the Web?

❑ **Customer information.** How do they view the site of your company or client? Do they use it? What do they think of the site's competitors?

❑ **Personal information.** This might include such information as age, gender, and location (for example, urban or rural).

❑ **Design preferences.** How would they define a "good" site design? While you might not ask them to leap into an art school–esque dissection of a given site's design, you might ask them to tell you some of their favorite sites. Try to find out why those sites are their favorites. Additionally, you could try to uncover what sites they like least, and why.

Of course, this isn't a comprehensive list—the goal of any user sampling is to get as much data as possible that will be helpful to you in your design effort. But rather than just seeing this as a data-mining initiative, think of it as a series of conversations with real people. While demographic information and technical statistics are vital to planning your site's development, collecting anecdotes and quotes from actual people will help to create a more effective persona. Remember that these are ostensibly the individuals that will be visiting your site, and whose needs your design will need to address. When you think of them as *users*, your design suffers; when you think of them as *people*, your site will be all the more successful.

Once you've collected as much data as possible, the analysis begins. By sifting through your notes, trends should emerge. An overwhelming percentage of your users might use the Macintosh version of Internet Explorer; a large minority of your users might be color blind, or suffer from poor vision; a high number might be working mothers, or perhaps teachers looking to acquire professional development credit. More than likely, your audience will be multifaceted, and could contain any or all of the above. But no matter the spectrum that your users cover, it's important to keep these seemingly disparate characteristics in mind as you sit down to write your personas—because just like your "real" users, your persona may not be able to be easily categorized.

In fact, the best place to start working on your persona is probably the narrative, or the persona's biography. This is the meat of the persona, and is where the credibility of this virtual user is established. If you have a gift for embellishment, this isn't a bad time to flex those creative muscles. While you might want to communicate your persona's lack of technical expertise (and, in doing so, remind the developers that your users aren't especially Web-savvy), try to think up a few fictional details about his or her life:

- ❑ Is your persona married?
- ❑ Does your persona have any children?
- ❑ What about hobbies? Perhaps your persona is a cigar aficionado, reads avidly, or was president of his or her high school chess club.

All of these details might seem superfluous when your project deadlines are looming, but this extra level of creativity can help your persona leap off the page and into the forefront of your mind while you're planning your site.

Once you've completed the narrative, add the finishing touches that will complete the picture:

- ❑ **Name.** A real name, such as Nathan, Molly, Jon, and so on.
- ❑ **Age.** The age of your persona.
- ❑ **Work environment.** What kind of computer does your persona use in the office? How fast is his or her connection to the Internet?
- ❑ **Technical frustrations.** What does your persona find difficult about working online? What makes him or her want to close her browser window in sheer frustration?
- ❑ **Photo.** A photo.

Ideally, your personas should be around one to two pages long, chock-full of important details about your users' needs, as well as those personal details that make the personas come alive. That said, there is no hard-and-fast rule to determine when you're finished working on your personas. Most projects will benefit from a relatively small number of personas; popular opinion ranges anywhere from two to seven personas. Ultimately, *you* are the best judge of your project's specific needs. By better understanding your audience, you can then begin to assess the second most important part of your site: its content, and how your users should access it.

Information Architecture

For a moment, take a look at this book that you're holding. It comprises several hundred pages, each of which might contain a few dozen (we hope worthwhile) concepts. Now, were you presented with all of those ideas printed on one huge piece of paper in a random order, you'd likely ask the bookseller for your money back. There is no way that you could easily find any information on CSS, and this book would be utterly useless to you. Thankfully, you're spared that experience. At every stage of the book's development, there has been a constant attempt to bring order out of this conceptual jumble, on levels both large and small. The goals of the book were established, and then the topics that the book needed to cover were outlined. From those general topics came chapters, and within each chapter came section outlines and headings.

But there's more at play here than simply creating an outline and then tossing in a few paragraphs (or at least, we hope it looks that way). Rather, thought has been given to how the order of these content areas must make sense to you, the reader. Without that consideration for how *you* will read the book—how you will *interface* with the content therein—we might as well have saved everyone some time and printed everything out on that long sheet of paper.

In contemporary Web-speak, *information architecture* (IA) is the term most used to refer to this process. On the face of it, information architecture is a means through which you can define the internal organization of a Web site: to take all of the content for your site, divide it up into easily digestible chunks, and subsequently create a logical navigation structure that makes those chunks easily accessible by your users.

But taken simply in those terms, IA could be seen as a glorified job for a librarian: write down some discrete piece of content on an index card, and file it away in a well-labeled drawer so that someone else might access it. At the heart of it, IA isn't simply about content categorization and site structure. Instead, think of it as imposing order on an otherwise chaotic set of information, in a method that will allow others to more easily interface with it. In fact, the word "interface" implies this two-way street between user and site. Your site might have the most compelling content available online, but what good is it doing your users if they can't locate it? It's our responsibility as designers—and yes, as information architects—to impose order on a seeming jumble of pages, so that others might more easily browse through them.

Of course, figuring out exactly what that jumble contains is the first step to making sense out of it.

Putting It into Practice

Let's say that we've been asked to redesign a small Web magazine named *WebMag 5000* (we never said we were especially strong at branding, but bear with us). In meeting with the site's stakeholders, we learn that *WebMag 5000* is a publication focused on writing articles for online professionals, primarily those working in the Web design industry. Their writers are culled predominantly from their readership, and all contribute on a volunteer basis. *WebMag 5000* has accrued quite the reputation over the past few years, and there is a considerable amount of prestige associated with publishing an article on the site. As a result, the submission rate of prospective articles has been gratifyingly high for the past year or so.

Because it's positively swimming in a sea of great content, *WebMag 5000* features a diverse array of content: articles that analyze new industry trends; tutorials for designers and developers; and reviews of software and books in which the audience would be professionally interested. Unfortunately, readership has dipped a bit. The one common thread in all the users' feedback is that the site is getting harder and harder to navigate. With all of the new content coming in, the original site's design is starting to show its age. Originally built to handle editions posted (sometimes) twice a month, the original design was never meant to handle the amount of content from the current site's tri-weekly editions. The home page is so cluttered with new, featured content that users are having trouble locking onto areas of interest. So, as part of your redesign, *WebMag 5000* has asked you to give the site a facelift that's not only more visually appealing, but is also more useable.

Taking Stock of Your Content

If you're a freelance Web professional, the word "audit" likely conjures up stressful images of unpleasant discussions with various tax authorities. But, in the context of *any* Web project (large or small), a content audit is the first step to bringing order out of Web chaos. It's a method through which you can create an inventory of your content, identify the strengths and weaknesses of what content your site contains, and begin to organize that information into discrete, user-digestible chunks.

For example, let's say that we wanted to organize the books in a bookstore. To do so, we would first take an inventory of all the books currently sitting on the store's shelves, and figure out the best way to organize them. Should we sort the inventory by author, title, genre, or some combination of the three? Should we put all paperback books on one shelf, with all of the hardcover titles on another? Other than the funny looks we're likely garnering from you, these questions are actually quite important. We could settle on an arbitrary order for our books, but it's more important to organize them in a way that will enable us to find our books more easily in the future.

Furthermore, as you sift through books in the store, you're sure to uncover a few that you could bear to part with. Perhaps you've not read one book in years, or you realize that you don't really need all eight copies of *Goodnight Moon*. If you should come across some of these less-valued books, you can either part with them to make your collection more lightweight, or relegate them to a lower shelf so that other books might be featured more prominently. Similarly, any online content audit you perform will probably enable you to identify and remove cruft from your Web site, reducing the number of extraneous pages your users will have to sift through to achieve their goals.

So, turning to *WebMag 5000*, let's examine what we've already learned. In our early requirements-gathering discussion, we've learned that articles, features, and tutorials are the meat of the site. In further discussions, and in clicking around the old site, we discover that there is a significant amount of other information not accounted for:

- ❑ A contact page
- ❑ Rates and information for advertisers
- ❑ The site's copyright information
- ❑ An accessibility statement (for users with special browsing needs)
- ❑ Profile pages for all of the articles' authors
- ❑ Information and tips for prospective writers
- ❑ Pages on the site's history and development
- ❑ A subscription page (which details various for-pay services into which readers might opt)

After creating this content inventory, we can evaluate the merits of each item with the site's stakeholders. Each piece of content should be thoroughly reviewed, and its relevance to the site considered carefully. Do users really need to know about how the site was constructed? How many users currently convert from non-paying readers to paid subscribers? Is the "subscribe" feature even worth maintaining?

Once we've determined which pieces of content are to be culled from *WebMag 5000*, we can sketch out a diagram of the content inventoried thus far. It might look something like Figure 1-2.

Granted, this sketch is purely informational. It lets us quickly see all of the information contained in the site. There's no thought given to how this content is to be ordered, or to how a user might navigate from one area of the site to another. But this is only the first step in our IA planning. Think of this inventory as having taken all of the books off of the shelves. Now we must organize our pages in an intelligent fashion, so that our users might be able to access them more easily.

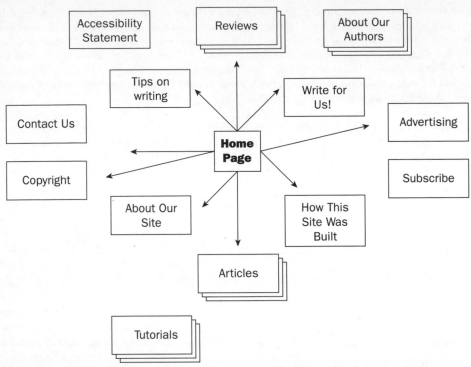

Figure 1-2: A rough content inventory for our site. How do we make sense of it all?

From Inventory to Hierarchy

So, how do we begin to make sense of our Web site so that others might do the same? To begin, it helps to consider your site not as a mass of pages, but as a hierarchy of information. In fact, it's no accident that most site maps look something like a tree: the home page sits at the top (or *root*) of the tree, with the various areas of the site branching out from it. As your users traverse through the different levels of the tree, each branch becomes more specialized than the one that precedes it. Traveling down from the root of the site down to the individual pages, the user is drilling down through these branches to find the content that matters most to them. Because of this, it's your responsibility to make the order of those branches as intuitive as possible.

So, let's say that after an exhaustive amount of research and user interviews, we discover that the audience for *WebMag 5000* can be broken into three types of users:

❑ **Readers.** These people are most interested in the reviews, articles, and tutorials published on our site. They're mainly consumers of information, so it's important to get them the information they need as quickly as possible.

❑ **Writers.** In one sense, this group is the lifeblood of our 'zine. Because all of our writers work on a volunteer basis, we must create a prestigious home on our site for the features they produce. Their name — and their work — should be featured prominently, in the hopes that they'll provide additional content in the future.

❑ **Prospective writers.** Of course, since we're looking for more volunteers to round out our queue of authors, we should have information for them on how to contribute, and what we're looking for. These people will (ideally) be drawn from our regular readership, and they should already be familiar with the topics we discuss.

From this, we can start to flesh out our site's hierarchy. To address the needs of these three groups of users, the highest level of our site might look like Figure 1-3.

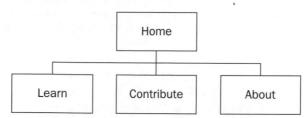

Figure 1-3: Identifying the main areas of our site

Because our primary audience is our readership, a section entitled Learn will house all of the articles, tutorials, reviews, and featured content for our webzine. The other main content area is the Contribute branch, which we hope will pique readers' interest in writing for our site and, therefore, increase our library of high-caliber articles. And finally, the About section contains information . . . well, *about* our little site that all three groups of users might need. Regular readers will get a better sense of our site's aims and philosophies. Writers will get a sense of how our site can give their work more exposure. Prospective writers can use this information to decide if our site would make a good home for their work.

> *There are very few "correct" answers in IA. The approach we've taken here to organizing our hypothetical site could easily be replaced with a number of alternatives. For example, we could have easily placed the site's reviews, articles, and tutorials in their own top-level sections. Whatever structure you settle upon for your own site, it's important to gather feedback from your users whenever possible. There is always the chance that assumptions you make about your users' behavior — no matter how well researched — might not meet with real-world user approval. If your project plan allows it, allotting some time for user testing and feedback can only help improve the result.*

Of course, the structuring effort doesn't end with these three branches. As we said earlier, each level of our site represents a higher, more fine-grained level of detail. Each of these three sections can contain pages, that's true — but they could also contain subsections, which in turn could contain pages and other subsections, and so on, as shown in Figure 1-4.

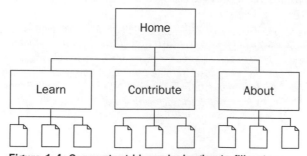

Figure 1-4: Our content hierarchy begins to fill out.

Chapter 1

This hierarchical categorization can easily be taken too far. Many sites fall into the trap of over-classifying their content, creating so many different tiers that users are unable to quickly access the content that's most vital to them. More often than not, these too-complex navigation structures arise from a lack of planning when thinking about a site's IA. The impulse to put the book somewhere, *anywhere* on the shelf becomes more important than placing it in an intelligent location, where others might easily locate it.

As tempting as it might be to organize your content beneath 12 levels of deeply nested navigation, that kind of information architecture is more a hindrance than a help to your users. This is another area in which our personas can help us, and enable us to reign in our impulse to over-classify. If we consider what language would be helpful to "Frank" to find a specific section of our site, or which categories make the most sense to "Natalie," then we can frame our IA work around our users' needs and goals. While planning your site's information architecture (and, in fact, throughout every stage of your project), it's important to keep your users' needs at the forefront of your mind. Paying attention to them now will only ensure their satisfaction later.

Building Our Site Map

Now that we've established the different high-level categories of our site, we can finally complete the organization process with a site map. A site map is a graphical, high-level overview that shows the title of each page or section in a Web site in a visually digestible, logical hierarchy (and if you can say that five times fast, we'll have to give you a gold star). The site map is the culmination of our IA work to date. It takes the content inventory we assembled, and organizes the content therein into a logical, navigable hierarchy.

As shown in Figure 1-5, every page and section of the site is listed and named in the site map, with "stacks" of pages to represent a group of related pages. We don't need to display every page in our Articles section, so we can easily group them through this notation. If we remember the content hierarchy diagram from before, then we can see exactly how this high-level tree structure drives the navigation for our site. There are three main navigation sections (Learn, About, or Contribute) and each page of our site has been placed within one of these sections. This means that from the home page, our users will most likely need to browse into one of these content areas *before* being able to navigate to one of the pages below.

Furthermore, we've relegated some pages to an area of "global navigation," which is accessible from every page of the site. These pages don't specifically fit within the bounds of our site's three main content areas, but are considered to be more universally relevant (that is, no matter which page of the site the user is currently reading, this information could potentially be relevant). If we were reading a *WebMag 5000* article and wanted to know about what options (if any) that we would have in reprinting it, we could easily select Copyright from the global navigation and find licensing info therein. Alternatively, while we may not be able to navigate directly from the site's colophon to Writing Tips in one click, both pages would allow users to access the accessibility statement directly.

> *There are a number of applications with which you can build your site maps. Designers often rely heavily on such applications as Adobe Photoshop or Illustrator; others might rely on more IA-specific graphing tools, such as Microsoft Visio (http://office.microsoft.com/en-us/FX010857981033.aspx) or OmniGroup's OmniGraffle (www.omnigroup.com/applications/omnigraffle/). Some IA professionals build all their deliverables in HTML, while others swear by their trusty pencil and paper. Try out a number of different tools, and settle on one that best meets your needs.*

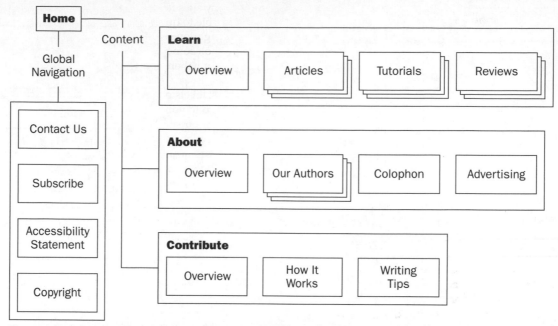

Figure 1-5: A site map for *WebMag 5000*, our imaginary Web site

But the boundaries aren't (and shouldn't be) as distinct as they might seem. Presumably, there will be content on the home page that will feature articles and other internal content. Because of this, it's also likely that there will be some facility on that front page allowing users to move directly into an individual article, two levels down in the navigation. Should our site map reflect this? If so, how should it?

In all honesty, it's your decision as to how exhaustively your site map charts the relationships between different sections of the site. If we were to graph every point in which users could move between each area, our site map might start to look like a map of downtown London, riddled with arrows and lines and making very little sense. Rather, we can outline some of the more important relationships between the different sections. For example, let's say that every article, tutorial, and review published on our site features a link to the author's profile page in the About section. Conversely, each author's profile will contain links to any articles, tutorials, and reviews that he or she has published on our site. If our site map needed to reflect this relationship, we might update the document to look like Figure 1-6.

This kind of cross-linking helps promote deeper relationships between different sections of your site, which allow users more than one way to access the information they're looking for. A user might come to your site looking for information on a particular piece of software, and could happen upon additional work by the author on his or her profile page. By creating relationships across the different content categories, we create a richer interface for our users, as well as a more scalable foundation for any future content we add to our site.

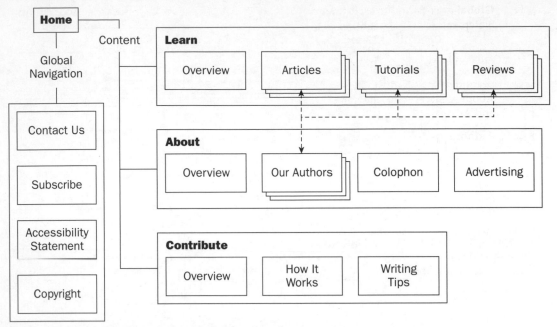

Figure 1-6: Annotating the relationship between sections

But once we've built our site map, our work is only halfway done. Now that we understand the "big picture" of our entire site's IA, how do we organize content on the individual pages?

Wireframes: Blueprints for Your Pages

A *wireframe* is a line drawing that represents the different areas of content on a page. Much in the same way that a site map gives us a sense of how different areas of our site relate to one another, a wireframe enables us to see how the different pieces of content on a given page will interact. These black-and-white line drawings imply structure *only*. Bereft of color, typography, or any other design elements, wireframes force us to establish a layout for our pages.

Typically, it's not necessary to build a wireframe for every single page of our site. Rather, we can sketch out a wireframe for each unique page layout in our site (such as your home page, search results, blog entry, and so on). By starting with these plain-looking documents, we can identify any possible usability issues before we've begun fleshing out our site's design.

Just as we started drafting our site map by taking inventory of the types of content our site would contain, we must identify the different areas of information that our page's layout will house. If we are building a wireframe for a *WebMag 5000* article, then let's assume that the page will contain the following information:

❑ **Content.** The article's content.

❑ **Related articles.** A listing of articles related to one the user is currently reading.

❑ **Logo.** The *WebMag 5000* logo.

- ❑ **Global navigation links.** From our site map, these are Contact Us, Subscribe, Accessibility Statement, and Copyright.

- ❑ **Primary navigation.** These are links to the Learn, About, and Contribute sections, which we defined in our site map.

- ❑ **Secondary navigation.** These are the navigation options within each section. If we were in the About section of our site map, the subnav options would be Our Site, Our Authors, Colophon, and Advertising.

- ❑ **Author's name.** This should link to the article's author profile.

- ❑ **Category listings.** These should list under which content categories the current article has been filed, so that users might view additional articles in these categories.

- ❑ **Advertising banner.** The client tells us it needs to be 280 pixels wide and 120 pixels tall, but we don't need to be concerned with layout at this stage.

Equipped with this list, we should now begin to group these chunks of content into different categories, which should speak to how the different content areas relate to each other. For example, with the content we've listed, we might create the following content hierarchy:

- ❑ Content:
  - ❑ The article's content
- ❑ Related content:
  - ❑ The author's name
  - ❑ Category listings
  - ❑ Related articles
- ❑ Branding:
  - ❑ The *WebMag 5000* logo
- ❑ Navigation:
  - ❑ Primary navigation
  - ❑ Secondary navigation
  - ❑ Global navigation
- ❑ Advertising:
  - ❑ The banner advertisement

These content groups are broken down largely into conceptual chunks (that is to say, that ancillary bits of information have been dumped into Related Content, the banner advertising has been oh-so-cleverly labeled Advertising, and so on). Were you working on a page that had a higher degree of interactivity (such a complex form that requires the user to enter a sizeable amount of data), you might use headers that describe the data contained therein (My Personal Information, My Company Information, Shipping Address, and so on).

Armed with this high-level list, we can turn these content groupings into a rough wireframe that demonstrates how these relationships might play out on a page.

In Figure 1-7, we've settled upon a rather traditional two-column layout for the wireframe. Most of our content categories have translated into discrete areas on the page, placed according to the amount of visual weight we need to allot them in our layout. For example, the client's logo has been placed at the top of the wireframe, in order to maximize the visibility of the *WebMag 5000* brand. The one content category that "straddles" the page layout is the site's navigation. While primary and secondary navigation have been placed immediately below the logo to facilitate easy navigation, the "global" navigation has been relegated to the footer of the page. While this might indicate to some users that it is perhaps the least important area of the page, we decided to position it at the bottom in the hopes that its consistent placement would enable users to find it more easily.

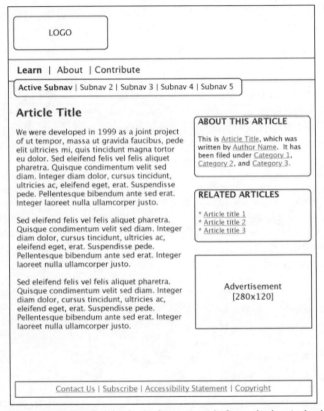

Figure 1-7: The finished wireframe, ready for a design to be hung upon it

The rest of the groupings play out largely as you might expect. The article's content area is of primary interest to the site's users, so that has been given the most weight on the page. In the right-hand column, many of the "related content" information has been stored to give it the most visibility, while remaining subordinate to the primary content area. The author's name and the article categories have been placed in a block named "About This Article." Other related articles have been moved into a separate area immediately below. The advertising banner is placed in the sidebar to give it maximum visibility without detracting from the content as a whole.

So, ultimately, the architecture dictated by the wireframe should reflect the needs of both your client and your users; the decisions we've made in this example wireframe might not be appropriate for your site or its requirements, but may at least present an idea of how to move forward. However you decide to perform this ever-delicate balancing act between client and user requirements, keep the goals of the page at the forefront of your mind. Build a clear, usable interface, and the rest will fall into place.

Sounds almost easy, doesn't it?

Jason Santa Maria's "Grey Box Methodology" (`www.jasonsantamaria.com/archive/2004/`*
`05/24/grey_box_method.php`) describes one graphic designer's approach to planning a design. His approach is a compelling read, and tackles the challenge of defining a page's architecture from a slightly different perspective. Whereas we took stock of the page's content before considering the layout, Santa Maria takes a more visual approach. The two methods achieve the same goals, however — both force the designer to think in terms of how the layout can help the user before planning the more aesthetic details of a design.*

Beginning the Design

So, the planning has been finished, the site map has been approved, and the wireframes are set. We can finally set aside all of this theoretical nonsense about "interface," "requirements," and "change management," and stop worrying about taking "notes" in "meetings" with "stakeholders." At long last, we can finally get into actually *designing* our site . . . can't we?

As much as we'd like to tell you otherwise, the actual construction of a site requires no less planning than the rest of the project. Sitting down to design and build a site is absolutely one of the most rewarding parts of any Web project, that's true. But this is the phase of the project in which all of your careful planning and analysis pay off. That's not to say that imposing a process upon the design process should remove any of the fun from it. Rather, some of the most compelling Web designs are a direct result of the constraints placed upon them.

That's not to say that there aren't many talented designers who can create a stunning personal site with little or no outside direction. However, it's another challenge altogether to create a design that simultaneously furthers a company's brand, ensures that the site is supremely user-friendly, *and* remains aesthetically appealing. From these competing needs, the true beauty of Web design originates.

Setting the Tone for Your Site

With a firm understanding of the scope of our project, we can then craft a design that speaks to the needs of both groups. In order to do so, however, we should establish the tone of our site. After all, we might settle upon a different design direction for a small law firm than we might for an online publication. Each company would have its own target audience, its own brand identity, and its own business requirements. As such, an understanding of what those goals are is integral to building a site that achieves them. Let's take a brief look at one site that exemplifies this attention to goal-driven design: Cinnamon Interactive (`www.cinnamon.nl/`).

In the early days of CSS adoption, far too many style sheet–driven sites were doomed to "look like Web standards" — their layouts were boxy, their palettes flat, and they made far from a compelling case for abandoning table-driven design techniques. Cinnamon Interactive was one of the earliest sites to showcase the true power of CSS as a tool for bringing gorgeous designs to the Web. Launched in January 2003, it featured an incredibly nuanced design (see Figure 1-8). The site's layered typography, beautiful use of color, and well-implemented access enhancements are facilitated by a foundation of CSS and valid XHTML, which ensures that the site is as impressive under the hood as it is above it.

Figure 1-8: Cinnamon Interactive. Fashionable and functional, this beautiful design floors random surfers while driving prospective clients into their portfolio.

But it's not just the jaw-dropping aesthetics (or the code behind it) that make Cinnamon a success. Rather, the goals of the site are beautifully reflected in its design. The cinnamon shaker logo is subtly mirrored in the photography on the home page, which creates a heightened sense of the company brand. This attention to the corporate identity is sure to impress not only random Web surfers, but also corporate clients looking for the same level of brand savvy for their own company.

Furthermore, the bulk of the home page is dedicated to links to the company portfolio. Not only is it the first link in the site's primary navigation (after the link back to the "*Voorpagina*," or home page), but the splash graphic on the home page is one big link directly into their body of work. This emphasis on advertising their portfolio is intended to not only draw interested users into some of their past projects, but ultimately move over to the "contact" page so that they might ultimately contract with Cinnamon for their own design initiatives.

Finding Inspiration

Of course, translating these goals into an attractive design isn't always the most elementary process. Just like a writer under deadline, it's easy for designers to get blocked. When presented with a creative brief, client requirements, and a mountain of documentation detailing your users' needs, a blank canvas in Photoshop can seem an almost impassable roadblock. So, how do we get started? How do we go from requirements to sleek, professional-looking design in nothing flat?

Simple — by seeing how others do it.

Don't worry, you bought the right book. This isn't *Professional Plagiarism* we're writing here. However, establishing and maintaining an awareness of current Web design trends is one of the keys to improving your own craft. the most rewarding part of working and designing online is that there is always something new to learn, another excellent resource you've not discovered yet. If we're feeling stumped by how to style a particular page element, uninspired by a corporate color palette, or just generally strapped for ideas, then seeing how other designers work in the face of adversity is always a welcome aid. So, whenever we start to feel as though we're pushing up against the constraints of our own design skills, we spend a bit of time browsing for inspiration.

This browsing could occur on-line or off-line. Whether walking through a museum, browsing through a magazine stand, or surfing through some well-designed Web sites, the medium you pick is less important than exposing yourself to well-reasoned, well-executed designs for an hour or two. Thankfully, we're able to keep that hour or two from turning into eight or nine by visiting a number of well-known design portals, or online communities dedicated to evangelizing some of Web design's brighter spots.

Over the past year, a number of sites evangelizing CSS-based Web designs have cropped up. The most recent addition is Stylegala (`www.stylegala.com/`). It features a design as compelling as the sites it covers. Each featured site in the gallery is accompanied by some thoughtful critiques by Stylegala's creator and designer-in-residence, David Hellsing. The site's users are allowed to vote for favorites within the gallery, as well as provide additional commentary. The discussions are always interesting, and the sites are all fine examples of what the Web (and CSS) can do.

Kaliber10000 (`www.k10k.net/`) isn't so much a community as an *authority*, providing a near-dizzying array of design-related news, tips, and tutorials on an even more dizzying basis. Founded in 1998 and staffed by some of the brightest designers in the industry, Kaliber10000 provides everything from screenshots of user desktops, to links to Flash-heavy portfolio sites. K10K won't just rid you of your design block — rather, it will help you obliterate it.

Selecting a Layout: Fixed or Liquid

Often characterized as one of the unholy wars of Web design, the debate between fixed or liquid layouts is the designer's version of "Chevy versus Ford" — each side has its fierce loyalists, with very little middle ground between the two poles. As we begin building our site, it's worth acknowledging this heated debate, so that you might choose a method that best fits your needs and those of your site.

Fixed Width

A fixed (or "ice") layout is one whose width is constant and unchanging. No matter how large or small the user's browser window becomes, the actual width of the page's content area will remain, well, fixed. The benefit to this approach is that it lends ultimate control to the designer, who always knows the dimensions of the canvas he or she is designing upon. For professionals coming from a print background, this is approach is a rather intuitive one. If the width of the content area is a fixed constant, then a designer can hang perfectly sized graphics upon that canvas with pixel-perfect precision.

However, the success of a fixed-width design is contingent upon an assumption: namely, the designer's assumption of the width of the user's browser window. Should the browser's width ever become narrower than that of the page, then a horizontal scroll bar will appear, forcing the user to manually scroll the page from left to right to see the site as its designer intended (see Figure 1-9).

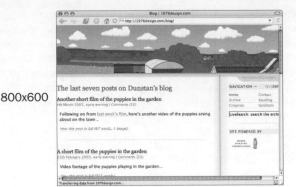

800x600

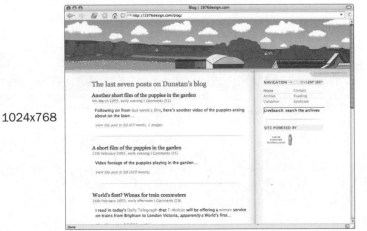

1024x768

1280x1024

Figure 1-9: 1976design.com is the weblog of Dunstan Orchard, one of this book's authors. It is built with a fixed layout, which causes a horizontal scroll bar to appear at smaller screen resolutions.

Conversely, fixed-width designs are often unkind to larger screen resolutions. When browsing at higher resolutions and with a fully maximized window, a design optimized for smaller window sizes can be drowned out by unused white space. Our users' displays are constantly increasing, which makes fixed-width designs less than future-proof—a site designed for the resolutions of today will likely need to be revisited in a year or two, as its users clamor for a more intelligent use of the window widths available to them.

Liquid Layouts

Proponents of liquid (or "fluid") layouts are quick to counter that fixed-width designs set an unfair technical assumption on our audience: there is no guarantee that our user's browser window is large enough to accommodate the width specified in our design, and users with smaller windows should not be penalized by the sites they visit. So, to that end, liquid layouts are designed to be entirely flexible. As the browser window expands or contracts, the page's layout will follow suit, ensuring that the content fills the display at any window size (see Figure 1-10).

Most apologists for fixed-width techniques will say that their users' screen resolutions have been increasing over recent years, and that designing for smaller screen resolutions is no longer necessary. Their server logs might tell them that an overwhelming majority of their users are running resolutions such as 1024 × 768 or 800 × 600, and that building a design that caters to smaller screens is less vital than it was in the early days of the Web. Designers on the other side of the debate will quickly counter with the fact that *screen resolution does not determine the size of the browser window*. If a user's screen resolution is set to a specific width, the browser isn't automatically maximized to occupy all of that space. By making that assumption (and serving up a fixed-width design to match), designers can potentially exclude users who browse at smaller window sizes, forcing them to resize their pages to meet the designer's design criteria. Instead, fluid layouts are agnostic when it comes to the size of the browser window. By definition, they attempt to subvert the design to the preferences of the user, rather than the other way around.

Of course, liquid layouts are not without their flaws—no design technique is a silver bullet, and this is no exception. Just as it is easier to read text that has been divided into separate paragraphs, it is also easier to read text that has been set to an optimal width. This is where most fluid layouts break down. By allowing their content to reflow as the size of the browser window increases, that content can be increasingly difficult to read at larger window sizes. Studies have shown that the user's ability to comprehend onscreen text suffers slightly when the length of the line being read exceeds 4 inches (http://psychology.wichita.edu/surl/usabilitynews/42/text_length.htm); so while a fluid layout might be ideal for small-to-medium browser window widths (see Figure 1-11), legibility can suffer quite a bit when the window expands beyond that threshold (see Figure 1-12).

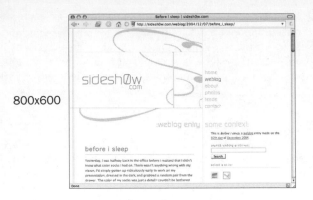

800x600

1024x768

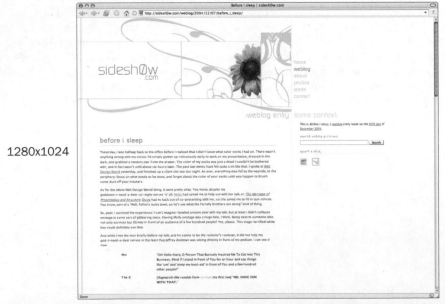

1280x1024

Figure 1-10: sidesh0w.com is the weblog of Ethan Marcotte, another of this book's authors. It features a liquid, resolution-independent layout, which some might find difficult to read at larger screen resolutions.

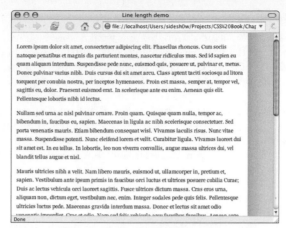

Figure 1-11: A page of text with a fluid width. Seems quite manageable at a narrow width, doesn't it?

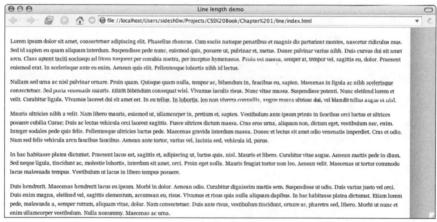

Figure 1-12: The same fluid block of text, but at a larger screen resolution. The line lengths have become unmanageable and are difficult to scan.

Furthermore, the lack of control over the content area's width can be difficult to balance when placing fixed-width elements within it. When a Web designer knows the physical dimensions of the page, then graphics can be designed specifically to fit within that space. Even the staunchest fluid-width proponents are envious of their fixed-width comrades' ability to place a perfectly sized graphic across the top of a content area. Most liquid designers are forced to use graphics of an arbitrary width, which could break the layout as the window becomes infinitely small.

> *Richard Rutter, Web designer and proponent of liquid layouts, has published a number of experiments with placing wide images within a fluid-width container (`http://clagnut.com/blog/268/`). He proposes a number of interesting CSS workarounds that may be of interest to those pursuing liquid layouts.*

Gaining Some Perspective

The truth is that both methods have their strengths and weaknesses. Neither is inherently superior to the other. In the hands of the right designer, either can be equally effective (or, in the hands of a less-talented designer, ineffective) in a site's design. Of course, the relative strengths of one approach can be debated *ad nauseam* at the expense of the other's faults — and as in most design communities, it is debated endlessly.

Rather than seeing either layout model as "The One True Path" of Web design, we would suggest that the two models are *tools*. The true key to success in either method is applying it intelligently to your work, with an overall sensitivity to the context of each element on your page. It's not the relative width of a design's content area that makes for a successful site, but rather the thinking before and behind the design that distinguishes it.

Summary

With this chapter, we've completed an overview of some of the highlights of a typical Web project. This overview is far from exhaustive and, in fact, could be called a bit of a gloss. Entire tomes have been written about project and client management, and we've dedicated only a few pages to it. However, we hope that this sketch of an entire project lifecycle demonstrates that there is far more than well-coded style sheets that make a site successful. In our experience, a successful project is rarely determined by process, documentation, and deliverables as much as it is by good communication. If the designer and the client make a concerted effort to work closely together throughout the project, then each will be more aware of the other's needs and expectations as both move toward meeting (and exceeding) the project's goals.

So with a better understanding of a project lifecycle, we can now turn to two of the more critical components of its design: XHTML and CSS. We'll examine the relationship between these two important technologies, as well as discuss some tips for more effectively integrating them into your design workflow.

2

Best Practices for XHTML and CSS

In its early years, the Web wasn't exactly the most attractive thing on the planet. Created by and for nuclear physicists, hypertext was simply a means by which content-heavy documents could be shared over an open, distributed network. Needless to say, high-caliber design wasn't a top priority for the Web's earliest authors. In fact, HTML's much-used (and, as we'll discuss, oft-abused) `table` element was created with one purpose in mind: the display of tabular data.

By the time we reached the heyday of late-1990s Web design, the "L" in HTML was often ignored. Many professionals felt that the code we used to build our Web pages wasn't a language *per se,* and, as such, wasn't beholden to the rules and restrictions of a real programming language. Besides, our clients weren't paying us for "compliant," "accessible," or "future-proof" code. In fact, many sites were produced with the requirement that they be "backward compatible." This was a misnomer if ever there was one because it simply required a consistent display in version 4.0 browsers or higher.

Browsers of that time were temperamental, to say the least. With poor support for the specifications written by the World Wide Web Consortium (`www.w3.org/`), or W3C, you could count on a page rendering differently in Browser A than in Browser B. So, while many of us were dimly aware of the "standards" the W3C produced, the browsers we had to support were less than tolerant of standards-compliant markup. In this sense, the divide between the science and the reality of the Web was far too great. We would deliberately invalidate our HTML with proprietary, browser-specific markup to ensure that things "looked good" in our target browsers. And for a time, all was good. We had narrow specifications, we had deadlines, we weren't paid by the hour, and as you can see, we had excuses.

Of course, designers learned early on that by zeroing out a `table`'s cellpadding, spacing, and border, we could create complex grid-based layouts, and bring a new level of aesthetic appeal to our sites. Granted, given browsers' poor support for CSS in those days, we had no alternative but to weigh our pages down with presentational cruft. The result was a Web that is bogged down by the weight of its own markup, saturated with kilobyte-heavy pages that are hard to maintain, costly to redesign, and unkind to our users' bandwidth.

Thankfully, there is a way out. XHTML and CSS are two standard technologies that will enable you to clear away the clutter in your pages, facilitating pages that are significantly lighter, more accessible, and easier to maintain. Of course, these two tools are only as effective as your ability to wield them. This chapter examines the need for XHTML and CSS, and introduces some practical strategies for applying them intelligently to your design.

Structure and Presentation: Shoehorned Together

Now, let's take a deep breath, and be honest with ourselves: Does this HTML snippet look familiar?

```
<body marginwidth="0" marginheight="0" leftmargin="0" topmargin="0">
```

In the heyday of early Web design, this was *the* way to place your pages' content flush against the browser window. Without these four attributes, our designs would be surrounded by a margin of 10 or so pixels—and yes, we're sufficiently finicky where something like this would keep us up at night.

This approach highlights the extent to which an emphasis upon "looking right" pervaded early Web design. Despite HTML's origins as a well-structured language, our pages evolved into a kind of "tag soup"—a not-so-tasty goulash of structural and presentational markup. Because contemporary browsers had nonexistent or imperfect support for cascading style sheets, we relied on transparent spacer graphics, font elements, and deeply nested tables to control our sites' designs. Our attribute-heavy body perfectly illustrates this mismatch of structure and style in our markup. While the body element itself performs an important structural purpose (it contains a Web page's content), the small army of attributes crammed into its opening tag is there only to make that structure *look* a certain way.

Granted, our little body element might not seem all that egregious—is it really worth wringing our hands over one little line of markup? For a concrete example of the problems with presentation-rich markup, let's look at the Harvard University home page (www.harvard.edu/). The site's design (see Figure 2-1) admirably reflects the University's well-established brand: a conservative, earth-toned color palette accentuates the distinctive Harvard crimson, while the centered two-column layout emphasizes content over flash, delivery over glitz. By all accounts, it's a successful site design—and one that garners more than a little traffic each day, we're sure.

> There are a number of browser utilities you can install to quickly affect the display of a page as we've done here. For the Mozilla browsers, the Web Developer Toolbar (http://chrispederick.com/work/firefox/webdeveloper/) is one such tool, and an excellent one at that. It's an invaluable part of our CSS toolkit, allowing designers to turn on borders of different page elements, quickly edit a page's CSS, and easily access various online code validators.

Figure 2-1: The Harvard University home page

As we said, this is an effective, straightforward design. But if we "turn on" borders for all table elements in the HTML, the site reveals something much less straightforward under the hood (see Figure 2-2).

Figure 2-2: The Harvard home page again, with table borders activated

Quite a change, isn't it? There's quite a lot of markup vested in such a simple layout: tables are pristinely nested five levels deep, logo graphics split with pixel precision into multiple files and strewn across multiple table rows. Even looking at the code for the primary navigation bar is a bit dizzying:

```
<table bgcolor="#cdd397" border="0" cellpadding="0" cellspacing="0" width="650">
<tbody><tr>
<td valign="top"><img src="images/shield3.gif" alt="Harvard University shield"
border="0" height="25" width="117"></td>
<td valign="top"><a href="http://www.harvard.edu/"><img src="images/home2.gif"
alt="Home" name="nav01" border="0" height="25" width="47"></a></td>
<td><img src="images/nav_bullet.gif" border="0" height="25" width="14"></td>
<td><a href="http://www.harvard.edu/admissions/" onmouseover="imgOn('nav02')" ;=""
onmouseout="navOff('nav02')"><img src="images/admissions.gif" alt="Admissions"
name="nav02" border="0" height="25" width="166"></a></td>
<td><img src="images/nav_bullet.gif" border="0" height="25" width="14"></td>
<td><a href="http://atwork.harvard.edu/" onmouseover="imgOn('nav03')" ;=""
onmouseout="navOff('nav03')"><img src="images/employment.gif" alt="Employment"
name="nav03" border="0" height="25" width="80"></a></td>
```

```
<td><img src="images/nav_bullet.gif" border="0" height="25" width="14"></td>
<td><a href="http://lib.harvard.edu/" onmouseover="imgOn('nav04')" ;=""
onmouseout="navOff('nav04')"><img src="images/libraries.gif" alt="Libraries"
name="nav04" border="0" height="25" width="59"></a></td>
<td><img src="images/nav_bullet.gif" border="0" height="25" width="14"></td>
<td><a href="http://www.harvard.edu/museums/" onmouseover="imgOn('nav05')" ;=""
onmouseout="navOff('nav05')"><img src="images/museums.gif" alt="Museums"
name="nav05" border="0" height="25" width="64"></a></td>
<td><img src="images/nav_bullet.gif" border="0" height="25" width="14"></td>
<td><a href="http://www.harvard.edu/arts/" onmouseover="imgOn('nav06')" ;=""
onmouseout="navOff('nav06')"><img src="images/arts.gif" alt="Arts" name="nav06"
border="0" height="25" width="33"></a></td>
</tr>
</tbody></table>
```

The table begins by setting the background color for the first navigation row (#cdd397, a light, desaturated green), and by zeroing out the table's border, as well as the padding within and spacing between each of its cells. Once that's completed, the site's author is left with an invisible grid, upon which graphics can be placed with pixel-perfect precision. Every other table cell contains nav_bullet.gif, the bullet graphic that abuts each navigation item. The remaining cells contain the navigation graphics themselves, each of which is surrounded by an anchor upon which onmouseover and onmouseout attributes are placed to control the graphics' rollover effects.

Remember, this is simply the markup for one of the navigation bars. The rest of the page follows this same layout model: Zero out a table's default attributes; place content, graphics, and additional markup therein; repeat as needed. After a while, reading through this page begins to feel something like running down the rabbit hole. Just when you think you've reached the end of one table, another presents itself, and you're reminded how much effort goes into seeking that Holy Grail of "looking right"—a truly consistent, bulletproof display across all target browsers.

Of course, that Holy Grail is a bit of a tin cup. Until recently, we've been concerned solely with the visual display of our sites on graphical desktop browsers. There are other devices and other users whose needs should be taken into account. If we view the Harvard University home page in an environment that can't render the carefully arrayed graphics, what happens then?

A screenshot of a text-only browser's view of the site holds the answer (see Figure 2-3). Without the aid of color or headings, it's certainly more difficult to navigate through this environment than in the context of the site's design. If it's difficult for us as sighted users, consider the difficulty that users with special browsing needs must encounter.

For example, a number of the graphics on the page are missing alt attributes, an important accessibility requirement. If a blind user were using a screen reader to read the Web pages' content aloud, the file-names of these alt-deprived graphics would be read out loud. To that user, our navigation menu might sound like "link Home nav underscore bullet dot gif link Admissions nav underscore bullet dot gif link Employment nav underscore bullet dot gif link Libraries," and so forth.

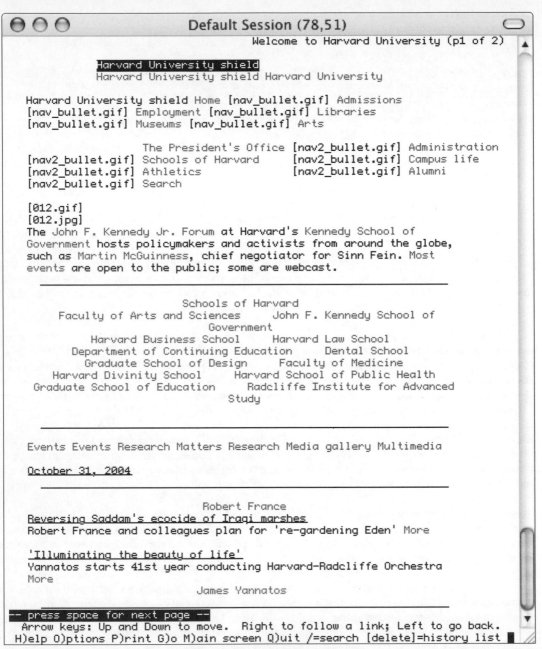

Figure 2-3: View of www.harvard.edu in Lynx, a text-only browser

First and foremost, this is not an indictment of the Harvard home page; in years past, we've built hundreds of pages with these exact same tactics. Rather, it is a reminder of the reality of the Web that, until only recently, we were *all* forced to work in. With such shoddy support for CSS, table-based layouts were a matter of course. We were devoted to ensuring an excellent display in all graphic browsers, at the expense of bandwidth-heavy markup and inaccessible site designs. Of course, this begs the question: What do we do about it?

By now, if you're thinking that there must be a better way, you're right — there most certainly is. Today's browsers have become much more intelligent, and we should, too. With greater support for cascading style sheets across the board, we no longer have to rely upon bandwidth-hogging markup to realize a site's design. We can instead focus on abstracting presentational cruft out of our markup, and move it into our cascading style sheets.

The promise of separating structure from style is at the heart of standards-based Web design, and makes for one of the most compelling arguments for creating page layouts with CSS. By drawing a line in the sand between our pages' content and their presentation, our pages will not only be drastically lighter, but far easier to maintain as well.

A Valid Foundation: Learning to Love Our Markup

Let's revisit our lonely little `body` element one last time:

```
<body marginwidth="0" marginheight="0" leftmargin="0" topmargin="0">
```

Don't worry, we won't retread that whole "presentation versus structure" conversation again. We can hear some snoring in the back of the audience, and aren't about to start pressing our luck.

It is worth remembering that none of these attributes were in any HTML specifications (www.w3.org/MarkUp/). `marginwidth` and `marginheight` were Netscape-only attributes and would work only in that browser. Conversely, while `leftmargin` and `topmargin` attributes had the same margin-trimming effect, they would work only in Internet Explorer. But valid or no, that didn't keep us from placing this proprietary markup on our sites. We were dealing with browsers offering non-standard (and often contradictory) implementations of HTML, and we did so with a smile on our face — as well as every snippet of invalid, proprietary code in our site builder's arsenal.

And, since we served up the same invalid, proprietary HTML to *all* browsers that visit our pages, this one line of HTML demonstrates just how tolerant browsers are of flawed markup. And that's by design. If we neglect to include a closing tag (such as `</tr>` or `</div>`) or introduce a proprietary element into our markup to work around a layout bug (as we did in the preceding `body` element), your Web browser has a recovery strategy in place. It has to "repair" your markup while parsing it, rendering the page despite any imperfect code found therein.

But the real headaches arise because each browser has its own internal logic for interpreting this invalid code, which invariably leads to unpredictable results when doing cross-browser testing. One browser might recover gracefully from a missing angle bracket, while another might break our entire layout because of it. These inconsistent rendering strategies make one thing certain: Invalid code means that we spend more of our time coding and testing to ensure that a site displays correctly across all target browsers. Rather than focusing on improving our site's design and content, we were forced to spend far too much time nursing broken markup. It's true. Our early reliance on malformed, proprietary, or otherwise invalid markup allowed our designs a consistent display on old-school browsers. But in availing ourselves of markup hacks, we create a dependency in every page of our site. We've placed code in our documents that targets a specific browser's idiosyncrasies. When today's browsers finally slip over the upgrade horizon and the next generation appears, each of those hacks is a potential landmine. Will newer browsers be as tolerant of our code, bloated as it is with such non-standard markup? Or will the next version of Internet Explorer ship with a bug that refuses to render a page when it encounters the `marginheight` attribute on a `body` element?

Yes, this is the kind of stuff we worry about. But the simple truth is that invalid markup creates a long-term liability that we can't afford to ignore. Rather than fretting about how our markup hacks will perform (or won't) in another year or eight, perhaps it's finally time to pay attention to the "L" in HTML.

XHTML: The New Hotness

XHTML is described by the W3C as "bring[ing] the rigor of XML to Web pages" (`www.w3.org/MarkUp/#xhtml1`). In short, XHTML was created so that site owners would have a cleaner upgrade path between HTML and a stricter document syntax, XML. Compare this snippet of HTML to its XHTML equivalent:

```
<!DOCTYPE HTML PUBLIC "-//W3C//DTD HTML 4.01//EN"
"http://www.w3.org/TR/html4/strict.dtd">
<html>
<head>
<title>My sample page</title>
<meta http-equiv="Content-Type" content="text/html; charset=utf-8">
</head>
<body>
<ul>
<li>Here's a sample list item,
<li>And yet another.
</ul>
<p>I like big blocks,<br>and I cannot lie.
<p>You other coders can't deny.
</body>
</html>
```

And now, look at the XHTML:

```
<!DOCTYPE html PUBLIC "-//W3C//DTD XHTML 1.0 Transitional//EN"
"http://www.w3.org/TR/xhtml1/DTD/xhtml1-transitional.dtd">
<html xmlns="http://www.w3.org/1999/xhtml">
<head>
<title>My sample page</title>
<meta http-equiv="Content-Type" content="text/html; charset=utf-8" />
</head>
<body>
<ul>
<li>Here's a sample list item,</li>
<li>And yet another.</li>
</ul>
<p>I like big blocks,<br />and I cannot lie.</p>
<p>You other coders can't deny.</p>
</body>
</html>
```

Don't feel bad if you didn't spot any changes—there are more similarities here than differences. And, in fact, both of these pages will render the same in any given browser. Your end users won't be able to tell the difference between the two languages. While the similarities in syntax do outweigh the differences between XHTML and its predecessor, those few differences are quite significant.

Begin with the DOCTYPE Declaration

The first item in the two sample pages is a DOCTYPE (geek-speak for "document type") declaration. Point your browser to the URL in the DOCTYPE element:

```
http://www.w3.org/TR/xhtml1/DTD/xhtml1-transitional.dtd
```

You'll be presented with a long, complex text document known as the DOCTYPE definition, or DTD. The DTD outlines the rules of the language to which the ensuing markup is supposed to conform. Declaring this DTD at the beginning of our markup signals what language is used on the page to "user agents," a blanket term for *any* device or program that can access our page. It's not just about graphical desktop browsers anymore. Printers, cellular telephones, and screen readers are all examples of user agents, and each benefits from knowing what markup language they will encounter on the rest of the page.

Online validation tools are another example of user agents, and they (above all others) benefit from our opening DOCTYPE declaration. This allows them to assess how effectively our code conforms to the DTD— in effect, whether it's valid or not.

Keeping Your Markup Well Formed

"Well-formed" is essentially a new name for an old rule. It simply means that your elements must be nested properly. Consider this example:

```
<p>Here's <em>my <strong>opening</em></strong> paragraph!</p>
```

Here, the em is opened first, and the strong opened second. However, markup follows a "first opened, last closed" rule. Since the em is opened before the strong, it must be closed *after* the strong's final tag. If we revise the markup so that it's well formed, the elements' nesting order makes a bit more sense:

```
<p>Here's <em>my <strong>opening</strong></em> paragraph!</p>
```

As you've no doubt noticed, this concept of proper nesting is an old one. While it's never been valid to write incorrectly nested markup, it is still quite common in many pages built today. As a result, browsers have become far too tolerant of the tag soup we feed them. Any given browser will have a different strategy in place for how to "fix" this incorrectly nested markup, which can often yield differing results once the page is rendered. XHTML is a language that explicitly demands structural soundness. By requiring our markup to be well formed, this stricter document syntax enables us to combat structural inconsistencies in our own code.

Of course, it's important to remember that "well formed" does not equal "valid." Consider this example:

```
<a id="content">
<em>
<div class="item">
<p>I'm not exactly sure what this means.</p>
<p>...but at least it's well-formed.</p>
</div>
</em>
</a>
```

This code is immaculately nested, but it's far from valid. HTML differentiates between *block-level elements* (div, p, table, and the like) and *inline elements* (such as a, em, strong). Inline elements can never contain the block-level elements, making our previous markup invalid. While browsers will be able to read this code correctly, it's almost certain to cause display errors when the CSS is applied. Depending on the browser, styles applied to the anchor element may or may not cascade down to the text contained in the div. It certainly would be an unpleasant surprise if all of your content suddenly gained the link's signature underline, or visibly changed when you hovered over it with your mouse.

This is yet another example of the importance of validation. By beginning your document with a DOCTYPE declaration and validating frequently, you can proactively squash layout bugs before they arise. This translates into less debugging time for you, which in turn translates into more time you can spend focusing on your site's design.

Close Every Element

When you opened an element in HTML, you weren't always required to supply the corresponding closing element. In fact, the HTML 4.01 specification differentiates between elements whose ending elements are optional (such as the paragraph element: www.w3.org/TR/REC-html40/struct/text.html#h-9.3.1), required (phrase elements such as em or strong: www.w3.org/TR/REC-html40/struct/text.html#h-9.2.1), and, in some cases, outright forbidden (the good ol' br: www.w3.org/TR/REC-html40/struct/text.html#h-9.3.2).

Thankfully, this ambiguity has been removed from XHTML, largely because of XHTML's insistence that our markup be well formed. If you open an element, a closing element is required — simple as that. The following is valid markup in HTML 4:

```
<ul>
<li>Here's a sample list item,
<li>And yet another.
</ul>
<p>I like big blocks,<br>and I cannot lie.
<p>You other coders can't deny.
```

However, the XHTML looks slightly different (the changes are shown here in bold):

```
<ul>
<li>Here's a sample list item,</li>
<li>And yet another.</li>
</ul>
<p>I like big blocks,<br />and I cannot lie.</p>
<p>You other coders can't deny.</p>
```

Because we're working in XHTML, we don't have the option of leaving our list items (<li></li>) and paragraphs (<p>) open. Before starting a new element, we'll need to close each with </li> and </p>, respectively. However, the sharp-eyed readers may be wondering exactly *what* we were thinking when we added a forward slash (/) to the br.

Trust us: we haven't gone slash-happy. Elements such as br, img, meta, and hr are considered "empty" elements because they don't contain any text content — which isn't the case for p, li, td, and, in fact, most elements in the HTML specification. But while empty elements traditionally have *not* had a closing element, XHTML doesn't play any favorites when it comes to keeping our document well formed. So, by ending an empty element with />, we can effectively close it. Structural consistency is a strong requirement for our new markup, and XHTML certainly delivers that consistency.

See the space between <br and /> in the previous example? This space ensures that legacy browsers developed before the XHTML spec can still access your content.

Lowercase Elements and Attributes

The HTML specification never mandated a particular letter case for our pages' markup elements. As a result, developers have become accustomed to writing elements and their attributes in any case at all:

```
<P CLASS=Warning>Alert!</P>
```

In XHTML, all elements and their attributes must be written in lowercase. This is because XML is quite case-sensitive. For example, <body>, <Body>, and <BODY> would be considered three different elements. Because of this, the authors of the XHTML specification standardized on lowercase:

```
<p class="Warning">Alert!</p>
```

You may notice that we've kept the value of Warning intact for our class attribute. This is perfectly acceptable in XHTML because attribute values may be in mixed case (for example, pointing the href of a link to a case-sensitive server). However, they must be quoted.

Every Attribute Requires a Value

Additionally, there were attributes in HTML that previously didn't require a value:

```
<input type="checkbox" checked>
<dl compact>
```

Both checked and compact are examples of "minimized" attributes. Because they didn't require a value; it was simply enough to declare the attribute and then carry on. However, XHTML mandates that a value must be supplied for all attributes. For "minimized" attributes, they can be easily expanded like so:

```
<input type="checkbox" checked="checked">
<dl compact="compact">
```

This is a small distinction but one that's integral to ensuring that your code remains valid.

Abstracting Style from Structure

Many standards advocates tout "the separation of style from structure" as the primary benefit of adopting CSS in your site's design—and we agree, with a slight qualification. As you'll see in the coming pages, there never is a true divorce between your markup and your style sheets. Change the structure of the former, and dozens of rules in the latter might become obsolete.

Because your markup and your CSS are quite interrelated, we prefer to think of style as *abstracted from* structure. Your markup primarily exists to describe your content, that's true—however, it will always contain some level of presentational information. The degree, however, is entirely up to you. If you so choose, you could easily offload the presentational work onto the XHTML—replete with font elements, tables, and spacer GIFs.

On the other hand, our style sheet can contain rules that determine all aspects of our pages' design: colors, typography, images, even layout. And if these rules reside in an external style sheet file to which your site's pages are linked, you can control the visual display of *n* HTML documents on your site—an appealing prospect not only for day-to-day site updates, but one that will pay off in spades during that next site-wide redesign initiative. Simply by editing a few dozen lines in a centralized style sheet, you can gain unprecedented control over your markup's presentation.

This should, we hope, make you and your marketing department very happy.

Because your CSS can reside in that separate file, your users could ostensibly cache your entire site's user interface after they visit the first page therein. This is quite a departure from the tag soup days of Web design, where users would be forced to re-download bloated markup on each page of our site: nested `<table>` elements, spacer GIFs, `<font>` elements, `bgcolor` declarations, and all. Now, they simply digest your site's look-and-feel once, and then browse quickly through lightweight markup on the rest of your pages.

This should, we hope, make your users very happy.

And finally, the most obvious benefit is how very simple your markup has become. This will further positively impact your users' bandwidth, allowing them to download your pages even more quickly. And, of course, this lighter markup will benefit your site in any search engine optimization initiatives you might undertake. If you think it's easy for *you* to sift through five lines of an unordered list, just think of how much more search engine robots will love indexing the content in your now-lightweight markup.

This should, we hope—oh, you get the point. Happy yet?

> Brandon Olejniczak has published an excellent article on "Using XHTML/CSS for an Effective SEO Campaign" (`http://alistapart.com/articles/seo/`). In it, he discusses some practical, commonsense strategies for reducing your markup and making it more search engine–friendly.

Avoid Divitis and Classitis

When abandoning tables for more lightweight markup, it's not uncommon for beginning developers to rely heavily on `class` attributes to replace their beloved `font` elements. So, we might have dealt with a navigation bar table that looked like this:

```
<!-- outer table -->
<table bgcolor="#000000" border="0" cellspacing="0" cellpadding="0">
<tbody>
<tr>
<td>
<!-- inner table -->
<table border="0" cellspacing="1" cellpadding="3">
<tbody>
<tr>
<td bgcolor="#DDDDDD"><font face="Verdana, Geneva, Helvetica, sans-serif"
size="2"><a href="home.html">Home</a></font></td>
<td bgcolor="#DDDDDD"><font face="Verdana, Geneva, Helvetica, sans-serif"
size="2"><a href="about.html">About Us</a></font></td>
<td bgcolor="#DDDDDD"><font face="Verdana, Geneva, Helvetica, sans-serif"
size="2"><a href="products.html">Our Products</a></font></td>
</tr>
</tbody>
</table>
<!-- END inner table -->
```

```
</td>
</tr>
</tbody>
</table>
<!-- END outer table -->
```

This version isn't much better:

```
<!-- outer table -->
<table class="bg-black" border="0" cellspacing="0" cellpadding="0">
<tbody>
<tr>
<td>
<!-- inner table -->
<table border="0" cellspacing="1" cellpadding="3">
<tbody>
<tr>
<td class="bg-gray"><a href="home.html" class="innerlink">Home</a></td>
<td class="bg-gray"><a href="about.html" class="innerlink">About Us</a></td>
<td class="bg-gray"><a href="products.html" class="innerlink">Our Products</a></td>
</tr>
</tbody>
</table>
<!-- END inner table -->
</td>
</tr>
</tbody>
</table>
<!-- END outer table -->
```

This is known as *classitis*, a term coined by designer Jeffrey Zeldman (www.zeldman.com/) to describe markup bloat from overuse of the class attribute. The monkey on our back has been exchanged for another. Rather than spelling out our presentational goals explicitly in the markup, this example uses the class attribute to achieve the same means. All that's been changed is that the values of the bgcolor attributes and font elements have been moved to an external style sheet — a fine start, but the markup is still unnecessarily heavy.

Even worse, it's far too easy to succumb to *divitis*, taking otherwise sensible markup and turning it into soup loaded with div elements:

```
<div id="outer-table">
<div id="inner-table">
<div class="innerlink"><span class="link"><a href="home.html"
class="innerlink">Home</a></span></div>
<div class="innerlink"><span class="link"><a href="about.html"
class="innerlink">About Us</a></span></div>
<div class="innerlink"><span class="link"><a href="products.html"
class="innerlink">Our Products</a></span></div>
</div>
</div>
```

If that made any sense to you, perhaps you'd be kind enough to call us up and explain it to us. There's no obvious attempt here to write well-structured markup. While div and span are excellent markup tools, an over-reliance upon them can lead to code bloat and hard-to-read markup. And not just hard for *you* to read, but your users as well. Remember our text-only screenshot from before (refer to Figure 2-3)? If someone has style sheets turned off, using generic markup will make it difficult for those in a non-graphical environment to understand the context of your content.

Toward Well-Meaning Markup

Alternatively, we can use markup elements as they were intended — using `divs` and `spans` to fill in the gaps where no other elements are available. In this section, we'll discuss some strategies for stripping your pages' markup to a well-structured, well-*meaning* minimum, getting it (and you) ready for the CSS tips and strategies contained throughout the remainder of this book.

In the following sections, we'll revisit some of the HTML used in the Harvard Web site (refer to Figure 2-1). We'll apply some more well-structured thinking to the old-school markup, and see if we can't produce something a bit sleeker.

Familiarize Yourself with Other Markup Elements

Here, we're in the process of *describing* content, not designing it. As such, the more well versed you are with the XHTML specification, the more adept you'll be at accurately depicting your site's structure with it.

Headers

Let's look at the markup for one of the news items in the right-hand column of the Harvard Web site:

```
<b>'Illuminating the beauty of life'</b>
<br>Yannatos starts 41st year conducting Harvard-Radcliffe Orchestra
<a href="http://www.news.harvard.edu/gazette/2004/10.21/23-yannatos.html"><font
size="-1"><b>More</b></font></a><font size="-1"><br></font>
</td>
<td width="120">
<a href="http://www.news.harvard.edu/gazette/2004/10.21/23-yannatos.html"><img
src="images/041029a.jpg" alt="James Yannatos" border="0" height="120"
width="120"></a><br><br>
```

In this news item, the content leads with a header displaying the title of the featured story. However, you wouldn't know it was a header from the markup:

```
<b>'Illuminating the beauty of life'</b>
```

Rather than using markup to describe how the element should look to sighted users on desktop browsers, why not use a header element?

```
<h4>Reversing Saddam's ecocide of Iraqi marshes</h4>
```

Here we've used an h4, which would be appropriate if there are three levels of headers above this one in the document's hierarchy. Now, any user agent reading this page will recognize the text as a header, and render it in the most effective way it can.

When building your well-meaning markup, it's helpful to think of your document as conforming to a kind of outline — the most important header sits at the top in an h1, beneath it are a number of h2s, beneath each of which is an h3 or two, and so on down to h6. How you envision your document's outline is entirely up to you. Settle upon a model that makes sense to you, and keep it consistent throughout your site's markup.

Paragraphs

After the news story's headline, a paragraph-long excerpt follows it—but, again, the markup belies the content's intent:

```
<br>Yannatos starts 41st year conducting Harvard-Radcliffe Orchestra
<a href="http://www.news.harvard.edu/gazette/2004/10.21/23-yannatos.html"><font
size="-1"><b>More</b></font></a><font size="-1"><br></font>
```

If this is a paragraph, then we should mark it up as such, and not just rely on break elements (<br>) to visually set it apart from the content surrounding it:

```
<p>Yannatos starts 41st year conducting Harvard-Radcliffe Orchestra <a
title="Harvard Gazette: &quot;Illuminating the beauty of life&quot;"
href="http://www.news.harvard.edu/gazette/2004/10.21/23-yannatos.html">More</a></p>
```

Here, you can see that we've included the More link within the paragraph—as we'll show you later in the chapter, we could easily use CSS to move the anchor down to the next line. So, while keeping the anchor inside the paragraph is intentional, you may opt to take a different approach.

Unordered Lists

As for the menus at the top of our page, what is a site's navigation but a list of links? We can replace the table-heavy navigation menus with unordered lists, each list item element containing a link to a different part of our site.

With a little bit of JavaScript magic, nested unordered lists can be quickly and easily converted into dynamic drop-down menus. One of the most popular examples of this is the "Son of Suckerfish" (SoS) menu script (www.htmldog.com/articles/suckerfish/dropdowns/) developed by designers Patrick Griffiths and Dan Webb. The SoS menu is a perfect example of how behavior (JavaScript) and style (CSS) can be layered atop a foundation of well-structured markup, all the while degrading gracefully to non-CSS or non–JS-aware Internet devices.

Take Stock of Your Content, Not Your Graphics

First and foremost, you should perform an inventory of your page's content areas. Taking another look at the Harvard University home page (see Figure 2-4), we can see that the site's layout quickly breaks down into the following outline:

- ❑ Header
- ❑ Navigation
  - ❑ Primary
  - ❑ Secondary
- ❑ Content
  - ❑ Main Content
  - ❑ Additional Content
- ❑ Footer Navigation
- ❑ Copyright Information

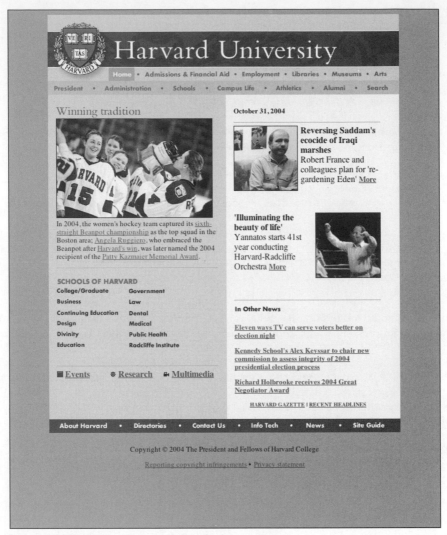

Figure 2-4: The entire Harvard University home page

Within the two columns, we can further describe the various blocks of content therein—which is exactly what we've done in Figure 2-5. Within the Main Content column, we have a featured story, a list of school links, and a list of miscellaneous other links. The second column is devoted primarily to news stories, with the first content block containing the news features we examined earlier, the second containing news items of lesser importance.

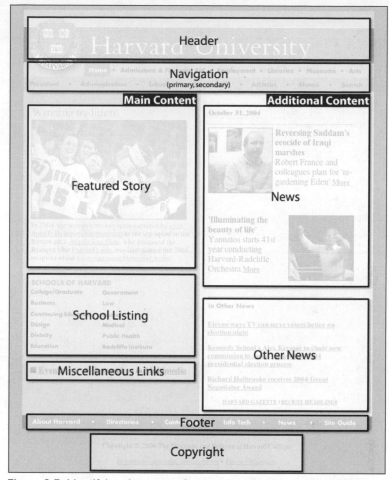

Figure 2-5: Identifying the areas of content on the Harvard home page

From this mental map of our page's content, we can then describe it through markup. Each one of the content areas can be described by a `div` with a unique `id`, and — in the case of the two content columns — nested child content blocks in `div`s as necessary. Once we've done so, we'll have an XHTML document that looks something like Figure 2-6. Every content area is marked up with a descriptively `id`'d `div`, with the nesting order reflecting the relationships we outlined in our content inventory (refer to Figure 2-5).

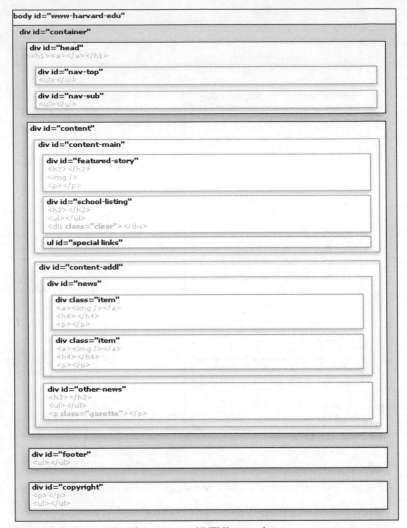

Figure 2-6: The outline for our new XHTML template

At this point, our markup is a kind of blank slate, upon which we can layer style accordingly. And for those users unable to see our styles, they're left with a well-structured, easy-to-follow markup structure (see Figure 2-7). In the rest of this chapter and throughout this book, we'll be examining strategies for how to best add this presentation layer on top of this foundation of valid markup.

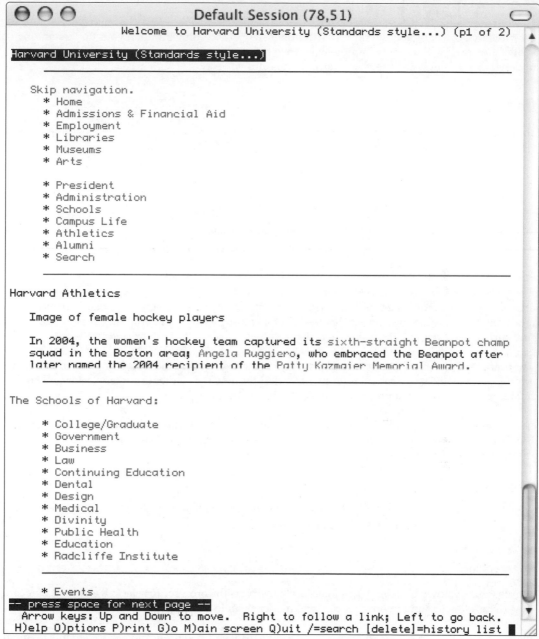

Figure 2-7: Lynx view of our revised Harvard XHTML

CSS: A Layer of Style

As with any other language, getting your bearings in CSS is contingent upon your understanding of its syntax. Doing so will not only improve your own fluency in writing style sheets, but increase your understanding of how the browser interprets the rules you write.

Selectors

Your CSS comprises style *rules* that are interpreted by the browser, and then applied to the corresponding elements in your document. For example, consider Figure 2-8.

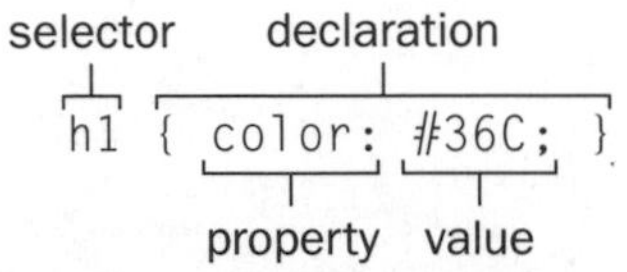

Figure 2-8: A simple sample style rule. Say that five times fast.

Every CSS rule comprises these two parts: a *selector*, which tells the browser which element(s) will be affected by the rule; and a *declaration block*, which determines which *properties* of the element will be modified. In Figure 2-8, we can see that the selector comprises everything up to, but not including, the first curly brace ({).

The braces encompass the *declaration block*, which is the real meat of the rule. It consists of one or more *declarations*, as well as a *property/value* pair that decides how the elements in the selector will be styled. In Figure 2-8, color is the property, and #36C is its declared value.

If you think this sounds simple, it certainly is. Commonsense logic pervades through the syntax of CSS. But this is just the beginning. We can use these very simple principles to build increasingly complex rules, and gain even more control over our sites' presentation.

Type Selectors

It's been only a couple paragraphs, but we know you've missed our simple h1 rule. Let's revisit it:

```
h1 {
color: #36C;
}
```

This is what's known as a *type selector* because it instructs the browser to select all elements of a certain type (here, all h1s found in our markup) and render them in a lovely blue.

In case you were wondering, that sound you just heard was a few thousand font elements taking their last gasping breath.

Wondering about that odd-looking #36C color value? That's a shorthand way of notating hex colors. You can abbreviate your RGB triplets in this way if each of the hex pairs is the same. So, rather than typing out #3366CC, we can instead write #36C because the red (33), green (66), and blue (CC) hex pairs all contain duplicate characters. We could similarly shorten #FFFF00 to #FF0, #000000 to #000, #CC3300 to #C30, and so forth.

The Universal Selector

Another selector with far-reaching authority, the *universal selector,* has a much broader scope than the type selector. Rather than selecting elements of a specific type, the universal selector quite simply matches the name of *any* element type. Aptly enough, its notation is the asterisk, or wildcard symbol, as shown here:

```
* {
color: #000;
}
```

This rule renders the content of every element in our document in black. This is simple enough, right? You might not encounter a rule like this too frequently because use of the universal selector is limited a bit by its intimidating scope. Furthermore, there are a few support issues with it that might warrant testing. However, we'll later discuss some specific uses for this selector, which sometimes leaves its mark by not showing up at all.

Descendant Selectors

Suppose for a moment that we were faced with the following markup:

```
<p>I just <em>love</em> emphasis!</p>
<ul>
<li>Don't <em>you</em>?!</li>
<li>Oh, certainly.
<ol>
<li>I <em>still</em> love it!</li>
</ol>
</li>
</ul>
```

By default, most browsers render em elements in italics—nothing new there. But what if we're feeling a bit arbitrary? Let's say that we want all em elements in our uls to be displayed in uppercase. Using what we've learned up to this point, we could write a rule that uses a type selector, and matches on all em elements:

```
em {
text-transform: uppercase;
}
```

However, we want to match only the ems within the ul — in other words, any ems in the opening paragraph should be unaffected by our rule. Simply using the em in our selector will match on *all* ems from our document, so we'll have to be a bit more specific:

```
ul em {
text-transform: uppercase;
}
```

This rule begins with a *descendant selector*, and tells the browser to "select all em elements that are descendants of ul elements." Just as you're a child of your parents, you're a *descendant* of your grandparents and your great-grandparents. In this way, em elements at every level of the unordered list would get the style applied—even those contained within the ordered list. Most important, our rule won't select the em element in the opening p, just as we'd intended.

Granted, there aren't too many occasions when you'll need to style your poor little ems in this way (though, if that happens to be your particular slice of heaven, we won't stand in your way). Instead, bear in mind that these kinds of selectors can afford you a highly granular level of control over your pages' design. Should you ever need to exempt certain sections of your content from otherwise global style rules, you now possess the means to do so.

Class Selectors

Looking for even finer-grained control? Style sheets can hook into even more aspects of your markup. Remember the class attribute we used in the Harvard University makeover? We used it to denote an "item" category of divs. Well, it's not just auspicious timing that brings us to the *class selector*:

```
input.text {
border: 1px solid #C00;
}
```

This selector allows CSS authors to select elements whose class attribute contains the value specified after the period (.). In this example, the rule would select all input elements whose class attribute contained the word "text," like so:

```
<form id="sample" action="blah.html" method="post">
<fieldset>
<p>
<label for="text-one">Box #1:</label>
<input type="text" id="text-one" size="15" class="text" />
</p>
<p>
<label for="text-two">Box #2:</label>
<input type="text" id="text-two" size="15" class="text" />
</p>
<input type="submit" id="submit" value="Submit!" />
</fieldset>
</form>
```

The submit button at the end of our sample form is unaffected, and the rule is applied to the two text fields — classed, aptly enough, as "text."

If we want our class selector to be even more generic, we can simply omit the "input" like so:

```
.text {
border: 1px solid #C00;
}
```

Though you might not recognize it, our universal selector is making an appearance here; if we wanted, we could write this rule:

```
*.text {
border: 1px solid #C00;
}
```

Both selectors achieve the same goal: both will select *all* elements whose class attribute contains the word "text".

id Selectors

Similar to class selectors, id selectors enable you to select an element based on the id attribute:

```
h1#page-title {
text-align: right;
}
```

Whereas the class selector used a period (.), the id selector relies on a hash (#). In this rule, we've selected the h1 element that has an id attribute whose value matches the text after the hash (namely, "page-title"). As with class selectors, we could again rely on the implicit universal selector here, leaving the h1 out of the picture altogether:

```
#page-title {
text-align: right;
}
```

How are we able to do this? Well, the value of an element's id attribute is unique, within the context of a valid XHTML document—no other element in our markup may share the "page-title" id with our h1. Therefore, we know that both rules will match only one element in our markup, making the results of the two rules equivalent.

Nothing especially exciting, you say? You ain't seen nothing yet, we say.

The true power of id selectors is when they're used as the foundation for descendant selectors, like so:

```
#content h2 {
text-transform: uppercase;
}
```

Rules such as this are the foundation of complex layouts. As CSS designers, this allows us to create style rules that are incredibly context-aware. For example, this rule will select all h2 elements that are descendants of the element with an id of "content," and *only* those h2s. All other second-level heading elements in the document will be unaffected by this rule.

Other Selectors

In this section, we'll examine some of the other selectors available to us in the specification (although it might be more accurate to surround "available" with quotation marks because we're not currently able to use the full power of these excellent styling tools). As you'll see, another title for this section might have been "The Best Ideas You Can't Really Use."

As of this writing, the Windows version of Microsoft Internet Explorer (MSIE/Win)—currently the world's most prevalent browser—does not support these selectors. While other modern browsers enjoy rich support for them, many of these selectors are new as of CSS2. MSIE/Win's implementation of that specification is nascent at best. Until Internet Explorer supports them, these useful selectors cannot be relied upon for everyday commercial use.

We mention these tools not to yank the rug out from under your feet, but for completeness. At some point in the (we hope) near future, these selectors will enjoy robust support from Microsoft's browser.

While these selectors can't be relied upon to fuel professional design projects as of the writing of this book, the day will come when browser implementation (or the lack thereof) is no longer an issue. As they say, luck favors the prepared.

Child Selectors

When we discussed descendant selectors, we discovered that we could write rules that instantly affect all elements beneath another element. Let's assume that we want to style all the paragraphs in the body of our document:

```
<body>
<p>I am the very model...</p>
<div class="news">
<p>Of a modern markup general.</p>
</div>
<p>I use every attribute, be it vegetable or mineral.</p>
</body>
```

To have all paragraphs display in bold, we could write either of the following:

```
p {
font-weight: bold;
}
```

or

```
body p {
font-weight: bold;
}
```

Both would have the same effect. As we've discussed previously, they would select all paragraphs contained within the document's `body` element, at any level.

But, what if we wanted to restrain the scope of our match a bit, and just select the paragraphs immediately beneath the `body` element in our document's hierarchy?

Enter *child selectors*:

```
body>p {
font-weight: bold;
}
```

The greater-than sign (>) instructs the user agent to select all *child* p elements, not all *descendants*. Therefore, the paragraphs contained by the `div` would not be affected because they are children of that element — not the `body`. However, the paragraphs immediately before and after the `div` would be affected because they both share the `body` as their parent element.

Attribute Selectors

Rather than peppering our form with `class` attributes, the CSS specification has defined *attribute selectors*. These selectors enable us to not only match on a given element's `class`, but on any other attribute it possesses. Denoted by a set of square brackets, attribute selectors can match in any of the four ways shown in the following table.

Attribute Selector Syntax	Result
[x]	Matches when the element has the specified x attribute, regardless of the value of that attribute.
[x=y]	Matches when the element's x attribute has a value that is exactly y.
[x~=y]	Matches when the value of the element's x attribute is a space-delimited list of words, one of which is exactly y.
[x|=y]	Matches when the value of the element's x attribute is a hyphen-separated list of words beginning with y.

Seem a bit confusing? A few concrete examples of attribute selectors, and the elements they would select, are shown in the following table.

Selector	What It Means	What It Selects	What It Won't Select
p[lang]	Selects all paragraph elements with a lang attribute.	`<p lang="eng">` `<p lang="five">`	`<p class="lang">` `<p>`
p[lang="fr"]	Selects all paragraph elements whose lang attribute has a value of exactly "fr".	`<p lang="fr">` `<p class="gazette" lang="fr">`	`<p lang="fr-Canada">` `<p lang="french">`
p[lang~="fr"]	Selects all paragraph elements whose lang attribute contains the word "fr".	`<p lang="fr">` `<p lang="en fr">` `<p lang="la sp fr">`	`<p lang="fr-Canada">` `<p lang="french">`
p[lang|="en"]	Selects all paragraph elements whose lang attributes contain values that are exactly "en", or begin with "en-".	`<p lang="en">` `<p lang="en-US">` `<p lang="en-cockney">`	`<p lang="US-en">` `<p lang="eng">`

The potential application for these selectors is exciting, to say the least. Revisiting our form from before, our work gets a lot easier:

```
<form id="sample" action="blah.html" method="post">
<fieldset>
<p>
<label for="text-one">Box #1:</label>
<input type="text" id="text-one" size="15" />
</p>
<p>
<label for="text-two">Box #2:</label>
<input type="text" id="text-two" size="15" />
```

```
</p>
<input type="submit" id="submit" value="Submit!" />
</fieldset>
</form>
```

Using an attribute selector, it would be very easy for you to hone in on all input elements whose type attribute exactly matched "text":

```
input[type="text"] {
border: 1px solid #C00;
}
```

The advantage to this method is that the <input type="submit" /> element is unaffected, and the border applied only to the desired text fields. No longer do we need to pepper our markup with presentational class attributes. Instead, we can use our XHTML itself as a kind of API for our style sheets, writing selectors that "hook" into the very structure of our document.

Lest we be accused of turning our nose up at class selectors, let us reassure you that we're not guilty of semantic grandstanding. At the end of the day, the selectors we're able to use — that is, those compatible with Microsoft's Internet Explorer — are excellent tools, if perhaps not the ideal ones. While using classes in our form might not be the most "semantically pure" solution, they afford us a great deal of flexibility and structural control in our designs today.

Multiple Declarations

Now, all of the style rules we've looked at so far have had only one declaration — thankfully, this doesn't have to be the case. Imagine how verbose our CSS would be if we had to restrict ourselves to this sort of syntax:

```
h1 { color: #36C; }
h1 { font-weight: normal; }
h1 { letter-spacing: .4em; }
h1 { margin-bottom: 1em; }
h1 { text-transform: lowercase; }
```

Were your browser to read your style sheet aloud to you, this snippet would be an incredible cure for insomnia. It might sound something like, "Select all h1 elements, and apply a color of #36C. Select all h1 elements, and weight the type normally. Select all h1 elements, and space the letters by point-four ems. Select all h1 elements, and apply a bottom margin of one em. Select all h1 elements, and transform the text to lowercase." Not exactly a gripping read, is it? Rest assured, it'll knock your kids out faster than *Goodnight Moon* ever could.

Thankfully, we've a way out of this over-verbose mess. Multiple declarations for the same selector can be compressed into one semicolon-delimited, easy-to-carry rule. With that, let's revisit our multiple h1 rules:

```
h1 {
color: #36C;
font-weight: normal;
letter-spacing: .4em;
margin-bottom: 1em;
text-transform: lowercase;
}
```

This is much better. As this example shows, we can style multiple properties of our h1 elements in one rule. This enables us to keep our style sheets clutter-free, and the cost of managing them way, way down. After all, brevity *is* the soul of style.

> *When writing a rule with multiple declarations, the semicolon is technically considered a delimiter — something to separate the end of one declaration with the start of another. As such, it's perfectly valid for you to omit the semicolon from the final rule in a style block because there isn't another subsequent declaration. For consistency's sake, we recommend ending every declaration with a semicolon. That way, if you need to change a declaration's position in a rule, or globally edit a property's value, you won't need to worry about whether or not a semicolon is actually present.*

Grouping

But what if we want to apply the style of our h1 rule to other elements in our document? If we wanted to have all h2 and h3 elements share the same style as our h1s, we could, of course, be quite explicit about it:

```
h1 {
color: #36C;
font-weight: normal;
letter-spacing: .4em;
margin-bottom: 1em;
text-transform: lowercase;
}
h2 {
color: #36C;
font-weight: normal;
letter-spacing: .4em;
margin-bottom: 1em;
text-transform: lowercase;
}
h3 {
color: #36C;
font-weight: normal;
letter-spacing: .4em;
margin-bottom: 1em;
text-transform: lowercase;
}
```

No small amount of code, you say? Right you are. But once again, the specification has provided us with another way to keep our CSS lean and bandwidth-friendly. Namely, when several rules share the same declarations, the selectors can be "grouped" into one comma-delimited list. For example, we can write our three header rules into one all-encompassing rule:

```
h1, h2, h3 {
color: #36C;
font-weight: normal;
letter-spacing: .4em;
margin-bottom: 1em;
text-transform: lowercase;
}
```

The order of the list is irrelevant. All the elements in the selector will have the corresponding declarations applied to them.

Of course, we can be even more intelligent about consolidating shared properties. If rules share only certain properties but not others, it's simple enough for us to create a grouped rule with the common values, and then leave the more unique properties in separate rules, as shown here:

```
#content {
border: 1px solid #C00;
padding: 10px;
width: 500px;
}
#footer {
padding: 10px;
width: 500px;
}
#supplement {
border: 1px solid #C00;
padding: 10px;
position: absolute;
left: 510px;
width: 200px;
}
```

We can see that all the previous rules share a padding of 10 pixels. The #content and #footer rules share the same width. #content and #supplement have a 1 pixel–thin red border applied to the matching elements. With these similarities in mind, we can consolidate like-valued properties into grouped selectors, like so:

```
#content, #footer, #supplement {
padding: 10px;
}
#content, #footer {
width: 500px;
}
#content, #supplement {
border: 1px solid #C00;
}
#supplement {
position: absolute;
left: 510px;
width: 200px;
}
```

It may not look like we've gained all that much — we're now left with 14 lines compared to the previous example's 16, and we've even gained an extra rule to keep track of. But the advantage to this intelligent grouping is cumulative, and will become more apparent once you begin writing more complex style rules. When we consolidate shared style declarations, we need edit only *one* style rule to change the border color of the #content and #supplement elements, or to increase the width of the #content and #footer elements. Once your style sheets become not a few dozen rules long but a few *hundred*, this grouping can be a real timesaver when it comes time to edit shared values.

Inheritance

When writing CSS rules, it bears remembering that some properties (and the values you assign to them) will be inherited to descendant elements. In fact, it helps to envision inheritance much in the same way you'd think of traits that you inherit from your family. A Web page isn't all that dissimilar, in fact. There are parent-child relationships, in which elements inherit style properties from the elements that contain them. In fact, you can almost draw a family tree of your page's elements, as shown in Figure 2-9.

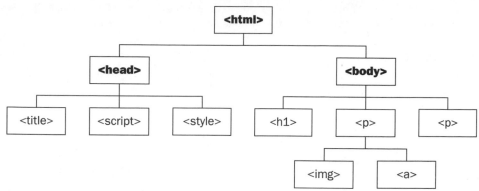

Figure 2-9: Your markup document tree

Element Hierarchy

The html element is the root element of your page, and, as such, is at the base of our "document tree." It is the *parent* of its *child* elements—namely, the head and body elements, which have their own children, which in turn have their own children, and so on down the line. Elements that share the same parent are called *siblings*. Tags placed more than one level down the tree from a given point are considered *descendants*. Conversely, elements near the top of the tree can be considered *ancestors* to those that are nearer the bottom. There you have it, all the neatly arranged hierarchy of a family tree, without such niceties as your Uncle Eustace's habit of telling off-color jokes during Thanksgiving dinner.

We're much better at writing Web design books than we are at making jokes about genealogy. Honest.

When thinking of our markup in this hierarchical manner, it's much easier to envision exactly how styles will propagate down the various branches. Consider the following example:

```
body {
color: #000;
font-family: Georgia, "Times New Roman", serif;
font-size: 12px;
}
```

According to the syntax rules we've already covered, we know that this rule tells the user agent to select all body elements and apply a serif typeface (looking on the client's machine for Georgia, Times New Roman, or a generic sans-serif font, in that order), sized at 12 pixels and colored in black (#000).

Now, applying the rules of inheritance to our document, these three properties will be handed down to all elements contained within the body of our document—or, to use the language of our document's family tree, to all elements that are *descendants* of the body. Already we've demonstrated why CSS is such a powerful presentation engine. With four lines of a single style rule, we've done the work of a small army of font elements.

While inheritance is perhaps the most powerful aspect of CSS, it can at times also be one of the more confusing. Keep in mind that *not all properties are inherited*. Margin and padding are two such examples. Those properties are applied solely to an element, and are not inherited by its descendants.

For a reference of what properties are passed along to an element's descendants, you're best served by the specification itself (`www.w3.org/TR/CSS21/about.html#property-defs`).

Overriding Inheritance

What if we don't want a specific section of our document to inherit some of its ancestors' traits? Consider the following example:

```
<body>
<p>I still like big blocks.</p>
<ul>
<li>...but lists are even cooler.</li>
</ul>
</body>
```

If the earlier CSS rule for the `body` element were applied here, then all of the text within the `p` and `li` would inherit the values declared therein. But when your client walks in and demands that all list items should be in a red (his wife's favorite color) sans-serif typeface? Simply write a rule to select the descendant elements you're worried about, like so:

```
body {
    color: #000;
    font-family: Georgia, "Times New Roman", serif;
    font-size: 10px;
}
li {
    color: #C00;
    font-family: Verdana, sans-serif;
}
```

This is our first glimpse at how the *cascade* part of "cascading style sheets" works. Because the list items are descendants of the `body` element, the second rule effectively breaks the chain of inheritance, and applies the declared styles to the selected elements — here, the `li`. However, because we've not declared a new font size for the list items, they'll still inherit that property's value (10px) from their ancestor, the `body`. The end result is that your users will see the list items rendered in the requested red, sans-serif font, while all other elements on the page will inherit the rules from the `body`. Let's hope you, your client, and your client's wife are happy with the result.

Putting It All into Action

Let's take another look at an example of some overworked markup. Consider the rather bare-bones navigation bar shown in Figure 2-10.

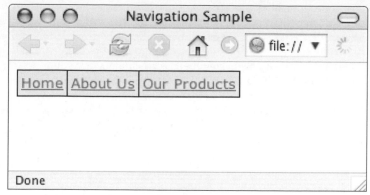

Figure 2-10: A simple navigation bar

Notice the three links in a light-gray, horizontal row, each surrounded by a 1 pixel–thin black border. This seems rather unassuming, until you consider the traditional markup method for creating it:

```
<!-- outer table -->
<table bgcolor="#000000" border="0" cellspacing="0" cellpadding="0">
<tbody>
<tr>
<td>
<!-- inner table -->
<table border="0" cellspacing-"1" cellpadding="3">
<tbody>
<tr>
<td bgcolor="#DDDDDD"><font face="Verdana, Geneva, Helvetica, sans-serif"
size="2"><a href="home.html">Home</a></font></td>
<td bgcolor="#DDDDDD"><font face="Verdana, Geneva, Helvetica, sans-serif"
size="2"><a href="about.html">About Us</a></font></td>
<td bgcolor="#DDDDDD"><font face="Verdana, Geneva, Helvetica, sans-serif"
size="2"><a href="products.html">Our Products</a></font></td>
</tr>
</tbody>
</table>
<!-- END inner table -->
</td>
</tr>
</tbody>
</table>
<!-- END outer table -->
```

There are two tables involved in creating this simple navigation bar. The first, outer table has a black background applied to it (bgcolor="#000000"). The inner table has no background color of its own, but has a cellspacing of 1 pixel. This allows the parent table's black background to bleed through, creating the "border" effect around each of the navigation items. We've also added 3 pixels of cellpadding on the inner table, so that there's some breathing room between the text of each link and the table cell (<td>) that contains it. Finally, the gray background color (bgcolor="#DDDDDD") is applied to each cell of the inner table, as well as a <font> element denoting the appropriate typeface and size.

Twenty-four lines of code—about 1KB of data—might seem rather innocuous when contained to one code snippet in a Web design book, but consider that the code spread across twenty pages of your site— or perhaps a hundred, even a thousand. What happens when you're asked to modify this code? Perhaps your marketing department needs the gray background universally changed to a light green, or they've since standardized on Arial as their corporate typeface. In either event, you'll need to edit, test, and redeploy the markup used on each of those 20, 100, or 1,000 pages to meet their requirements.

Suffice it to say that this isn't exactly an appealing prospect to us. Thankfully, we can use what we've learned about XHTML and CSS to improve this navigation bar, as well as make our lives easier. First, we'll start with some fresh markup. Rather than relying on the bloated, font-heavy table from before, let's take a different approach.

```
<ul id="nav">
<li class="first"><a href="home.html">Home</a></li>
<li><a href="about.html">About Us</a></li>
<li><a href="products.html">Our Products</a></li>
</ul>
```

That's right, this is a simple unordered list. As we mentioned earlier in the chapter, we don't need to be worried about presentation at this level. We just need to ensure that we're marking up our content in a sensible way, which is exactly what we've done. So, we have our humble beginnings, as shown in Figure 2-11.

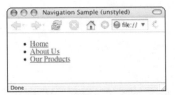

Figure 2-11: A simple unordered list

First, let's get rid of that unseemly bulleted look—that's so 1996.

```
ul#nav, ul#nav li {
list-style: none;
margin: 0;
padding: 0;
}
```

Figure 2-12 shows the result.

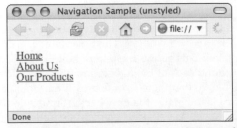

Figure 2-12: An unordered list . . . but *sans* bullets

As you can see, we're using ID selectors quite liberally here. By specifying ul#nav in our rules, we'll be able to style our navigation list (and the elements within it) independently of the rest of the markup on our page. And by grouping the ul#nav and ul#nav li rules into one comma-delimited selector, we can simultaneously remove the bullets from the list items (list-style: none;) *and* remove superfluous margin and padding at the same time (margin: 0; padding: 0;).

Of course, our original navigation table was horizontal, and our list currently isn't anything remotely resembling that. However, that's easily fixed.

```
ul#nav, ul#nav li {
float: left;
list-style: none;
margin: 0;
padding: 0;
}
```

Figure 2-13 shows the result.

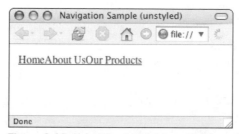

Figure 2-13: Using floats to get our list in order

Adding the float property to our rule gets our list back in line, literally. Each list item floats to the left of the one before it, pulling them out of their vertical stacking order and into the horizontal line we see here.

> *The float model is a powerful CSS construct, and is, in fact, the basis for many CSS-based layouts. Eric Meyer's article "Containing Floats"* (www.complexspiral.com/publications/containing-floats/) *explains floats in more detail, and clears up some common misconceptions about this remarkably handy layout tool.*

Now that we've established the basic layout, we can begin adding a few more of the visual components. We're sure you've missed the black border and gray background, so let's make those our next priority:

```
ul#nav {
font-family: Verdana, Geneva, Helvetica, sans-serif;
font-size: .82em;
background-color: #DDD;
}

ul#nav li a {
border: 1px solid #000;
display: block;
float: left;
padding: 3px;
}
```

61

Figure 2-14 shows the result.

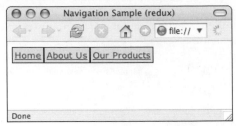

Figure 2-14: Applying borders and color to our navigation list

As you can see, we've applied the gray background color to the unordered list directly. And by setting the font attributes on the list as well, we can use inheritance to apply a sans-serif font to all elements therein. By default, anchors are rendered as inline elements. This presents a slight problem for us, because any padding we apply to them will affect only their horizontal edges. Because we want 3 pixels of padding on each side of our navigation links, we must turn our links into block-level items with `display: block;`.

However, things aren't quite right. You'll notice that the border is too thick between the Home and About Us links, and again between About Us and Our Products. This is because the border on each item abuts against its siblings, creating a doubled-up effect when two of the links touch. So, we'll have to rethink our style slightly:

```
ul#nav li a {
border-color: #000;
border-width: 1px 1px 1px 0;
border-style: solid;
display: block;
float: left;
padding: 3px;
}
```

Figure 2-15 shows the result.

Figure 2-15: Rethinking the borders

That's more like it. Our more verbose border declarations (`border-color`, `border-width`, *and* `border-style`) achieve the same effect as our earlier `border: 1px solid #000;`, but the final 0 in our `border-width` declaration instructs the browser to leave off the left-hand border from each list item, whereas the top, right, and bottom edges each get a 1px-wide border applied. Now, we simply need to restore the border to the first list item, and *only* the first list item — we don't need that double-border effect again, thank you very much. To do that, let's apply a `class` attribute to the first list item in our markup:

```
<ul id="nav">
<li class="first"><a href="home.html">Home</a></li>
<li><a href="about.html">About Us</a></li>
<li><a href="products.html">Our Products</a></li>
</ul>
```

Now that we've supplied ourselves with that "hook" into our document's structure, it should be pretty straightforward to write a style rule that applies a border to that element, and that element alone:

```
ul#nav li.first a {
    border-width: 1px;
}
```

Figure 2-16 shows the result.

Figure 2-16: The final list

And that's done it! Here's the entire set of rules we've written:

```
ul#nav, ul#nav li {
float: left;
list-style: none;
margin: 0;
padding: 0;
}

ul#nav {
font-family: Verdana, Geneva, Helvetica, sans-serif;
font-size: .82em;
background-color: #DDD;
}

ul#nav li a {
border-color: #000;
border-width: 1px 1px 1px 0;
border-style: solid;
display: block;
float: left;
padding: 3px;
}

ul#nav li.first a {
border-width: 1px;
}
```

We've successfully combined grouping, ID, and class selectors, and some well-placed inheritance to turn a humble navigation list into a horizontal navigation menu. Instead of resting on our laurels (comfy though they are), let's consider the benefits of this approach. Is this really any better than building this in a `table`?

Absolutely. Granted, the number of lines of code hasn't changed all that much, when you tally up the XHTML and the CSS together. However, we've achieved a measure of abstraction of our content's style from its structure. Rather than muddying our markup with presentational cruft, we can instead let cascading style sheets do all the heavy lifting in our user interface. Now, if we need to add another link to our menu, we simply add another `li` to the end of our navigation list, and the CSS handles the rest of the presentation.

Understanding the Cascade

Now that we've figured out the basics of CSS syntax, let's take a closer look at the mechanics behind it, to determine how it is that a user agent determines what styles are delivered to users.

Style Origin

To do so, we must first identify the appropriate rules because the origin of the style rule determines how much "influence" it has in the cascade. Following are the three areas from which style sheets may originate:

❑ **User agent.** To fully conform to the CSS specification (`www.w3.org/TR/CSS21/conform` `.html#conformance`), a user agent must apply a default style sheet to a document before any other style rules are applied. This internal set of CSS rules establishes the default display rules for every HTML element. This is how your browser knows to display an `h1` in a garishly huge serif font, or to put a bullet before every unordered list item.

❑ **The user.** Yes, that's right—your users can write CSS, too. User style sheets were introduced in the CSS2 specification, and conceived as a means of allowing users to override an author's chosen fonts and colors for any given page. While some designers might blanch at the thought, this is a very important accessibility initiative. Under certain design conditions, some users might be unable to perceive your site. Writing custom CSS enables users to increase font sizes that may be illegible, or avoid certain color/contrast combinations that are otherwise invisible to them.

❑ **Author.** This means you. These are the style sheets you include in your markup, and are the primary focus of this book.

When a user agent is faced with evaluating style rules from these three distinct sources, it must figure out which style sheet's rules should be presented to the end user. To do so, it assigns a certain degree of importance (or "weight") to each. The listing of the origins is ordered in an increasing level of importance (that is to say, the browser's default style rules are considered less important than the user's, which are in turn less important than the rules you specify in the CSS files that reside on your site's server).

However, both the author and the user can define `!important` rules:

```
h2 {
font-size: 2em !important;
color: #C00 !important;
}
```

According to the CSS specification (`www.w3.org/TR/CSS21/cascade.html#important-rules`), the `!important` rules "create a balance of power between author and user style sheets." As we mentioned, rules contained in a user style sheet are typically weighted less than those in the author's CSS. However, the presence of an `!important` rule turns this relationship on its head; a user's `!important` declarations are always weighted *more* than the author's, as shown in Figure 2-17.

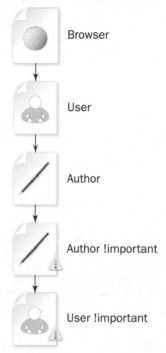

Figure 2-17: Style origin and the cascade, from least to most important

How does this affect our CSS? Let's say that a browser is trying to determine the style for a basic paragraph element (p). After parsing all available style sheets—browser, user, and author—all relevant styles are evaluated, as shown in Listings 2-1, 2-2, and 2-3.

Listing 2-1: The Browser's Style Sheet

```
p {
color: #000;
font-size:
1em;
margin: .9em;
}
```

Listing 2-2: The User's Style Sheet

```
p {
color: #060 !important;
}
```

Listing 2-3: The Author's Style Sheet

```
p {
color: #300;
font-size: 1.2em;
line-height: 1.6em;
padding: 10px;
}
```

Let's set aside the user style sheet for a moment. Therefore, for general users, paragraphs will be styled according to this final, calculated rule:

```
p {
color: #300;              /* author overwrites browser rule */
font-size: 1.2em;         /* author overwrites browser rule */
line-height: 1.6em;       /* specified only by author */
margin: .9em;             /* specified only by browser */
padding: 10px;            /* specified only by author */
}
```

Now, if someone views your page with the user style sheet from Listing 2-2, the final result is changed somewhat:

```
p {
Color: #060;              /* user !important rule overwrites author rule */
font-size: 1.2em;         /* author overwrites browser rule */
line-height: 1.6em;       /* specified only by author */
margin: .9em;             /* specified only by browser */
padding: 10px;            /* specified only by author */
}
```

Sort by Specificity

Every selector is given a *specificity rating*, which is yet another qualitative assessment of a selector's importance in the cascade (www.w3.org/TR/CSS21/cascade.html#specificity). The higher a rule's specificity, the more influence it is granted when your browser sifts through all the rules in the cascade. For example, id-based selectors are inherently more specific than class-driven selectors, as the id by design occurs once in each document.

Specificity is calculated by the selector's syntax itself, and is weighted according to four separate factors.

A. Whether or not the selector is the "style" attribute of an element, rather than a true selector.

B. The number of id attributes in the selector.

C. The number of other attribute (for example, [lang], [rel], [href]) and pseudo-class (for example, :hover, :visited, :first-child) names in the selector. Remember that class selectors (such as li.active) are a type of attribute selector, and are tallied up in this category.

D. The number of element (for example, a, li, p, and so on) and pseudo-element (for example, :before, :after, and so on) names in the selector.

With these four components in hand, it's rather easy to calculate a given selector's importance in the cascade. The following table shows a list of selectors, from least to most specific (columns A–D).

Selector	A	B	C	D	Specificity
a	0	0	0	1	1
h3 a	0	0	0	2	2
ul ol+li	0	0	0	3	3
ul ol li.red	0	0	1	3	13
li.red.level	0	0	2	1	21
#other-news	0	1	0	0	100
style="..."	1	0	0	0	1000

With this information in hand, let's return to our humble paragraph styles from before, and calculate their specificity, as shown in Listings 2-4, 2-5, and 2-6.

Listing 2-4: The Browser's Style Sheet

```
p { color: #000; font-size: 1em; margin: .9em; }
/* A:0, B:0, C:1, D:1  = specificity of 1 */
```

Listing 2-5: The User's Style Sheet

```
p { color: #060 !important; }
/* A:0, B:0, C:1, D:1  = specificity of 1 */
```

Listing 2-6: The Author's Style Sheet

```
p { color: #300; font-size: 1.2em; line-height: 1.6em; padding: 10px; }
/* A:0, B:0, C:1, D:1  = specificity of 1 */
p.gazette { color: #0C0; }
/* A:0, B:0, C:1, D:1 = specificity of 11 */
p#footer { color: #FFF; }
/* A:0, B:1, C:0, D:1  = specificity of 101 */
```

We can see from this that p#footer has the highest specificity, with p.gazette coming in second. Assuming that your site's visitor doesn't have a user style sheet (and is, therefore, unaffected by the !important rule):

1. The paragraph element with an id of `footer` will be displayed in white (#FFF).

2. Those paragraphs with a class of `gazette` will display in green (#0C0).

3. All others will display in a dark red (#300).

All paragraphs in the document obey the property values declared in the original p rule: a font size of 1em, line height of 1.6ems, and 10 pixels of padding. However, the browser's default margin of .9em still reaches the user's display because the author's CSS didn't override it.

Sort by Order

Let's assume that, for some odd reason, an author style sheet declared these two rules, one after the other:

```
p { color: #C00; }
p { color: #000; }
```

When multiple rules have the same specificity, weight, and origin, origin always wins. According to this rule, all paragraphs will be rendered in black. Of course, we could change the weight:

```
p { color: #C00 !important; }
p { color: #000; }
```

The rules are no longer equivalent because !important author rules are weighted more heavily than regular author rules—therefore, all paragraphs will be rendered in red.

From Theory to Practice

Of course, talking at length about the CSS specification gets us only so far (and does wonders for your attention span, we're sure). Integrating the standards to practice into our daily workflow is another matter entirely. To do so, let's examine two critical items in a modern Web designer's toolkit—and no, neither of them has a magic wand tool or a layers palette in sight.

Build to a Reliable Browser

If you build a site when testing in a broken browser, you're building code that relies upon broken rendering. It's as though you're building a house on a foundation of sand. Once you begin testing on other browsers or platforms, the flaws in your work will become far too apparent. Instead, start with a modern browser with an acknowledged level of standards-compliance. As you'll see later in this chapter, you can write hacks into your code that will address lesser browsers' rendering quirks.

This isn't a browser snob's apology, nor is it an attempt to switch your favorite browser. Rather, this approach will save you time and resources when building your site. If you begin building to a flawed browser's bugs, you will spend far more time debugging when you test in a more standards-compliant one. As of this writing, this means one of three options: Opera, Safari, or a Gecko-based browser such as Camino, Mozilla, or Firefox.

You'll note that Internet Explorer doesn't appear in this list, and that's unfortunately intentional. While its standards implementation has increased dramatically over recent years, the Windows version of Internet

Explorer is universally regarded as lagging behind other modern browsers, with regard to support for standards like CSS and XHTML.

However, there is some exciting news on the horizon for IE. Despite announcements from Microsoft that development on standalone versions of Internet Explorer had been halted (`http://slashdot.org/articles/03/05/31/1650206.shtml`), a new version of Internet Explorer has been promised for the summer of 2005, with improved support for Web standards (`http://blogs.msdn.com/ie/archive/2005/03/09/391362.aspx`). While the scope of that support is up for conjecture, we're excited to see a stated commitment to Web standards from IE's developers.

Regardless, we're not yet at the point where clients ask by name for better Firefox support, or improved Opera layouts. While each is an excellent browser in its own right, they have some work to do before capturing the hearts, minds, and — let's face it — the market share of our clients.

The Need for Hacks

Of course, issues are bound to arise when working with CSS-based layouts. While browser implementations have vastly improved over the past few years, the playing field still isn't level. Unless you're supporting just one browser on just one platform, you'll most certainly run into bugs when testing across different browser/platform combinations. Proponents of `table`-layout techniques might interpret these issues as weaknesses in cascading style sheets as a viable layout method. However, the fault lies with the browsers, rather than the CSS specification itself.

But while every browser has its own rendering issues, we're in a rather enviable position. Most of these issues — and their causes — have been well documented and, in many cases, solved outright. What follows is an example of one of the most widespread browser bugs. It's not the only one you'll encounter, but it's a fine example of some of the workarounds available to you. When the chips are down and the browsers aren't behaving, there's almost always a way out.

The Bug

According to the CSS specification (`www.w3.org/TR/CSS21/box.html`), every element in your document tree has a content area; this could be text, an image, or so forth. Additionally, padding, border, and margin areas may surround that content area, as shown in Figure 2-18.

Figure 2-18: The box model

If seeing the box model in resplendent black-and-white leaves you scratching your head, Web designer Jon Hicks has built a full-color, three-dimensional diagram that might be worth checking out as well (www.hicksdesign.co.uk/journal/483/3d_css_box_model/).

Now, the dimensions of those three "extra" areas — padding, border, and margin — add to the total calculated width and height of the content area. Let's look at a style rule that demonstrates this in action:

```
p#hack {
border: 20px solid #C00;
padding: 30px;
width: 400px;
}
```

The width property declares that the content within our paragraphs will not exceed 400 pixels. On top of that, we add 10 pixels of padding and a 10 pixels–thick red border *to each side of the box* — top, right, bottom, and left. So, if we're trying to figure out the full, calculated width of our paragraphs, we'd move from left to right across the box's properties and tally the final width:

```
Left Border:       20   +
Left Padding:      30   +
Content:           400  +
Right Padding:     30   +
Right Border:      20   =
TOTAL WIDTH:       500  PIXELS
```

In short, the padding and border are outside the declared width of the content area, as the specification requires.

However, there are older versions of Internet Explorer on Windows that have an incorrect (or more specifically, a "non-standard") implementation of the box model, and instead put the border and padding *inside* the declared width. Version 6 of that browser is the first to get the calculations right, but only if the browser is in standards-compliant mode — that is, if there's a DOCTYPE at the top of your markup. Otherwise, these browsers incorrectly see our declared 400 pixels as the space into which all of the box's properties — content width, padding, and border — must be placed. So, the calculation in one of these browsers would look something like this:

```
Declared Width:    400  -
Left Border:       20   -
Left Padding:      30   -
Right Padding:     30   -
Right Border:      20   =
CONTENT WIDTH:     300  PIXELS
```

When you're trying to ensure a consistent design across all browsers, a difference of even 1 pixel is unacceptable — a few hundred are enough to make you want to run back to your trusty tables. Thankfully, there's way out.

It's worth noting that this rendering bug happens only when an element has a declared width and either padding or borders. Another strategy to avoid all this CSS hackery is to apply the padding to an element's parent and leave the width on the child — or vice versa. Understanding the cause of a rendering bug is, at times, more important than knowing the hack or fix, and can help you more strategically plan your style sheet's architecture.

The Solution

CSS hacks provide us with a workaround for browser inconsistencies such as this IE bug, and ensure that we can have our layout looking sharp across the board. Typically, these hacks exploit a parsing bug in a browser's CSS implementation, allowing us to hide or display sections of our CSS to that browser. In effect, this allows us to serve up the "correct" value to more CSS-compliant browsers, while delivering the "incorrect" value to the ones with the poor math skills.

To work around our little IE bug, we'll resort to using some hacks to ensure our display is looking sharp across all our target browsers:

```
p#hack {
border: 20px solid #C00;
padding: 30px;
width: 400px;
}

* html p#hack {
width: 500px;
w\idth: 400px;
}
```

We've turned our single CSS rule into two. The first rule contains the `border` and `padding` information to be applied to our paragraph, as well as the desired width of 400 pixels.

The second rule (beginning with the universal selector, *) contains our hackery. If we were to read out the `* html p#hack` rule in plain English, it would tell us to "Select all `p` elements with an `id` attribute of 'hack' that are descendants of an `html` element *that is itself a descendant of any element*." We've emphasized the last part of the rule because that's where the hack lies. Because `html` is the root of our HTML and XHTML documents, it can't be a descendant of any other element. So, if this second rule shouldn't match any element, why include it?

Actually, this rule will return a valid match in all versions of Internet Explorer (Windows and Macintosh), which erroneously disregard the universal selector and interpret the rule as `html p#hack`. As a result, this rule is seen *only* by Internet Explorer, and disregarded by all other browsers. The first property declares an "incorrect" width of 500 pixels, ensuring that the buggy browsers leave sufficient space for our content. Because they put the padding and border *inside* the declared width, we must send them a pixel width that matches a correct browser's interpretation of the spec. And because our `html p#hack` selector is more specific than the last, this new width value overrides the previous value of 400 pixels.

But we can't rest on our laurels yet because we've one last hack to perform. Internet Explorer 6 on Windows and Internet Explorer 5.*x* on the Mac implement the box model correctly, so we've just fed two good browsers that "incorrect" value of 500px. To remedy this, the second width property contains the proper value of 400px. However, by escaping the "i" with a backslash (`w\idth`), we can exploit a bug in older versions of Internet Explorer and hide this rule from that browser. And with this hack-within-a-hack approach, we've fixed our bug!

If your head's spinning a bit, we feel your pain. Thankfully, there are some excellent resources available to help you better understand this and other CSS hacks. We recommend reading through the CSS-Discuss Wiki (discussed in greater detail in the next section), which has an in-depth analysis of the box model hack

we've used, as well as other approaches (`http://css-discuss.incutio.com/`
`?page=BoxModelHack`). *Its near-exhaustive list of other style sheet hacks is worth poring over*
(`http://css-discuss.incutio.com/?page=CssHack`), *as are its tips for avoiding needless*
hacks (`http://css-discuss.incutio.com/?page=AvoidingHacks`).

The Road Is Long

As you've seen, the number of idiosyncratic browsers to which we build makes testing our CSS a necessary part of a site's development cycle. While browser support for the standard is excellent (especially when compared with that of a few years ago), you're bound to encounter some of these browser bugs in your own code. But don't worry: it's a natural part of the site-development process.

Every CSS designer hits a roadblock at some point. If someone tells you that every site they've built went off without a hitch, feel free to back away slowly — they're either lying, or just downright talkin' crazy-talk. When your own debugging fails to fix the problem (you *did* validate your code, right?), there are some excellent sites to which you can and should turn.

If you're facing an inexplicable bug in your layout, knowing the resources available to you is often more important than immediately knowing the solution. If nothing else, it should lend you some security as that deadline approaches. The chances are excellent that, at some point, someone's encountered the same issue that you are facing.

CSS-Discuss

The CSS-Discuss mailing list (`www.css-discuss.org/`) was founded in early 2002, and is currently administered by Eric Meyer, CSS guru and former Netscape standards evangelist. According to the site's manifesto, the mailing list is "intended to be a place for authors to discuss real-world uses of CSS." As such, the list is an incredible success; a small army of helpful, CSS-aware Web designers and developers are subscribed to the list. Each is willing and eager to help other Web professionals work through the trials of CSS, so that they might better understand the joys of working with it.

Just as valuable as the list itself is the CSS-Discuss Wiki (`http://css-discuss.incutio.com/`), a community-authored and -edited site containing information regarding font sizing (`http://css-discuss.incutio.com/?page=FontSize`), layout strategies (`http://css-discuss.incutio.com/?page=CssLayouts`), CSS editors (`http://css-discuss.incutio.com/?page=CssEditors`), and of course, CSS hacks (`http://css-discuss.incutio.com/?page=CssHacks`). The Wiki is a site worth poring over and, once you're ready, adding your own contributions.

Position Is Everything

The Position Is Everything (PIE) site (`www.positioniseverything.net/`) is an exhaustive CSS resource, and one to which you should refer whenever you're stumped by a browser issue. Maintained by John Gallant and Holly Bergevin (two extremely capable CSS developers), PIE contains a dizzying number of browser quirks, workarounds, and unresolved bugs — all written up in the clear, easy-to-understand style for which John and Holly have become known.

The Problem with Hacks

Of course, it's perfectly acceptable to write hacks directly into your CSS: find a bug in Internet Explorer 5 on Macintosh OS X, isolate the problematic rule, add a hack, move on to the next issue. This "as-you-go" approach is one that most style sheet developers take, and it *does* afford you great flexibility in dealing with browser inconsistencies. Besides, there comes a certain level of security with writing the workaround directly into your code, anyway: write it, test it, and move on. Simple, right?

By now, our ability to lead with a loaded question should be obvious. While quite effective, this improvisational approach to hack management does pose some problems for the long-term viability of your code. First and foremost, it's all too easy for your code to become weighed down with an unseemly number of hacks, like so:

```
#album-thumbs {
float: left;
list-style-image: none;
list-style: none;
margin: 0;
padding: 0;
}


/* hide from MacIE5 \*/
* html #album-thumbs {
display: inline;
height: 1%;
width: auto !important;
width /**/: 90%;
}
/* hide from MacIE5 */

#album-thumbs a {
display: block;
float: left;
padding: 6px;
margin: 5px;
width: 70px;
}

#album-thumbs a {
\width: 60px;
w\idth: 50px;
}
```

Does this look like gibberish? It's not too far from it. Granted, this style sheet's author left us with nearly no comments to lead us through this goulash of style rules. The backslash in the first comment (/* ... */) will cause the Macintosh version of Internet Explorer to stop parsing the CSS until reaching a properly formed comment (/* ... */). Only the 5.*x* versions of Internet Explorer will read the declaration with the backslash before the "w" in \width, and so forth down the daisy-chain of broken CSS implementations.

What if you had to look at code like this, day in and day out? If this code is difficult for you to sift through, you can bet it's going to be difficult for someone else to maintain. Team members, coworkers, interns, stray dogs—if anyone else is ever going to be responsible for editing your CSS, this approach to hack management isn't a viable one. But putting code readability (or the lack thereof) aside for a moment, these rules *are* valid CSS, and they *do* serve their purpose—they fix bugs in different browser/platform combinations, and they do it well. So what's the problem?

Well, imagine that your CSS is littered with code like this. What happens when you need to obsolete a given hack? Perhaps one of the problematic browsers passes over the upgrade horizon, or the next version of Internet Explorer will stop reading your style sheet when it encounters a hack for the Opera browser. At some point, you might need to edit your CSS and remove some of the hacks you introduced. But what if these hacks aren't spread over 30 lines of CSS, but over 3,000? What then?

Hacking Artfully

Rather than muddying our style sheet with browser-specific hacks, we're much better served by placing our workarounds into browser-specific style sheets. While this kind of "hack quarantine" isn't strictly necessary, it does have the benefit of keeping our "clean" CSS distinct from the hacks required to get it working in less-compliant browsers. Consider Figure 2-19.

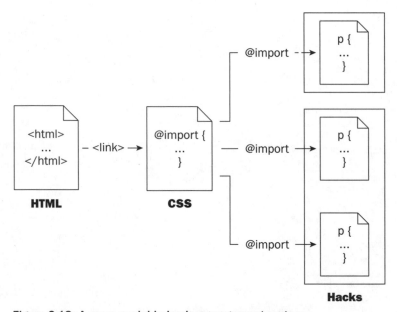

Figure 2-19: A more scalable hack management system

In this model, there's a `link` to our style sheet — nothing unusual there. But this first style sheet simply acts as a gateway to multiple other style sheets, which are invoked through the `@import` rule. The first imported style sheet is the one that contains our site's presentation, clean and hack-free. Thereafter, we simply import browser-specific style sheets that contain the hacks necessary to ensure our site displays consistently across all target browsers.

> *There are other ways to manage your hacks, of course. Web developer Mark Pilgrim describes how he uses user agent detection on his Web server to deliver up browser-specific CSS hacks (`http://diveintomark.org/archives/2003/01/16/the_one_ive_never_tried`). This kind of server-side content negotiation is excellent, though it requires knowledge of, and an ability to configure, the Apache Web server and its `mod_rewrite` component. So while the technical bar's set a bit higher than the solution offered here, this sort of server-side solution is an excellent alternative.*

For the first line of our gateway CSS file, let's call in our core style sheet:

```
@import url("core.css");
```

There is nothing surprising there. A simple `@import` rule pulls in `core.css`, which has been well tested in the more reliable CSS-aware browsers.

Now, were we to simply `@import` in additional files, there's nothing to prevent all browsers from parsing them. Instead, we need a way to serve these CSS files up selectively, so that only the problem user agents digest the rules there. If possible, the "good" browsers should remain blissfully unaware of our little hacks. How do we do this, you ask? Well, fire *is* the best way to fight fire. We'll use CSS hacks to hack more intelligently.

First, let's deal with Internet Explorer 5.*x* on Windows. Its implementation of the CSS box model is notoriously problematic, and is bound to cause some issues for your layout. So, rather than adding our workarounds to the core style sheet, we'll make use of a wonderful technique known as the Mid Pass Filter:

```
/* Import IE5x/Win hacks */
@media tty {
    i{content:"\";/*" "*/}} @import 'hacks.win.ie5.css'; /*";}
}/* */
```

Developed by CSS pioneer and Web developer Tantek Çelik, the Mid Pass Filter allows you to deliver a style sheet to the 5.*x* versions of Internet Explorer on Windows, and to those browsers alone. All other user agents will skip right over this rule because they don't fall prey to the same parsing bug as IE5.*x*/Win.

While the Macıntosh version of Internet Explorer 5 is considered to have CSS support that's far superior to its Windows-based cousins, it's not without its bugs. Development on the browser ended in mid-2003, leaving us to deal with its occasional layout quirks. Thankfully, we've another filter at our disposal, the IE5/Mac Band Pass Filter:

```
/* Import IE5/Mac hacks */
/*\*//*/
@import url("hacks.mac.ie5.css");
/**/
```

Also developed by Tantek Çelik and popularized by Web designer Doug Bowman, the IE5/Mac Band Pass Filter will serve up only the imported CSS to — you guessed it — Internet Explorer 5 on the Mac OS. Still, the effect is the same as the Mid Pass Filter. Other browsers will disregard the style sheet that's targeted for one browser's quirks.

> *For a discussion of other CSS filters and hack-management techniques, read Molly Holzschlag's article "Integrated Web Design: Strategies for Long-Term CSS Hack Management" (*www.informit.com/ articles/article.asp?p=170511*). This section owes much to her excellent essay, in which Molly discusses additional filters not mentioned here.*

You might be asking yourself why these parsing bugs are the best way to manage other hacks. We're not trying to be needlessly abstract, honest. By isolating browser-specific hacks into one CSS file, and keeping our core style sheet relatively pure, we've gained two rather tangible benefits. First and foremost, these workarounds are easier for other folks to locate, maintain, and modify. Second, we've resolved the issue of hack obsolescence. Now, if we need to stop supporting a browser, we simply delete a few lines from our core style sheet and move forward.

Summary

In coming chapters, you'll learn real-world, professional strategies for getting the most out of your style sheets. We hope this chapter has shown you some of the foundations for high-octane XHTML/CSS design, ideas and goals that you can bring forward into the more applied chapters that await. By beginning with a foundation of valid, well-structured markup, we can use CSS to layer our pages' presentation thereupon. This lightens our pages' weight, lowers the cost of maintenance and future redesigns, and increases our sites' accessibility.

In the next chapter, we'll take an in-depth look at the first of several companies to be profiled in this book, Google. Taking to heart some of these benefits, their recent redesign of the Blogger site makes for a compelling case study, and demonstrates that it's an exciting time indeed to be pursuing CSS-driven design.

3

Blogger: Rollovers and Design Improvements

In August 1999, a small company known as Pyra Labs released a new product called "Blogger" to the Web. Not only would it go on to earn that team fame and fortune, it would also kick-start the blogging revolution.

Blogger lets people such as you, your friends, and really anyone publish a Web site, or more specifically, a blog. It makes this process simple, fast, and really very friendly indeed. It's also free, which is a bit of a bonus on the Web, where no one wants to pay for anything.

In February 2003, a company called Google (you *might* have heard of them) whipped out their checkbook and acquired Pyra Labs, bringing Blogger into the Google fold. Along with the contracts and funding came something rather nice as far as the Blogger Team was concerned: the appearance of a BlogThis! button on the Google Toolbar. The overwhelming number of people using the Google Toolbar each day has enabled blogger.com to experience a huge surge in traffic. Sign-ups should have gone through the roof. But they didn't. What was going on?

A few phone calls later and user experience experts Adaptive Path were on the case. With them came designer and CSS maestro Douglas Bowman of Stopdesign. Together they would examine the behavior of visitors to blogger.com and realize that something fundamental was stopping the conversion of these new visitors into new customers: the design of the site itself.

Plans were drawn up, ideas bandied about, and eventually, after 6 months of development, a new design was released. Blogger.com had a new face, and with it would come (one hoped) a mass of new customers.

Bowman's redesign of blogger.com involved a number of subtle (yet effective) design touches: rounded corners, rollovers on links, graphical buttons, boxes whose borders faded to nothing, and a delightfully simple method of style-switching put in place not to help visitors, but to aid the Blogger Team in the production of the site.

This chapter discusses some of these design touches and looks at how to re-create them using the cleanest XHTML and the cleverest CSS around today. We also touch upon issues these solutions have with Internet Explorer (IE), and provide workarounds (where possible) for this troublesome browser.

This chapter should provide some understanding of what is possible if your first thought is not, "Does this work in Internet Explorer?" but rather "What is the cleanest, most forward-looking way I can build this?"

The solutions provided here might not be suitable for you to push into production today (that decision is up to you), but they provide a starting point in the whole development process. Kick off with an *ideal* solution, and then work your way backward until you reach a *practical* solution. For many developers, those two points may be one and the same, in which case the techniques described here can be slotted in to the next site they build. For others, there may be some distance between those two points, with more weight being given to ensuring a design works 100 percent on IE and less weight being given to the cleanliness of the solution.

So, read the chapter, take in the lessons, and decide, project by project, Web site by Web site, to what extent you compromise your ideal solution.

Interviewing the Designer

Douglas Bowman is an influential designer whose highly publicized and hugely successful redesigns of sites such as Blogger, Wired News, and Adaptive Path have pushed him to the forefront of standards-compliant Web design. He is the principal of Stopdesign, a design consultancy based in San Francisco, California.

Q: *First off, are you pleased with how things have turned out?*

A: I'm quite pleased with results of the entire project. The first measure of success in any project for me is whether or not it met or exceeded the client's goals. Usually, if the client is happy, I'm happy. In this case, one of the project's goals was to increase user sign-ups. Another goal was to increase use (by its existing user base) of Blogger in general. I can't be specific about numbers, but I can say that end results far exceeded Google's expectations.

This project had multiple facets to it; all of them contributed to the ultimate success of the Blogger redesign. Adaptive Path and Stopdesign worked with Google to redesign and simplify Blogger's home page and registration system. In addition to this site redesign, Stopdesign contracted 5 other designers to help create over 30 new user templates. Adding to the impact, Google worked really hard to up the ante by expanding Blogger's feature set and capabilities. User profiles, commenting, new ad-free hosted blog pages on BlogSpot, and blog search were just some of the new features that were added at or around the same time as the redesign.

Q: *Which bit of the design is the internal team most pleased with? And which part are the site's visitors most pleased with?*

A: I think this probably depends on whom you ask on the team. From talking with the developers and engineers at Google, I think they're most pleased with the design system, and how easy it is to expand and tweak the pages. The design is simple and straightforward. Obviously, it uses very simple HTML and an all-CSS layout. Google ended up taking the XHTML templates and CSS we provided for the home page and registration pages, and used them as a base to redesign the entire application. In addition to the required page types Google needed from us, we also provided some generic templates that they're able to quickly grab and repurpose for new sections of the site.

If you were to ask a product manager, they might say they like the simplified design the best. Especially in regards to how much better the new home page helps communicate what a blog is, and the benefits of starting one immediately by using Blogger.

Blogger's visitors probably don't notice the site's design as much. In fact, if we did our job right, users might have a small affinity to the look of Blogger, but they wouldn't really pay as much attention to the design. They should be able to immediately grasp the benefits, and see a clear path to publishing their own blog in as short amount of time as possible.

Users immediately noticed the huge increase in number of available templates from which they could choose for their own blog. When it comes to customization, an abundance of pre-fabbed choices gives them lots of options with which to express their voice and personality.

Q: *Later on in this chapter, we look at the code behind the rounded corners on blogger.com, but present a different solution to the one you used on the site. Our method requires no additional divs, but sacrifices some cross-browser performance, with IE receiving no corner styling. If you were doing the project again would you consider such an approach, or, as a designer, do you demand that each and every element of the design be adhered to?*

A: If the choice were strictly up to me, and I was the only one working with the code, I'd go for the leaner, no-additional-divs option. I have the benefit of understanding exactly what the benefits and tradeoffs are, and exactly how the more advanced CSS operates. Leaner, simpler HTML is always a plus, especially if HTML can be removed that was inserted specifically for the purpose of style hooks. Page module code would not only be simpler, but more stable, and less reliable on a precise number of classed divs.

I've made several choices with recent personal projects to give IE only a base set of styling, and then give other more CSS-capable browsers additional advanced styles. The term for this approach is "Progressive Enhancement," coined by Steven Champeon, in an article he wrote for *Webmonkey* a couple of years ago. Give some browsers an acceptable base design that functions well, give more capable browsers a more and more advanced design that builds on the base.

But the choice isn't only mine to make. In this case, the rounded corners throughout the site design were pretty big players in helping to give Blogger a simple, friendly feeling. A large number (possibly the majority) of Blogger users are still using IE as their default browser. If we had gone with the progressive enhancement approach, those IE users would see a page design that didn't quite mesh with the new Blogger "appearance."

With other projects, getting all the design details in IE correct may not have been important. But because Google was specifically targeting a wider, less-techy audience with this Blogger redesign — one that is also more likely to be using IE as their browser — compromising on this design aesthetic in IE browsers for the sake of leaner HTML wouldn't necessarily have been a good choice.

Q: *Has Blogger noticed any benefits from the redesign, either financial or just in the number of customers they're attracting?*

A: As stated previously, I can't be specific with numbers. But I can say that the number of new user registrations Blogger receives went up dramatically after the redesign of the home page and registration system. The revamped home page drove more users into the registration system. The simpler registration system had fewer pages than the previous system. And it was designed to guide the user all the way through as quickly and as effortlessly as possible, allowing them to set up a blog and be posting to it in less than 5 minutes. Those changes basically guaranteed success. But not even Google knew how big the success would be.

Q: *Would you have done anything differently, looking back?*

A: Ask any designer who coded her or his own design a year after the fact, and I bet every one of them would do something differently. We're all in a constant state of learning when it comes to design on the Web. No one person has figured out how to do everything perfectly. Technology changes, techniques evolve, and new methods are discovered.

With each major redesign I complete, I usually discover a better way to do something within a week or two of completing that redesign. A light bulb that turns on. A tweak to the design that could have made coding it so much easier. A CSS selector that I never tried to use before suddenly makes sense and I can see all its various uses.

Specifically, with Blogger's CSS, there are lots of floats used that I wish didn't need to be there. Some were used solely to fix bugs in one or two browsers. Others were used for more legitimate purposes, like containing other nested floated elements.

I also wish I could have been involved in more of the latter aspects of the project. The team at Google did a great job at expanding the designs and templates we provided. But I wish I could have helped or overseen some of that expansion in order to maintain the consistency and quality of the design approach. Budget is always a limiting factor in this regard, and there simply wasn't enough of it to have Stopdesign or Adaptive Path involved at every major step of the project.

Q: *How much interest has the Blogger redesign produced for you, personally? Are other large companies looking at the finished product and wanting to go the same route?*

A: The Blogger redesign was a great project all around. Collaborating with Adaptive Path is always a fun learning experience; working with the Blogger team produced good results because they naturally "get it." Having the opportunity to execute successfully on a big project for Google brought lots of attention to both Adaptive Path and Stopdesign. Both companies have picked up a few projects as a result of people really noticing the Blogger redesign, and with the help of a few referrals from Google.

I think the Blogger redesign is just one more solid example, added to the heaps of others, that helps convince large companies that standards-based design is really the only way to go now. Pair all the benefits of standards together with the strengths and talents of a couple design consultancies. Then add on top of that the fact that the project was done for a high-profile client with a product that tons of people use and write about on a daily basis. No doubt there has been, and will be, a lot of attention given to the Blogger redesign. It stands out as a good example of the importance of effective design and a sound implementation of that design. Let's hope that Blogger bolsters another developer's case, and gives one more reason for a designer's plea to value properly executed design.

Q: *Two of Blogger's three "competitors" have been using standards-based design for some time now. Do you think this was the main driving force behind Blogger's adoption of standards, or was it just a natural progression to commission the site in this way?*

A: I don't necessarily think Google was thinking, "Uh-oh, our competitors are all using standards-based design, we need to get on the ball and do the same." When they came to us, they had a few simple objectives in mind. They probably hadn't thought out exactly how those objectives were to be achieved. But they knew we were capable of helping them solve their problems and greatly improve the user experience. Both Google and Adaptive Path also knew, by default, Stopdesign's philosophy when it comes to implementing its designs, so I think a standards-based solution was probably assumed by default.

Sometimes, clients are remotely aware of the benefits of standards. But they really start to understand and get excited about a standards-based approach once they start working with one for their own site. The benefits are logical on paper, but they're tactical once the benefits are experienced.

No matter what CMS or scripting language is used to output code, simpler leaner HTML is always appreciated. It's just easier and faster to work with, and it's usually immediately parsable without needing to dissect multiple tables and rows and cells. Once the basic design was approved and fairly stable, the fact that Google's engineers and developers were able to continue making changes to the underlying code base, while we hosted the CSS files and continued making small changes to the design proved a convenient method of simultaneous iteration from both sides.

Bounding Boxes

Sooner or later, every article, book, or workshop on CSS gets around to talking about the box model. It's one of the fundamental elements of cascading style sheets, and if you want to strengthen your CSS-foo, you better have a good understanding of the box model's ins and outs.

To refresh your memory, here are examples to explain the box model basics. Figure 3-1 contains a three dimensional (3D) version of the model, showing the creation of a simple `div`, and then highlighting the order in which the `div`'s elements are stacked.

It's important to note that the box's `content`, so often shown to be layered "below" the `border`, is actually the topmost of all elements. In the following pages, we'll see how vital that fact is in letting us create one of Blogger's trademark looks: rounded corners.

Figure 3-2 contains a series of images that show the effect `padding`, `border`, and `margin` have on the overall width and height of an element.

```
<div>
<p>Here is some sample content. It is constrained by
the width of its containing element.</p>

<p>Here is some sample content. It is constrained by
the width of its containing element.</p>

<p>Here is some sample content. It is constrained by
the width of its containing element.</p>
</div>
```

```
div {
    background-color: #EF0F6A;
    background-image: url('lamb.jpg');
    border: 10px solid #000;
    margin: 20px;
    padding: 20px;
}

p{
    margin: 0 0 20px 0;
    padding: 0;
}
```

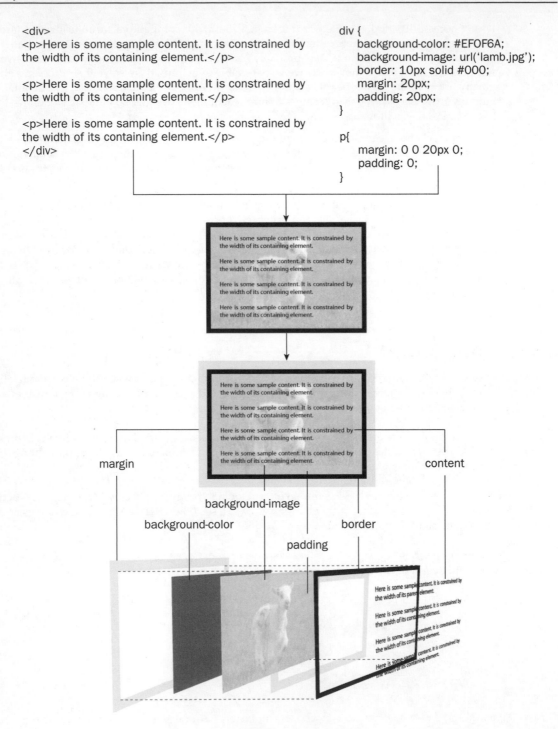

Figure 3-1: A 2D and 3D representation of the box model in action

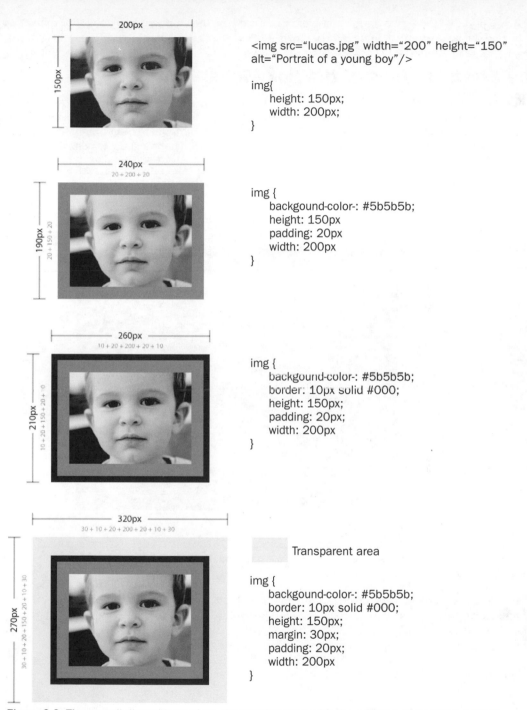

Figure 3-2: The overall dimensions of an element increase with the addition of padding, border, and margins.

If you find that those two figures completely confuse you, then it might be a good idea to read up on the box model before you continue (www.w3.org/TR/REC-CSS2/box.html).

The Straight Lines of the Box Model

Given the name and nature of the box model, it's not terribly surprising that the vast majority of Web sites using CSS end up looking a little "boxy." Straight lines abound in CSS-centric designs because the edges of CSS elements are straight. Pointy corners poke out everywhere from CSS-based sites because the corners of CSS elements are pointy, as shown in Figure 3-3. That's just the way it is.

Figure 3-3: All the elements of the box model have pointy corners and straight edges.

In the past, designers were too busy struggling with browser bugs to confront this issue. When four different browsers display your markup in four different ways, you don't have much time to think of life "outside the CSS box."

Today, though, is a different story. Our understanding of CSS, and the browsers' ability to interpret CSS, has risen to such a level that designers are now asking, "Why do our sites have to look like this? Why am I limited in this way?"

Having a million Web sites that all look fundamentally the same isn't a good advertisement for CSS, nor is it going to impress our clients or bosses. Sure, our sites are easier to maintain, and, yes, we can make site-wide changes by altering single CSS files. But who cares when our work looks just like every other boxy CSS creation out there?

What we need, and what CSS needs to ensure its popularity, is a way of blurring these straight lines and of rounding these corners. We must find a way to hide the fact that our site is made up of a series of rect-angles, and present a more varied, more designed front. Because we can't alter the way CSS functions, we must create an illusion of change.

To take an example we're all familiar with, let's think of photographs and the frames we use to display them. Photographs pretty much come in one shape: rectangles, but photo frames come in an amazing variety of shapes. Photos displayed in these differently shaped frames appear to be the shape of the frame, even though they are still rectangular.

Figure 3-4 shows an example of this illusion in action, using a teddy bear picture frame bought at a local market, and a photo of a cute child.

The lesson to learn here is that you can take one photo, slip it into any kind of frame, and give the illusion of having changed the shape of that photo. That's exactly what we're trying to achieve with CSS and our site designs: hiding the dull, dictated, underlying structure, and instead presenting an interesting, person-alized front. Take one set of XHTML markup and slip it into a variety of exciting CSS-driven front-ends.

The question you're probably asking now is, "Exactly how do I apply that idea to my Web site?" Well, before we get into markup-specifics, let's see how Douglas Bowman used it in his 2004 redesign of blogger.com.

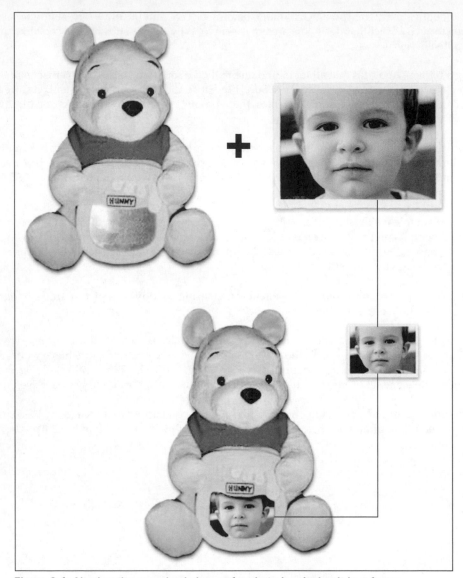

Figure 3-4: Altering the perceived shape of a photo by placing it in a frame

Blogger's Curvy Corners

If, as a designer, you're seeking to banish sharpness and rigidity from your work a natural place to start is by rounding off any pointy corners a design has. When the site you're working on is information-centric (as blogger.com is) and you've used boxes to compartmentalize sections of information (as blogger.com does) then there are a significant number of corners to smooth out.

Glance at Figure 3-5 and you'll notice that practically every element of the Blogger design has smooth, rounded corners. The sidebar, the main content panel, the buttons, even the logo and the header background are all curved.

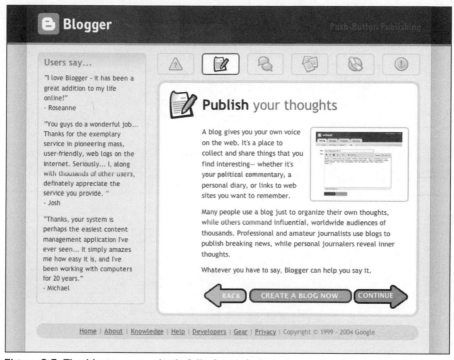

Figure 3-5: The blogger.com site is full of rounded corners.

Bowman hasn't gone crazy in his efforts to mellow out the design. He's taken a subtle approach, matching shape and color to create a comfortable, calm, and friendly site. And, as we've already noticed, key to that are those lovely rounded corners.

Creating Fixed-Width, Round-Cornered Boxes

There are many ways to produce rounded corners, from the horrible, hacky use of tables, to lovely, advanced use of CSS. This book obviously favors CSS solutions, and one of the best of those utilizes CSS's `:before` and `:after` pseudo-element selectors. It may be a fairly advanced technique, but it's probably the cleanest and most forward-looking method available as of this writing. And, with a little care, it can degrade nicely for older, less-capable browsers as well.

Figure 3-6 shows part of the Blogger Tour. Take a good look at the left-hand side of the page, which contains a box entitled "Users say . . . "; it's going to be our focus in these next few sections. (Note also that all of blogger.com's boxes are fixed-width, which means their `width` won't change as you resize your browser window or alter your browser's `font-size`. You can't tell they're a fixed width from Figure 3-6, but visit the site and you'll see they are.)

"Users say..." box

Figure 3-6: The "Users say . . . " box used throughout this section

Let's take a quick look at the XHTML we'd need to re-create the "Users say . . . " box using this advanced CSS technique.

The XHTML

Following is the XHTML:

```
<div id="sidebar">
<div class="box">
<h2>Users say...</h2>

<p><q>I love Blogger - it has been a great addition to my life online!</q> -
Roseanne</p>

<p><q>You guys do a wonderful job... Thanks for the exemplary service in pioneering
mass, user-friendly, web logs on the internet. Seriously... I, along with thousands
of other users, definately appreciate the service you provide.</q> - Josh</p>

<p><q>Thanks, your system is perhaps the easiest content management application
I've ever seen... It simply amazes me how easy it is, and I've been working with
computers for 20 years.</q> - Michael</p>
```

```
</div>

<!-- more "boxes" can be placed in this sidebar -->
</div>
```

That's pretty clean markup, with only one encompassing `div` needed to create the "box." Let's see if the CSS is just as tidy.

The CSS

Following is the CSS:

```
#sidebar {
width: 200px;
}

.box {
background-color: #f5ece3;
border: 2px solid #e1d4c0;
padding: 8px;
}

.box:before {
content: url(box-top.gif);
display: block;
line-height: 0.1;
margin: -10px -10px -22px -10px;
}

.box:after {
clear: both;
content: url(box-btm.gif);
display: block;
line-height: 0.1;
margin: 0 -10px -10px -10px;
}

.box h2 {
margin-top: 0;
}
```

That looks good as well. And don't worry if you don't understand any of that. We're going to break it down, line by line, in just a moment.

The Images

Finally, here are the two images we'll use, one for the top set of rounded corners (see Figure 3-7), and one for the bottom set (see Figure 3-8).

Figure 3-7: The box-top.gif file at 200 × 30px

Figure 3-8: The box-btm.gif file at 200 × 8px

What Does It All Mean?

Now, you're no doubt scratching your head a little and wondering what all that CSS does, so here's a more detailed explanation of each bit.

Rounding the Top of the Box

Because this is a fixed-width example, the first thing we need to do is set the width for the sidebar div (#sidebar), as shown in Figure 3-9. We set the width here, and not on the box (.box) itself because this way we avoid any problems with Internet Explorer's faulty handling of the box model (www .positioniseverything.net/articles/box-model.html).

```
#sidebar {
width: 200px;
}
```

Figure 3-9: Setting the width of the sidebar

Next we'll style the box itself, giving it a background-color and a border, as shown in Figure 3-10:

```
.box {
background-color: #f5ece3;
border: 2px solid #e1d4c0;
}
```

Figure 3-10: Styling the box

If you're wondering about the space at the top of the box, that's the h2's top margin; we'll be removing that later on.

Now we'll add some padding to the box, to put some space between the text and the border, as shown in Figure 3-11:

```
.box {
background-color: #f5ece3;
border: 2px solid #e1d4c0;
padding: 8px;
}
```

Now it's time for the cleverness. The problems we now face are slightly complicated, so we're going to take this bit quite slowly:

❑ **Problem 1.** We must find a way to apply two sets of images to our box, one at the top, and one at the bottom.

❑ **Problem 2.** However we apply these images, they must be able to overlap the box's borders, hiding its sharp corners with smooth, rounded, graphic corners.

Let's think back to our 3D box model. If the images need to overlap the box's borders, then there's only one bit of the box model in which they can appear: the "content." Only the box's "content" layer appears on top of the border layer. If we placed the images anywhere else and tried to move them, they'd just slide under the border.

Figure 3-11: Adding padding to the box

So, we know we have to place them in the content section, but how? We don't have any extra, blank divs to use . . . Hmm, could we maybe use the h2 and p tags?

Well, that does seem like a good idea, doesn't it? They're there, and they have no other images applied to them, so why not use them?

Basing an Element's Style on the Contents of That Element

A good rule in CSS is to never use the contents of an element to style the element itself. Unless you have absolute and total control over every tiny piece of your site, you can't be sure that the necessary content will be there to aid in the styling of its parent. (And, if you insist that the content be there, then you're doing something very odd indeed: you're letting your CSS dictate the content of your site, and that's certainly not the way to go.)

Let's say we set up the .box style to be reliant on an h2 at the start, and a p tag at the end, applying a background-image to each one. Blogger.com has thousands of users, so what are the odds that every single one of them will always use those two elements in every "box" they create?

And if we get clever and say, okay, let's not specify actual tags in our CSS, let's use :first-child and :last-child, or let's insert a .first and .last class in the XHTML, we'll still run into problems. Not every browser understands :first-child and :last-child, and not every user will remember to insert .first and .last classes into their documents. Do they even know what classes are?

And finally, what happens if the box contains only one element? How can you apply two background images to a single element? You can't.

So, you see, it really is a bad idea to base an element's style on the contents of that element. It is much better to find a way to style it directly.

Let's look at what we now know:

❑ We must insert the images into the box's content area.

❑ We can't use the box's contents (the h2 and p tags) to style the box.

Isn't that a bit of a contradiction? How are we going to solve this problem? What else is there in the box's content area, except for the content the user puts in?

Bending Our Own Rules with the :before and :after Pseudo-Elements

Hurrah for CSS, and hurrah for its surprising ability to create and insert content into a document.

The :before and :after pseudo-elements (www.w3.org/TR/REC-CSS2/generate.html#before-after-content) are two spankingly gorgeous (and fairly advanced) bits of CSS and they are exactly what we're looking for. They allow us to insert content (in this case, two images) into the box's content area, and then style it as we wish. In this way, we're not relying on content generated by the user to style our box. We're inserting some of our own.

Once they've been inserted, we can treat these pseudo-elements like spare divs, adding in content (via the content property), giving them padding, borders, margins, background colors — whatever we want, and all through a few additional lines in our style sheets.

Now, you may be thinking, "Ahem, didn't we just agree not to use an element's contents to style the element itself?" You're right, but that's why this section is entitled "Bending Our Own Rules . . ." If we insert the content, and we do so using CSS, then we skip around all the problems mentioned in the previous section. It is our (virtually) perfect solution.

But enough sidetracking; let's get back to making these curves work. If we once again look at our XHTML, we can see where our CSS is going to insert the :before pseudo-element:

```
<div id="sidebar">
<div class="box">
OUR :BEFORE PSEUDO-ELEMENT IS INSERTED HERE
<h2>Users say...</h2>

<p><q>I love Blogger - it has been a great addition to my life online!</q> -
Roseanne</p>

<p><q>You guys do a wonderful job... Thanks for the exemplary service in pioneering
mass, user-friendly, web logs on the internet. Seriously... I, along with thousands
of other users, definately appreciate the service you provide.</q> - Josh</p>

<p><q>Thanks, your system is perhaps the easiest content management application
I've ever seen... It simply amazes me how easy it is, and I've been working with
computers for 20 years.</q> - Michael</p>
</div>
</div>
```

Figure 3-12 shows where the new element will appear.

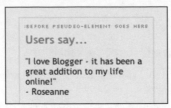

Figure 3-12: Indication of where the :before pseudo-element will appear

This is a pretty powerful thing to be able to do when you think about it. We're using CSS not just to style something, but to actually generate content and insert it into the document.

Here's how we do it. First we create our pseudo-element:

```
.box:before {

}
```

Then we use the content property to insert an image into the document. You can see the new image appear in Figure 3-13, just above the heading "Users say . . . "

```
.box:before {
content: url(box-top.gif);
}
```

Figure 3-13: New image

Although we've managed to insert an image using the CSS content property, it's not exactly perfectly aligned. Why is this? Well, remember the 8px of padding and 2px of border that we applied to the box earlier on? Those two properties are vertically and horizontally offsetting the pseudo-element, by a total of 10px, as shown in Figure 3-14.

We must find a way to counteract this offset, and move the new image into its correct position, at the top of the box.

Figure 3-14: Padding and border applied to the box offset the :before pseudo-element.

We start doing that by giving the pseudo-element a top-margin of -10px. This "pulls" the pseudo-element up and sits it flush with the top of the box. We also set display: block because only block-level elements can have margins applied to them, as shown in Figure 3-15:

```
.box:before {
content: url(box-top.gif);
display: block;
margin: -10px 0 0 0;
}
```

Figure 3-15: "Pulling" the pseudo-element up

We then add in negative values for both the left and right margins, to pull the pseudo-element into place horizontally, again counteracting the 8px of padding and 2px of border we gave the box, as shown in Figure 3-16:

```
.box:before {
content: url(box-top.gif);
display: block;
margin: -10px -10px 0 -10px;
}
```

It's looking pretty good now, but we have two more things left to do.

Figure 3-16: Positioning the pseudo-element horizontally

First we have to pull the text up, so the heading ("Users say . . . ") sits in the correct place. We do this by applying another negative margin to the pseudo-element, this time a bottom margin of -22px. We also apply a top margin of 0 to the h2, as shown in Figure 3-17:

```
.box:before {
content: url(box-top.gif);
display: block;
margin: -10px -10px -22px -10px;
}

h2 {
margin-top: 0;
}
```

Figure 3-17: Positioning the heading text

And, finally, we must take care of a little problem caused by line-height.

Line-height is the vertical distance between two lines of text. Set a large line-height and it increases the vertical gap between the lines; set a small line-height and the lines of text can start to overlap, as shown in Figure 3-18.

Although we haven't specifically set a line-height on the :before pseudo-element, it's inherited a value from the default styles applied to the HTML document by the Web browser.

This vertical spacing can often cause problems when playing with pixel-perfect design, and in this case it's introducing a very small gap underneath our box-top.gif image. We don't notice this gap because the background of the pseudo-element is transparent. But, if we change the background-color to green, the gap becomes more apparent, as shown in Figure 3-19.

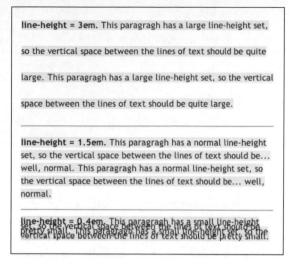

Figure 3-18: The CSS property line-height affects the vertical spacing between lines of text.

Figure 3-19: Line-height can cause unexpected vertical spacing problems (shown here as a darker line).

Even though it's not affecting our design at this moment, it's a good idea to cancel out `line-height` when you can. In this case, we'll do it by setting the `line-height` to `0.1`, as shown in Figure 3-20:

```
.box:before {
content: url(box-top.gif);
display: block;
line-height: 0.1;
margin: -10px -10px -22px -10px;
}
```

Figure 3-20: Rounded corners on the top of the box

97

And now we have rounded corners and a nicely blended background, all through the power of CSS, and not an extra `div` or `table` in sight.

All that's left to do now is use the same technique to apply rounded corners to the bottom of the box as well.

Rounding the Bottom of the Box

This time we'll be using the `:after` pseudo-element, which is inserted after the rest of the box's content:

```
<div id="sidebar">
<div class="box">
<h2>Users say...</h2>

<p><q>I love Blogger - it has been a great addition to my life online!</q> -
Roseanne</p>

<p><q>You guys do a wonderful job... Thanks for the exemplary service in pioneering
mass, user-friendly, web logs on the internet. Seriously... I, along with thousands
of other users, definately appreciate the service you provide.</q> - Josh</p>

<p><q>Thanks, your system is perhaps the easiest content management application
I've ever seen... It simply amazes me how easy it is, and I've been working with
computers for 20 years.</q> - Michael</p>

OUR :AFTER PSEUDO-ELEMENT IS INSERTED HERE
</div>
</div>
```

Figure 3-21 shows where the new pseudo-element will appear.

"Thanks, your system is perhaps the easiest content management application I've ever seen... It simply amazes me how easy it is, and I've been working with computers for 20 years."
- Michael
:AFTER PSEUDO-ELEMENT GOES HERE

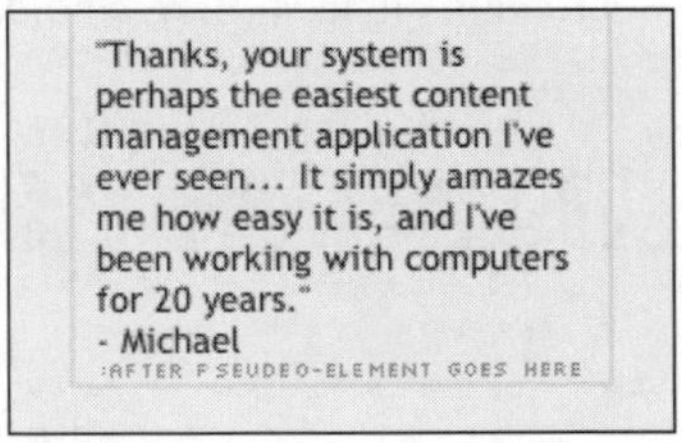

Figure 3-21: Indication of where the :after pseudo-element will appear

First, let's create the `:after` pseudo-element:

```
.box:after {

}
```

Now let's insert the image (`box-btm.gif`) using the `content` property, and make the whole pseudo-element block-level (see Figure 3-22):

```
.box:after {
content: url(box-btm.gif);
display: block;
}
```

> "Thanks, your system is
> perhaps the easiest content
> management application I've
> ever seen... It simply amazes
> me how easy it is, and I've
> been working with computers
> for 20 years."
> - Michael

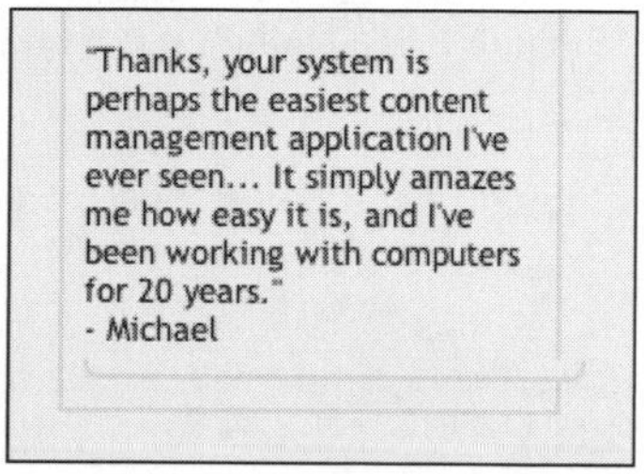

Figure 3-22: Inserting the image and making the pseudo-element block-level

Next we apply a negative bottom margin, to pull the pseudo-element down toward the bottom of the box, as shown in Figure 3-23. (Remember, it's being offset by the 8px of `padding` and 2px of `border`.)

```
.box:after {
content: url(box-btm.gif);
display: block;
margin: 0 0 -10px 0;
}
```

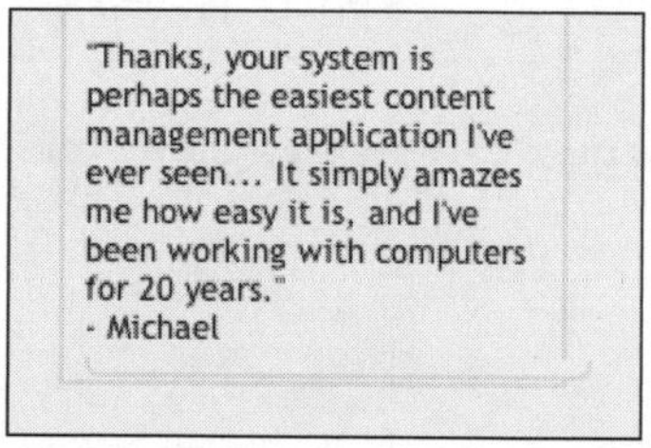

> "Thanks, your system is
> perhaps the easiest content
> management application I've
> ever seen... It simply amazes
> me how easy it is, and I've
> been working with computers
> for 20 years."
> - Michael

Figure 3-23: Pulling the pseudo-element toward the bottom of the box

Notice that it hasn't been pulled perfectly into place? That's `line-height` at work again. If we set that to `0.1`, we'll see the image line up perfectly with the bottom of the box (see Figure 3-24):

```
.box:after {
content: url(box-btm.gif);
display: block;
line-height: 0.1;
margin: 0 0 -10px 0;
}
```

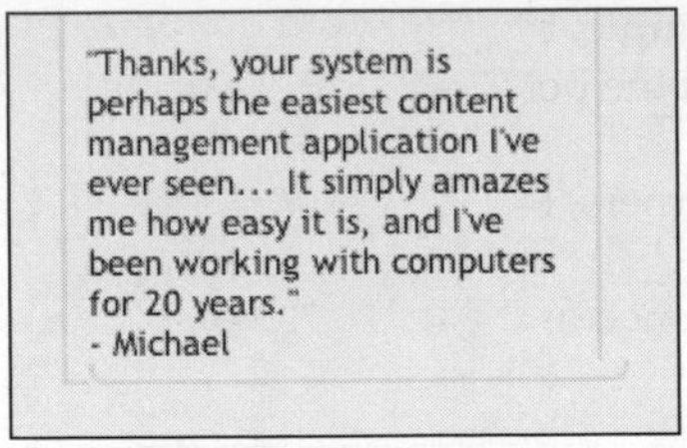

"Thanks, your system is perhaps the easiest content management application I've ever seen... It simply amazes me how easy it is, and I've been working with computers for 20 years."
- Michael

Figure 3-24: Lining up the image with the bottom of the box

We then apply negative left and right margins to pull the pseudo-element into place, horizontally, as shown in Figure 3-25:

```
.box:after {
content: url(box-btm.gif);
display: block;
line-height: 0.1;
margin: 0 -10px -10px -10px;
}
```

"Thanks, your system is perhaps the easiest content management application I've ever seen... It simply amazes me how easy it is, and I've been working with computers for 20 years."
- Michael

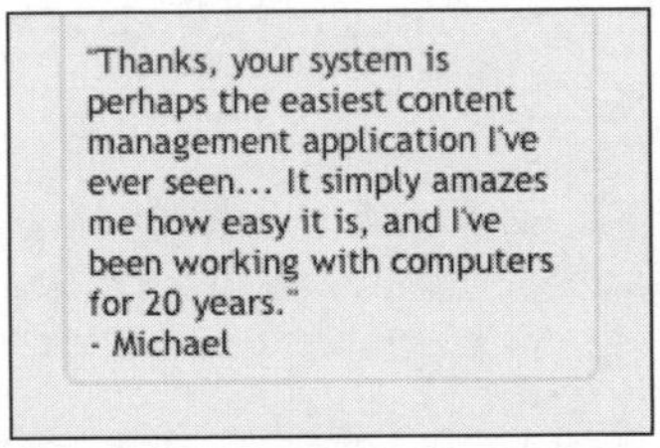

Figure 3-25: Pulling the pseudo-element into place horizontally

And finally, just to be on the safe side, we'll apply a clearing rule to the pseudo-element:

```
.box:after {
content: url(box-btm.gif);
clear: both;
display: block;
line-height: 0.1;
margin: 0 -10px -10px -10px;
}
```

That rule has no effect in this example, but it's helpful to have in there for safety's sake. If we didn't insert it, and the final elements in the box were floated, it could potentially cause a problem.

And there we have it: rounded corners, lovely clean markup, and some fancy-pants CSS (see Figure 3-26).

Well, that may be it for browsers such as Firefox, Opera, and Safari, but what about Internet Explorer? How does that handle our code?

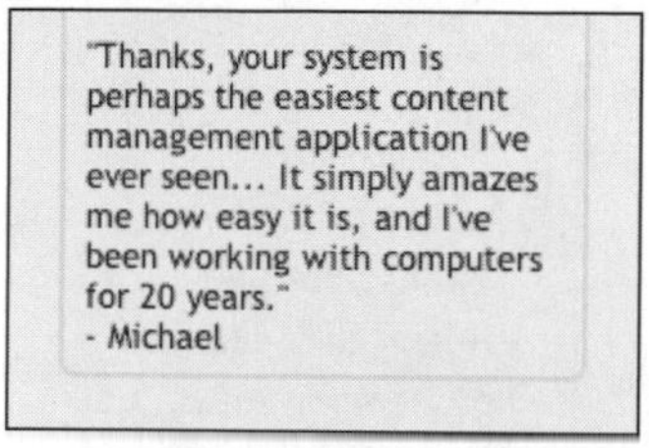

> "Thanks, your system is perhaps the easiest content management application I've ever seen... It simply amazes me how easy it is, and I've been working with computers for 20 years."
> - Michael

Figure 3-26: Rounded corners on the top and bottom of the box

Dealing with Internet Explorer

Unfortunately IE doesn't interpret `:before` and `:after` and, as a consequence, our lovely curves and that attractive gradient fill are lost, as shown in Figure 3-27.

What can we do? Well, IE may not interpret `:before` and `:after`, but it does understand the `background-image` property. With a little bit of a rethink, we can take the image we used for the `:before` pseudo-element and insert it as the background to the h2.

Let's see how that works.

Users say...

I love Blogger - it has
been a great addition
to my life online!
- Roseanne

You guys do a
wonderful job...
Thanks for the
exemplary service in
pioneering mass, user-
friendly, web logs on
the internet.
Seriously... I, along
with thousands of
other users, definately
appreciate the service
you provide.
- Josh

Thanks, your system is
perhaps the easiest
content management
application I've ever
seen... It simply
amazes me how easy it
is, and I've been
working with
computers for 20
years.
- Michael

Figure 3-27: Internet Explorer applies no rounded corner styling.

First we set the `background-image` on the h2 (see Figure 3-28):

```
.box h2 {
background: transparent url(box-top.gif) no-repeat top left;
}
```

Figure 3-28: Setting the background image on the h2

Now we need to counteract the 8px of `padding` and 2px of `border` we applied to the box. We'll do so using negative margins, pulling the h2 and its `background-image` up and to the left, as shown in Figure 3-29:

```
.box h2 {
background: transparent url(box-top.gif) no-repeat top left;
margin: -10px -10px auto -10px;
}
```

Figure 3-29: Counteracting the padding and border

We'll then add in some padding to nudge the heading text back to its normal position, as shown in Figure 3-30:

```
.box h2 {
background: transparent url(box-top.gif) no-repeat top left;
margin: -10px -10px auto -10px;
padding: 10px 10px 0 10px;
}
```

Figure 3-30: Altered styling for IE

And *voilà*, this is a nice fix for IE users . . . or is it?

Well, it's certainly a fix, but is it necessarily "nice"? In this instance, we're fortunate enough to know that (a) the h2 is there, (b) it doesn't already have a `background-image` applied to it, and (c) we can tweak our h2's `padding` after the fact to return the text to its normal position. But what if we didn't know those three things? What if we didn't know what kind of content the box would contain? Could we put this out as part of a template for Blogger's clients to use and still expect our IE hack to work? The answer is probably not.

Although we bent our "it's not a good idea to base an element's style upon the contents of that element" rule with the use of `:before` and `:after`, we've totally shattered it with the IE-specific CSS shown previously. We're on dangerous ground here.

So, is the IE hack outlined here "good"? In this instance, yes, it's okay. Could we implement it on blogger.com and guarantee it would work every time? No, we couldn't. Should you use it on your site? Well, that's up to you . . .

Fixing the Fix

That may well be it for IE, but we've a little bit of housekeeping to do now before we can say we're entirely done.

The IE-focused CSS that we've just written isn't just understood by Internet Explorer; it's understood by all the main browsers. Browsers such as Firefox, Opera, and Safari now have three sets of images on-screen: the image we inserted using `:before`, the image we inserted using `:after`, and the image we inserted behind the h2.

Luckily we've been so accurate in our placement of these images that you can't tell the top section has two images applied to it, as shown in Figure 3-31.

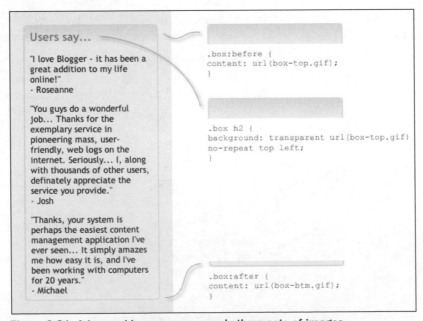

Figure 3-31: Advanced browsers now apply three sets of images.

However, it's silly having them both there, so let's write some CSS that will tell Firefox, Opera, and Safari to remove the extra h2 styling, but that IE will skip over and ignore.

To do this, we'll use something called a child selector (www.w3.org/TR/2001/CR-css3-selectors-20011113/#child-combinators). The child selector does exactly what its name suggests. It helps us select one element that is the *child* (not the grandchild or other descendant) of another element. Here's a quick example to illustrate that:

```
span {
     background-color: green;
}

div > span {
     background-color: yellow;
}

<div>
     <span> <!-- child of div -->
          I will be yellow
     </span>
     <span> <!-- child of div -->
          I will also be yellow
               <span> <!-- grandchild of div -->
                    But I will be green
               </span>
     </span>
</div>
```

In this instance, only the spans that are *children* of the div will have a background color of yellow. The one span that is a grandchild of the div will keep its green background.

Not only does the child selector add a bit more finesse to our style sheet, but it has the added benefit of being one of the CSS elements that IE doesn't interpret. Because browsers skip over rules they can't understand, we are able to use the child selector to feed CSS to the more advanced browsers, while hiding that CSS from IE.

In this instance we are able to use the child selector to return the h2 to its pre–IE hack self. We must remove its background-image, reset its margin, and set its padding back to zero. Let's do that (see Figure 3-32):

```
.box > h2 {
background-image: none;
margin: 0 0 auto 0;
padding: 0;
}
```

Figure 3-32: The finished article as seen in Firefox, Opera, and Safari

As far as Firefox, Opera, and Safari are concerned, things are back to normal. It's as if this "Dealing with Internet Explorer" section never happened.

IE, on the other hand, now has something a bit nicer to show, as shown in Figure 3-33.

It's not perfect, but it's perfectly acceptable if we understand the limitations. We've dealt with IE in a very friendly manner, and, unless users were to compare the two browser displays side-by-side, they'd never be aware that they were being fed a degraded design.

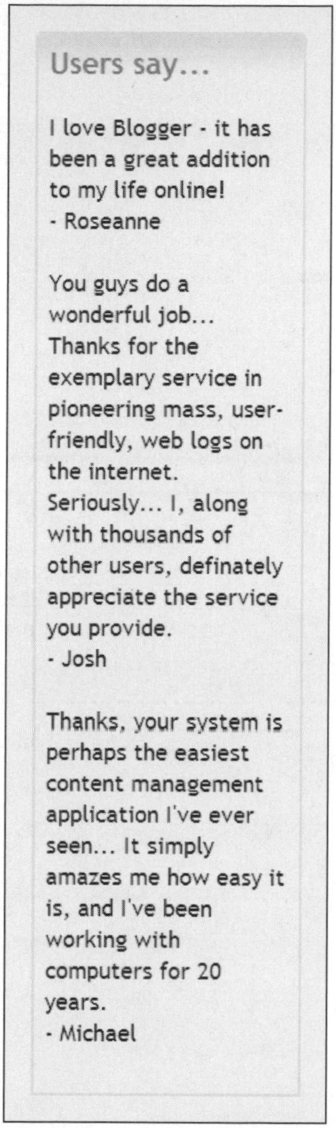

Figure 3-33: The finished article in IE6

Creating Fluid-Width, Round-Cornered Boxes

The previous section looked at creating rounded corners on boxes of a known and fixed width (200px wide in that case). A much harder challenge is to add rounded corners to a box whose width you don't know — a fluid box.

Blogger.com uses only fixed-width boxes, but many sites on the Web use a fluid layout — one that changes with the width of the browser window or the size of the browser's text.

Figure 3-34 shows a tweaked version of the blogger sidebar. Its width has been set at 50 percent of the width of the document's body. See how the content flows to match the changes in width of the browser window? That's fluid design.

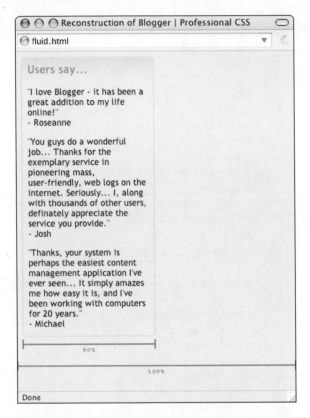

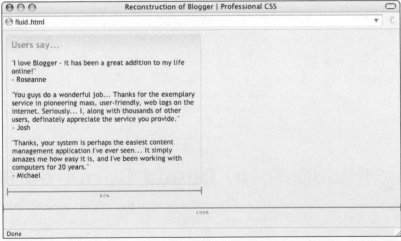

Figure 3-34: A box with a width of 50 percent reflows and resizes along with the browser window.

Let's take a quick look at the XHTML we'd need to create rounded corners for such a design.

The XHTML

Following is the XHTML:

```
<div id="sidebar">
<div class="box">
<h2>Users say...</h2>

<p><q>I love Blogger - it has been a great addition to my life online!</q> -
Roseanne</p>

<p><q>You guys do a wonderful job... Thanks for the exemplary service in pioneering
mass, user-friendly, web logs on the internet. Seriously... I, along with thousands
of other users, definately appreciate the service you provide.</q> - Josh</p>

<p><q>Thanks, your system is perhaps the easiest content management application
I've ever seen... It simply amazes me how easy it is, and I've been working with
computers for 20 years.</q> - Michael</p>
</div>

<!-- more "boxes" can be placed in this sidebar -->
</div>
```

That's exactly the same XHTML as we used in the first example. See how great this is? The same XHTML, different CSS, provides a new look. That's the benefit of CSS right there.

Let's see our new CSS.

The CSS

The following is the CSS:

```
#sidebar {
width: 50%;
}

.box {
background: #f5ece3 url(box-tm.gif) repeat-x top left;
border: 2px solid #e1d4c0;
padding: 8px;
}

.box:before {
background: transparent url(box-tr.gif) no-repeat top right;
content: url(box-tl.gif);
display: block;
line-height: 0.1;
margin: -10px -10px -12px -10px;
}

.box:after {
background: transparent url(box-br.gif) no-repeat bottom right;
clear: both;
```

```
content: url(box-bl.gif);
display: block;
line-height: 0.1;
margin: 4px -10px -10px -10px;
}
```

Well, well, that's really not that different from the fixed-width CSS we wrote in the previous section. In fact, the only changes are the addition of background images to both pseudo-elements, and the tweaking of some padding and margins.

The Images

The images themselves are too small to print with any clarity. So, to help out, we've placed expanded versions (8x) of each image next to the originals, as shown in Figure 3-35.

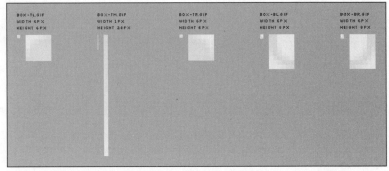

Figure 3-35: The images used to create rounded corners on a fluid-width box. Zoomed-in versions are presented alongside their "actual size" counterparts.

Here's an odd thing. It seems these images we're inserting into the pseudo-elements must be 5px or more in height. If they're not, and we try to insert, say, a 4px high image, then we get some odd spaces appearing in our layout.

In Figure 3-36, the corner images are only 4px high, and the pseudo-element's background has been set to green to help illustrate the 1px gaps that have appeared.

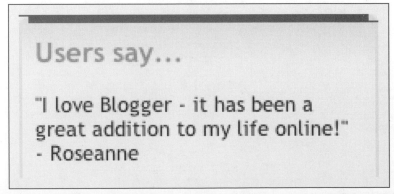

Figure 3-36: Images below 5px in height cause layout problems that can't be solved using line-height or height (shown with a line).

Why these gaps should appear is a mystery, but they do, and no amount of fiddling with `line-height` and `height` will make them go away.

So, always ensure your images are at least 5px high when using the techniques outlined in the following sections.

What Does It All Mean?

Once again, let's take a closer look at each bit of the CSS.

Rounding the Top of the Box

First we must set the `width` of the sidebar div (`#sidebar`). We set the `width` here, and not on the box (`.box`) itself because this way we avoid any problems with the faulty handling of the box model in IE (`www.positioniseverything.net/articles/box-model.html`).

We're using an arbitrary figure of `50%` for the width, but this can be anything you like, whatever it takes to fit in with your design (see Figure 3-37):

```
#sidebar {
width: 50%;
}
```

Users say...

"I love Blogger - it has been a great addition to my life online!"
- Roseanne

"You guys do a wonderful job... Thanks for the exemplary service in pioneering mass, user-friendly, web logs on the internet. Seriously... I, along with thousands of other users, definately appreciate the service you provide."
- Josh

"Thanks, your system is perhaps the easiest content management application I've ever seen... It simply amazes me how easy it is, and I've been working with computers for 20 years."
- Michael

Figure 3-37: Setting the width of the sidebar

Next we'll style the box, giving it a border and some padding (to keep a gap between the text and the border). We also add in a background color and a background image. This image produces the gradient at the top of the box, as shown in Figure 3-38.

```
.box {
background: #f5ece3 url(box-tm.gif) repeat-x top left;
border: 2px solid #e1d4c0;
padding: 8px;
}
```

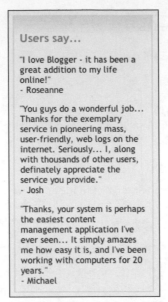

Figure 3-38: Producing the gradient at the top of the box

Now for the clever bits. First, let's create our `:before` pseudo-element:

```
.box:before {

}
```

Next, we'll insert our top-left rounded-corner image into the pseudo-element (see Figure 3-39):

```
.box:before {
content: url(box-tl.gif);
}
```

Figure 3-39: Inserting the top-left rounded-corner image

Now we'll add in the top-right rounded-corner image. We do this by setting a `background-image` on the pseudo-element, and making the whole thing block-level (see Figure 3-40):

```
.box:before {
background: transparent url(box-tr.gif) no-repeat top right;
content: url(box-tl.gif);
display: block;
}
```

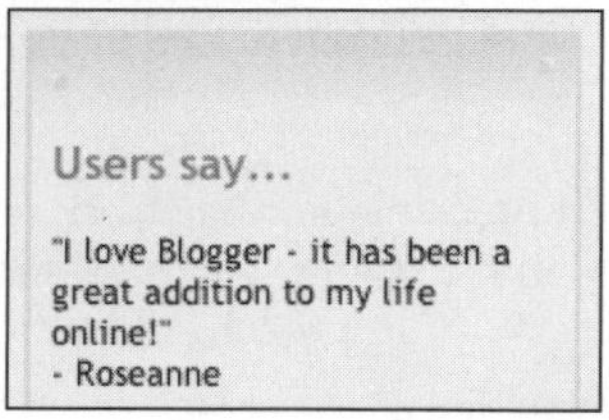

Figure 3-40: Adding the top-right rounded-corner image

We have to counteract the 8px of padding and 2px of border we applied to the box. We do this by applying negative top, right, and left margins to the pseudo-element, pulling it into place, as shown in Figure 3-41:

```
.box:before {
content: url(box-tl.gif);
background: transparent url(box-tr.gif) no-repeat top right;
display: block;
margin: -10px -10px 0 -10px;
}
```

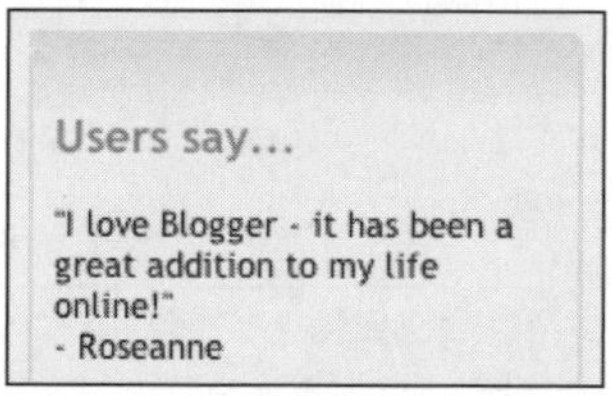

Figure 3-41: Counteracting the border and padding

Finally, we apply a line-height to the pseudo-element (to fix that problem with the left-hand corner) and a negative bottom margin, to pull the heading ("Users say . . . ") up, and back to its proper place, as shown in Figure 3-42:

```
.box:before {
background: transparent url(box-tr.gif) no-repeat top right;
content: url(box-tl.gif);
display: block;
line-height: 0.1;
margin: -10px -10px -12px -10px;
}
```

And that's it. Rounded corners, a gradient background, and fluid width, as shown in Figure 3-42.

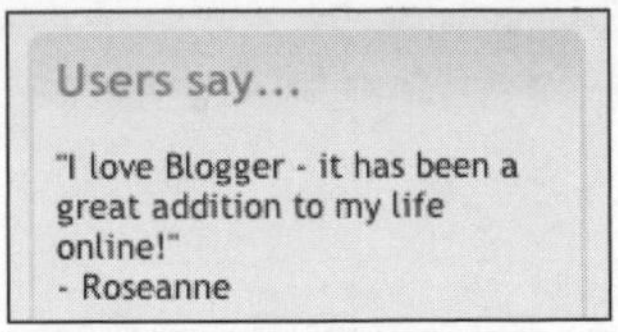

Users say...

"I love Blogger - it has been a
great addition to my life
online!"
- Roseanne

Figure 3-42: Rounded corners at the top of a fluid-width box

What's neat about this method is that by using both the `background-image` and `content` properties, we've managed to insert two images into a single pseudo-element. Without that ability this fluid layout would be beyond our "minimalist markup" approach, and we'd have to resort to hacky CSS or even adding in extra `divs`.

Now, having mastered the top of the box, let's do the same for the bottom corners.

Rounding the Bottom of the Box

First, we create our `:after` pseudo-element:

```
.box:after {

}
```

Next we'll insert our bottom-left rounded-corner image into the pseudo-element, via the `content` property (see Figure 3-43):

```
.box: after {
content: url(box-bl.gif);
}
```

Users say...

"I love Blogger - it has been a
great addition to my life
online!"
- Roseanne

Figure 3-43: Inserting the bottom-left rounded-corner image

Now we'll add in the bottom-right rounded-corner image. We do this by setting a `background-image` on the pseudo-element and making the whole thing block-level, as shown in Figure 3-44:

```
.box: after {
background: transparent url(box-br.gif) no-repeat bottom right;
content: url(box-bl.gif);
display: block;
}
```

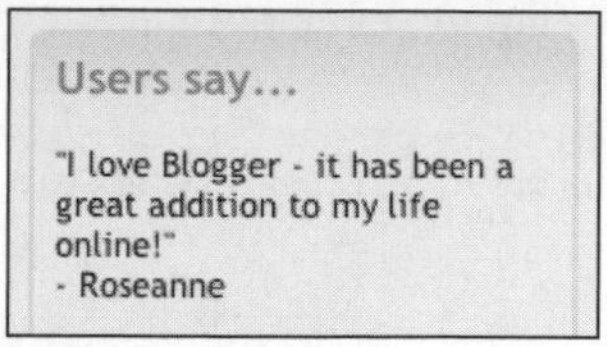

Figure 3-44: Inserting the bottom-right rounded-corner image

We must counteract the 8px of padding and 2px of border we applied to the box. We do this by applying negative bottom, right, and left margins to the pseudo-element, pulling it into place. We also add in 4px of top margin to make the gap between the text and bottom border a bit nicer (see Figure 3-45).

```
.box:after {
background: transparent url(box-br.gif) no-repeat bottom right;
content: url(box-bl.gif);
display: block;
margin: 4px -10px -10px -10px;
}
```

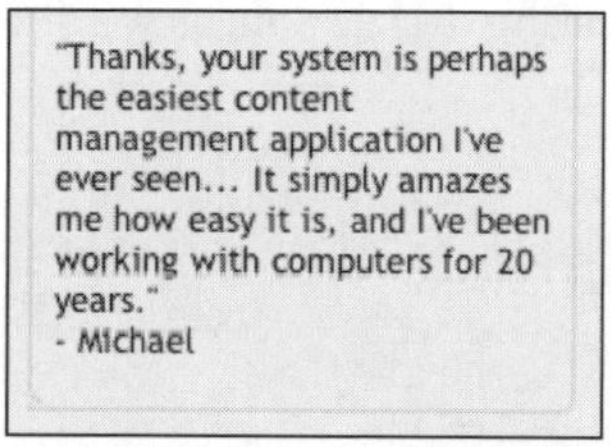

"Thanks, your system is perhaps
the easiest content
management application I've
ever seen... It simply amazes
me how easy it is, and I've been
working with computers for 20
years."
- Michael

Figure 3-45: Counteracting the padding and border

The right-hand side looks fine, but what's happening on the left side of Figure 3-46? Ah, it's line-height at work again.

Figure 3-46: Line-height can cause vertical spacing problems.

Let's set a value of 0.1 and fix it (see Figure 3-47):

```
.box:after {
background: transparent url(box-br.gif) no-repeat bottom right;
content: url(box-bl.gif);
display: block;
line-height: 0.1;
margin: 4px -10px -10px -10px;
}
```

> "Thanks, your system is perhaps
> the easiest content
> management application I've
> ever seen... It simply amazes
> me how easy it is, and I've been
> working with computers for 20
> years."
> - Michael

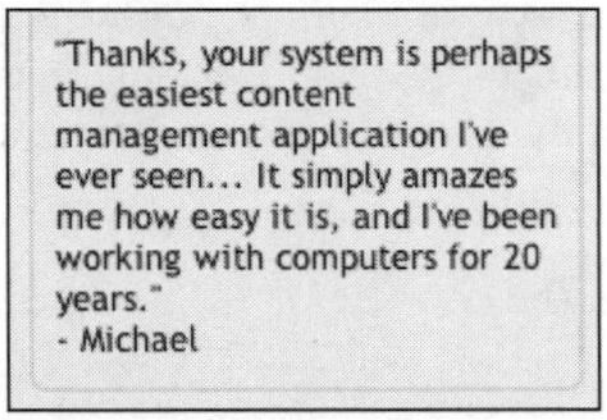

Figure 3-47: Fixing the rounded corners on the left side

To finish up, we simply add in a clearing declaration, as we did in the fixed-width example, and that's it (see Figure 3-48).

```
.box:after {
background: transparent url(box-br.gif) no-repeat bottom right;
clear: both;
content: url(box-bl.gif);
display: block;
line-height: 0.1;
margin: 4px -10px -10px -10px;
}
```

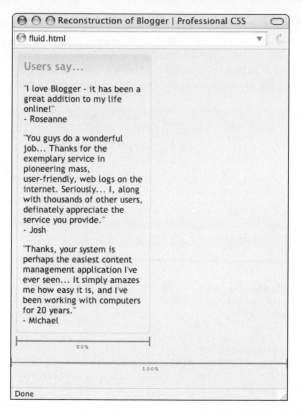

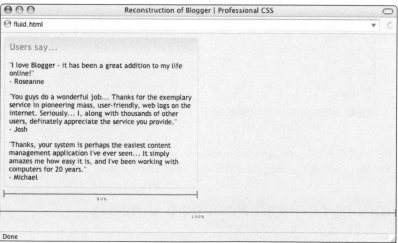

Figure 3-48: The finished article as seen in Firefox, Opera, and Safari

Dealing with Internet Explorer

Unfortunately, and unlike in the previous section, there's no wonderfully easy way to give IE users a taste of what we've done here (see Figure 3-49). After a bit of margin-tweaking to remove the gaps at the top and bottom of the box, IE users will have to be satisfied with the carefully thought-out color scheme, the excellent use of white space, and the overall feeling of calm that blogger.com's layout brings.

Figure 3-49: No lovely styling for IE

Of course, if it's vital that IE users see your rounded corners, then you can't use this technique. You'll have to resort to the slightly less elegant method of inserting a series of extra `div`s in your XHTML.

Better Thinking Through Pseudo-Elements

You should now have a fair understanding of the capabilities of the `:before` and `:after` pseudo-elements. They really are wonderfully powerful tools.

One of their main benefits is that they allow you to change your markup mindset. No longer should your first thought be "Well, I'll have to add in a whole bunch of extra `div`s to build this layout." You now have a set of tools that let you say, "Can I build this layout without altering the XHTML markup in any way?"

As CSS grows more powerful, and as browsers become better at interpreting it, this thought process will become second nature to all of us.

Implied Boxes

If rounded corners go a long way toward mellowing out Blogger's boxy design, then Bowman's second idea, the implied box, finishes the job.

There's really no easier way to explain what an implied box is than to show you one of them *in situ*. Figure 3-50 shows one in use on the front page of blogger.com.

Figure 3-50: An implied box (top right) on blogger.com

See it? It's the bit in the top-right corner of the page. Figure 3-51 shows it close-up.

Figure 3-51: An implied box in action in the Sign In form

There's nothing super-clever about the CSS here. It's just the application of a simple `background-image` to a `form` or `div`, but the effect is very soothing and allows the design to retain a level of openness while still providing a way for visually demarcating sections of the document. In essence, it removes visual clutter and lets our brains fill in the blanks. It's a very clever move in such a busy site.

Here's the relevant CSS for that example:

```
#header form {
background: url(ibox-login.jpg) no-repeat left top;
padding: 12px 15px 0;
width: 290px;
}
```

Figure 3-52 shows the image being used.

Figure 3-52: The ibox_login.jpg image at 320 × 290px

So, you don't always have to use advanced CSS to implement a nice piece of design. This is about as simple as it gets, and it does the job admirably.

Writing CSS That Benefits Your Site Maintainers

There's something rather clever going on at blogger.com, although at first glance you won't be able to tell what it is. In fact, the only people who really appreciate this cleverness are the people who have to maintain the site, the Blogger Team.

This section looks at the styling of Blogger's content `div`s and shows how, with the addition of a simple `class`, the Blogger Team can quickly (and easily) change the layout of their site by moving from one column to two, or from sidebar positioned on the left to a sidebar positioned on the right.

To find out how this style-swapping works, we must first understand the basic structure of Blogger's pages.

Basic Page Structure

Each of the pages on blogger.com is divided into two mains sections: a "header" (`<div id="header">`) containing the logo and tagline, and a "body" (`<div id="body">`) containing everything else. (Don't get that "body" `div` confused with the `body` tag (`<body>`); they're two separate things.)

To put this in perspective, here's a quick outline of a Blogger page:

```
<html>
<head>
<title></title>
</head>

<body>

<div id="header">
```

```
    </div>

    <div id="body">
        <div id="main">
        </div>

        <div id="sidebar">
        </div>
    </div>

    </body>
    </html>
```

We're going to be looking closely at `<div id="body">` and its descendants.

Inside the body div

Almost every page on blogger.com contains a "body:" div (`<div id="body">`). Its sole purpose is to constrain the site contents to a width of `710px`, and center it horizontally, as shown in Figure 3-53.

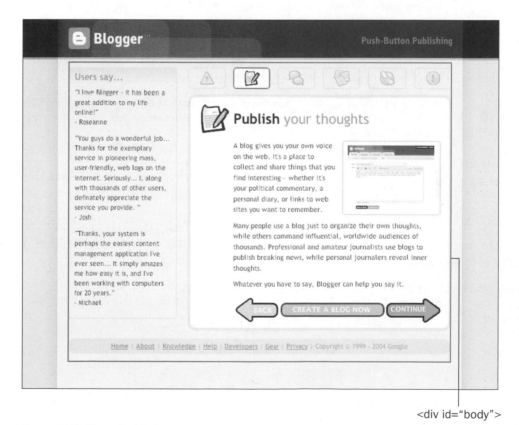

<div id="body">

Figure 3-53: The <div id="body">

Almost every page on blogger.com also contains a "main" div (<div id="main">), which sits inside the body div and holds the main content of the page, as shown in Figure 3-54.

<div id="main">

Figure 3-54: The <div id="main">

This main div can either be presented on its own (as in Figure 3-54), taking up all the available width, or it can be narrowed and displayed in conjunction with a "sidebar" div (<div id="sidebar">), which can appear on the left or on the right of the page, as shown in Figure 3-55.

<div id="sidebar">   <div id="main">

Figure 3-55: The <div id="sidebar"> and <div id="main">

Providing alternate layouts is nothing terribly clever, but what is rather nice is the way that Bowman triggers such layout changes: by altering the value of a `class` applied to the `body` tag.

Assign a `class` of `"ms"` to the `body` tag and the main `div` (m) and sidebar `div` (s) will display alongside each other — main on the left, sidebar on the right (see Figure 3-56).

```
<body class="ms">
```

Figure 3-56: The result of <body class="ms">: <div id="main"> is on the left and <div id="sidebar"> is on the right.

Swap that around and assign a `class` of `sm` to the `body` tag and the two `div`s swap places. Now the sidebar (s) is on the left and the main `div` (m) on the right (see Figure 3-57).

```
<body class="sm">
```

Figure 3-57: The result of <body class="sm">: <div id="sidebar"> is on the left and <div id="main"> is on the right.

Leave the `class` attribute out entirely and the main `div` will expand to fill the full width of the body `div`. The sidebar, if it exists, will be hidden (see Figure 3-58):

```
<body>
```

Figure 3-58: The result of setting no class attribute on <body>. Only <div id="main"> displays.

See how easy that is? See how easy Bowman has made it for the Blogger Team to mix and match the layout of their pages?

Let's see the XHTML and CSS that enables this layout swapping to occur.

The XHTML

The following is the XHTML:

```
<body>

<div id="header">
</div>

<div id="body">
    <div id="main">
    </div>

    <div id="sidebar">
    </div>
</div>

</body>
```

The CSS

The following is the CSS. (This is a simplified set of styles, dealing with layout only. Colors, borders, and so on have been left out.)

```
div#body {
    margin: auto;
    width: 710px
}

div#sidebar {
    display: none;
}

body.ms div#main,
body.sm div#main {
    width: 490px;
}

body.ms div#sidebar,
body.sm div#sidebar {
    display: block;
    width: 200px;
}

body.ms div#main,
body.sm div#sidebar {
    float: left;
}

body.sm div#main,
body.ms div#sidebar {
    float: right;
}
```

What Does It All Mean?

Okay, let's break that CSS down rule by rule.

First off, let's look at the styling for the `body` `div`. This `div` helps constrain everything and provides room for the two `div`s (main and sidebar) to sit side by side (when they need to). We set its `width` at `710px`, and set `margin-left` and `margin-right` values to `auto` to center the content:

```
div#body {
    margin: 0 auto;
    width: 710px
}
```

Next is the default style for `div#sidebar`. Unless some kind of class is specified in the `body` tag, the sidebar `div` will not be displayed and will be removed from the document flow.

```
div#sidebar {
    display: none;
}
```

If a class has been specified, then the following rule will constrain the width of div#main to 490px (from its browser default of 100 percent) to make room alongside it for the sidebar:

```
body.ms div#main,
body.sm div#main {
    width: 490px;
}
```

If a class has been specified, we also must set some styles that will be applied to the sidebar div:

```
body.ms div#sidebar,
body.sm div#sidebar {
    display: block;
    width: 200px;
}
```

The display: block counteracts the display: none (which we set as our default style for the sidebar), making it visible again. We also set the sidebar's width at 200px.

Now that we've set up the display and widths of the main and sidebar divs, it's time to position them on the left or right. We'll do this by using floats, and to save space in our CSS file, we're going to combine what should be four rules (two for the main div, and two for sidebar div) into just two rules.

The first rule floats the divs left. For the main div, this rule will be applied when the body tag has the class ms applied to it. For the sidebar div, this rule will be applied when the body tag has class sm applied to it.

```
body.ms div#main,
body.sm div#sidebar {
    float: left;
}
```

The second rule floats the divs right. For the main div, this rule will be applied when the body tag has the class sm applied to it. For the sidebar div, this rule will be applied when the body tag has class ms applied to it.

```
body.ms div#sidebar {
float: right;
}
```

And that's all there is to it. By simply altering the class of the body tag, members of the Blogger Team can easily (and quickly) affect the layout of the page. This is yet another example of why CSS is so darned good.

CSS-Enabled Rollovers

If there's one thing that CSS has helped to simplify on the Web, it's the humble rollover — the act of swapping one image (or color) for another when the user moves the mouse over a section of the page. Until about 2001, the only reliable way to achieve such an effect was by breaking out JavaScript and writing something like this:

```html
<html>

<head>
<title></title>
<script type="text/javascript">
<!--
function SwapOut()
    {
    document.getElementById('picture').src = 'picture-rollover.jpg';
    return true;
    }

function SwapBack()
    {
    document.getElementById('picture').src = 'picture.jpg';
    return true;
    }
-->
</script>
</head>

<body>

<p><a href="" onmouseover="SwapOut()" onmouseout="SwapBack()"><img id="picture"
src="picture.jpg" width="100" height="150" /></a></p>

</body>
</html>
```

CSS, thank heavens, has given us a number of different ways to achieve the same goal, and they're all delightfully simple. Let's take a look at them. . . .

Changing the Color and Background Color of Links (Simple)

This is the simplest (and most common) of all CSS rollover techniques. It is used to alert the user that the mouse is placed over a hyperlink.

Figure 3-59 shows some examples of the rollover in action.

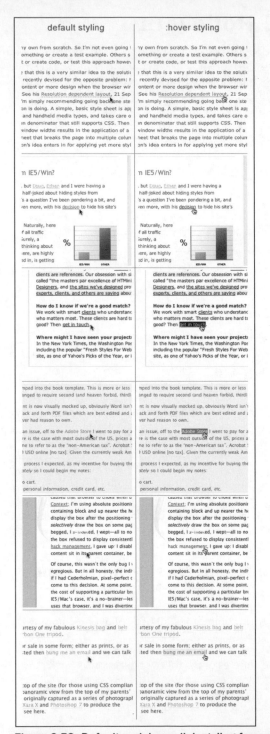

Figure 3-59: Default and :hover link styling from stopdesign.com, simplebits.com, 37signals.com, mezzoblue.com, sidesh0w.com, and 1976design.com

Let's look at that last example and see how it might be copied.

The XHTML

Following is the XHTML:

```
<p> If you're interested then <a href="">bung me an email</a> and we can talk about
what you want </p>
```

So, all that's needed is a simple a tag. How about the CSS?

The CSS

Following is the CSS:

```
a {
border-bottom: 1px solid #eee;
color: #d17e62;
text-decoration: none;
}

a:visited {
border-bottom: 1px solid #eee;
color: #9d604c;
text-decoration: none;
}

a:hover {
background-color: #ffffda;
border-bottom: 1px solid #ddd;
color: #c30;
text-decoration: none;
}
```

It's important to note the order in which those rules are written. The first rule, a {}, affects all links. The second rule, a:visited {}, affects those links that the user has already visited (this is determined by the browser's cache). The third rule, a:hover {}, affects those links that the mouse is currently hovering over.

Following the logic of the CSS Cascade (www.htmlhelp.com/reference/css/structure.html#cascade) each of those rules has precedence over the one before it. So, a normal link will have its styles overwritten by a visited link, and a visited link will have its styles overwritten when the user hovers over it. Simple, really, but you'd be surprised how many people get those in the wrong order.

Changing the Color and Background Color of Links (Complex)

This is a great trick for fast, low-bandwidth rollovers, and it's something Bowman has used on the front page of Blogger. It involves nothing more than altering the background color of an element, while keeping the image on top of that background (be it an inline image or a CSS background image) the same.

To see it in action, Figure 3-60 shows four links on the front page of blogger.com.

Figure 3-60: Four links on the front page of blogger.com. (The rest of the page has been dimmed so you can clearly identify the links.)

Figure 3-61 shows what happens when you move the mouse over one of those links.

Figure 3-61: One of the rollover links in action

You'll see that the background color has changed color and the word "thoughts" has become black. The actual button image, however, hasn't changed at all.

How has this been achieved? Well, first off, let's look at the XHTML, CSS, and images that make up this section.

The XHTML

Following is the XHTML:

```
<ul>
<li id="publish"><a href="tour_publish.g"><strong>Publish</strong> thoughts
</a></li>
<li id="feedback"><a href="tour_feedback.g"><strong>Get</strong> feedback</a></li>
<li id="people"><a href="tour_people.g"><strong>Find</strong> people</a></li>
<li id="more"><a href="tour_more.g"><strong>And</strong> more...</a></li>
</ul>
```

The CSS

Following is the CSS:

```
ul {
list-style: none;
margin: 0;
padding: 0;
}

ul li {
float: left;
margin: 0;
padding: 0;
}

ul li a {
color: #777;
display: block;
padding: 80px 10px 5px;
text-align: center;
text-decoration: none;
width: 75px;
}

ul li#publish a {
background: #fff url(icon_publish.gif) no-repeat top left;
}

ul li#feedback a {
background: #fff url(icon_feedback.gif) no-repeat top left;
}

ul li#people a {
background: #fff url(icon_people.gif) no-repeat top left;
}

ul li#more a {
```

```
    background: #fff url(icon_more.gif) no-repeat top left;
    }

    ul li#publish a:hover,
    ul li#feedback a:hover,
    ul li#people a:hover,
    ul li#more a:hover {
    background-color: #f8f2eb;
    }

    ul li a strong {
    color: #000;
    display: block;
    font-size: larger;
    }

    ul li a:hover {
    color: #000;
    }
```

The Images

For this to work, the images being used must have transparent sections that let the background color of the image (or of the parent element) show through. In each case, the images shown in Figure 3-62 have had their transparent sections replaced with a checkered pattern, so you can see which bits are see-through, and which aren't.

Figure 3-62: The checkered pattern indicates transparent areas.

What Does It All Mean?

Figure 3-63 shows our starting display.

- Publish thoughts
- Get feedback
- Find people
- And more...

Figure 3-63: The unstyled display

Now, let's go through the CSS line by line and see what effect each part has. First off, we'll remove the bullets (dots) that precede each list item, as shown in Figure 3-64:

```
    ul {
    list-style: none;
    }
```

Figure 3-64: Removing the bullets

Then we'll remove any margin and padding the unordered list might have, as shown in Figure 3-65. We do this so that when we come to position the finished list in the page, we're not fighting against the default browser settings for padding and margin on unordered lists.

```
ul {
list-style: none;
margin: 0;
padding: 0;
}
```

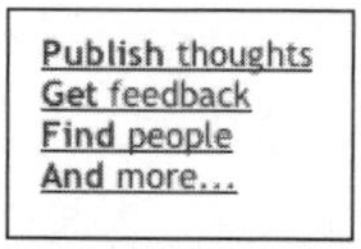

Figure 3-65: Removing margins and padding

Next, we style the list items. First, we float each item left, so that they no longer display vertically, and instead line up next to each other, horizontally, as shown in Figure 3-66. We also remove their margin and padding.

```
ul li {
float: left;
margin: 0;
padding: 0;
}
```

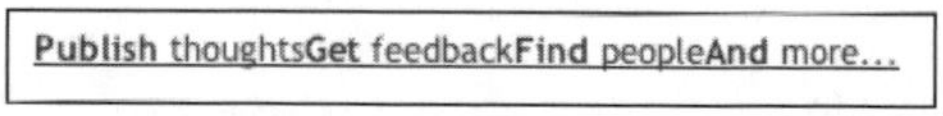

Figure 3-66: Floating each item in the list

Now we style the links. First we set a font color (see Figure 3-67):

```
ul li a {
color: #777;
}
```

Figure 3-67: Setting a font color

Next we set the links to `display: block`, and apply a `width` of `75px`, as shown in Figure 3-68. (This is equivalent to the width of the images we'll be using.)

```
ul li a {
color: #777;
display: block;
width: 75px;
}
```

Figure 3-68: Blocking the elements

Now we must insert some white space so that our images (which we'll be adding in a short while) will have somewhere to sit, as shown in Figure 3-69. We do this by adding in 80px of padding at the top (75px for the image, and 5px to make a gap between the image and the text).

```
ul li a {
color: #777;
display: block;
padding: 80px 0 0 0;
width: 75px;
}
```

Figure 3-69: Inserting white space for placement of the images

Next we add in 10px of padding on the left and padding on the right, and 5px of padding on the bottom (see Figure 3-70):

```
ul li a {
color: #777;
display: block;
padding: 80px 10px 5px;
width: 75px;
}
```

Figure 3-70: Adding padding

And, to finish off the generic link styling, we center align the link text and remove its underline (see Figure 3-71):

```
ul li a {
color: #777;
display: block;
padding: 80px 10px 5px;
text-align: center;
text-decoration: none;
width: 75px;
}
```

Figure 3-71: Centering text and removing underlining

Now it's time to add in the background images for each of the links, as shown in Figure 3-72:

```
ul li#publish a {
background: transparent url(icon_publish.gif) no-repeat top center;
}

ul li#feedback a {
background: transparent url(icon_feedback.gif) no-repeat top center;
}

ul li#people a {
background: transparent url(icon_people.gif) no-repeat top center;
}

ul li#more a {
background: transparent url(icon_more.gif) no-repeat top center;
}
```

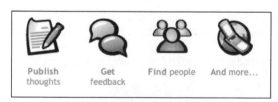

Figure 3-72: Adding background images

Things are coming together nicely. Next, we'll make the first word of each link darker and larger, as shown in Figure 3-73:

```
ul li a strong {
color: #000;
font-size: larger;
}
```

Figure 3-73: Making the first word of the links darker and larger

We'll also add in a rule to ensure that the second word of each link is forced onto a new line (see Figure 3-74):

```
ul li a strong {
color: #000;
display: block;
font-size: larger;
}
```

Figure 3-74: Forcing the second word of the link to a new line

That's all looking very nice, so let's add in the CSS that will make the rollovers work.

This rule alters the background color of each link as the user hovers the mouse over it (see Figure 3-75):

```
ul li#publish a:hover,
ul li#feedback a:hover,
ul li#people a:hover,
ul li#more a:hover {
background-color: #f8f2eb;
}
```

Figure 3-75: Altering the background color

To finish things off, this little rule will alter the color of the text on `:hover` so that it changes from gray to black, as shown in Figure 3-76:

```
ul li a:hover {
color: #000;
}
```

Figure 3-76: The finished product in action

And we're done!

Dealing with Internet Explorer

The previous example works perfectly for users of IE. However, if you're not careful, you can cause problems for the few people out there who claim IE5 for the Mac as their browser of choice. It turns out that this browser has an odd disliking for quotation marks around image filenames in CSS.

For example, this will work:

```
ul li#publish a {
background: #fff url(icon_publish.gif) no-repeat top left;
}
```

But this will not:

```
ul li#publish a {
background: #fff url('icon_publish.gif') no-repeat top left;
}
```

And neither will this:

```
ul li#publish a {
background: #fff url("icon_publish.gif") no-repeat top left;
}
```

Many coders like to put quotation marks around such filenames, triggering color-coding in their text editors, as shown in Figure 3-77. Unfortunately, it seems that by doing so, they're depriving IE5 Mac users of the full, visual experience.

```
ul li#publish a {
background: #fff url('icon_publish.gif') no-repeat top left;
}


ul li#publish a {
background: #fff url(icon_publish.gif) no-repeat top left;
}
```

Figure 3-77: Using quotation marks activates friendly code-coloring in some text editors.

This is an odd little bug, and one that can easily slip past you when you're not concentrating, so watch out.

Changing the Background Color of Table Rows

The use of alternating row colors in tables has become a well-recognized design touch (think of iTunes), providing structure to long tables, and letting the eye scan easily across a row of information.

If this is combined with a hover effect to highlight the row under the mouse pointer, it can produce an attractive and functional look, as shown in Figure 3-78.

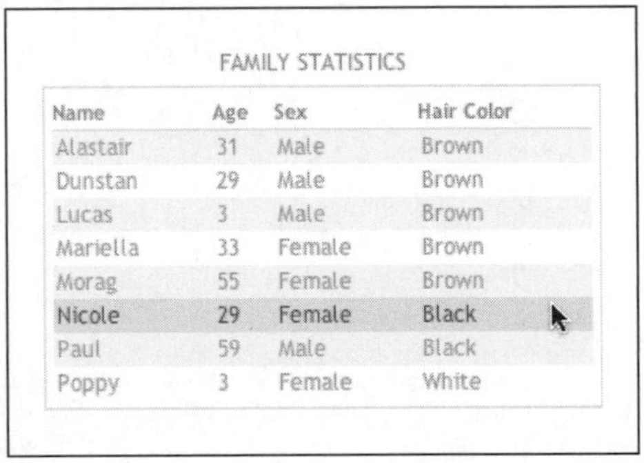

FAMILY STATISTICS			
Name	Age	Sex	Hair Color
Alastair	31	Male	Brown
Dunstan	29	Male	Brown
Lucas	3	Male	Brown
Mariella	33	Female	Brown
Morag	55	Female	Brown
Nicole	29	Female	Black
Paul	59	Male	Black
Poppy	3	Female	White

Figure 3-78: An example of alternate row coloring and row highlighting

The code for this hover effect couldn't be simpler. Using the previous example, here's the XHTML and the CSS needed to style the table rows.

The XHTML

Following is the XHTML:

```
<table cellpadding="5" cellspacing="0" border="1">
<caption>Family Statistics</caption>

<thead>
<tr>
    <th>Name</th>
    <th>Age</th>
    <th>Sex</th>
```

```
        <th>Hair Color</th>
    </tr>
    </thead>

    <tbody>
    <tr class="odd">
        <td>Alastair</td>
        <td>31</td>
        <td>Male</td>
        <td>Brown</td>
    </tr>
    <tr class="even">
        <td>Dunstan</td>
        <td>29</td>
        <td>Male</td>
        <td>Brown</td>
    </tr>
    <tr class="odd">
        <td>Lucas</td>
        <td>3</td>
        <td>Male</td>
        <td>Brown</td>
    </tr>
    <tr class="even">
        <td>Mariella</td>
        <td>33</td>
        <td>Female</td>
        <td>Brown</td>
    </tr>
    <tr class="odd">
        <td>Morag</td>
        <td>55</td>
        <td>Female</td>
        <td>Brown</td>
    </tr>
    <tr class="even">
        <td>Nicole</td>
        <td>29</td>
        <td>Female</td>
        <td>Black</td>
    </tr>
    <tr class="odd">
        <td>Paul</td>
        <td>59</td>
        <td>Male</td>
        <td>Black</td>
    </tr>
    <tr class="even">
        <td>Poppy</td>
        <td>3</td>
        <td>Female</td>
        <td>White</td>
    </tr>
    </tbody>
    </table>
```

The CSS

Most of the following CSS is needed to style the table. The rules that actually do the hover effect have been boldfaced for you.

```
table {
        background-color: #fff;
        border: 1px solid #ddd;
        empty-cells: show;
        font-size: 90%;
        margin: 0 0 20px 0;
        padding: 4px;
        text-align: left;
        width: 300px;
}

table caption {
        color: #777;
        margin: 0 0 5px 0;
        padding: 0;
        text-align: center;
        text-transform: uppercase;
}

table thead th {
        border: 0;
        border-bottom: 1px solid #ddd;
        color: #777;
        font-size: 90%;
        padding: 3px 0;
        margin: 0 0 5px 0;
        text-align: left;
}

table tbody tr.odd {
        background-color: #f7f7f7;
}

table tbody tr.even {
        background-color: #fff;
}

table tbody tr:hover {
     background-color: #ffe08e;
}

table tbody td {
     color: #888;
     padding: 2px;
     border: 0;
}

table tbody tr:hover td {
     color: #444;
}
```

What Does It All Mean?

We're not going to go through each and every line of that CSS because it's not all relevant to this rollover section. However, let's look at the last few rules in detail.

The first thing to note is that we've given each of the two row classes (.odd and .even) a background color. This lets us create our alternating row-color effect.

```
table tbody tr.odd {
    background-color: #f7f7f7;
}

table tbody tr.even {
    background-color: #fff;
}
```

Next, we set a rule that changes the background color of a row when the user hovers over it:

```
table tbody tr:hover {
    background-color: #ffe08e;
}
```

And finally, we change the color of the text contained within the row that is being hovered over, making it darker to stand out against its new background color:

```
table tbody tr:hover td {
    color: #444;
}
```

It really is wonderfully simple stuff.

Changing the Color of Text

The final hover application we're going to look at in this section is highlighting text (be it plain text or linked text) when a user hovers over a div or similar element.

Why might this be useful? Imagine a site that contains many links. Developers usually style their links so that they're a bright color, making them stand out from the surrounding text. That's all very well when you have a few links per page, but what happens if your site contains hundreds of links per page? The eyes of the user will be assaulted by a mass of bright color as hundreds of links vie for their attention. How can you expect to pick out the subtleties of your design if all you can see is a sea of color?

The solution (or one of them) is simple. If we hide the bright colors of these links until the user hovers the mouse over the relevant section of the page, then we can present users, at first glance, with a much calmer site. We'll make the links obvious only when the user is indicating that he or she is interested in that section of the page, by moving the mouse over it.

Figure 3-79 shows that approach in action.

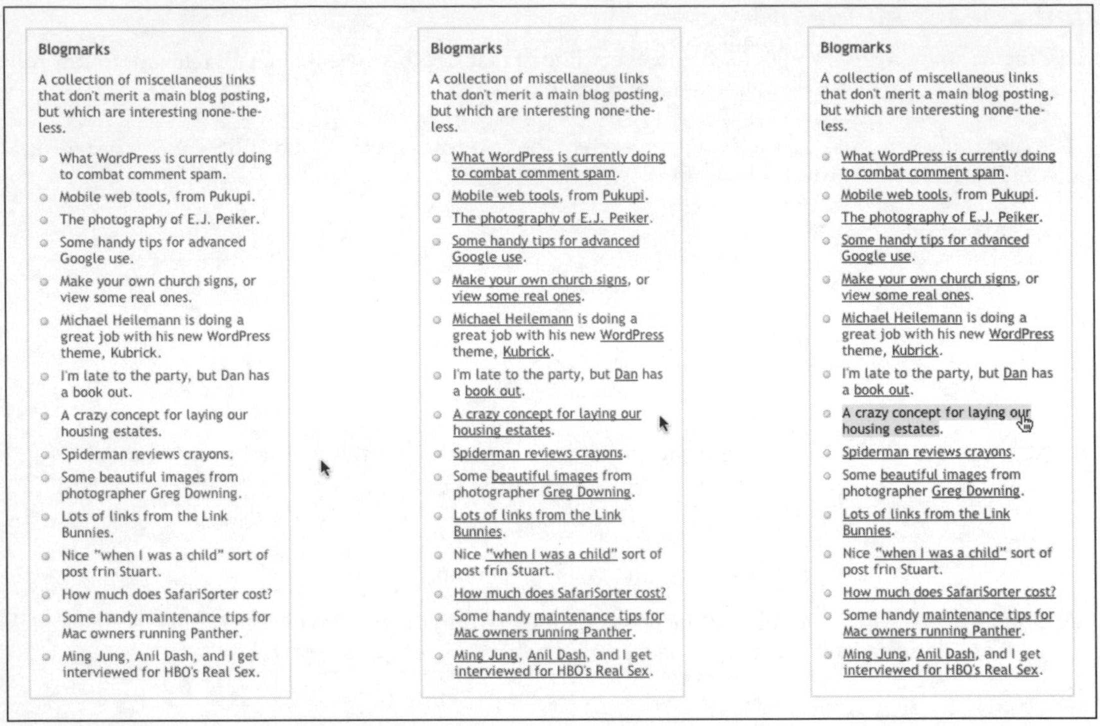

Figure 3-79: Text can be highlighted when the mouse hovers over divs or links.

See how effective that is? Let's see how we might re-create that.

The XHTML

Following is the XHTML:

```
<div id="links">
<h3>Blogmarks</h3>

<p>A collection of miscellaneous links that don't merit a main blog posting, but
which are interesting none-the-less.</p>

<ul>
<li><a href="">What WordPress is currently doing to combat comment spam</a>.</li>
<li><a href="">Mobile web tools</a>, from <a href="">Pukupi</a>.</li>
<li><a href="">The photography of E.J. Peiker</a>.</li>
<li><a href="">Some handy tips for advanced Google use</a>.</li>
<li><a href="">Make your own church signs</a>, or <a href="">view some real
ones</a>.</li>
<li><a href="">Michael Heilemann</a> is doing a great job with his new <a
href="">WordPress</a> theme, <a href="">Kubrick</a>.</li>
<li>I'm late to the party, but <a href="">Dan</a> has a <a href="">book
out</a>.</li>
<li><a href="">A crazy concept for laying our housing estates</a>.</li>
```

```
<li><a href="">Spiderman reviews crayons</a>.</li>
<li>Some <a href="">beautiful images</a> from photographer <a href="">Greg
Downing</a>.</li>
<li><a href="">Lots of links from the Link Bunnies</a>.</li>
<li>Nice <a href="">&#8220;when I was a child&#8221;</a> sort of post frin
Stuart.</li>
<li><a href="">How much does SafariSorter cost?</a></li>
<li>Some handy <a href="">maintenance tips for Mac owners running Panther</a>.</li>
<li><a href="">Ming Jung</a>, <a href="">Anil Dash</a>, and I get <a
href="">interviewed for HBO's Real Sex</a>.</li>
</ul>
</div>
```

The CSS

Following is the CSS:

```
div#links {
    color: #333;
    border: 2px solid #ddd;
    padding: 10px;
    width: 240px;
}

html > body div#links {
    width: 220px;
}

div#links ul {
    margin: 0 0 0 19px;
    padding: 0;
}

div#links ul li {
    list-style-image: url('list-dot.gif');
    margin: 0 0 .5em 0;
}

html > body div#links ul li a {
    color: #333;
    text-decoration: none;
}

div#links:hover ul li a {
    color: #0000ff;
    text-decoration: underline;
}

div#links ul li a:hover {
    background-color: #ffff66;
    color: #000;
    text-decoration: none;
}
```

Images

All we're using is a little "dot" image to replace the browser's default "list dot" (or bullet), as shown in Figure 3-80.

Figure 3-80: A replacement list dot (or bullet)

What Does It All Mean?

Again, we're not going to look at every little bit of that CSS code because it's not all relevant to the rollover technique we're discussing. However, here are a few bits that are worth examining.

First, we set the default text color for everything in the div. We choose a shade of gray because gray is a nice calm color, and that's one of the things we're trying to achieve here—calm.

```
div#links {
    color: #333;
}
```

Next, we style the links so that they fit in with the gray text, removing anything that would make them stand out from their surroundings:

```
html > body div#links ul li a {
    color: #333;
    text-decoration: none;
}
```

We use the child selector (>) to style the links so that IE (which doesn't interpret rules containing the child selector) won't apply the rule. For a full explanation of why we do this, see the following section, "Dealing with Internet Explorer."

Now come our two :hover rules. The first will be activated when the user moves the mouse over the div. It will cause the links to change from gray to blue and to show their underline text decoration.

```
div#links:hover ul li a {
    color: #0000ff;
    text-decoration: underline;
}
```

The second :hover rule activates when the user moves the mouse directly over a link. It changes the text color to black, removes the underline, and makes the background of the link bright yellow.

```
div#links ul li a:hover {
    background-color: #ffff66;
    color: #000;
    text-decoration: none;
}
```

And that's all there is to it.

Dealing with Internet Explorer

As mentioned earlier, IE doesn't understand the `:hover` selector on elements other than links.

So, Firefox, Opera, Safari, and IE all understand this:

```
a:hover {
color: red;
}
```

But only Firefox, Opera, and Safari understand these:

```
div:hover {
color: yellow;
}

div:hover a {
color: green;
}
```

Why is that relevant? Well, it affects what we've just done in this demonstration. Imagine that you're using Firefox to browse a Web site. The page loads, and CSS turns all the text and links gray, to mellow things out for you. You zero in on a section that interests you. You move your mouse over it and, ah! The links turn bright blue. You can now see what's a link and what's plain text.

Now, imagine that you're browsing the same site using IE. The page loads, and CSS turns all the text and links gray. You zero in on a section that interests you. You move your mouse over it and nothing. No links pop out at you and you're just left with a sea of unresponsive gray text. Why? Because IE doesn't understand that you're hovering over a `div`, and so it can't apply a different, brighter style to the links. Disaster!

So, you can see why we have to stop the links being turned gray right at the start in IE. There's no point turning them gray if the browser can't turn them back to blue at the appropriate moment. Hence, we use the child selector.

Now, here's the bugger of using a child selector to hide styles from IE: IE for the PC doesn't understand the child selector (great!), but IE5 for the Mac does!

So, any time we use > to block IE, we must remember we're blocking only IE for the PC, not IE for the Mac.

This wouldn't be a problem if IE5 for the Mac handled things like `:hover` on any element, but it doesn't. It's just as bad there as its PC cousin.

What this means is that if you're at all worried about annoying IE5 for the Mac users, be very aware of CSS techniques that use the child selector to hide rules from IE.

Changing the Background Position on Links

The second approach to CSS-based rollovers is one that focuses on swapping not just background color, but images as well, and does so using the increasingly important method of background positioning.

If you've never heard of this idea, then don't worry; it's easy as pie, but it does require a little explanation.

Making Rollovers from Embedded Images

Let's say we've been given the page layout shown in Figure 3-81 and we've been asked to jazz up the photo a bit—add in a rollover, maybe a bit of a drop shadow, something a bit more interesting.

Figure 3-81: Can we replace this photo using CSS?

We can do that, right? Well, what if we were told that we have to make those changes without touching the XHTML? Could we still do it?

```
<div id="sidebar">
<div class="box">
<h2>Lucas says...</h2>

<div id="photo-lucas">
<img src="lucas.jpg" width="150" height="100" alt="Portrait of small boy" />
</div>

<p>Hello there, my name is Lucas. I am 3-years old and the bi-lingual monkey-child
of an English man and an Italian woman.</p>

<p>I like cars and trucks and buses and trains and almost anything that moves. I'm
not so keen on sprouts or the Welsh.</p>

<p>My Grandma has a dog, called Poppy. She's small and cute and she widdles when
she gets excited.</p>

<p>When I grow up I want to be like my Uncle... what a guy he is...</p>
</div>
</div>
```

Well, if you're fortunate, and you're working with well thought-out XHTML, then this sort of thing is a breeze to do. It may sound daunting, but with a bit of Adobe Photoshop magic and some CSS, we can very quickly have a layout that not only inserts a new image, and not only repositions that image, but also makes that image function as a rollover whenever the user moves the mouse into the "Lucas says . . . " box.

Figure 3-82 shows the finished result. It's shown twice so you can see the page in its normal state (on the left) and in its "rolled-over" state (on the right).

Figure 3-82: The finished layout and rollover in action. Mousing-over the text causes the rollover to trigger and the color image to be revealed.

Let's see how that was achieved.

The XHTML

This is pretty much the same XHTML as we used to create the "Users say . . . " box beginning in the earlier section "Creating Fixed-Width, Round-Cornered Boxes." The new markup, and the bit worth paying attention to, has been boldfaced for you:

```
<div id="sidebar">
<div class="box">
<h2>Lucas says...</h2>

<div id="photo-lucas">
<img src="lucas.jpg" width="150" height="100" alt="Portrait of small boy" />
</div>

<p>Hello there, my name is Lucas. I am 3-years old and the bi-lingual monkey-child
of an English man and an Italian woman.</p>

<p>I like cars and trucks and buses and trains and almost anything that moves. I'm
not so keen on sprouts or the Welsh.</p>

<p>My Grandma has a dog, called Poppy. She's small and cute and she widdles when
she gets excited.</p>

<p>When I grow up I want to be like my Uncle... what a guy he is...</p>
</div>
</div>
```

The CSS

We're not going to repeat the CSS used to style the box because we covered that earlier in this chapter. Instead, let's just look at the new, interesting pieces:

```css
.box {
    position: relative;
}

html > body div#photo-lucas img {
    left: -5000px;
    position: absolute;
}

html > body div#photo-lucas {
    background: transparent url(lucas-rollover.png) no-repeat top left;
    height: 124px;
    left: 185px;
    position: absolute;
    width: 160px;
}

div.box:hover div#photo-lucas {
    background-position: top right;
}
```

The Images

Figure 3-83 shows the original JPG image referenced in the XHTML.

Figure 3-83: The original image, referenced in the XHTML (lucas.jpg at 150 × 100px)

Figure 3-84 shows a PNG file we're going to use as the replacement image. We're using a PNG file because we want to have a realistic, semi-transparent drop shadow, and neither JPG files nor GIF files can do that.

Figure 3-84: The image used for the rollover: Lucas-rollover.png 320 × 124px (transparent sections are denoted by the checkered pattern)

What Does It All Mean?

The XHTML isn't worth examining in any more detail, but let's have a look at what the CSS does.

Figure 3-85 shows our starting point.

Figure 3-85: Starting point

First off, we must remove the original `lucas.jpg` image. There are a number of ways to do this using CSS, but the best all-round method is to set its position to absolute and then fling it as far off the edge of the screen as possible (see Figure 3-86).

```
html > body div#photo-lucas img {
    left: -5000px;
    position: absolute;
}
```

We use `position: absolute` and not `position: relative` because absolutely positioning an object removes it completely from the document flow. In this case, it causes its parent element (`div#photo-lucas`) to collapse, and lets the text below it move up and reflow to fill the now-blank space.

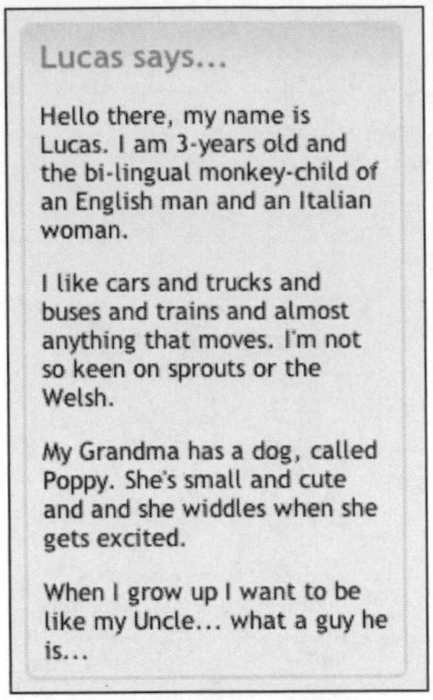

Figure 3-86: Removing the image

Having cleared out the old image, it's time to insert the new one. We're going to insert it as a background image to `div#photo-lucas`, the `div` that contained the original image (see Figure 3-87):

```
html > body div#photo-lucas {
        background: transparent url(lucas-rollover.png) no-repeat top left;
}
```

Figure 3-87: Inserting the new image

Hmm, well, we've inserted it, so where is it?

Well, remember that this is a background image to div#photo-lucas, the element that contained the original photo. But, because we threw the original photo off the edge of the screen, div#photo-lucas has no content, and no content means no dimensions. So, yes, our new background image is there, but we must give div#photo-lucas a width and a height in order to be able to see it, as shown in Figure 3-88.

```
html > body div#photo-lucas {
        background: transparent url(lucas-rollover.png) no-repeat top left;
        height: 124px;
        width: 160px;
}
```

Figure 3-88: Revealing the hidden image

Ah! There it is, very nice. Notice that the height we set corresponds to the height of the new rollover image (lucas-rollover.png), and the width is exactly half that image's width. This way we see only one-half of lucas-rollover.png at a time, which is just what we want.

With the new image on-screen, let's reposition it off to the right. To do that, we once again use position: absolute (see Figure 3-89):

```
html > body div#photo-lucas {
        background: transparent url(lucas-rollover.png) no-repeat top left;
        height: 124px;
        position: absolute;
        width: 160px;
}
```

Figure 3-89: Repositioning the image

Now, don't worry, it hasn't gone wrong. All that's happened is that `div#photo-lucas` has been removed from the document flow, meaning that it no longer interacts with anything around it. Instead it floats above everything else (or underneath if we want to start using `z-index`) and can be positioned anywhere on-screen.

Because that's the case let's move it to its new position on the right of the box. The first thing to do is to alter a bit of that original box CSS and insert the following rule:

```
.box {
    position: relative;
}
```

This means that whatever XY coordinates we give to `div#photo-lucas`, we will be positioning it relative to its containing element, the box (`.box`). The `top left` will be the top-left corner of the box, `bottom right` will be the bottom-right corner of the box, and so on.

Now that our reference point is established, let's move our image. First of all, let's set the left position, as shown in Figure 3-90:

```
html > body div#photo-lucas {
    background: transparent url(lucas-rollover.png) no-repeat top left;
    height: 124px;
    left: 185px;
    position: absolute;
    width: 160px;
}
```

Figure 3-90: Setting the left position

Perfect. And, in fact, we don't need to set a top position because it's already in the right place. Now, all that's left to do is activate the main point of this demonstration: the rollover, as shown in Figure 3-91. We hope, by now, you're starting to understand just how easy this final step always is.

```
div.box:hover div#photo-lucas {
    background-position: top right;
}
```

Figure 3-91: Activating the rollover

Dealing with Internet Explorer

IE gets rather short shrift here. Not only does it not interpret :hover on divs, but it also doesn't handle semi-transparent PNGs. As a consequence, we've blocked it from implementing any of these changes by using the child selector, as described earlier in this chapter.

There are certainly instances where you could use an IE-friendly version of this technique. You could use a regular JPG, instead of a PNG. (You wouldn't get the drop shadow, but that's not always a bad thing.) As long as your original image sat inside a link then the rollover would work as well (in a limited way).

You may be thinking, "Stop showing me demos that don't work in IE!" However, what you should be taking away from this is an idea of what's possible with today's best browsers. Once you realize what's possible, you can start to adjust these demos until you reach a happy balance—a balance between CSS and cross-browser functionality; between lean, mean XHTML, and making the site work on your client's machine.

But okay, let's make this demo work in IE. Changes to the code have been boldfaced in the following example. All we are doing is inserting one image for IE (a JPG), and then replacing that image for Firefox, Opera, and Safari. As always, we're using the child-combinator selector to do this.

```css
.box {
    position: relative;
}

div#photo img {
    left: -5000px;
    position: absolute;
}

body div#photo-lucas {
    background: transparent url(lucas-ie.png) no-repeat top left;
    border: 2px solid #e1d4c0;
    height: 113px;
    left: 175px;
    position: absolute;
    width: 156px;
}

html > body div#photo-lucas {
    background: transparent url(lucas-rollover.png) no-repeat top left;
    border: none;
    height: 124px;
    left: 185px;
    position: absolute;
    width: 160px;
}

div.box:hover div#photo-lucas {
    background-position: top right;
}
```

Figure 3-92 shows the new, IE-only image.

Figure 3-92: The lucas-ie.jpg file at 156 × 113px

And how does that all look in IE? Figure 3-93 shows how the complete package looks.

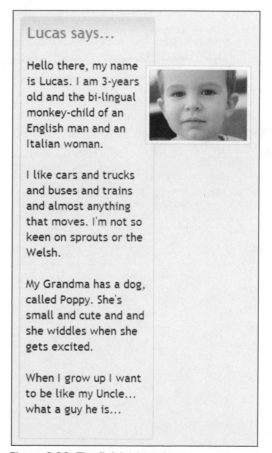

Figure 3-93: The finished product

Not bad.

Summary

This chapter began by discussing two methods of inserting rounded corners into boxes, complete with a glimpse at the power behind the `:before` and `:after` pseudo-elements. We briefly examined a way to further blur the rigid box structure that underlies all our sites, through the use of implied boxes. We also looked at (and bent) an interesting rule and discussed the pitfalls of using the content of an element as hooks to style the element itself.

We then highlighted the benefits of sensible and well thought-out design. We showed how, with the manipulation of a simple CSS class, blogger.com's site maintainers are able to select one of three layouts for a page — hiding, showing, and repositioning content with no fuss, and not a hint of nonsense.

We looked at rollovers that manipulate text color and background color, and we looked at rollovers that manipulate the position of background images. We've seen that Internet Explorer lets us down with its incomplete support of `:hover`, and we've also seen that IE for the PC and IE for the Mac behave in different ways.

This chapter should provide you with an understanding of the underlying principles of the techniques discussed, and not leave you blindly copying code examples. If you find that you can't put these ideas to work on your client's site, at least you can play with them, and try to duplicate your work using these techniques. You'll be amazed at how simple it can be, and you'll also be amazed at how easy it is to cut-and-paste one set of code to get it working.

In the next chapter, we'll take a look at the inner workings of a successful event-driven site: The PGA Championship.

The PGA Championship

The PGA Championship is one of the world's premier sporting events. Presented in the late summer each year by the PGA of America, the tournament is the final major event of the golf season, features the best players in professional golf, and is followed by millions of fans around the world.

Turner Sports Interactive, a division of Time Warner, was responsible for the site development and editorial content during the event. The technological goal was to create a dynamic, rich, standards-compliant site using CSS for all layout and presentation, easily digestible XHTML markup, and Flash for special features. The creative goal was for a Web presence that was visually unique, sophisticated, and most of all, without any of the typical golf design clichés. A palette of desaturated, warm neutral tones was chosen, plus white and black to emphasize original photography and place as much attention on the textual content as possible.

Soon after its launch in July 2004, the PGA Championship site received overwhelmingly positive feedback from both golf fans and the Web-development community for its unique presentation, adherence to Web standards, and overall design. Traffic exploded on the first day of competition, as the PGA.com editorial team delivered a steady stream of news, scores, and multimedia content to millions of users per hour. Thanks to the lightweight CSS/XHTML markup, there was plenty of bandwidth to spread around.

This chapter provides detailed walkthroughs of some of the techniques used for a few of the site's original features. Included in this discussion are general CSS/XHTML tips and tricks, as well as real-world caveats to watch out for in your own projects. The topics discussed in this chapter include the following:

- ❑ How to create the layered, drop-shadow effect using CSS and Photoshop
- ❑ A powerful, ultra-light method for adding CSS-powered drop-down menus
- ❑ Embedding Flash content without breaking standards compliance

Drop-Shadow Effect

One of the more eye-catching features of the PGA Championship site was the nearly three-dimensional (3D), layered separation of content. The effect was subtle, but if you look closely at the home page (www.pga2004.com/) shown in Figure 4-1, the left column appears to hover above its surrounding content. This wasn't just a cool visual trick, but served an editorial purpose. The left column contained the most up-to-date Championship news and features. By giving the area a subtle (but noticeable) sense of visual lift, end-users could quickly discern where the freshest Championship content was published.

The left column couldn't simply be "higher" than its neighbors, but needed to partially obscure content so that the space appeared to realistically float above the page. This was the idea behind the "Top Story" header at the top of the left column. Because it appeared to be connected to the left column, and provided the right edge for the beginning of a drop shadow running down the page, it *seemed* to be part of the XHTML and to be sitting on top of the Flash movie. But the illusion was just that.

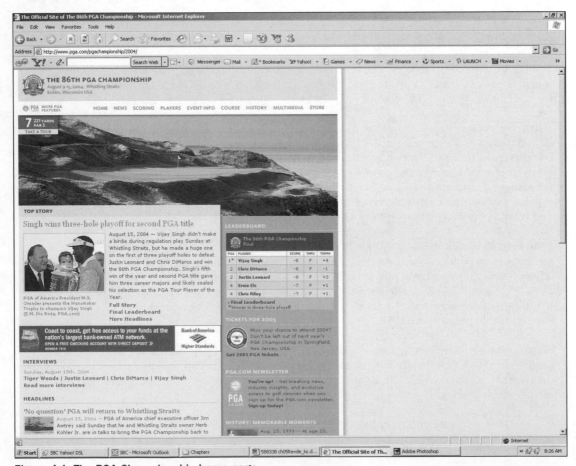

Figure 4-1: The PGA Championship home page

The total effect may look complex and bandwidth-intensive, but it was actually very light in byte size and code, and fairly straightforward to create with a little advance planning. This section examines the effect by using Photoshop, Flash, CSS, and XHTML, and offers an extra tip for pushing the effect to an even greater height.

Creating the Illusion

Before we begin with the nuts and bolts, let's back up for a moment and revisit the goal — to visually meld the Flash movie at the top of the page with the content below, and create the appearance that the left column is on a higher layer than its surrounding content by running a drop shadow down the length of the document. It's tricky because if the shadow in either the Flash movie or the XHTML were 1 pixel off, the effect would have been ruined. But, thanks to the preciseness of both CSS and XHTML, it was possible.

Flash movies, like any embedded content, are always square. It's impossible for a Flash object to have an irregular shape. To "break the bounding box" and create the illusion of layers, part of the left column's design was placed inside the bottom of the Flash movie and positioned (to the pixel) so that, when the Flash and XHTML content were placed next to each other, they snapped together to complete the illusion.

To start, a new document was created in Photoshop, and filled with the same hex color used by both the Flash movie and the right column running down the right side of the page. A new layer (named "bar") was created, a space the same width as the left column was selected (using the Rectangular Marquee tool), and then filled the area with the color of choice. A Drop Shadow layer effect was applied to "bar," and the shadow options were set to produce a look that wasn't too pronounced or heavy, but enough so that it provided a subtle sense of separation.

When completed, the document looked like Figure 4-2.

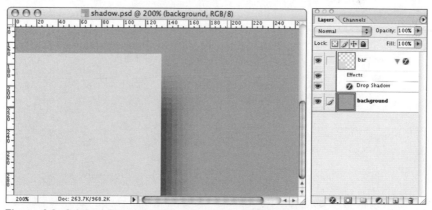

Figure 4-2: Original Photoshop document magnified 200 percent for a closer look at the shadow

Once the shadow looked about right, the visibility of the "background" layer was turned off and the Rectangular Marquee Tool was used to select the shadow itself (see Figure 4-3). The shadow was copied to the clipboard (Edit ➪ Copy Merged), a new Photoshop document with a transparent background was created, and the shadow was pasted inside. The graphic was saved as a PNG file and placed in the Flash movie (where a vector shape the same width and height of the "bar" from the Photoshop document already existed).

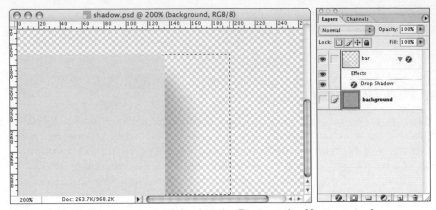

Figure 4-3: Shadow area selected using the Rectangular Marquee tool

You may be wondering why the graphic was saved as a PNG instead of the more commonplace GIF or JPEG file types. This is because PNG is the preferred format to use when importing bitmaps into Flash. Why? Because the PNG file format offers alpha channels with 256 levels of transparency. This enables you to export highly detailed images from your favorite bitmap editor (Photoshop, Fireworks, and so on), import them into Flash, and publish movies that retain their transparent data while simultaneously applying lossy JPEG compression. It's literally the best of both worlds — the visual quality of the PNG file format with the small file size of a JPEG.

With the Flash movie done, next up was replicating the shadow using CSS/XHTML. Because the shadow would run all the way down the length of the page, and the browser had to automatically repeat the shadow effect for as long as there was content, a "replicable" section of the graphic was needed. This required a graphic that could be vertically tiled (one after another after another) without gaps, seams, or anomalies. So, as shown in Figure 4-4, an area 1 pixel high was selected, making sure to include some of the background color for a smooth blend.

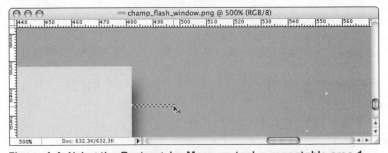

Figure 4-4: Using the Rectangular Marquee tool, a repeatable area 1 pixel high including the shadow and a little of the background was selected and copied to the clipboard.

Once copied, a new document was created (which Photoshop automatically set to the exact width and height of the clipboard) and the selection was pasted inside, as shown in Figure 4-5.

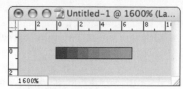

Figure 4-5: The clipboard area pasted into a new document and magnified for detail

That took care of the shadow itself, but the lighter gray background that ran under the left column had to be addressed. To do this, the canvas size of the graphic was increased to the pixel width required and with the shadow aligned to the right. And as shown in Figure 4-6, the transparent area was filled with the left column's hex color, and the whole graphic was saved as a GIF file.

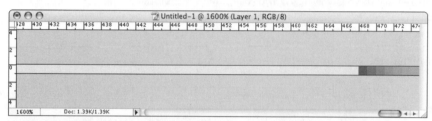

Figure 4-6: Final background image containing the left column's background color and drop shadow

Let's back up a moment and discuss image file formats again. Why was GIF used here, but not PNG as discussed earlier? The culprit is Internet Explorer, and its infamously poor support of PNG. Nearly eight years ago, Microsoft touted in a white paper that version 4.0 of their browser would "provide native support" for PNG, unlike "other browser manufactures [who] include PNG support as a third-party option." Well, 4.0 didn't fulfill their claim, and eight years later they've yet to fully support it in their browser. Sadly, it'll be years before Web developers will be able to tap into the incredible power of PNG in their designs — if, of course, Microsoft ever follows through.

So, for now, GIF was the way to go for both cross-browser acceptance and the lossless compression the non-photographic content required.

Now, let's look at the CSS magic. In the style sheet, a "container" was created with a `div` — an invisible block that would provide an outer framework for positioning groups of content (which, in this case, were the left and right columns). As the content inside either column grew vertically, the outer container would expand accordingly. This is precisely why the background image was applied to the container and not to the columns — the image would be repeated regardless of the interior content's length. To set this up in CSS, the following was created in the style sheet:

```
#colwrap {
    width:740px;
    background:#96968C
url(http://i.pga.com/pga/images/pgachampionship/img/bg_home_content.gif) repeat-y;
}
```

A specific pixel width was set with `div`, followed by the background attribute (which is where all the action took place. We use a hex value that is the same as the background of the Flash movie and the right column, a `url` to the desired image, plus an instruction to the browser to repeat the image vertically (`repeat-y`) for the complete length of the `div`.

Without `repeat-y`, the browser (by default) would have not only tiled the graphic vertically, but *horizontally* as well. This would have caused the left edge of the graphic to appear again after the right edge of the shadow. This obviously wouldn't have worked with the design so `repeat-y` was used to tile the image in only one direction (down). If your design required a horizontally tiled graphic, you could use `repeat-x`.

Because CSS allows you to apply both a hex color *and* an image to a single element, you can (with a little planning) shave a few bytes from your file size by using CSS to draw areas of consistent color (known as "spot" colors in the print world). This is the reason why the container's background image was cropped at the edge of the drop shadow. The remainder of the background (the dark gray area the shadow bled into) was drawn by the browser using the stipulated color value. While this method was not required (all of it could have been included in the background GIF file), a few bytes were saved by doing so. As we all know, every little bit helps.

When completed, the `div` appeared as shown in Figure 4-7.

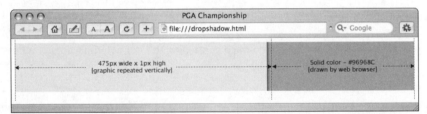

Figure 4-7: The container div with background graphic applied and viewed in a Web browser. Extra notation has been added to illustrate which area is an image and which area is drawn by the browser.

With the `div` background completed, the Flash movie was placed above the container `div`, and the two pieces snapped together perfectly, as shown in Figure 4-8.

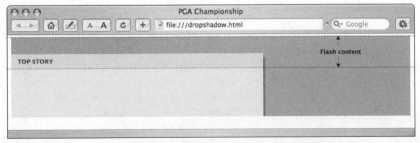

Figure 4-8: Flash movie placed above container div from Figure 4-7

Before moving on, here's a tip to consider. Ensure that your design is nailed down ahead of time, prefer-ably on a grid with elements snapped to the pixel. An effect like this requires you to know the exact placement of content beforehand. If you get ahead of yourself and try to apply effects such as these while layout considerations are still taking place, you'll have to retrace your steps more than once. Think of effects such as these as a "sweetening" stage of your design workflow. A little patience and planning will save you many headaches and a significant amount of time down the road.

Extra Realism

This is a good spot to include a bonus tip that can add extra visual definition and realism to the drop-shadow effect built thus far.

In reality (yes, that place outside your monitor), the opacity of a shadow changes according to appear-ance of the surface it falls across. If the surface were white, the drop shadow would appear in gradations of light gray. If the surface were dark, the shadow would appear even darker. This all may be rather obvious, but in the flat world of computer screens, it isn't so straightforward.

So, with the PGA Championship site, the concept was pushed further by manipulating the drop shadow's appearance whenever it came in contact with areas of a different background color. Most of the content in the right column had a transparent background and thus used the existing color underneath, but the news links were a unique problem (refer to Figure 4-1). Without some sense of visual separation, it was hard for users to tell them apart. So, the background of every other news item was darkened (like alternating row colors in a table), followed by manipulating the drop shadow wherever applicable.

To do this, the original Photoshop document used to create the drop shadow was re-opened and the background color was changed to a slightly darker value (#828279) that would harmonize well with the overall layout. An area 1 pixel high in the middle of the shadow was selected (as was done earlier for the main area shadow) and copied into a new document. And, as shown in Figure 4-9, the finished graphic looked just like the first one, but a little darker.

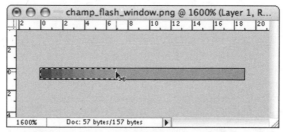

Figure 4-9: Shadow sitting on top of a slightly darker background and selected with the Rectangular Marquee tool

For the XHTML, an unordered-list was created to mark up the content. Semantically, list elements are perfect for wrapping grocery-list bits of data (and navigation, as we'll see a little later in this chapter). When paired with a style sheet, they provide all kinds of presentational opportunities.

So, in the right column of the XHTML template, an unordered list of news items was created, like so:

```
<ul class="stories">
    <li>DiMarco and Riley play their way into Ryder Cup</li>
    <li>'No question' PGA will return to Whistling Straits</li>
    <li>Sullivan lowest club professional at PGA since 1969</li>
    <li>PGA of America adjusts Sunday yardages at Whistling Straits</li>
</ul>
```

The class assigned to the unordered list element, stories, was then added to the style sheet:

```
ul.stories {
    margin:0;
    padding:0;
    color:#E9E9DF;
}
```

First, stories was assigned as a subclass of the unordered-list element. The default properties Web browsers would automatically apply to the unordered-list elements were then reset. This was accomplished by setting both the margin and the padding to zero. A color property was then added, which affected all text inside the list.

Technically, you could leave out the "ul" and create a standalone class named "stories." But assigning classes directly to HTML elements is not just good form, but makes your style sheets much easier to read. Think of elements as inline comments that describe their function at a glance, so whether you're returning to a style sheet months later to make an edit, or your style sheet is shared among multiple developers, it's easy to see which classes belong to which elements. A little organization can pay off big time down the road.

After taking care of the unordered-list object, it was time to tackle each of the list elements inside:

```
ul.stories li {
    list-style:none;
    margin-bottom:2px;
    padding:4px 4px 4px 10px;
}
```

Let's walk through this line by line. First, the list-style property was set to none, which killed the browser's default behavior of attaching a rounded bullet to the list item. From there, a smidgen of margin was added to push the list items a little further apart vertically, plus padding (4 pixels to the top, right, and bottom, as well as 10 pixels to the left).

By default, each list item generated inside the stories unordered list received these values. At this stage, they all had the same background (using the color underneath), but here's where the extra effect came into play:

```
ul.stories li.odd {
    background:#828279
url(http://i.pga.com/pga/images/pgachampionship/img/bg_stories_shadow.gif) repeat-
y;
}
```

Through the beauty of inheritance, this odd class came pre-loaded with all the attributes assigned previously, leaving only what was necessary to produce the change—the background. The darker background color's hex value was applied, then the url for the shadow graphic, and the browser was instructed to repeat the background vertically, but not horizontally.

The unordered-list code was added to the XHTML, and the odd class was applied (manually, although this could also be done programmatically with JavaScript, PHP, and so on) to every other list item:

```
<ul class="stories">
    <li class="odd">DiMarco and Riley play their way into Ryder Cup</li>
    <li>'No question' PGA will return to Whistling Straits</li>
    <li class="odd">Sullivan lowest club professional at PGA since 1969</li>
    <li>PGA of America adjusts Sunday yardages at Whistling Straits</li>
</ul>
```

All together, the unordered-list appeared to be part of the right column and underneath the main content area's drop shadow, but actually sat *above* the background created earlier (see Figure 4-10). The trick was to position the right column (which contained the unordered-list) directly up against the right edge of the left column. This created the illusion that the list item's darker background color was a part of the existing drop shadow on the page, when actually it was layered on top of it.

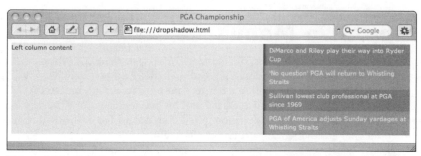

Figure 4-10: List items with darker shadow background placed in the XHTML container div

Here's the CSS for the left and right columns:

```
#lcol {
    width:468px;
    float:left;
}
#rcol {
    width:271px;
    float:right;
}
```

The basic XHTML necessary to create the effect is as follows:

```
<div id="colwrap">
 <div id="lcol">
     <!--Left column content -->
 </div>
 <div id="rcol">
     <ul class="stories">
         <li class="odd">DiMarco and Riley play their way into Ryder Cup</li>
         <li>'No question' PGA will return to Whistling Straits</li>
         <li class="odd">Sullivan lowest club professional at PGA since 1969</li>
         <li>PGA of America adjusts Sunday yardages at Whistling Straits</li>
     </ul>
 </div>
</div>
```

And with that, our extra drop-shadow effect was complete.

If you take one idea away from this exercise, remember this. By leveraging the Web browser's ability to automatically repeat background images and also apply color to the same element, there are countless creative opportunities to add visual depth and richness to an otherwise flat, static layout with barely any effect on overall document weight. All it takes is a little patience, planning, and experimentation.

CSS Drop-Down Menus

In the dot-com gold rush of the late 1990s, the hallmark of a sophisticated, cutting-edge site was often signaled by the inclusion of fancy drop-down navigational menus. They may have been pleasing to the eye, but behind their glitzy façade was often a hornet's nest of JavaScript, bloated HTML, or even worse, proprietary browser API methods. For all a site's intent on making the user experience more fluid and straightforward, early drop-down solutions more often than not added additional levels of frustration (especially when they failed to operate) and unnecessary bloat.

Then along came CSS and the magical :hover attribute. Gurus like Eric Meyer published tutorials on how to tap into the capabilities of an anchor tag's :hover attribute, which when used with regular ol' unordered lists, could create drop-down menus similar in appearance yet a fraction of the weight and complexity of conventional methods.

But for all the promise of pure CSS menus, there was one huge problem: Internet Explorer for Windows. By far the most popular browser accessing the Web, the browser had limited support for the :hover attribute (and CSS in general, but that's another story), and thus couldn't render the drop-downs. As a result, CSS menus were relegated to a hobbyist tool at best.

But that started to change in November 2003, when Patrick Griffiths and Dan Webb set the CSS community on fire with *Suckerfish Dropdowns* (www.alistapart.com/articles/dropdowns), a lightweight, CSS-powered, drop-down system that worked in nearly every browser available, including Internet Explorer for Windows. Suckerfish was not just a revelation in file weight, but in cross-browser compatibility, compliance to Web standards, semantic richness, and accessibility.

Suckerfish drop-down menus were also incredibly easy to build. If you knew how to create an unordered list in XHTML, you were halfway home. All of the presentation and functionality was controlled with a small set of style properties.

A few months after the initial release of Suckerfish, Griffiths and Webb upped the ante with *Son of Suckerfish Dropdowns,* an even lighter version of the original with greater compatibility and multiple drop-down menus to boot. It was the "Son" flavor of Suckerfish that the PGA Championship site used, but this discussion won't delve into the basic structure (which you can download examples of for free at www.htmldog.com/articles/suckerfish/drop-downs/). We will discuss the customizations made, potential caveats, and a few general usage tips.

Customization: Positioning the Drop-Down Menus

The first issue encountered when modifying Suckerfish for the PGA Championship site's navigation involved positioning of the drop-down menus. By default, the nested drop-down menus appeared directly below their parent list item, depending on the height of the graphic or text contained therein. In the case of the PGA Championship site, the parent graphics were cut shorter than the surrounding area (to conserve file weight). So, instead of appearing below the white navigational bar (as they do in the final form of the site), the drop-down menus were popping out below the graphical links.

The graphical links could have been edited with extra white space on the bottom to "push" the drop-down menus where desired, but that would have increased the file size of each graphic and created a "hot" link space where no content was present. The challenge, then, was to find a way to push the drop-down menus below the white navigation bar without adversely affecting or changing the existing content.

The first step was simple. Each nested unordered list (the drop-down menus) was already using absolute positioning, so a `top` property was added to push them down where they needed to be:

```
#nav li ul {
    position:absolute;
    left:-999em;
    top:20px;
}
```

This successfully moved each drop-down menu 20 pixels below its parent list item and thus below the white navigational bar. But a new problem emerged. The area between the main links and the drop-down menus (the same blank area that shouldn't have been clickable) was now disengaging the rollover when the pointer moved downward. So, the next step was to find a way to maintain the visibility of the drop-down menus whenever the mouse pointer entered this vacant area.

By default, a list element is only as tall as the content it contains. But we can change that behavior with CSS:

```
#nav li {
    position:relative;
    float:left;
    margin:0 15px 0 0;
    padding:0;
    width:auto;
    height:20px;
}
```

The important part here was the `height` property. By specifying a custom height and thus overriding the aforementioned default behavior, the invisible bounding box of each list element expanded downward to fill the gap. The list items now behaved as if they contained graphics 20 pixels tall, but were actually much shorter. But the browser couldn't tell the difference, and thus, the drop-down menus operated as expected.

To see how the list items and graphical elements were affected, take a look at Figure 4-11. Using Chris Pederick's free Web Developer extension (www.chrispederick.com/work/firefox/Webdeveloper/) for Firefox, the invisible bounding boxes of the list elements and images were turned visible by adding a temporary black stroke. This offered a visual confirmation of the style sheet modifications, and to see-what-the-browser-was-seeing in real time. The extension came in handy many times during development of the PGA Championship site, and it is recommended to anyone involved with Web development and design.

Figure 4-11: The PGA Championship viewed in Firefox and with all list elements and images outlined using the Web Developer extension

Customization: Styling the Drop-Down Menus

Now that the drop-down menus were functioning properly and appearing in the proper place, it was time to tweak the appearance of the menu options.

To start, nested unordered lists were given a background color of white, and assigned a uniform width (based on the longest menu item title) to all the drop-down menus:

```
#nav li ul {
    margin:0;
    padding:0;
    position:absolute;
    left:-999em;
    top:20px;
    background:#fff;
    width:146px;
}
```

As shown in Figure 4-12, it was easy to see the problem. The left edge of each drop-down menu was aligned with the left edge of its parent list item, and there wasn't enough visual separation between each option.

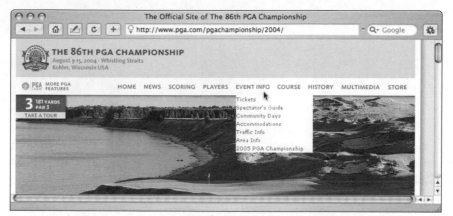

Figure 4-12: Misaligned drop-down shadow with visually bland options

So, some additional edits were made to the nested list items:

```
#nav li li {
      height:auto;
      margin:0;
      padding:0;
      width:100%;
      font-size:9px;
      border-bottom:1px solid #F5F5F0;
}
```

By setting the width of each nested list item to 100 percent, their boxes expanded to the width of their parent element — which, in this case, was 146px. Had the default width of the list items not been modified, the browser would have drawn a bottom border for only as long as the text contained inside. By setting the list item to a width of 100 percent, the menu options had a uniform appearance, regardless of how much text was contained in each item.

Next, the textual content was addressed:

```
#nav li li span {
      display:block;
      margin:0;
      padding:3px 4px 3px 7px;
      position:relative;
}
```

To better control the positioning of each block of text within its respective list items, each option was wrapped with a span tag because span avoided another subclass with a unique name and semantically made more sense than a div, paragraph tag, or what-have-you. So, the display properties of span were changed to a block element (which by default it was not). This allowed block attributes such as margin and padding. After the padding was successfully tweaked, the menus appeared, as shown in Figure 4-13.

171

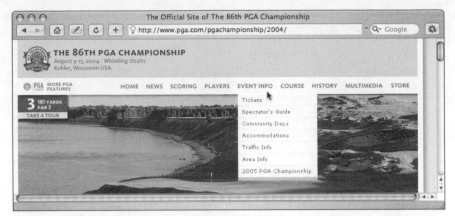

Figure 4-13: Drop-down options styled, but misaligned with left margin of the main navigation links

The drop-down menus looked complete but with one remaining issue. The textual menu options were no longer aligned with the left edge of their respective parent list items. Although they didn't have to be changed, it was decided they would look better with a slight adjustment to the left. Fortunately, this was as easy as forcing each unordered list to the left, like so:

```
#nav li ul {
    margin:0 0 0 -8px;
    padding:0;
    position:absolute;
    left:-999em;
    top:20px;
    background:#fff;
    width:146px;
}
```

Thank goodness for negative values! By changing the left `margin` from zero to -8 (the order of margin values was top, right, bottom, left), each nested unordered list shifted 8 pixels to the left (as opposed to the right if the number were positive). This brought the left edge of each textual option perfectly in line with its parent list item, as shown in Figure 4-14.

Caveats to Consider

Now that we've discussed ways to modify the original source, let's consider some potential issues to watch out for when using Suckerfish drop-down menus:

❑ **Caveat #1: Suckerfish requires JavaScript in IE/Windows.** Chalk this up as another example of Internet Explorer's lackluster support of CSS. Suckerfish is activated purely by CSS in Mozilla, Firefox, and Safari, but in order for it to work in Internet Explorer for Windows (IE/Windows), a little bit of JavaScript must be included in any document using the drop-down menus. The "hack" is quite small, and simply oversteps IE's lack of support for the `:hover` pseudo-link element by attaching custom behaviors to the Document Object Model (DOM). But here's the rub. If your IE/Windows users have JavaScript turned off, your drop-down menus won't appear. Very few people actually turn this off, but it's a reality you should be aware of.

Figure 4-14: The completed drop shadow with options fully styled and properly aligned

❑ **Caveat #2: IE/Mac doesn't like it one bit.** Many people have tried to work around the lack of Suckerfish support in Internet Explorer for the Macintosh (all versions, in OS X and older), but as of this writing, it remained a lost cause. The failure is thankfully silent (the menus simply don't appear), and they shouldn't interfere with your main navigation. Microsoft has ended development of the Mac version of the browser, so don't expect this situation to change. To look on the bright side, thanks to Safari, Firefox, and other popular OS X browsers, you can expect to see less and less traffic from Internet Explorer for the Macintosh.

❑ **Caveat #3: Early builds of Safari don't like it either.** Safari, the Mac OS X Web browser based on the KHTML layout engine from Konqueror and bundled into the operating system, has its own share of Suckerfish issues. Builds of Safari earlier than 1.2 (which was released in February 2004) won't display your drop-down menus either. Safari 1.2, on the other hand, *does* display Suckerfish drop-downs just fine. That is, unless . . .

❑ **Caveat #4: Safari, Suckerfish, and Flash don't get along at all.** If you embed Flash content in your document below the Suckerfish drop-down menus, your menus will "flicker" on and off when engaged in *every* build of Safari, with version 2.0 being the latest release as of this writing.

Usage Tips

Now that we have the browser support issues out of the way, the following are some real-world usability tips when implementing CSS drop-downs in your own work:

❑ **Tip #1: Provide backup.** Because of the cross-browser issues detailed earlier, it is imperative that your site layout include a secondary level of navigation should your drop-down menus fail to operate. Otherwise, your visitors won't be able to navigate your site. This should be standard procedure for any type of drop-down navigation—Suckerfish or otherwise.

❑ **Tip #2: Be careful with Internet Explorer, Suckerfish, and Flash.** When Internet Explorer for Windows encounters Flash content (whether it's an advertisement or a movie created by you), the browser will push it to the very top of the z-index layer stack. What does that mean? It means your menus could potentially appear underneath your Flash content; obscuring the ability to click on any of the covered options. The solution is to include a `wmode` tag in Flash's object/embed code. (Details can be found at `www.macromedia.com/support/flash/ts/documents/flash_top_layer.htm`.)

❑ **Tip #3: Include a** `z-index` **property if your document has layers.** If your layout has layered objects using a `z-index` property, your Suckerfish navigation must have one as well, but on a higher level than everything else. The `z-index` can be added to either your navigation's parent unordered list element, or (in the case of the PGA Championship site) you can wrap your navigation with a container `div`, and apply the `z-index` to that element. Doing so will raise your navigation above the rest of the fray, so the menus drop down and *over* anything they may come in contact with.

The Bottom Line

So, after all that, you may be wondering why Suckerfish is recommended. The answer is simple. Despite the issues noted here, Suckerfish remains the most accessible, cross-browser–friendly drop-down menu solution out there. It's also far, far lighter in bytes than anything else, and much easier to update and maintain. If you implement the menus on a highly trafficked site (the PGA Championship site, for example, was hit millions of times per hour), then having a light drop-down menu solution is optimal.

Web Standards–Compliant Flash Embedding

One of the common problems Web developers face when creating standards-compliant XHTML markup is embedding Flash content. Most developers simply copy and paste the standard set of `object/embed` tags Flash creates when publishing a movie. However, because they come loaded with all kinds of invalid attributes and elements, they wreak havoc on a document's conformance to Web standards.

Fortunately, there are workarounds. Here are the three most popular methods used today to embed standards-compliant Flash content.

The Flash Satay Method

The Flash Satay method (`www.alistapart.com/articles/flashsatay/`) removes the `embed` tag (a proprietary element not found in any W3C specification) and removes some "unnecessary" proprietary attributes in the `object` tag. It works great, but with one *huge* caveat: Flash movies in Internet Explorer for Windows won't start until they are 100 percent loaded.

The Satay method does offer a workaround, which includes fooling Internet Explorer for Windows by embedding an empty "container" movie set to the same parameters (width, height, and so on) as the "real" movie, and using the container clip to load the actual content. Internet Explorer will then successfully stream the movie, and the markup will validate, but at a cost to any developer's sanity — each and every embedded movie requires an accompanying empty container movie, thus creating a lot of extra directory trash and headaches.

Write the object/embed Tags Using JavaScript

In this scenario, the object/embed elements remain as they are, but are moved to an external JavaScript file. Flash content is then written into the document using a series of document.write JavaScript methods. Validators (the W3C has an excellent one at http://validator.w3.org/) see only the valid JavaScript element—not Flash's object/embed code contained inside—so the object/embed tags pass with flying colors.

This was the workaround used for the PGA Championship site. The XHTML not only remained valid, but because JavaScript was used, offered an opportunity to perform some light browser or plug-in detection should alternate (non-Flash) content be required.

Once the external JavaScript file was created (too long to reproduce here—load www.pga.com/pgachampionship/2004/js/flash_home.js in your Web browser to see the source), it was linked in the XHTML document like so:

```
<script type="text/javascript"
src="http://www.pga.com/pgachampionship/2004/js/flash_home.js"></script>
```

This method is not without issues. First of all, Web standards purists will argue that the JavaScript file is essentially a Trojan horse that slips invalid, unsupported markup into XHTML and past the eyes of validators (which is exactly the point). Second, by relying on JavaScript to write our content, we are assuming that users have it enabled in their browsers (most everyone does, but some disable it for extra speed and avoidance of ads). Finally, each and every Flash movie requires its own external .JS file (not a big deal with a handful of movies, but things could quickly get out of control).

FlashObject

Released a few months after the 2004 PGA Championship site, FlashObject is the most sophisticated and robust embedding method currently available. Created by Geoff Stearns, the JavaScript package is a direct response to the limitations of both of the aforementioned methods, while providing simpler markup that validates as XHTML 1.0 Transitional and up.

FlashObject offers everything a Flash developer would need—player detection, ability to offer alternate content to those without the plug-in, methods to pass additional parameters and variables through FlashVars, div targeting for embedding an swf in a specific area, and even a variable to bypass player detection and force the display of a Flash movie, whether the user has the plug-in or not.

FlashObject is also search engine–friendly, which you rarely see with Flash content. Users simply create a div in their document and fill it with normal HTML textual content, which can then be indexed by search engines and displayed for visitors without the Flash plug-in. If a visitor has the Flash plug-in, the div's content is replaced with the Flash movie. This enables both the haves and the have-nots to easily receive rich content, without a lot of work for the Web developer.

For more information about FlashObject (which is free to download and use), see http://blog.deconcept.com/2004/10/14/web-standards-compliant-javascript-flash-detect-and-embed/.

Summary

We covered a lot in this chapter, from creating visual effects in Photoshop to positioning elements with CSS to working around common Flash validation issues in XHTML. The techniques used here should inspire further exploration and experimentation when using CSS in your own work.

Next up is a look at the redesign of The University of Florida's Web site, including the history of the site, the challenges in updating legacy content, and a walkthrough of the CSS markup used.

5

The University of Florida

The University of Florida (UF) is among the world's most academically diverse public universities with fields of study across 16 colleges. UF, which traces its roots to the East Florida Seminary in 1853, has a long history of established programs in international education, research, and service, with extension offices in all 67 Florida counties.

UF's student body, with just shy of 50,000 students, is one of the five largest among U.S. universities. UF has more than 4,000 distinguished faculty members with nearly 100 Fulbright scholars, more than 50 eminent scholars, and numerous other faculty members who are nationally and internationally recognized in their fields.

The University of Florida's Web presence has somewhat mirrored the trends you would see when looking at the Web as a whole. Shifts in the foci of Web developers (and the developers of the browsers in which they are viewed) can be seen by microcosm through the UF Web site. In this chapter, we'll explore some of the decisions UF made with regard to its Web presence and take a look at the techniques used to carry them out. Let's get started.

University of Florida's Web Site

UF posted a home page in 1995 that was typical of sites of the time. Well-built pages were generally structural in nature and light on aesthetics. The 1995 page, in fact, was rather utilitarian with links to much of the same information one would find on the current UF site (see Figure 5-1).

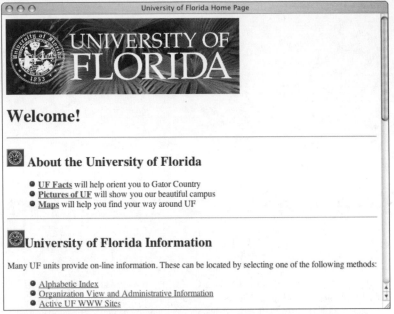

Figure 5-1: The University of Florida home page launched in 1995

Here's a bit of the markup from the first UF site:

```
<H2><IMG alt=** src="images/placeholder.gif" align=bottom width="32" height="32">
About the University of Florida</H2>
<UL><IMG alt=* src="images/ball.gif" width="14" height="14">
<B><A href="#">UF Facts</A></B> will help orient you to Gator Country<BR>
<IMG alt=* src="images/ball.gif" width="14" height="14">
<B><A href="#">Pictures of UF</A></B> will show you our beautiful campus<BR>
<IMG alt=* src="images/ball.gif" width="14" height="14">
<B><A href="#">Maps</A></B> will help you find your way around UF<BR>
</UL>
<HR>
```

As you might notice, a number of semantic elements are well identified. Headings were given the proper weight and unordered lists were marked as such. Glaringly omitted are the list item elements. Instead of the li element, the creators used images and br tags to start and end list items. This was done, presumably, to style the lists.

Revisions

The subsequent revisions of the university's site trended toward using a role-based navigational system consisting primarily of five major groups (see Figure 5-2):

- ❑ Prospective Students
- ❑ Current Students
- ❑ Campus Visitors
- ❑ Faculty & Staff
- ❑ Alumni, Parents & Friends

Figure 5-2: A revision to the University of Florida home page launched in 1999

Within each of these groups, the visitor would find all the information the university thought each of the different types of visitor would need. Inside "Prospective Students" would be admissions information, directions on taking a campus tour, facts about the university, and so on. Each group would have similar role-targeted information. The tendency to shift to role-based navigation as a primary means of navigation was seen across both university Web sites and the Web at large.

This new graphics-heavy design did not come without a price. While UF received more positive than negative feedback in response to the aesthetics of the 1999 design, there were a number of complaints centered on the time needed to load the site. In this design, the visitor's browser had to make more than 30 HTTP requests to the UF servers for various pieces of the page: HTML, images, JavaScript, and so on. Each request lengthened the total time needed to load the site.

The more semantic markup found in the first design was lost in these revisions. The unordered lists and header elements in the first design were scrapped for multiple image maps, JavaScript rollovers, and tables.

The Current Site

With the expansion in usage of standards-compliant browsers, UF decided to attack these problems and others with a new design (see Figure 5-3). To redesign the site, UF needed the following:

- ❑ An assessment of the university's major audiences and development of user profiles (discussed in Chapter 1) to include Web technology usage and accessibility needs

- ❑ Structuring of the information within the site

- ❑ In-depth user testing

- ❑ Reviews of peer Web sites

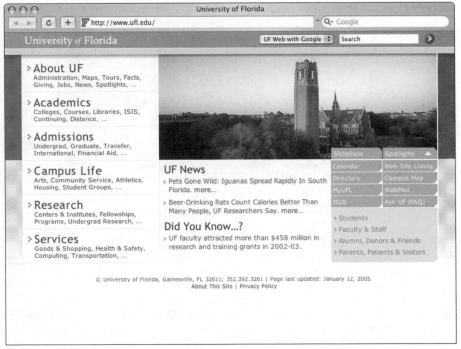

Figure 5-3: Revision of the site launched in 2004

The current site was launched in February 2004 and receives approximately 100,000 visits per day. The remainder of this chapter provides you with a look into how this new site was developed.

Defining the Site

When identifying success for a university site, issues such as the financial bottom line and clicks-through to a shopping cart take a backseat to broader issues such as visitor satisfaction and perception. This makes identifying the goals of the site's fairly simple: talk to the site's visitors, watch them use it, and give them what they want.

Building the Team

Many members of the UF community have multiple roles. With visitors looking for so many different types of content coming through a single site, it was imperative to have the design driven by not only the site's visitors, but also the members of UF's staff and faculty that deal directly with those visitors. Early on, a team representing 20 of these areas from around campus developed a nested list of the types of visitors to the UF site. For example, a main type of visitor would be "student." Within "student" would be "undergraduate," "graduate," "international," and so on. Then further nesting: "prospective graduate," "transfer undergraduate," and so on. The team then identified tasks that each type of visitor would perform.

User Research

As with most organizations, people at UF often find themselves wearing many different hats. A staff member might also take courses and attend athletic events, while a graduate student may teach courses and be an undergraduate alumnus. This manifested itself in user research where visitors to the previous UF site would have to guess which group they fell within to find the information they were looking for.

Visitors would also choose different groups based on their desired membership, not necessarily their current role. For example, many potential UF students (namely, those in high school) would choose the Current Students link from the UF home page instead of Prospective Students. When asked, the visitors gave responses that fell into three general categories:

❑ I am currently a student at my high school.

❑ What does "prospective" mean?

❑ I wanted to see what real UF students are doing, not some brochure. (This type of response was the most prevalent—and the one we found the most interesting—among those potential students who chose something other than Prospective Students.)

It became clear quite quickly that the way the university classifies people, while valid and useful to the university, is not necessarily the way visitors classify themselves. This also suggests that role-based navigation should not be relied upon as the primary means of navigating the site.

UF needed to marry this look at its visitors with the current trends in university Web sites.

Peer Review

An important part of defining the site was looking at how sites throughout academia define themselves. While many university sites primarily use a role-based navigational system, we knew through our user research that this wouldn't be ideal for UF. That being said, we could use other universities' sites to ensure we were staying within the *lingua franca* of academia. The phrases universities use to define different pieces of content, if agreed upon, can serve as the basis for a primary navigation.

We understood from the beginning that the final structure of the UF site would be unique. However, looking at macroscopic trends like these pulled out the phrases that are common to most. To look into this, UF surveyed more than a thousand university Web sites looking for commonly used terms. Idioms such as "About (University/College X)," "Academics," "Admissions," and "Alumni" quickly rose to the top. These matched up well with the user research (namely, card sorting) and were adopted as main phrases within the navigation.

> *Card sorting is a fairly low-tech (but very useful) method of enlisting a site's visitors when creating an information architecture. Essentially, test participants are asked to group index cards that contain short descriptions of pieces of content and tasks from the site, and then name these new stacks. More on this methodology can be found in Mike Kuniavsky's book* Observing the User Experience: A Practitioner's Guide to User Research *(Morgan Kaufmann, 2003).*

Many sites fell prey to frequent use of acronyms and other proprietary phrases. While this is unpreventable in some cases, it should be avoided and certainly done sparingly. We also noted that acronyms were very rarely defined.

Technical Specs

The increased download times created by the myriad images of the previous design was something UF wanted to tackle without returning to the vanilla site launched in 1995. Also, the university wanted a return to (and improvement upon) the semantics found in the initial design. If by and large, the visitors' environment supported a shift to a strictly standards-compliant design, this would be UF's path.

Web Standards

Early on, the decision was made to strive for a site where content and aesthetics were separated. This could be implemented only if UF knew the following:

- ❑ How many visitors would be adversely affected by taking a standards-based approach?

- ❑ How quickly are these visitors moving away from non-compliant browsers?

UF felt comfortable proceeding with standards-compliant markup and semantic use of XHTML elements because of the following:

- ❑ The steady movement of Netscape users to Netscape 7 and, ultimately, Mozilla or Firefox. (We'll explore this in greater detail later.)

- ❑ Generally speaking, users of non-compliant browsers access the Web through a slower connection. The decrease in load time (from 50K and 30 HTTP requests to 30K and, more important, only 3 HTTP requests for users of non-compliant browsers) heavily outweighs any simplification of aesthetics. This is especially true for these visitors who are regularly subjected to pages that react very poorly to ancient browsers.

- ❑ The addition of an enterprise resource management system that rejects ancient browsers to handle the university's financials forces users to move to modern browsers. (About 40 percent of UF home page traffic comes internally from students, faculty, and staff using the university's statewide network.)

- ❑ By using style sheets, users of non-compliant browsers that do not support the @import rule would receive a document with the browser's very simple default styling.

Ancient Browsers

Of the ancient browsers, the most popular and the one causing the most concern was Netscape 4. In June 2003, Netscape 4 had a 2.6 percent share of site traffic (approximately 2,000 visitors using Netscape 4 per day) and it would be difficult to explain a page being "broken" to that large of an audience. After tracking Netscape 4's usage over a number of months, it became apparent that its usage was steadily declining at a rate of about 20 percent per month. This trend led to a much more acceptable level — 1 percent in December 2003 (see Figure 5-4).

Month (2003)	NS4 Usage of ufl.edu
June	2.6%
July	2.2%
August	1.8%
September	1.5%
October	1.3%
November	1.1%
December	1.0%

Figure 5-4: Netscape 4 usage per month in the second half of 2003

As you might guess, this movement has continued. Netscape 4 users comprised less than 0.15 percent of UF's site visitors at the end of 2004.

Accessibility

UF was very concerned with creating a site that was accessible to all members of the UF community through whichever medium they choose to use. This includes those who must use alternative Web browsing technologies due to hearing, visual, or mobility impairment. A standards-based approach served as a way to advance accessibility as part of the entire development process, not simply an add-on before launching a site — or even worse, realizing a site isn't accessible and creating a "text only" version.

> *More information on assistive technologies such as screen readers, Braille displays, and talking browsers can be found in the book* Building Accessible Websites *by Joe Clark (New Riders Press, 2002).*

Creating a Main Navigational Structure

The University of Florida has more than a million pages on the Web covering topics from aerospace engineering to zoology. Its site navigation must both (at a glance) convey the diversity of research and teaching activity at the university and allow intuitive access to all its resources.

An inherent drawback to rollovers as navigational tools is the concealing of the underlying architecture. The visitor can't scan the page's content in its entirety. The visitor must guess what items are hidden beneath each branch of the structure, and then act on that guess to see if that section of navigation contains what is sought.

Although rollovers allow a site's visitor to see the site structure one branch at a time, an entire architectural overview that requires no guessing on the part of the visitor can be much more useful when a site's navigation is not completely visceral. The six major sections that give an overview of the university are much better served by openly displaying some of their contents near the section headers (see Figure 5-5).

Figure 5-5: The University of Florida's primary navigation

The XHTML

On the UF home page, the primary navigation is not merely a means of getting from one page to another. It is some of the most important content of the page and the markup used in the navigation should reinforce that importance.

Unordered Lists

Grouping similar sets of information (as is done when lists are used) allows for the following:

❑   Styling through CSS

❑   Semantic grouping of similar objects

❑   Easier traversal through groups of content, especially in screen readers

Nested Unordered Lists

At first glance, the UF primary navigation might seem best handled as nested, unordered lists. There is an unordered list of main topics, with each topic having a set of links that apply to them (see Figure 5-6). This would look something like the following:

```
<ul id="priNav">
    <li><a href="/aboutUF/">About UF</a>
    <ul>
      <li><a href="/aboutUF/administration.html">Administration</a>,</li>
      <li><a href="http://campusmap.ufl.edu/">Maps</a>,</li>
      <li><a href="http://virtualtour.ufl.edu/">Tours</a>,</li>
      <li><a href="/facts/">Facts</a>,</li>
          .
          .
          .

    </ul>
    </li>
    <li><a href="/academics/">Academics</a>
    <ul>
      <li><a href="/colleges/">Colleges</a>,</li>
      <li><a href="http://www.reg.ufl.edu/soc/">Courses</a>,</li>
      <li><a href="http://www.uflib.ufl.edu/">Libraries</a>,</li>
      <li><a href="http://www.isis.ufl.edu/">ISIS</a>,</li>
          ...
    </ul>
    </li>
      ...
</ul>
```

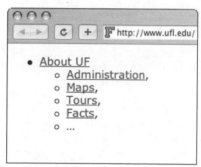

Figure 5-6: Unstyled, nested
unordered lists

Although certainly valid, the list items inside the navigation acting as headers ("About UF," "Academics," and so on) are not separately defined with heading elements, weakening the document's semantic strength. When treated as list items, major areas of the site are understated.

Weighting for Semantics

To give the main headings the proper meaning within the page and site as a whole, the navigation is placed inside a div and represented as a series of headers followed by unordered lists (see Figure 5-7):

```
<div id="priNav">
    <h2><a href="/aboutUF/">About UF</a></h2>
    <ul>
      <li><a href="/aboutUF/administration.html">Administration</a>,</li>
      <li><a href="http://campusmap.ufl.edu/">Maps</a>,</li>
```

```
      <li><a href="http://virtualtour.ufl.edu/">Tours</a>,</li>
      <li><a href="/facts/">Facts</a>,</li>
         ...
   </ul>
   <h2><a href="/academics/">Academics</a></h2>
   <ul>
      <li><a href="/colleges/">Colleges</a>,</li>
      <li><a href="http://www.reg.ufl.edu/soc/">Courses</a>,</li>
      <li><a href="http://www.uflib.ufl.edu/">Libraries</a>,</li>
      <li><a href="http://www.isis.ufl.edu/"><acronym title="Integrated Student
Information System">ISIS</acronym></a>,</li>
         ...
   </ul>
   ...
</div>
```

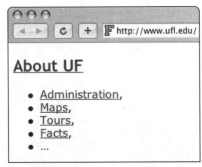

**Figure 5-7: Unstyled, unordered lists
with topical headers**

The headers here assign meaning to both the current page and the entire site. This benefits users of screen readers such as Jaws and IBM's Home Page Reader, allowing rudimentary navigation from header to header. As an added bonus, many search engines give more weight to text inside headings.

Because the initial letters of Integrated Student Information System (UF's Web-based system to register for classes and pay tuition, which is seen inside the list item for Academics) form a pronounceable word, ISIS is considered an *acronym*. (ISIS is pronounced "eye-sis.") If the initial letters formed a word called an *initialism* where each letter is pronounced (as in HTML), the word would be considered an abbreviation and the abbr tag used. The acronym and abbr elements allow contextual expansion of the text presented to the visitor. This should be done to describe the first occurrence of any acronyms or abbreviations in a document. This assists screen reader users by reading out the meaning of the abbreviations and acronyms. It also explains what would be esoteric phrases to search engines such as Google.

> *Every instance of an acronym can be annotated, but such annotation is not really needed and can quickly become cumbersome.*

The CSS

Following is the CSS:

```
*  {
     padding: 0;
     margin: 0;
}

ul { list-style: none; }
li {
 font-size: 11px;
 color: #444;
}
h2 {
     font-weight: normal;
     font-size: 21px;
}

a { text-decoration: none; }
a:link, a:visited { color: #0021a5; }
a:hover, a:active { color: #ff4a00; }

acronym {
 border: 0;
 font-style: normal;
}

#priNav {
     width: 248px;
     float: left;
     padding: 6px 2px 0 0;
     margin: 0 2px;
}

#priNav h2 {
     padding: 7px 0 0 20px;
     letter-spacing: 1px;
     line-height: 22px;
     background: url(images/pointer.gif) no-repeat 9px 14px;
}

#priNav ul {
     padding: 0 0 7px 20px;
     height: 26px;
     border-bottom: 1px solid #eee;
}

#priNav li {
     display: inline;
     line-height: 13px;
     padding-right: 4px;
     float: left;
}
```

The Images

UF uses two images to display its primary navigation: navDropShadow.jpg (see Figure 5-8) and pointer.gif (see Figure 5-9). The first is borrowed from the main container.

Figure 5-8: navDropShadow.jpg

Figure 5-9: pointer.gif

The `background.gif` image in the `body` element can be seen on the sides of Figure 5-3.

Brick by Brick

To start, we'll use the universal selector to set the default `margin` and `padding` to zero (0) for all elements:

```
* {
    padding: 0;
    margin: 0;
}
```

Next, remove the default bullets from all unordered lists and shine up the `h2` and `li` elements:

```
ul { list-style: none; }
li { font-size: 11px; }
h2 {
    font-weight: normal;
    font-size: 21px;
}
```

UF's official colors are orange and blue, so we'll turn all links UF blue and set the hover and active states to UF orange:

```
a:link, a:visited { color: #0021a5; }
a:hover, a:active { color: #ff4a00; }
```

The UF home page is very link-heavy (`ufl.edu` has more than a million pages) and having every word on the page underlined could be a bit messy so we'll lose the underline on all links:

```
a { text-decoration: none; }
a:link, a:visited { color: #0021a5; }
a:hover, a:active { color: #ff4a00; }
```

Several `acronym` elements are used on the site. Keeping the default `border-bottom` that some user agents apply would be distracting and draw the eye to the links that have acronyms. We don't want that so let's remove the underlining effect from `acronym`, too:

```
acronym { border: 0; }
```

Building the Box

The primary navigation has a fixed width, so we'll set that first:

```
#priNav {
    width: 248px;
}
```

We used a left float to ensure that the navigation would appear on the left, and the rest of the content to the right:

```
#priNav {
    width: 248px;
    float: left;
}
```

The content container uses a `padding` of 2 pixels on the left and right that should be matched here by adding a similar `margin` to the right side of the primary navigation. We'll use `margin` instead of `padding` to keep the writable area of the box 2 pixels from the edge of the main container and 2 pixels from the main content area:

```
#priNav {
    width: 248px;
    float: left;
    margin-right: 2px;
}
```

To give the header's drop-shadow gradient some room and keep the text from running to the right edge of the section dividers, we'll add padding to the top and right of the navigation:

```
#priNav {
    width: 248px;
    float: left;
    padding: 6px 2px 0 0;
    margin-right: 2px;
}
```

That'll do it for the primary navigation's container. Let's move on to style the section elements.

Styling the Section Headers

Each `h2` in the primary navigation covers one of the six major areas of UF's site. We've already set the `font` properties for the `h2` element globally, but here, we'll let it breathe a little by adding positive `letter-spacing`:

```
#priNav h2 {
    letter-spacing: 1px;
}
```

The bounds are well set for the `width` of the section header by the primary navigation container so we don't need to set it explicitly here. That being said, the h2 element must be given some `padding` from the top and left edge of the section dividers:

```
#priNav h2 {
        padding: 7px 0 0 20px;
        letter-spacing: 1px;
        }
```

The `background-image`, `background-repeat`, and `background-position` properties can be combined in the `background` property. We do it, in this case, to put a bullet (`pointer.gif`) in front of each h2. The upper-left corner of the bullet is placed 9 pixels to the right of and 14 pixels below the upper-left corner of the padding area we just set. The `background-color` and `background-attachment` properties can also be combined in the `background` property, but they are not needed here.

```
#priNav h2 {
        padding: 7px 0 0 20px;
        letter-spacing: 1px;
        background: url(images/pointer.gif) no-repeat 9px 14px;
}
```

To ensure that descenders (the portion of a letterform that drops below the baseline in letters such as *p* and *y*) don't affect the lines below them, we'll define the `line-height`:

```
#priNav h2 {
        padding: 7px 0 0 20px;
        letter-spacing: 1px;
        line-height: 22px;
        background: url(images/pointer.gif) no-repeat 9px 14px;
}
```

Styling the Lists

To style the unordered lists below each heading, we'll start by adding the vertical complement of the padding set for the h2 elements to the ul. (The h2 element is a block element by default.)

```
#priNav ul {
        padding: 0 0 7px 20px;
}
```

Next, to place the li elements one after the next inside the ul block, we'll override the li elements' default `block` state to display it `inline`:

```
#priNav li {
        display: inline;
}
```

To set the height of the list, we'll add the `height` property to the ul elements and `line-height` to the li elements:

```
#priNav ul {
        padding: 0 0 7px 20px;
```

```
        height: 26px;
}

#priNav li {
    display: inline;
    line-height: 13px;
}
```

Now, we'll add the border that separates each section:

```
#priNav ul {
    padding: 0 0 7px 20px;
    height: 26px;
    border-bottom: 1px solid #eee;
}

#priNav li {
    display: inline;
    line-height: 13px;
}
```

That was fairly straightforward, wasn't it? We kept the semantics of the primary navigation intact and styled the headers and subsequent lists to match the desired design.

Now that we've tackled the primary navigation, let's look at another type of unordered list: the supplementary navigation.

Making the Supplementary Navigation

A supplementary navigation does exactly what it sounds like it would do. It supplements the primary navigation. The supplementary navigation we will discuss here consists of two parts: the utility navigation and the role-based navigation (see Figure 5-10).

Figure 5-10: UF's supplementary navigation

The XHTML

Because the supplementary navigation is made of two distinct parts, we'll define each separately. The structures that house both of them are quite similar. Let's look at the utility navigation first.

Utility Navigation

Utility navigation is simply a set of links to frequently used tools. At UF, this includes a map of the campus, calendar of events, campus directory, ufl.edu e-mail access, and so on. In the past, groups of disparate utilities have often been handled using pipes or images to separate items. This neither adds meaning to the items used for separation nor allows for the function afforded by the browser.

The best method of applying a sensible grouping to these types of utilities is through (you guessed it) an unordered list. The list we'll create looks like this:

```
<ul id="utilNav">
  <li><a href="http://calendar.ufl.edu/">Calendar</a></li>
  <li><a href="/websites/">Web Site Listing</a></li>
  <li><a href="http://phonebook.ufl.edu/">Directory</a></li>
  <li><a href="http://campusmap.ufl.edu/">Campus Map</a></li>
     ...
</ul>
```

Each utility gets its own list item inside a containing `ul` with the `id` of `utilNav`. That's the first part of the supplementary navigation; let's handle the second part.

Role-Based Navigation

Previously in this chapter, we discussed the movement away from role-based navigation as a primary means of navigation in the design. That being said, UF did not want to completely remove that as a means of grouping information.

We'll keep the role-based navigation, but downplay its importance by moving it down the page in the XHTML and placing it in a box in the bottom-right corner of the design:

```
<ul id="roleNav">
  <li><a href="/students/">Students</a></li>
  <li><a href="/facstaff/">Faculty &amp; Staff</a></li>
  <li><a href="/friends/">Alumni, Donors &amp; Friends</a></li>
  <li><a href="/visitors/">Parents, Patients &amp; Visitors</a></li>
</ul>
```

Similar to the utility navigation, each role is a list item inside an unordered list called `roleNav`.

Wrapping the Two Together

Now that we've created the utility and role-based navigation, we can group them together as supplementary navigation. We'll simply wrap it all in a `div` called `suppNav`.

```
<div id="suppNav">
<ul id="utilNav">
  <li><a href="http://calendar.ufl.edu/">Calendar</a></li>
  <li><a href="/websites/">Web Site Listing</a></li>
  <li><a href="http://phonebook.ufl.edu/">Directory</a></li>
    <li><a href="http://campusmap.ufl.edu/">Campus Map</a></li>
      ...
  </ul>
  <ul id="roleNav">
```

```
    <li><a href="/students/">Students</a></li>
    <li><a href="/facstaff/">Faculty &amp; Staff</a></li>
    <li><a href="/friends/">Alumni, Donors &amp; Friends</a></li>
    <li><a href="/visitors/">Parents, Patients &amp; Visitors</a></li>
  </ul>
</div>
```

This works, but the two navigational groups lack definition. We must give headers that describe what is inside each list to both the utility and role-based navigation.

```
<div id="suppNav">
      <h2>Frequently Used Sites</h2>
  <ul id="utilNav">
    <li><a href="http://calendar.ufl.edu/">Calendar</a></li>
    <li><a href="/websites/">Web Site Listing</a></li>
    <li><a href="http://phonebook.ufl.edu/">Directory</a></li>
        <li><a href="http://campusmap.ufl.edu/">Campus Map</a></li>
        ...
  </ul>
      <h2>Information For:</h2>
  <ul id="roleNav">
    <li><a href="/students/">Students</a></li>
    <li><a href="/facstaff/">Faculty &amp; Staff</a></li>
    <li><a href="/friends/">Alumni, Donors &amp; Friends</a></li>
    <li><a href="/visitors/">Parents, Patients &amp; Visitors</a></li>
  </ul>
</div>
```

Now that we have a well-structured pair of lists to work with, let's polish them up.

The CSS

We have three distinct items with which to work: the utility navigation, role-based navigation, and the supplementary navigation container. The container should be dealt with first.

Styling the Supplementary Navigation

The first thing we'll want to do is place a limit on the width of the supplementary navigation container, suppNav:

```
#suppNav {
    width: 200px;
}
```

The entire supplementary navigation must be moved outside the normal flow, and off to the right side of the page. To do that, we'll place the container absolutely:

```
#suppNav {
    width: 200px;
    position: absolute;
    top: 195px;
    right: 2px;
}
```

For more on positioning and document flow, read the section "CSS Positioning: The Fundamentals" in Chapter 7.

We added headers to each of the two navigational groups, but we're about to start styling each of those groups. This styling should be enough to separate the lists from the information around them, so let's hide the headers inside the supplementary navigation:

```
#suppNav h2 { display: none; }
```

Because this style is inside the style sheet brought in through @import, the headers will still be displayed in their proper formatting not only in search engines, but in ancient browsers as well.

This styled supplementary navigation div gives us a good container in which to place our utility and role-based navigation.

Styling the Utilities

Here we want the list of utilities to flow and fill up the width of the container. We'll start by setting the li element to display inline as we did with the lists inside the primary navigation:

```
#utilNav li {
    display: inline;
}
```

Next, we must build the box inside of which each of the utilities will reside. Because we have an exact width and height we would like to specify for each box, we'll set both. To take advantage of the default center vertical alignment inside the box, let's use the line-height attribute to set the height.

```
#utilNav li {
    width: 99px;
    line-height: 21px;
    display: inline;
}
```

The container is 200 pixels wide and allows us to give the list items some space. The 1-pixel margin added to the left should be matched by a 1-pixel margin on the bottom:

```
#utilNav li {
    width: 99px;
    line-height: 21px;
    margin: 0 0 1px 1px;
    display: inline;
}
```

Now that we have list items sized and spaced, we should handle the links inside them. To have the a element handle the rollover properly, the default display type must be overridden by rendering it as a block. The size of the box that holds the link should match the size of the box created by the list item, so we'll size the a element accordingly:

```
#utilNav li a {
     width: 99px;
     height: 21px;
     display: block;
}
```

We want to give the text inside a little padding to the left, but also want to avoid the hassles caused by differences in box model interpretations. We can do this by indenting the text in lieu of padding it:

```
#utilNav li a {
     text-indent: 3px;
     width: 99px;
     height: 21px;
     display: block;
}
```

An introduction to the box model is given in Chapter 2.

To shine up the links, we'll add some color and an image. Placing the image in the lower right of each link bevels the corner at 45 degrees:

```
#utilNav li a {
     text-indent: 3px;
     width: 99px;
     height: 21px;
     color: #fff;
     display: block;
     background: #94a2d9 url(images/chamfer.gif) no-repeat right bottom;
}
```

Adding a splash of feedback to the links is as simple as setting the hover state. Here we'll make them change color slightly by changing the `background-color` but leaving the `chamfer` image intact.

```
#utilNav li a:hover { background-color: #566cc3; }
```

That Tricky Box Model

Using list items in this way can cause problems in Internet Explorer 5 for Mac and Windows. We were able to avoid most of the problems by indenting the text inside the links instead of padding them. That fixes the rendering in all of the browsers except IE5. When text is indented inside list items, IE5 creates a *de facto* margin outside the box equal to the size of the indentation, thus making the effective size of the box wider and throwing off the proper wrapping inside the container.

A quirk in these browsers can fix the problem as easily as it was created. To trick IE5 for Mac and Windows into gobbling up this extra girth it creates, simply float everything left:

```
#utilNav li {
     width: 99px;
     line-height: 21px;
     margin: 0 0 1px 1px;
     display: inline;
     float: left;
}
```

```
#utilNav li a {
    text-indent: 3px;
    width: 99px;
    height: 21px;
    color: #fff;
    display: block;
    background: #94a2d9 url(images/chamfer.gif) no-repeat right bottom;
    float: left;
}
#utilNav li a:hover { background-color: #566cc3; }
```

By the way, notice that we didn't need to style the #utilNav ul element at all in making our design work. To style our next navigational item, we will make use of the ul element.

Styling the Roles

The role-based navigation has a few similarities to the utility navigation we just styled, but quite a few differences. Here, we want to give the effect of text inside a containing box, not individual buttons for each list item. In this case, we'll handle some of the manipulation inside the unordered list element.

The method we used in the utility navigation to get around the extra width caused by text indentation in Internet Explorer 5 for Mac and Windows has its repercussions here. Because the utility list items were floated left, the point at which the browser renders the current element never moved. We'll get around this by clearing any elements that are floated to the left:

```
ul#roleNav {
    clear: left;
}
```

The ul element should stretch to fit the width of its container, so there is no need to set a width. The height will be handled naturally, as well. To make the left-hand side of the role-based navigation line up with the left-hand side of the individual list item boxes we created earlier, we'll add a 1-pixel left margin:

```
ul#roleNav {
    clear: left;
    margin-left: 1px;
}
```

The chamfer.gif image we used to bevel the corner of the utility list items can be reused here to bevel the corner of the role list container:

```
ul#roleNav {
    background : #dbe0f2 url(images/chamfer.gif) no-repeat right bottom;
    clear: left;
    margin-left: 1px;
}
```

The list box needs some room to stretch top and bottom, so let's add 6 pixels:

```
ul#roleNav {
    padding: 6px 0;
    background : #dbe0f2 url(images/chamfer.gif) no-repeat right bottom;
```

```
        clear: left;
        margin-left: 1px;
    }
```

We want to create some spacing between the list items and vertically center each of the items. To do so, we'll set the `line-height`:

```
ul#roleNav li {
    line-height: 22px;
}
```

To remove extra spacing created by IE5 below each of the list items, we'll fool it into gobbling the space up by setting `display` to `inline`:

```
ul#roleNav li {
    line-height: 22px;
    display: inline;
}
```

As with the links inside the utility list, we should set the `height` of the links inside the list items. The `display` property should also be overridden here to `block`. Like the list items and the unordered list they are in, this will stretch to fit the width of the container.

```
ul#roleNav li a {
    height: 22px;
    display: block;
}
```

To move the text off the left side of the box, add a `padding-left` large enough to give the bullets we will add some breathing room:

```
ul#roleNav li a {
    padding-left: 16px;
    height: 22px;
    display: block;
}
```

As we did in the primary navigation, we'll place a bullet inside the left padding using a background image 8 pixels from the left edge and centered vertically. (When the second parameter of the `background-position` property is omitted, it defaults to `center`.) Let's set the color and size of the font, too:

```
ul#roleNav li a {
    padding-left: 16px;
    font-size: 12px;
    height: 22px;
    display: block;
    color: #596ec4;
    background: #dbe0f2 url(images/pointer_small.gif) no-repeat 8px;
}
ul#roleNav li a:hover { color: #0021a5; }
```

The Final Outcome

So, here you have it: a complete look at the style behind the supplementary navigation.

```
#suppNav {
    width: 200px;
    position: absolute;
    top: 195px;
    right: 2px;
}
#suppNav h2 { display: none; }
#utilNav li {
    width: 99px;
    line-height: 21px;
    margin: 0 0 1px 1px;
    display: inline;
    float: left;
}
#utilNav li a {
    text-indent: 3px;
    width: 99px;
    height: 21px;
    color: #fff;
    display: block;
    float: left; /* For IE5 */
    background: #94a2d9 url(images/whiteCornerNik.gif) no-repeat right bottom;
}
#utilNav li a:hover { background-color: #566cc3; }
ul#roleNav {
    padding: 6px 0;
    background : #dbe0f2 url(images/whiteCornerNik.gif) no-repeat right bottom;
    clear: left;
    margin-left: 1px;
}
ul#roleNav li {
    line-height: 22px;
    display: inline;
}
ul#roleNav li a {
    padding-left: 16px;
    font-size: 12px;
    height: 22px;
    display: block;
    color: #596ec4;
    background: #dbe0f2 url(images/pointer_small.gif) no-repeat 8px;
}
ul#roleNav li a:hover { color: #0021a5; }
```

That's it. That's the list.

Flash Embedding Revisited

UF wanted to display a rotating series of three spotlights on faculty and decided Flash (instead of Java or JavaScript image rotators) was the way to do it, as shown in Figure 5-11.

Using Flash also meant that it couldn't be a deal-breaker. In other words, if the visitor doesn't have Flash installed, the site still must function properly. To be appropriate for this site's audience, Flash must be an augmentation of the site's content—not a barrier to those without Flash.

The previous chapter discussed methods of properly including Flash into your designs. Let's look at one of these in some more detail: Flash Satay (`www.alistapart.com/articles/flashsatay/`).

Flash Satay

As discussed in Chapter 4, the Flash Satay method of including Flash in Web sites addresses the `embed` element used by older browsers and the proprietary attributes commonly used inside the `object` element.

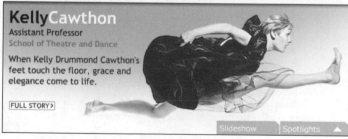

Figure 5-11: Examples of the Flash spotlights used on the UF site

To better understand what we're trying to do here, let's take a look at what a typical piece of markup would look like to include Flash on a page:

```
<object classid="clsid:D27CDB6E-AE6D-11cf-96B8-444553540000"
codebase="http://download.macromedia.com/pub/shockwave/cabs/flash
/swflash.cab#version=6,0,0,0" width="516" height="194" id="movie">
   <param name="movie" value="spotlights.swf">
   <embed src="spotlights.swf" width="516" height="194"
      name="movie" type="application/x-shockwave-flash"
      plug inspage="http://www.macromedia.com/go/getflashplayer">
</object>
```

The Flash Satay method takes a big chunk out of this and leaves off with some rather clean markup:

```
<object type="application/x-shockwave-flash" data="loader.swf" width="516"
height="194">
<param name="movie" value="loader.swf" />
</object>
```

This new loader movie (a small file of around 4K) simply loads the larger movie with all the content (see Figure 5-12). This gets around an issue in IE for Windows where the movie loaded in the object parameter won't stream, causing the visitor to have to wait until the entire Flash movie has loaded before it starts.

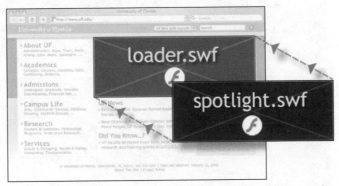

Figure 5-12: Flash Satay uses a loader movie in addition to the main Flash content.

If the visitor does not have Flash installed, we want to put alternate content in its place. The `object` module has a very useful method of allowing us to do that by simply adding the alternate content after the first parameter. In this case, we'll place an image of a campus landmark, as shown in Figure 5-13.

```
<object type="application/x-shockwave-flash" data="loader.swf" width="516"
height="194">
<param name="movie" value="loader.swf" />
<img src="images/tower.jpg" alt="Century Tower Photo" width="516" height="194" />
</object>
```

Figure 5-13: Elements passed after the movie parameter are used as alternate content.

Elsewhere on the page in the primary navigation, there is a link to the same XHTML-based spotlights that the Flash-based spotlight movie links to. So, if a visitor does not have Flash installed or enabled, the same content is still accessible.

This works well for all modern browsers, or so it would seem. An unfortunately widespread glitch caused by a corrupt Flash Player Active X control when users of IE 5.5 upgraded from IE 5.01 causes a text area to be rendered instead of the requested object (in this case, our Flash spotlights loader) in the absence of the classid attribute. For IE to play nicely with our new, sleek, standards-compliant markup, we will need to resort to a little trickery.

Flash Satay with Server-Side Detection

Flash Satay suggests using the object element without an embed attribute to allow standards-compliant addition of Flash content to XHTML. UF took the Flash Satay method of Flash inclusion described earlier and circumvented problems in IE 5.5 by making a minor revision: server-side browser detection.

Apache and the BrowserMatch Directive

To handle the classid attribute properly, we must pass it only to visitors using Internet Explorer for Microsoft. We can discern what browser a visitor is using (for the most part) through the request it makes to the server for a Web page. The server normally records some basic information about the request: the name of the file, the time, whether the request was successful, the size of the file (and most important for our needs here) the type of browser.

The method we will use here assumes the site is hosted on an Apache Web server. Approximately two-thirds of all Web sites (including the UF site) are hosted using the Open Source Web server software Apache. This method can be modified for usage by sites hosted on Microsoft's IIS or other Web servers.

To begin, create or locate the .htaccess file in either the root directory of the site or in the directories where the documents are that use Flash. The .htaccess file is a simple text file containing directives that configure how a server handles documents and directories. If not done already, tell the server to parse

the type of document used. We are using (X)HTML documents, so we will do this by adding an
`AddHandler` directive for the suffix of our content to the site's `.htaccess` file:

```
AddHandler server-parsed .html
```

If the content is already in a server parsed format, the `AddHandler` directive is not needed.

Now, we want to set an environment variable that will allow us to identify the content in our documents
(namely, the `classid`) we want to pass to Internet Explorer for Windows. Inside the `.htaccess` file,
add the following line:

```
BrowserMatch MSIE msie
```

This directs the server to set an environment variable called `msie` to true if the `User-Agent` is `MSIE`
(Internet Explorer for Windows).

Let's take another look at the markup as it is now:

```
<object type="application/x-shockwave-flash" data="loader.swf" width="516"
height="194 classid="clsid:D27CDB6E-AE6D-11cf-96B8-444553540000">
<param name="movie" value="loader.swf" />
<img src="images/tower.jpg" alt="Century Tower" width="516" height="194" />
</object>
```

Because we now have a variable that lets us know when the visitor is using IE for Windows, we can
selectively add the `classid` back in by checking for the `msie` variable. The code to tell the server to do
so looks like this:

```
<object type="application/x-shockwave-flash" data="loader.swf" width="516"
height="194" <!--#if expr="${msie}"-->
classid="clsid:D27CDB6E-AE6D-11cf-96B8-444553540000"
<!--#endif --> >
<param name="movie" value="loader.swf" />
<img src="images/tower.jpg" alt="Century Tower" width="516" height="194" />
</object>
```

*For more information on how to use the BrowserMatch directive, it is explained in more detail in the
Apache documentation describing the* mod_setenvif *module at* http://httpd.apache.org/
docs/mod/mod_setenvif.html.

Drawbacks and Barriers to Flash Satay with Server-Side Detection

As is mentioned in Chapter 4, if a site has a sizeable number of Flash movies, then the creation of container movies for each one can become cumbersome. The UF site uses a small number of Flash movies
(well, just one), so we're okay here.

For the method described here, the site's server must be configured to allow directives and the content
creator must have access to create those permissions. This is the case at UF.

The directive must parse through each page served, placing an additional (though nominal) load on
the server. This wasn't an issue for UF because it already parses every page to allow for server-side
includes (SSIs).

Missteps

After going through a 7-month process to redesign its site, UF found some things it would do differently.

Leading Only by Example

When UF released the new site, colleges and departments around campus were clamoring to incorporate the techniques and manner of design used on the home page. To stay on schedule, the site was launched without the completion of a definitive style guide and set of templates to be distributed across campus.

A set of templates has since been developed, but the delay stymied campus Web development. The time to manage a shift in how UF develops Web sites was when its most visible section was going through that change.

"Force of Habit" or "Who Moved My Input Field?"

With any redesign, especially on a site with a large number of repeat visitors, managing change becomes critical to acceptance. There are often users (especially staff members) whose site usage is something like this:

> *"I go to the home page and click 'Link X', scroll down and click 'Link Y', type what I need into 'Box Z,' and click 'Go'."*

While a well-tested redesign should certainly create a more usable site for any new visitor, repetitive users of the site (like the one quoted here) will likely react violently to an interrupt in their Pavlovian conditioning.

Mismanagement and lack of attention to the transition of these repeat visitors can lead to a great deal of angst and wasted resources.

While the site was shared with the test audiences, a protracted public beta might have alleviated some of the growing pains that came along with the redesign.

Summary

The evolution of the University of Florida Web site has provided a look into some of the challenges that await changing Web sites, the decisions UF made to combat them, and the techniques that did the job. We've looked at styling headers and unordered lists in different types of navigation and why they should be used. We've also made some modifications to widely used Flash inclusion markup to allow for both standards compliance and across-the-board application. We hope this will help you tackle your next big project.

Now let's take a look at the move to CSS in one of world's most popular sports sites, ESPN.com.

6

ESPN.com: Powerful
Layout Changes

If you're an American, or a fan of American sports, then ESPN probably needs no introduction. If you're not familiar with ESPN then you need to know only five simple facts about the company to understand how large it is:

❑ Its Web site, ESPN.com, serves between 1 and 1.3 billion pages a month (a figure roughly equivalent to that of the BBC's mass of Web sites).

❑ The site has approximately 15.3 million unique visitors a month.

❑ These visitors spend an average of 9 minutes a day on ESPN.com.

❑ ESPN.com is the largest and most popular sports Web site in the world.

❑ Disney owns 80 percent of ESPN.

That's impressive stuff.

So, now that we've established that it's not a Mickey Mouse outfit (well, only 80 percent Mickey Mouse), you may be wondering why its site, ESPN.com, has made it into a book on CSS. Surely sites that large don't make the transition from controlled, table-based layouts to the more fluid, and less predictable (so to speak) world of CSS, do they?

Do they?

ESPN and CSS Sitting in a Tree

Not only has ESPN.com made the leap from Tag Soup and Table Layouts to CSS, but it was one of the first major commercial organizations to do so, flicking the switch back in May 2003. How did they dare to do it? Well, the numbers just made sense. Careful analysis of traffic logs showed that the month prior to launching its new design, around 97 percent of visitors arrived using some form of compliant browser (IE 5+, Netscape 6+, Mozilla, Opera 6+, Safari, Chimera, and Konqueror), the remaining 3 percent being either undetectable or noncompliant.

Combined with projected bandwidth savings of 730 terabytes (TB) a year, promises of lowered maintenance costs, faster story turnarounds, and more adaptable page layouts, the team had enough evidence to convince the suits at the top that their plan was a good one.

The new site would be cost-effective, attractive, maintainable, forward-thinking, and the first step in embracing a Web standards–based future.

Interviewing the Designer

Mike Davidson is Senior Associate Art Director and Manager of Media Product Development at the Walt Disney Internet Group, in Seattle. In 2003, as Associate Art Director of ESPN, he was a driving force behind the ESPN.com redesign.

Q: *First off, Mike, are you pleased with how things have turned out?*

A: Absolutely. Running a site as big as ESPN is not a question of getting a redesign done and then throwing it on autopilot. I would say that the majority of Web sites out there need very little "rejigging" on a daily basis because usually only text and other simple data is changing. But with ESPN, entire sections change on a weekly basis. And formats change several times a year. New sponsorships can completely change the way a certain page grid is laid out. The list goes on and on.

We work in an environment that must act swiftly to adapt to changes in our industry and every "redesign" is just a big fresh start every two to three years. We measure how pleased we are with any given redesign by how far forward it propels us past our competitors and past where we were before. The 2003 redesign, now almost two years old, propelled us into the world of Web standards awareness and browser agnosticism.

Everyone who works on the site now thinks in those terms. It's no longer "make sure it works in IE," but rather "make sure it's coded correctly." With well over 100 people on staff contributing to the site, we knew we couldn't get everything perfect, and likely never will, but as these last couple of years have gone by, we're getting it more and more right every day.

Q: *Which bit of the design is the internal team most pleased with? And which part are the site's visitors most pleased with?*

A: The most important achievement to us was simply changing the way we think about code. It's no longer acceptable for a newbie to come in, hack together a table, and throw it onto the site for the sake of speed. We indeed do things sometimes for the sake of speed, but there is a certain level of pride now in doing things right first, and fast second. That said, a news site will always be driven by business objectives first (which include timeliness), but to the extent that technical teams can produce great work without sacrificing that timeliness, we are well ahead of the game.

As far as visitor benefits go, the originality of layouts we provide has always been tops in the industry, in my opinion. We have three major publishing modes for our front page, depending on how big a certain news event is, and users appreciate the importance-based design we give them. Why show users an 18-point plain black headline for a regular-season NBA game report and the same treatment for when the Red Sox win their first World Series in a million years?

Importance-based design has been evident in newspapers for centuries, and through the magic of CSS-P, it's available on ESPN.com as well.

Q: *How long had the idea for using standards-based design been in your mind before it got the green light?*

A: About a year. We tend to plan our redesigns about a year out, so we got to thinking about this around the middle of 2002. One major complicating factor was that ESPN.com had been run out of Seattle (where I live) for its entire life, but the decision was made to relocate it to the ESPN headquarters in Bristol, Connecticut, in the middle of 2003. So we pretty much started the redesign in Seattle and then ended it all the way across the country in Bristol. This included moving servers, employees, code, production facilities, and just about everything else. I'm a West Coast guy, so I elected to stay in Seattle and continue employment with ESPN's parent company, Disney, but a good bit of the staff ended up relocating. We still help out on a lot of ESPN-related projects from the Seattle office, but it's not a 100 percent time commitment anymore.

Q: *How much internal marketing did you have to do to convince, first, your own team, and, second, your bosses of the soundness of your plan?*

A: There was no internal marketing within the team as everyone agreed that it was the right thing to do, and honestly, there was very little convincing of the higher-ups necessary either. The technology teams are paid to know what's best for the site from a technology standpoint. So, as long as a move to standards-based design did not represent any extra costs or sacrifices in site features, then ESPN brass had no reason not to fully support it.

In fact, this move actually reduced our costs by quite a bit and let us do more with the site, so it really wasn't a tough argument to make. Executives might not care what a `div` or a spacer `gif` is, but they certainly do care about bandwidth bills and ad inventory.

Q: *Did you start by converting a small, sub-site of ESPN.com? Or did you leap straight in at the deep end and swap the high-profile front page over? And, regardless of your answer, can you explain your reasoning?*

A: ESPN.com is so enormous that you could never redesign the whole thing in one fell swoop and then just flip a switch when you were ready. Sure, everyone wants to do that, but it's just not possible, given the tens of thousands of templates involved.

We generally start with the front page, move on to the section index pages, and then do the story pages. I suppose it doesn't matter too much which order this is done in, but the speed at which all pages can eventually be converted is important. We wanted to set an example with our most trafficked page that all other pages could be molded after.

Q: *Would you have done anything differently, looking back?*

A: Well, I don't have veto power over every bit of the design/production process, so, obviously, not every decision made was mine, but I think we got most of the major things right. The one thing I guess that disappoints me a bit is how crufty things can get with time. Every time a major site redesigns (not just ours), code quality tends go down gradually until the next redesign. This occurs for many reasons:

- ❑ New people working on the site.
- ❑ Changing business needs require modified layouts.
- ❑ Advertising and sponsorship deals require less rigidity in layouts and more flexibility to put stuff wherever.
- ❑ Third-party tracking, survey, and ad code finds its way into the system.
- ❑ Documentation doesn't stay current.
- ❑ New features need to be shoehorned in.

It's an inescapable aspect of running a revenue-driven media site like ESPN, and we are just thankful for the opportunity every two to three years to assess what has changed, what's needed for the future, and wipe the slate clean. With each wipe, things get exponentially better.

Q: *Has this success given you the appetite and the political power to convert more of ESPN's on-line properties to standards-based designs?*

A: Absolutely. Our group has been intimately involved in the standards-based redesigns of ABCNews.com, Disneyworld.com, Disneymeetings.com, Wideworldofsports.com, and other Disney properties as well. ESPN is a technology leader within our company and where they lead, other vertical markets tend to follow.

Q: *And finally, do you envision your competitors' sites making similar changes in the near future, or do you think your site will remain unique within your industry for some time to come?*

A: You know what? When Eric Meyer interviewed me right after the ESPN redesign almost two years ago, I told him that I fully expected our competitors to be right behind us in the push toward Web standards. Unfortunately, that hasn't happened. I won't name names, but if you look at ESPN's major competitors in the sports media space and ABCNews's competitors in the mainstream media space, not a single one that I know of has dropped table-based design yet. Some of these companies have gone through two redesigns in the last two years, including as recently as January 2005, and still the same coding standards exist. I am not placing blame on any particular group since there are so many moving parts in most of these organizations, but it certainly would be nice to see some more progress. Oh well. Web sites are the sole property of their owners so those owners have the right to do with them as they please. Eventually, everyone will come around. And in the meantime, we'll just keep moving ahead.

Importance-Based Design

One of the nicest things about EPSN.com's new design is that there exists a mechanism for its editors to reformat the site in reaction to the importance of the news being presented. Mike Davidson refers to this per-article formatting as "importance-based design." To clarify the need for this, consider one of his responses in the previous interview:

> We have three major publishing modes for our front page, depending on how big a certain news event is, and users appreciate the importance-based design we give them. Why show users an 18-point plain black headline for a regular season NBA game report and the same treatment for when the Red Sox win their first World Series in a million years? Importance-based design has been evident in newspapers for centuries, and through the magic of CSS-P, it's available on ESPN.com as well.

As Davidson says, this sort of thing has been around in newspapers for a very long time. Following are two examples from the sports section of *The Daily Telegraph* (Britain's best-selling quality daily paper), showing the difference in layout that a "Holy Cow!" story can elicit. Figure 6-1 shows a normal day in the sports world, with no big story dominating the news. Figure 6-2 shows a cover from a special day, when Ellen MacCarthur broke the circumnavigation world record. The difference in layout, and, therefore, the difference implied in the importance of the stories, is obvious.

Now, let's compare the newspaper's implementation of importance-based design to ESPN.com's own layout changes. The following section describes the three major publishing modes ESPN can call into play at any time: Regular, Skirmish, and War.

Figure 6-1: An example of a newspaper cover in Regular mode

Figure 6-2: An example of a newspaper in War mode (Main photo copyright DPPI/ Offshore Challenges)

Regular

According to Davidson, "*Regular* mode gets published over 90 percent of the time and is for the most part completely automated. The editors select a photo, write a headline for it, and hit publish. It's a very streamlined workflow. The Flash headline at the top automatically scales depending on how long of a headline we write."

Figure 6-3 shows an example.

Skirmish

"*Skirmish* mode occurs when there is a news item of great significance in the sports world," Davidson said. "In this case, we generally know what's going to happen ahead of time (for example, Ichiro [a baseball player] breaking the all-time single-season hits record), so the photo-editing department spends a bit of time putting a composition together in Photoshop. Once the event occurs, we publish the site in Skirmish mode and through the magic of well-placed `div`s we take over the entire top story area with the hand-produced piece. Generally, all text in a Skirmish layout is set in Photoshop."

Figure 6-4 shows an example.

Figure 6-3: The front page of ESPN.com in Regular mode

Figure 6-4: The front page of ESPN.com in Skirmish mode

War

According to Davidson, "The last publishing mode is what's known as *War* mode and it is reserved for only the most important news events. The Red Sox winning the World Series, Dale Earnhardt dying, and the Super Bowl preview are all examples of when we'd publish in War mode. In this mode, a hand-composited Photoshop piece takes up almost the entire above-the-fold area of the screen, and browser text is laid on top of the right side of the photo."

Figure 6-5 shows an example.

"People seem to like both War and Skirmish modes quite a bit but we use them sparingly to preserve their dramatic effect. Were ESPN designed with tables, features like War and Skirmish would not be possible without negatively affecting other parts of the layout, but since the entire layout is CSS-P, everything slides around rather gracefully," Davidson said.

Putting It All Together

So, we've learned that importance-based design has firm roots in traditional media, and we can see for ourselves that ESPN has used CSS to port this approach to the Web, but how exactly are they doing it?

❑   Their method must be simple and quick to apply, for it must be understood and easily implemented by non-technical staff.

❑　It must be future-proof and easily adaptable, for the site's contents and structure may vary.

❑　It must be powerful, to transform a complex page so completely.

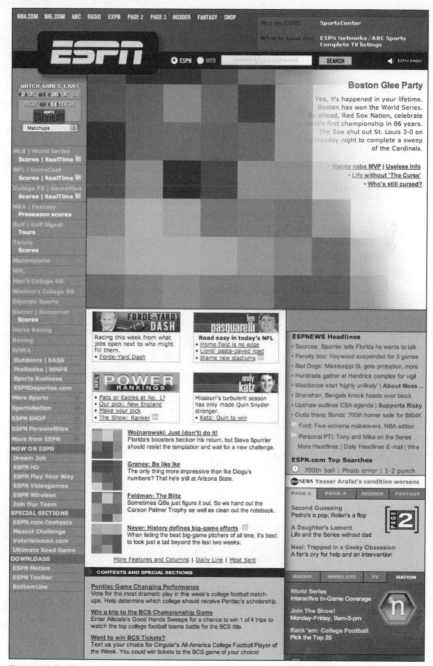

Figure 6-5: The front page of ESPN.com in War mode

That sounds like quite a challenge, but as you'll see in the next section there's actually a very simple solution, and it's a solution that you can start incorporating into your own sites right away.

Love Your <body>

You may have guessed from the clever title of this section that the key to ESPN's secret is the body element. By assigning a unique id to the body element, the staff at ESPN is able to use it as a starting point to make sweeping style changes to a page. For example, to provide different headline sizes on Regular, Skirmish, and War pages, they might use these rules:

```
body#regular h1 {font-size: 2em;}
body#skirmish h1 {font-size: 4em;}
body#war h1 {font-size: 8em;}
```

Once these rules were in place, it would be up to the editorial staff to decide which publishing mode was applicable for that day's headline. For example, let's say someone new to the team decides to publish an article in Regular mode; here's what the (simplified) HTML might look like:

```
<html>
<body id="regular">

<h1>No.1 Hit Wonder</h1>

<p>Ichiro records his 258th hit of the season, breaking George Sisler's 84-year-old
record.</p>

</body>
</html>
```

Figure 6-6 shows what that might look like in the browser.

However, when the Editor-in-Chief reads the story he decides that someone breaking the all-time single-season hits record is deserved of being published in Skirmish mode. So, what does he do? Simple: He slaps the new guy upside the head and swaps the value of the body's id attribute to skirmish. The outcome? The new guy learned a thing or two about his boss, and the CSS rules shown earlier transform the story's headline, making it larger and visually more important:

```
<html>
<body id="skirmish">

<h1>No.1 Hit Wonder</h1>

<p>Ichiro records his 258th hit of the season, breaking George Sisler's 84-year-old
record.</p>

</body>
</html>
```

Figure 6-7 shows what that might look like in the browser.

Easy as pie.

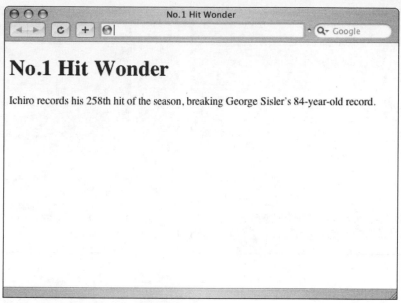

Figure 6-6: The story in Regular mode

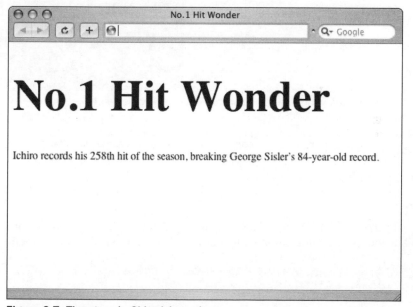

Figure 6-7: The story in Skirmish mode

Now, as we've seen from the screen shots in Figures 6-3, 6-4, and 6-5, swapping between Regular, Skirmish, and War modes on ESPN.com does much more than just change the size of the headline. It restructures the whole top section of the site, moving navigation, submenus, and advertising panels to less-prominent positions and focusing attention on the main story. Figure 6-8 shows a side-by-side comparison between Regular and War modes.

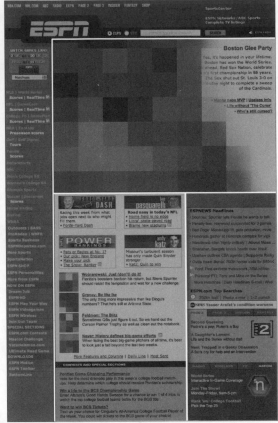

Figure 6-8: Comparing the various sections of ESPN.com in Regular and War modes

Given the amount of information ESPN.com has to cram into its pages, you might find it a little hard to see exactly what's going on, so let's clear away all the clutter and try to emulate the layout changes by creating a simple HTML page.

The HTML

Following is the section of HTML we'll be using for our demonstration. The value for the body's id has been left blank, but we'll be filling it in with regular, then skirmish, then war, for our three examples.

```
<!DOCTYPE html PUBLIC "-//W3C//DTD XHTML 1.0 Transitional//EN"
"http://www.w3.org/TR/xhtml1/DTD/xhtml1-transitional.dtd">
<html xmlns="http://www.w3.org/1999/xhtml">
<body id="">

<div id="container">
    <div id="content">
```

```
                <h1>No.1 Hit Wonder</h1>

                <p>Ichiro records his 258th hit of the season, breaking George Sisler's
        84-year-old record.</p>
            </div>

            <div id="sidebar">
                <h2>Other News</h2>

                <ul>
                <li>Man hits ball.</li>
                <li>Dog swims channel.</li>
                <li>Woman climbs hill.</li>
                </ul>
            </div>

            <div id="footer">
                <p>Footer info</p>
            </div>
        </div>

        </body>
        </html>
```

The CSS

The CSS is split into four main sections. The first section sets the default values for the `container` div, the `content` div, the `sidebar` div, and the `footer` div. The second section specifies rules that will be applied only to a page whose `body id` equals `regular`. The third section specifies rules that will be applied only to a page whose `body id` equals `skirmish`. And finally, the fourth section specifies rules that will be applied only to a page whose `body id` equals `war`.

```
/*** defaults
***********************/
div#container {
    border: 1px solid black;
    width: 500px;
}

div#content {
    background-color: green;
}

div#sidebar {
    background-color: pink;
}

div#footer {
    background-color: orange;
    clear: both;
    text-align: center;
}
```

```
/*** regular
**********************/
body#regular div#content {
    float: left;
    width: 250px;
}

body#regular div#sidebar {
    float: right;
    width: 200px;
}

body#regular h1 {
    font-size: 2em;
}


/*** skirmish
**********************/
body#skirmish div#content {
    float: left;
    width: 300px;
}

body#skirmish div#sidebar {
    float: right;
    width: 150px;
}

body#skirmish h1 {
    font-size: 4em;
}


/*** war
**********************/
body#war div#content {
    float: left;
    width: 480px;
}

body#war h1 {
    font-size: 8em;
}
```

Now then, let's see what happens when we alter the id of the body element in our demo page. First off, Figure 6-9 shows the Regular layout (`<body id="regular">`).

There is nothing too dramatic there. The story and the "Other News" section are laid out side-by-side, and the story, while drawing the eye, doesn't really dominate the page. Now, what happens if we swap over to the Skirmish layout (`<body id="skirmish">`), as shown in Figure 6-10?

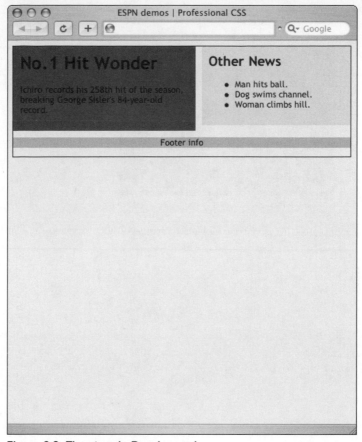

Figure 6-9: The story in Regular mode

Okay, we see a subtle (but significant) change. The story, which our editors have decided is fairly important, has grown in visual stature. It now takes up more width on the page, and the headline font size has increased.

So, let's see what happens when we swap to War layout (`<body id="war">`), as shown in Figure 6-11.

This is a big change. The headline, now deemed to be very important, has taken over the entire top section of the layout. Its font size has increased yet again, and it now dominates the whole page, which is exactly what the War layout is all about — pushing the big story into people's faces, giving it some oomph, letting the public know *"This is an important story!"*

The excellent thing about this demo is how amazingly easy it was to do. All we did was write a few additional styles and switch the `id` of the `body` element around; it really couldn't be simpler. But as basic as it was, it's essentially what ESPN is doing to alter its homepage so dramatically — providing a huge return on a very small amount of work.

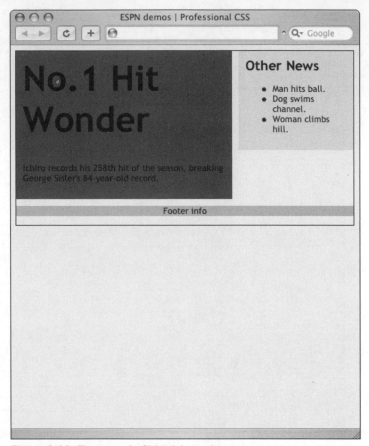

Figure 6-10: The story in Skirmish mode

Where Else Is This Applicable?

The short answer to the question "Where else is this technique applicable" is "Virtually everywhere!" Every time you insert a class or id, you should be asking yourself, "Is this the most efficient place for this, or can I move it higher up the document tree? Can I apply it to this element's parent? How do I get the maximum benefit from this?"

If another real-life example will help to clarify this idea, take a look at the following markup. (Figure 6-12 shows the result.) It's a simple set of navigation links, presented as an unordered list. The class of nav has been applied to each of the four links, and a CSS rule written to style them. The markup is valid, and the CSS works just fine, but is it the best way to approach the problem?

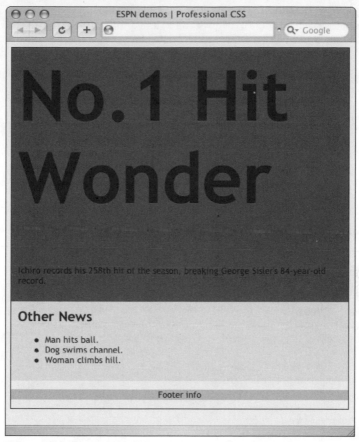

Figure 6-11: The story in War mode

```
a.nav {background-color: yellow;}

<ul>
<li><a class="nav" href="/">Home</a></li>
<li><a class="nav" href="/archive/">Archive</a></li>
<li><a class="nav" href="/about/">About</a></li>
<li><a class="nav" href="/contact/">Contact</a></li>
</ul>
```

- Home
- Archive
- About
- Contact

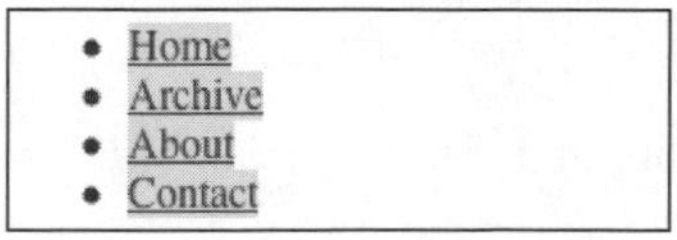

Figure 6-12: Links styled yellow

We hope you've spotted that adding `class="nav"` to all four anchors is not the most efficient thing to do. A much better approach would be to move the `class` application point up the document tree to the enclosing `ul`, and then alter the CSS rule to reflect the change (see Figure 6-13):

```
ul.nav li a {background-color: yellow;}

<ul class="nav">
<li><a href="/">Home</a></li>
<li><a href="/archive/">Archive</a></li>
<li><a href="/about/">About</a></li>
<li><a href="/contact/">Contact</a></li>
</ul>
```

- Home
- Archive
- About
- Contact

Figure 6-13: Links still styled yellow

The end result is still the same, but the second method has several advantages over the first. First, our HTML file will be smaller, and will download faster. Second, our markup is less cluttered and is easier to understand and edit. Third, by applying the `class` to the `ul`, we are able to style not only the anchors (`a`) but also the list-items (`li`) and `ul` itself (see Figure 6-14):

```
ul.nav {background-color: blue;}
ul.nav li {background-color: pink;}
ul.nav li a {background-color: yellow;}

<ul class="nav">
<li><a href="/">Home</a></li>
<li><a href="/archive/">Archive</a></li>
<li><a href="/about/">About</a></li>
<li><a href="/contact/">Contact</a></li>
</ul>
```

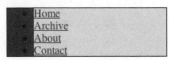

Figure 6-14: Links, list-items, and the unordered-list itself, all styled

Once again, we see a (relatively) large return for a small initial amount of work.

Now, you might scoff at this little demo and say that the difference between the two sets of code is minimal. But if you extrapolate these ideas out to a site that contains more than 100,000 pages (as ESPN.com does), you'll have some idea of the savings to be made.

Up a Bit . . . a Bit More . . . Stop!

It's important to realize that the ideas laid out here aren't demanding that you never assign a `class` or `id` to anchors or list-items. They're simply trying to get across the idea that moving the point of `class`/`id` application further up the document tree can have some major benefits for you.

That said, in all instances you'll reach a point where moving the application point higher just doesn't make any sense and will actually make your job more difficult. It's up to you to work out where that point is, and stop before you reach it.

For example, using our little list of navigation links from before, let's say we wanted to style the `About` link in such a way that it stands out from the other three. Where do we put our class?

A poor approach would be to do this:

```
ul.nav li a {background-color: green;}
ul.nav li a.selected {background-color: purple;}

<ul class="nav">
<li><a href="/">Home</a></li>
<li><a href="/archive/">Archive</a></li>
<li><a href="/about/" class="selected">About</a></li>
<li><a href="/contact/">Contact</a></li>
</ul>
```

A better method would be to move the application point up the document tree to the list-item:

```
ul.nav li a {background-color: green;}
ul.nav li.selected a {background-color: purple;}

<ul class="nav">
<li><a href="/">Home</a></li>
<li><a href="/archive/">Archive</a></li>
<li class="selected"><a href="/about/">About</a></li>
<li><a href="/contact/">Contact</a></li>
</ul>
```

This would let us style not only the `About` anchor, but also the list-item that contains it:

```
ul.nav li {background-color: yellow;}
ul.nav li a {background-color: green;}
ul.nav li.selected {background-color: red;}
ul.nav li.selected a {background-color: purple;}

<ul class="nav">
<li><a href="/">Home</a></li>
<li><a href="/archive/">Archive</a></li>
<li class="selected"><a href="/about/">About</a></li>
<li><a href="/contact/">Contact</a></li>
</ul>
```

Now we have to ask ourselves a question: Can we move the application point even further up the document tree? Can we apply it to the ul, for example? The answer, in this case, is "No." Not only do we already have a class on the ul, but applying class="selected" to the ul wouldn't help us specifically target the About anchor, would it? So, we'll just stay where we are, and apply the class to the list-item. It gives us maximum benefits for the minimum amount of work.

We hope you can now see that in each case this process has a logical starting point and a logical stopping point; it just requires a bit of mental trial-and-error to work out where those points are and where to apply your class or id.

Lesson Learned

The lesson to learn from this exercise is that you will see untold benefits from aiming high in the placement of your ids and classes. By placing an id in the body element, we are quickly able to make enormous changes to a page's layout, with very little extra effort or markup. The further down the document tree that we aim, the more markup we will end up writing, and the messier and more convoluted our pages will become.

So, each time you decide to add in a class or id to your HTML, ask yourself if it's really necessary to target that one specific element. Could you aim higher? Is there a containing element to which you could apply the class/id and still target the initial element, or have you reached the logical ceiling?

At some point you *are* going to reach that ceiling, and it's important that you realize ahead of time that it may be lower than you'd like. This desire to minimize the number of classes and ids in our documents has to be balanced against the abilities of today's Web browsers in understanding advanced CSS selectors. Sometimes we have no choice but to place classes on specific elements. It's not a failure on your part, it's just a side effect of having to live and work in the real world.

However, it's important that you retain some form of idealism. This kind of forward thinking will become increasingly useful as our Web browsers become more adept at understanding advanced CSS selectors. In the coming years, we'll be able to raise the application points for our CSS rules higher and higher until our HTML becomes almost devoid of the mass of classes and ids we rely on today.

A Glimpse into a Classless Future (Not a Socialist Manifesto)

At the end of the previous section, we touched briefly on the notion of "forward thinking" — the idea that as browsers become better at understanding advanced CSS selectors, the classes and ids so prevalent in today's markup will soon become a scarce commodity. This section explores that concept in a little more detail, and, in doing so, provides a glimpse of what the future might bring.

The Selectors of Tomorrow

If you mosey on over to the W3C's page on Selectors (www.w3.org/TR/2001/CR-css3-selectors-20011113/), you'll find a whole bunch of CSS that has rarely seen the light of day in a production environment. That document covers selectors not only from CSS Level 1 and 2, but also from Level 3, the

CSS of tomorrow. Some of today's browsers (Firefox, Opera, Safari) already support bits of CSS Level 3 (`:first-child` and `:last-child` being two examples), but on the whole, that page tends only to disappoint the adventurous coder. That said, it's still an important document. It gives us a glimpse of the world we'll all be working in tomorrow, and if we use our brains a little, adds practical weight behind the idea of separating structure and style.

Let's take a look at some of the goodies CSS has in store for us . . .

A Big List of Exciting Selectors

The following table shows the syntax of selectors, the result, and the selector type.

Selector Syntax	Result	Selector Type
E[foo]	Matches an E element with a foo attribute.	Attribute selector
E[foo="bar"]	Matches an E element whose foo attribute value is exactly equal to "bar".	Attribute selector
E[foo~="bar"]	Matches an E element whose foo attribute value is a list of space-separated values, one of which is exactly equal to "bar".	Attribute selector
E[foo^="bar"]	Matches an E element whose foo attribute value begins exactly with the string "bar".	Attribute selector
E[foo$="bar"]	Matches an E element whose "foo" attribute value ends exactly with the string "bar".	Attribute selector
E[foo*="bar"]	Matches an E element whose foo attribute value contains the substring "bar".	Attribute selector
E[foo|="bar"]	Matches an E element whose foo attribute has a hyphen-separated list of values beginning (from the left) with "bar".	Attribute selector
E:nth-child(n)	Matches an E element, the nth child of its parent.	Structural pseudo-class
E:nth-last-child(n)	Matches an E element, the nth child of its parent, counting from the last one.	Structural pseudo-class
E:nth-of-type(n)	Matches an E element, the nth sibling of its type.	Structural pseudo-class
E:nth-last-of-type(n)	Matches an E element, the n-th sibling of its type, counting from the last one.	Structural pseudo-class
E:first-child	Matches an E element, first child of its parent.	Structural pseudo-class
E:last-child	Matches an E element, last child of its parent.	Structural pseudo-class
E:first-of-type	Matches an E element, first sibling of its type.	Structural pseudo-class
E:last-of-type	Matches an E element, last sibling of its type.	Structural pseudo-class
E:only-child	Matches an E element, only child of its parent.	Structural pseudo-class

Table continued on following page

Selector Syntax	Result	Selector Type
E:only-of-type	Matches an E element, only sibling of its type.	Structural pseudo-class
E:target	Matches an E element that is the target of the referring URL.	User action pseudo-class
E:lang(foo)	Matches an E element in language foo.	:lang() pseudo-class
E:enabled or E:disabled	Matches a user interface E element that is enabled or disabled.	UI element state pseudo-class
E:checked or E:intermediate	Matches a user interface element that is checked or in an intermediate state (like a checkbox or radio button).	UI element state pseudo-class
E:contains("foo")	Matches an E element containing the substring foo in its textual contents.	Content pseudo-class
E::first-line	Matches the first formatted line of an E element.	:first-line pseudo-class
E::first-letter	Matches the first formatted letter of an E element.	:first-letter pseudo-class
E::selection	Matches the portion of an E element that is currently highlighted/selected by the user.	UI element fragments pseudo-elements
E::before	Matches generated content before an E element.	:before pseudo-element
E::after	Matches generated content after an E element.	:after pseudo-element
E:not(s)	Matches an E element that does not match simple selector s.	Negation pseudo-class
E + F	Matches an F element immediately preceded by an E element.	Direct adjacent combinator
E ~ F	Matches an F element preceded by an E element.	Indirect adjacent combinator

Seem a bit confusing? Well, the next section shows a few concrete examples of those selectors in action along with a description and demonstration of the elements they would select.

Examples of Exciting Selectors in Action

The examples in this section show how these advanced CSS selectors might be put to use on real HTML markup. The examples aren't exhaustive, but for each instance, consider how you would achieve the same effect using today's techniques. Most of the time the answer will be the liberal addition of classes and IDs to the HTML, but in many cases the answer is that it's impossible to re-create this functionality today.

Once you've done that, run through the selectors again and consider how you would duplicate the effects if you didn't have access to the HTML and so couldn't insert classes and IDs all over the place. In each and every case, short of using JavaScript, the answer will be that you can't. That's how big a change tomorrow brings.

The following selects all images that have a `title` attribute:

```
img[title]
```

Following is an example of what it selects (shown in bold):

```
<img src="pants.png" />
<img src="socks.png" title="These are my socks!" />
<img src="shoes.png" />
```

The following selects all input elements whose `type` attribute has a value of `text`:

```
input[type="text"]
```

Following is an example of what it selects:

```
<form>
<input type="text" name="name" />
<input type="text" name="email" />

<input type="submit" value="submit form" />
</form>
```

The following selects all links whose `rel` attribute value is a list of space-separated values, one of which is exactly equal to `met`:

```
a[rel~="met"]
```

Following is an example of what it selects:

```
<ul>
<li><a href="http://sidesh0w.com/" rel="colleague friend met">Sidesh0w</a></li>
<li><a href="http://mezzoblue.com/" rel="colleague">Mezzoblue</a></li>
<li><a href="http://photomatt.net/" rel="friend met colleague">Matt</a></li>
</ul>
```

The following selects all links whose `rel` attribute value begins exactly with `colleague`:

```
a[rel^="colleague"]
```

Following is an example of what it selects:

```
<ul>
<li><a href="http://sidesh0w.com/" rel="colleague friend met">Sidesh0w</a></li>
<li><a href="http://mezzoblue.com/" rel="colleague">Mezzoblue</a></li>
<li><a href="http://photomatt.net/" rel="friend met colleague">Matt</a></li>
</ul>
```

The following selects all links whose `rel` attribute value ends exactly with `colleague`:

```
a[rel$="colleague"]
```

Following is an example of what it selects:

```
<ul>
<li><a href="http://sidesh0w.com/" rel="colleague friend met">Sidesh0w</a></li>
<li><a href="http://mezzoblue.com/" rel="colleague">Mezzoblue</a></li>
<li><a href="http://photomatt.net/" rel="friend met colleague">Matt</a></li>
</ul>
```

The following selects all links whose `href` attributes contain the substring `.com`:

```
a[href*=".com"]
```

Following is an example of what it selects:

```
<ul>
<li><a href="http://sidesh0w.com/" rel="colleague friend met">Sidesh0w</a></li>
<li><a href="http://mezzoblue.com/" rel="colleague">Mezzoblue</a></li>
<li><a href="http://photomatt.net/" rel="friend met colleague">Matt</a></li>
</ul>
```

The following selects all links whose `hreflang` attribute has a hyphen-separated list of values beginning with `it`:

```
a[hreflang|="it"]
```

Following is an example of what it selects:

```
<p>You can view our <a href="/fr/" hreflang="fr">French translation</a>, our <a
href="/it/" hreflang="it">Italian translation</a>, or our <a href="/nl/"
hreflang="nl">Dutch translation</a>.</p>
```

The following selects all odd-numbered list-item elements:

```
li:nth-child(odd)
```

The following breaks the list-items up into groups of two and then selects the first list-item from each group:

```
li:nth-chid(2n+1)
```

Following is an example of what these select:

```
<ul>
<li>Dotty</li>
<li>Lotty</li>
<li>Squeak</li>
<li>Patch</li>
<li>Scrap</li>
<li>Poppy</li>
</ul>
```

The following selects all even-numbered list-item elements:

```
li:nth-child(even)
```

The following break the list-items up into groups of two and then select the second list-item from each group:

```
li:nth-child(2n+2)
```

or

```
li:nth-child(2n+0)
```

or

```
li:nth-child(2n)
```

Following is an example of what these select:

```
<ul>
<li>Dotty</li>
<li>Lotty</li>
<li>Squeak</li>
<li>Patch</li>
<li>Scrap</li>
<li>Poppy</li>
</ul>
```

The following breaks the list-items up into groups of three and then selects the second list-item from each of those groups:

```
li:nth-child(3n+2)
```

Following is an example of what it selects:

```
<ul>
<li>Dotty</li>
<li>Lotty</li>
<li>Squeak</li>
<li>Patch</li>
<li>Scrap</li>
<li>Poppy</li>
</ul>
```

The following select the fourth list-item:

```
li:nth-child(0n+4)
```

or

```
li:nth-child(4)
```

Following is an example of what these select:

```
<ul>
<li>Dotty</li>
<li>Lotty</li>
<li>Squeak</li>
<li>Patch</li>
<li>Scrap</li>
<li>Poppy</li>
</ul>
```

The following selects the first three list-items:

```
li:nth-child(-n+3)
```

Following is an example of what it selects:

```
<ul>
<li>Dotty</li>
<li>Lotty</li>
<li>Squeak</li>
<li>Patch</li>
<li>Scrap</li>
<li>Poppy</li>
</ul>
```

Counting from the last list-item, the following selects all odd-numbered list-item elements:

```
li:nth-last-child(odd)
```

Counting from the last list-item, the following breaks the list-items up into groups of two and then selects the first list-item from each group:

```
li:nth-last-child(2n+1)
```

Following is an example of what these select:

```
<ul>
<li>Dotty</li>
<li>Lotty</li>
<li>Squeak</li>
<li>Patch</li>
<li>Scrap</li>
<li>Poppy</li>
</ul>
```

Counting from the last list-item, the following selects all even-numbered list-item elements:

```
li:nth-last-child(even)
```

Counting from the last list-item, the following breaks the list-items up into groups of two and then selects the second list-item from each group:

```
li:nth-last-child(2n+2)
```

or

```
li:nth-last-child(2n+0)
```

or

```
li:nth-last-child(2n)
```

Following is an example of what these select:

```
<ul>
<li>Dotty</li>
<li>Lotty</li>
<li>Squeak</li>
<li>Patch</li>
<li>Scrap</li>
<li>Poppy</li>
</ul>
```

Counting from the last list-item, the following breaks the list-items up into groups of three, and then selects the first list-item from each of those groups:

```
li:nth-last-child(3n+1)
```

Following is an example of what it selects:

```
<ul>
<li>Dotty</li>
<li>Lotty</li>
<li>Squeak</li>
<li>Patch</li>
<li>Scrap</li>
<li>Poppy</li>
</ul>
```

Counting from the last list-item, the following select the fourth list-item:

```
li:nth-last-child(0n+4)
```

or

```
li:nth-last-child(4)
```

Following is an example of what these select:

```
<ul>
<li>Dotty</li>
<li>Lotty</li>
<li>Squeak</li>
<li>Patch</li>
<li>Scrap</li>
<li>Poppy</li>
</ul>
```

Counting from the last list-item, the following selects the last three list-items:

```
li:nth-last-child(-n+3)
```

Following is an example of what it selects:

```
<ul>
<li>Dotty</li>
<li>Lotty</li>
<li>Squeak</li>
<li>Patch</li>
<li>Scrap</li>
<li>Poppy</li>
</ul>
```

The following selects all odd-numbered images:

```
img:nth-of-type(odd)
```

The following breaks the images up into groups of two and then selects the first image from each group:

```
img:nth-of-type(2n+1)
```

Following is an example of what these select:

```
<img src="one.png" />
<img src="two.png" />
<img src="three.png" />
<img src="four.png" />
<img src="five.png" />
<img src="six.png" />
<img src="seven.png" />
<img src="eight.png" />
```

The following selects all even-numbered images:

```
img:nth-of-type(even)
```

The following break the images up into groups of two and then select the second image from each group:

```
img:nth-of-type(2n+2)
```

or

```
img:nth-of-type(2n+0)
```

or

```
img:nth-of-type(2n)
```

Following is an example of what these select:

```
<img src="one.png" />
<img src="two.png" />
<img src="three.png" />
<img src="four.png" />
<img src="five.png" />
<img src="six.png" />
<img src="seven.png" />
<img src="eight.png" />
```

Counting from the last image, the following selects the last four images:

```
img:nth-last-of-type(-n+4)
```

Following is an example of what it selects:

```
<img src="one.png" />
<img src="two.png" />
<img src="three.png" />
<img src="four.png" />
<img src="five.png" />
<img src="six.png" />
<img src="seven.png" />
<img src="eight.png" />
```

The following selects the first list-item. (Actually, this is the same as `li:nth child(1)`.)

```
li:first-child
```

Following is an example of what it selects:

```
<ul>
<li>Dotty</li>
<li>Lotty</li>
<li>Squeak</li>
<li>Patch</li>
<li>Scrap</li>
<li>Poppy</li>
</ul>
```

The following selects the last list-item. (Actually, this is the same as `li:nth-last-child(1)`.)

```
li:last-child
```

Following is an example of what it selects:

```
<ul>
<li>Dotty</li>
<li>Lotty</li>
<li>Squeak</li>
```

```
<li>Patch</li>
<li>Scrap</li>
<li>Poppy</li>
</ul>
```

The following selects the first instance of the definition title element in each list of child elements. In this case, it selects `Orchard`, `Alastair`, and `Mariella` definition-titles, but not `Dunstan`, `Pelosi`, or `Fabrizzio` (because those are not the first siblings of their type in the lists of children of their parent elements).

```
dt:first-of-type
```

Following is an example of what it selects:

```
<dl>
<dt>Orchard</dt>
<dd>
   <dl>
   <dt>Alastair</dt>
   <dd>The oldest son</dd>
   <dt>Dunstan</dt>
   <dd>The youngest son<dd>
   </dl>
</dd>
<dt>Pelosi</dt>
<dd>
   <dl>
   <dt>Mariella</dt>
   <dd>Only daughter</dd>
   <dt>Fabrizzio</dt>
   <dd>The youngest son</dd>
   </dl>
</dd>
</dl>
```

The following selects the last instance of the definition title element in each list of child elements. In this case, it selects `Dunstan`, `Pelosi`, and `Fabrizzio` definition-titles, but not `Orchard`, `Alastair`, or `Mariella` (because those are not the last siblings of their type in the lists of children of their parent elements).

```
dt:last-of-type
```

Following is an example of what it selects:

```
<dl>
<dt>Orchard</dt>
<dd>
   <dl>
   <dt>Alastair</dt>
   <dd>The oldest son</dd>
   <dt>Dunstan</dt>
   <dd>The youngest son<dd>
   </dl>
</dd>
<dt>Pelosi</dt>
```

```
<dd>
  <dl>
  <dt>Mariella</dt>
  <dd>Only daughter</dd>
  <dt>Fabrizzio</dt>
  <dd>The youngest son</dd>
  </dl>
</dd>
</dl>
```

The following selects list items whose textual contents contain the substring `"otty"`:

```
li:contains("otty")
```

Following is an example of what it selects:

```
<ul>
<li>Dotty</li>
<li>Lotty</li>
<li>Squeak</li>
<li>Patch</li>
<li>Scrap</li>
<li>Poppy</li>
</ul>
```

The following selects all elements except paragraph elements:

```
*:not(p)
```

Following is an example of what it selects:

```
<h1>My Shoes</h1>

<p>I have four pairs of shoes:</p>

<ol>
<li>Some brown ones;</li>
<li>Some green ones;</li>
<li>Some dirty ones;</li>
<li>Some smelly ones.</li>
</ol>

<p>If you're nice to me I'll let you see my shoes.</p>
```

The following selects all paragraph elements which do not have a `class` value of `hide`:

```
p:not(.hide)
```

Following is an example of what it selects:

```
<p>Poppy is my dog.</p>
<p>Poppy had five puppies.</p>
<p class="hide">I like to eat puppies.</p>
<p>There are three girl puppies and two boys.</p>
```

The following selects all list-items whose textual content does not contain the substring "otty":

```
li:not(:contains("otty"))
```

Following is an example of what it selects:

```
<ul>
<li>Dotty</li>
<li>Lotty</li>
<li>Squeak</li>
<li>Patch</li>
<li>Scrap</li>
<li>Poppy</li>
</ul>
```

The following selects the first line of a paragraph's textual content, as rendered by the browser:

```
p::first-line
```

Following is an example of what it selects:

```
<p>Oh, my old man's a
dustman, he wears a
dustman's hat, he wears
cor blimey trousers,
and he lives in a council
flat.</p>
```

The following selects the first letter of a paragraph's textual content:

```
p::first-letter
```

Following is an example of what it selects:

```
<p>Oh, my old man's a dustman, he wears a dustman's hat, he wears cor blimey
trousers, and he lives in a council flat.</p>
```

The following selects any paragraph that comes immediately after an h2, but only when they share the same parent in the document tree:

```
h2 + p
```

Following is an example of what it selects:

```
<div>
<h2>Soup, the untold story</h2>

<p>This document will tell you everything you ever wanted to know about soup.</p>

<p>And some things you didn't want to know.</p>
</div>
```

```
<div>
<h2>Soup in the middle ages</h2>
</div>

<p>Sir Galahad loved soup. Oh yes, he couldn't get enough of it, I tell you.</p>
```

The following selects any paragraph that comes after (not necessarily immediately after) an h2, but only when they share the same parent in the document tree:

```
h2 ~ p
```

Following is an example of what it selects:

```
<div>
<h2>Soup, the untold story</h2>

<p>This document will tell you everything you ever wanted to know about soup.</p>

<p>And some things you didn't want to know.</p>
</div>

<div>
<h2>Soup in the middle ages</h2>
</div>

<p>Sir Galahad loved soup. Oh yes, he couldn't get enough of it, I tell you.</p>
```

Love Your <body> Even More Tomorrow

Now then, given that the CSS selectors of tomorrow will let us target every single element on the page (based on their position in the document tree, on the presence and contents of their attributes, or simply based on their textual contents), what do you think the future holds for the humble class and id attributes?

Well, it would seem that the CSS of tomorrow provides the granularity needed to do away with such things. Why fill your markup with classes that (let's be honest) are almost always placed specifically to suit your current design, when you could use powerful structural pseudo-classes and attribute selectors to target the same elements?

There is, however, one vital use for classes and ids that will remain, and it's one we looked at in the first section of this chapter. By applying a class or id to the body element in each page we will be able to specify which rules should be applied to which pages. Sure, some of our CSS will be generic, but some will require this rule-page pairing that only a class or id on the body element can bring.

So, the future holds a powerful new set of CSS selectors for us to use, enabling us to remove *almost all* instances of classes and ids from our markup. Our HTML will be neater, our CSS will be more creative, and our sites will be *truly* skinnable.

Summary

In this chapter, we've seen the benefits that can come from applying `class` or `ids` high up in the document tree and how ESPN.com uses this simple technique to induce drastic layout changes in their site. We've also looked at CSS 3, the CSS of tomorrow, and glimpsed the power that its advanced selectors will bring to our work. By obtaining an awareness of the high-end of CSS selectors, we're not only preparing ourselves for tomorrow, but we're also raising our expectations of the capabilities of CSS. This, in turn, leads to a more inventive and adventurous approach to solving CSS issues.

In the next chapter, we'll take a look at creating three-column layouts with a case study of Fastcompany.com.

7

FastCompany.com: Building a Flexible Three-Column Layout

By the time 2003 began in earnest, a rather sizeable snowball was rolling. In October of 2002, Wired News abandoned traditional `table`-driven layout methods for a CSS-driven design. At that time, Wired wasn't the first redesign of its kind, but it was certainly the most highly trafficked. The site's chief designer, Douglas Bowman (see Chapter 3 for a discussion of his work on the Blogger.com redesign), took a highly visible and well-established brand, and delivered a compelling new design — all with standard technologies such as CSS and XHTML that would, as Bowman put it, help "lift the Web out of the dark ages" (*Wired News*, "A Site for Your Eyes": `www.wired.com/news/culture/0,1284,55675,00.html`).

For the next few months, you could almost hear the crickets chirping. Wired News had lifted style sheets out of the realm of academics and saber-waving standards advocates, and placed it squarely and confidently in the realm of mainstream media. Until the Wired redesign, most companies had never heard of cascading style sheets, much less considered them a viable alternative to the tried-and-true methods of designing with `tables`. The industry (and those of us in the saber-waving section of the audience) waited to see who, if anyone, would follow suit.

As it turns out, we didn't have to wait long.

Fast Company: Picking Up the Gauntlet

In April 2003, Fast Company (`http://fastcompany.com/`) was the next high-profile site to drop old, bloated page-building techniques for sleeker, standards-compliant methods, and it did so in style. The site serves two purposes:

❑ It is an archive of features from the popular magazine of the same name.

❑ It publishes various Web-only features, such as the popular FC Weblog (`http://blog .fastcompany.com/`).

Balancing both of these needs, the new Fast Company (FC) design was at once stylish and easy to navigate. Users could quickly sift through content-rich pages that could have easily become bogged down beneath the abundance of advertising and article content, as shown in Figure 7-1.

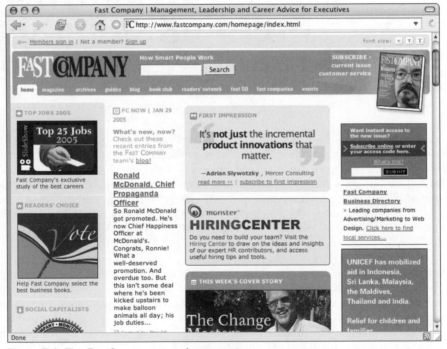

Figure 7-1: The FastCompany.com home page

Furthermore, Fast Company's nuanced design is eminently flexible. Rather than succumbing to the temptation of building a fixed-width design, FC built its site to accommodate the user's preferred window size (see Figure 7-2). However, notice how the width of the content area expands and contracts as the browser window increases or decreases—but *only up to a point*. At larger window widths, the page's layout stops expanding, thus ensuring that line lengths never reach unfriendly (and illegible) lengths.

800x600

1024x600

1280x600

Figure 7-2: The Fast Company home page, viewed at three different popular window sizes

The visual aspect of the site's design aside, however, the new site was a technical win as well. With pages that were half the weight as their `table`-heavy predecessors, the site was not only easier for Fast Company's production staff to maintain, it was also extremely kind to users' occasionally limited bandwidth. When the designers separated presentational information out of the site's markup and into external style sheets, FastCompany.com became accessible to a wider range of browsing devices that would be otherwise hindered by the site's design. These devices included not only ancient browsers and such alternative technology as assistive and handheld equipment, but also search engines.

So, all in all, the redesign was a success — for the company, for its users, and for the burgeoning CSS design community. Who, then, was responsible for it all?

Meet the Designer: Dan Cederholm

The architect behind Fast Company's high-profile redesign was Dan Cederholm, a multitalented designer, developer, and author. A vocal proponent of founding high-powered design upon CSS and XHTML, Cederholm is also the founder and author of SimpleBits (`http://simplebits.com/`), a site that serves as a home to his Boston-area Web design consultancy (`http://simplebits.com/work/`) as well as a personal journal of sorts (`http://simplebits.com/notebook/`).

While Cederholm first came into the spotlight with his one-two all-CSS redesigns of Fast Company and its sister site, Inc.com (`http://inc.com/`), he's remained prolific with such clients as Google, ESPN, and Staples. The reason is that much of Cederholm's philosophy can be summed up in one word: detail. A noted aficionado of pixel art, Cederholm's attention to even the finest points of a page's design is inspiring. Whether it's a project as expansive as Fast Company or as small as a single search results page, he creates designs that are simultaneously beautiful, meticulous, and painfully well-coded.

In the following question-and-answer session, Cederholm discusses some of his influences, his career on the Web, the impact of video games on a designer's development — all while giving us a glimpse into his creative process.

Q: *Mr. Cederholm, welcome — kindly pull up a chair.*

A: Why, thank you. Don't mind if I do.

Q: *From reading SimpleBits, one will come to know you as a man of many interests: you're a prolific writer, one-time rock musician, and an aficionado of fine black pepper. So, how is it, exactly, that you got into Web design?*

A: For me, getting into Web design was an evolutionary process. One could trace the birth back to an obsession with early video games — the ability to control colored pixels on a screen. But there are a few milestones that helped more than others, and I imagine other Web designers have similar stories.

My first Mac was the all-in-one Classic II, and it was used heavily around the time that AOL first surged in popularity just before the Web took off. I was immediately fascinated by this "online world" of chat rooms, e-mail, instant information, and so on. Soon after that, I was sitting in a desk job at a record label here in the Boston area (Rounder Records) and for the first time had the following: a constant Internet connection, access to the burgeoning World Wide Web, and a disinterest in what my actual job entailed. I was captivated by the Web — its convergence of design and information — the artistic and the functional. I loved being able to instantly capture information about my favorite bands, or the latest advancements in pepper mill technology. It was all out there.

From there, I bought a computer again for home, and studied HTML by viewing source on anything and everything — learning by trial-and-error mostly. You could say it was (and is?) an obsession to figure out how things work.

Over the years, the studying has never stopped, but it's constantly kept me interested. I think it's the combination of being able to do something creative and structured at the same time.

Q: *I understand you had something to do with the standards-based redesigns of Fast Company and its sister site, Inc.com. What was your role, exactly?*

A: I came to work at *Fast Company* magazine in 2000 as Web Production Guru (my, how I miss the job titles of the pre–dotcom boom). My position sort of evolved over the following three years into design. This was a fantastic atmosphere to tinker with and hone Web design skills — surrounded by creative and talented people that were putting out a killer magazine. It was impossible not to soak up the knowledge shared by the entire team.

In early 2003, we began the long process of redesigning both the Fast Company and Inc. sites using Web standards.

Q: *Well, tell us a bit about the redesign. As one of the earliest high-profile sites to adopt an all-CSS design, FC set the bar pretty high for the rest of us. What prompted the switch to style sheets?*

A: Around the same time that I had been experimenting with CSS-based layouts on my personal sites for a while, we had been planning the redesigns of FC and Inc. to also coincide with a new, homegrown CMS. I had the desire to move the sites to Web standards, but it wasn't until Wired News relaunched using a 100 percent CSS-based layout that we started thinking of that as a reality. Wired paved the way for other commercial sites to follow.

The reasoning for the switch was fast becoming obvious. The decreased code would speed up our sites, increase accessibility, make it easier to accommodate different advertising units, and make it easier to integrate into our new CMS. The CSS-based layout would also make it easier to integrate partner sites, change the look-and-feel at the flip of a switch, and so on.

Q: *How did you approach the move within the company? There must have been a fair amount of selling to do.*

For more information about the Wired News redesign, see `http://stopdesign.com/portfolio/web_interface/wired_news.html`.

A: I have to admit, I had it rather easy. The convincing was a matter of walking over to Rob Roesler's (the site's director) desk, showing him the Wired News redesign and saying "I've been experimenting with this stuff — we need to do this." And his response of, "Yes. We definitely need to do this," sealed the deal. We have Wired to thank for blazing the trail for other commercial publications.

Not every team is going to have that kind of support. The rest of the Web team at the time also got behind the switch to standards. For instance, when our developers David Searson and Bob Joyal saw how simple the template structure could be by using CSS for the site's design, they immediately recognized the advantage this would have from an application and development point of view.

Sometimes it takes showing, rather than explaining. But I think as more and more sites are utilizing CSS, it's only getting easier to sell the technology to clients and internal Web teams. It will soon, we hope, become commonplace and assumed.

Q: *In a time when most sites were adopting rather straightforward fixed-width layouts as they bootstrapped themselves with CSS skills, Fast Company chose to go with a flexible approach. What drove that decision?*

A: The decision to go flexible hinged on a few different things. Probably the main reason was the large advertisement that was required to "float" inside the article body text. At a resolution of 800×600, this particular unit would scrunch up the article's text to an almost unreadable line length. But this advertisement also paid the bills — it was a requirement that we had to work around. So, going with a flexible-width layout meant that users with a higher screen resolution could adjust the window to a more readable size. We at least wanted the option to be there for a portion of our audience.

But going flexible also meant a certain level of design constraint. We had to account for the fact the window could be any size at any time — and that can be challenging when designing.

Q: *Are there any aspects of the site's design that you're most proud of?*

A: I'm proud of the image-based tab navigation that I built for the site after the redesign was complete. I really just combined a few CSS techniques that were being invented at the time — but the result was a navigation system that used semantic markup [an unordered list], yet was image-based in order to fit a large number of options in a fixed horizontal space.

I'm also proud of the lengths we took to make things easy to change and update later on. For instance, the little icons that sit next to the site's headings are transparent, and the color filled in with CSS. Changing the color palette of the entire site was as easy as changing a few lines of code.

Related to that, I guess I'm most proud that the site has stood the test of time. It certainly was never perfect, and there are many things I would do differently if redesigned today — but the fact that the core design has been used so long [as of this writing] is a testament that it was a success.

Q: *What about second thoughts? After a few years, are there any things you wish you'd done differently?*

A: Oh, I'm sure there are *many* things I wish I had done differently. I was still learning CSS during the redesign of Fast Company, and while there were others generously sharing their knowledge and experience at the time, far more knowledge is out there *now*. For instance, the accessibility concerns regarding image replacement techniques weren't documented at the time. New ways to combat IE bugs weren't invented yet. I'm sure many, many things could've been simplified from a CSS and markup angle.

But it's a constant learning experience. Even the sites I build today, I'm sure I'll want to change down the road. The ebb and flow of the Web is what makes it interesting and fun.

Q: *Speaking more generally, so what is it that keeps you interested in Web design? What keeps you fired up after all these years?*

A: Well, I think that constant ebb and flow I just mentioned is part of it. I love how there's always something new happening — a new technique to learn, a new technology to explore. It seems to never settle. The flip side is that it can be frustratingly unstable. It's the balance in between that's the sweet spot.

I also love Web design because of its marriage of art and technology. I have a certain need to create things — anything. Music, food, photography, and so on, and Web design seems like a natural way to combine all of these creative impulses together. It's a creative outlet as well as a technical one.

The work of colleagues also keeps me fired up—being motivated by what others are doing, learning from their experiences, the sharing of knowledge—it's always been a wonderful give-and-take community.

Q: *You must have some design influences; care to drop a few names?*

A: I think design-wise, my influences are less *people,* than what I see and experience every day. Early on, I was influenced by the music packaging of indie bands, and later by the stellar design of *Fast Company* magazine and its designers. But I feel that even walking through the supermarket has an influence on design. Even if it just makes me think of what I like and what I don't like. Traveling also is a big influence—I love seeing architecture, signage, and packaging from different parts of the U.S. and abroad. Just looking at anything visual has an impact on me.

Having no *formal* design training, I can confess that at times I feel like I just get lucky if something comes out right. I tend to design from the gut, based on the experiences and environments I've soaked in.

As far as inspiration, however, there are plenty of Web designers whose work I admire. This tends to motivate me, get me excited about design. People like Douglas Bowman, Todd Dominey, Dave Shea, and Jeffrey Zeldman, whose work speaks for itself.

Q: *So, what about your own design process? How do you usually work?*

A: I usually start with a blank Photoshop canvas. I use Photoshop like a sketchpad, working out color palettes and dimensions. From there, I usually code certain page components, screen grab them, and bring them back into the Photoshop file. So, a combination of code and graphics editing takes me to the "mock-up" phase. When the client is happy, I begin pulling it apart.

It's worked for me thus far—but it's the only way I know. I've been thinking lately about ways in which I can streamline the process. For instance, I'm usually left with 100 Photoshop layers—unlabeled—to wade through. Making changes after the fact is a large problem.

There are times when I've tried coding first, and then designing something completely with CSS. I haven't had as much luck going this route. I believe that if you're aware of what you can do with CSS and what you can't, then sketching in Photoshop (or on paper) is perfectly fine. One must keep in mind how all the pieces will eventually fit together on top of an optimal markup structure.

Q: *We've all faced it: You're under a tight deadline, the client wants a quick status update, and you've a blank Photoshop canvas that's not being very cooperative. Ever been stuck with designer's block? How do you get out of it?*

A: Oh yeah. This is a tough one—and one that every designer has probably run into. I'm a little hesitant to recommend the consumption of alcoholic beverages, but lately, a glass of red wine has been my savior. Especially when designing into the evening hours. It clears my mind, helps me to concentrate more. I can't explain it, but it works.

Also, I go for a walk. This helps immensely. Coming back, even after a half hour, can help you gain a new perspective on what you need to accomplish.

Another idea I've tried, if the visuals just aren't working, is to start working on the markup structure instead. Start applying some base CSS, and it can start to take shape, in a very basic, but functional, way.

CSS Positioning: The Fundamentals

Before we can begin replicating Fast Company's layout, we should first step back and examine some of the mechanics behind CSS positioning. As we've seen in previous chapters, every element in your markup occupies a position within the document's flow. *Block-level elements* — such as headings, `div`s, lists, and paragraphs — are stacked like boxes atop each other, each expanding horizontally to occupy the full width of their containing element. On the other hand, *inline elements* are laid out horizontally within a containing block-level element, one after another. Some examples of inline elements include links, images, and phrase elements such as `em` and `strong`.

Initially, each element in your unstyled document is considered to have a "static" position — in other words, its position has not been modified from its default. That's why that paragraph is placed directly beneath that `h2`, and why that image appears within that `div`.

The official term for this default positioning scheme is the "normal flow" of the document. If we look at an unstyled HTML document, we see that boxes elements (such as `p`, `h1`, or `div`) "flow" vertically within their containing block, each stacked immediately below the preceding one. However, inline boxes (such as `span`, `a`, or `img`) will simply flow horizontally within their container. And without any additional style rules from us, this default flow will remain intact.

But, of course, we're about to change all that. We're nothing if not predictable.

What makes CSS such a compelling layout tool is its ability to override these default positioning rules, and create incredibly complex layouts without opening a single `td`. An element can be removed from its normal, static position by writing a simple CSS selector that sets a new value for — you guessed it — the element's `position` property, like so:

```
p {
    position: absolute;
}
```

Besides `static`, there are three valid values for this `position` property:

- ❏ `fixed`
- ❏ `relative`
- ❏ `absolute`

Setting the property to any of the three non-`static` values will give us different means of removing the element from its place in the normal document flow, and positioning it in a different section of the document. The mechanism at the heart of Fast Company's three-column layout uses a combination of the latter two — relative and absolute positioning. Let's examine these two property values and the relationship between them, and how we can better apply them to our own sites' designs.

Absolutely Fabulous Positioning

When absolutely positioned, an element's position is specified through some combination of `top`, `right`, `bottom`, and `left` properties, as we see here:

```
div#content {
    position: absolute;
    left: 10px;
    top: 100px;
}
```

Here, the `left` and `top` properties specify offsets for the `div` with an `id` attribute of "content." Rather than appearing sandwiched between the block-level elements immediately before and after it in the markup, the content `div` is instead removed from the document flow. But *where* is it placed, you ask?

To find an answer, let's look at the following markup structure which, for the sake of brevity, we'll assume is placed within the `body` of a valid XHTML document:

```
<div id="outer">
    <p>This is a paragraph in the <cite>outer</cite> block.</p>

    <div id="inner">
        <p>This is a paragraph in the <cite>inner</cite> block.</p>
    </div>
</div>
```

These are two rather unassuming `div`s, one (with an `id` of "inner") nested inside the other (named, cleverly enough, "outer"). Each `div` contains one child paragraph—nothing award-winning here, we're sure. Just to move this beyond the realm of angle brackets and into a screenshot or two, let's apply some basic style to this markup:

```
#outer {
    background: #DDF;
    border: 4px solid #006;
    height: 300px;
    margin: 120px 20px 0;
}

#inner {
    background: #FDC;
    border: 4px solid #930;
}
```

Again, these two selectors aren't designed to floor our clients. The first rule applies to the `div` with an `id` of "outer." We're setting an oh-so-comely blue border and background to the `div`, setting its height to 300 pixels, and then increasing its margins to offset it from its normal position (120 pixels down, and 20 pixels on either horizontal side). The second rule simply applies a light red background color and matching border to the `inner` div.

Yes, that's right: red on blue. We never said we were discriminating when tossing together code examples.

But before you slam this book shut in a fit of palette-driven indignation, let's examine how these two elements appear on the page. As you can see in Figure 7-3, we've taken the liberty of applying some basic type information to our document as well (Times New Roman is *so* 1995). But with our (somewhat garish, we'll admit) colors and borders activated, we can see that the two divs are placed in the normal document flow—the inner block is a child of the outer block, and the page's current display reflects that.

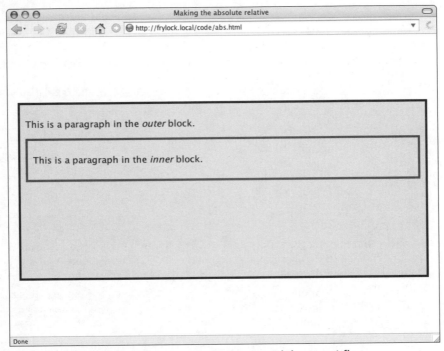

Figure 7-3: Our bland-looking elements in the normal document flow

However, by using CSS to change the value of the inner element's position property, our design doesn't *have* to be reflect this parent-child relationship. We can add three brief lines to our #inner selector:

```
#inner {
    background: #FDC;
    border: 4px solid #930;
    position: absolute;
    right: 20px;
    top: 20px;
}
```

The difference is rather marked, as Figure 7-4 shows. We've visually broken the parent-child relationship between the two divs. While the inner block is still a child of the outer one in the markup, we've used CSS to override the former's position in the normal document flow. Instead, we've positioned it absolutely, offsetting it 20 pixels from the topmost and rightmost edges of the body of our document.

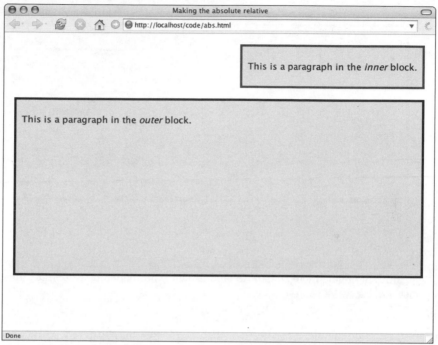

Figure 7-4: In the markup, the topmost block is a child of the bottom one. However, using position: absolute; removes the block from the document flow and positions it relative to the viewport.

The inner block typically appears in the normal flow of the document, in the context established by the other block-level elements that surround it in the markup. Our rule has *redefined* that context, and placed it in one that is relative to the boundaries of the browser window. This is why the body root of our document — the html element — is also known as the *initial containing block*, as it typically provides the positioning context for all elements contained within it.

Furthermore, this new positioning context for #inner has redefined that of its child elements — namely, the paragraph contained therein. In other words, we've not only repositioned the div, but any and all elements contained therein. This becomes a bit more apparent if we add a few more paragraphs to our absolutely positioned block, as we see in Figure 7-5.

When two new paragraphs are added to #inner (our absolutely positioned block), they inherit their parent's positioning context — which is all a fancy way of saying that since their parent block is absolutely positioned, it will expand to contain its new children.

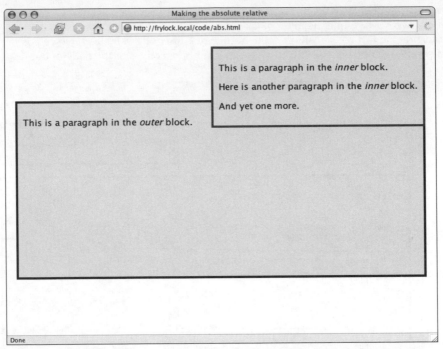

Figure 7-5: Adding more content to our absolutely positioned block demonstrates just how far we've come.

Another important thing to note in Figure 7-5 is that after increasing the height of our absolutely positioned block, the outer block is partially obscured. Remember that by applying `position` to the block, we've removed it from the normal flow — and in the case of absolutely positioned elements, the browser doesn't reserve any space for it within the document. Because of this, absolutely positioned elements are designed to overlap other elements on the page, be they positioned or not. This is a very important issue to consider when building a layout with absolute positioning, and one we'll return to later in greater detail.

Positioning That's Absolutely Relative

But what if we want to exercise a bit more control over the position of that inner block? What if we don't want to position it relative to the `browser window`, but to the outer `div`? As it turns out, the absolute positioning we've seen so far is only the *default* behavior. If an absolutely positioned element isn't placed within another positioned element — that is, if all of its ancestor elements are in their default, static position — then it will be placed as our example is in Figure 7-4: relative to the boundaries established by the initial containing block, the `body` element.

If you noticed that the last sentence contained quite a few "if"s," we're happy we haven't put everyone to sleep. So, if our absolutely positioned element *is* contained within another positioned element, what happens then? Let's see what happens when we apply this bit of logic to the outer `div`, which, as we determined previously, is the parent to our absolutely positioned element:

```
Done--em.#outer {
     background: #DDF;
     border: 4px solid #006;
     height: 300px;
     margin: 120px 20px 0;
     position: relative;
}
```

As shown in Figure 7-6, the changes to our inner div are quite striking. Because the outermost div is now a positioned element, it establishes a new positioning context for all absolutely positioned descendant elements — in this case, the #inner block. So, the offset of right: 20px; and top: 20px; no longer position the inner div in relation to the root of our markup, but to the container div to which we applied the position: relative; rule. Just to hammer the point home, let's change the top: 20px; in our #inner selector to bottom: 20px;, like so (see Figure 7-7):

```
#inner {
     background: #FDC;
     border: 4px solid #930;
     position: absolute;
     right: 20px;
     bottom: 20px;
}
```

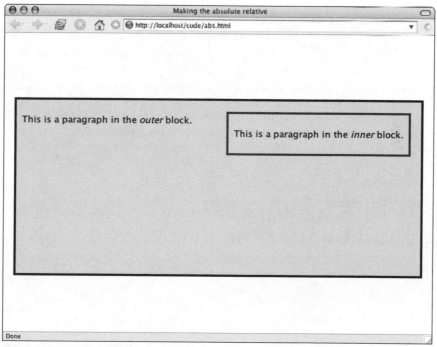

Figure 7-6: By setting the outer block to position: relative; the inner block is now positioned in relation to its parent.

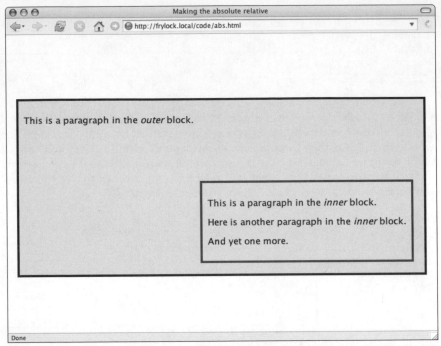

Figure 7-7: Courtesy of CSS: bulletproof bottom-edge positioning. Ain't technology grand?

Rather than creating a vertical offset between the inner box's top edge and that of its parent, we've instead positioned it 20 pixels from the bottom—all by changing one line in our selector. As we continue through this chapter, we'll discuss the benefits of this approach in more detail. For now, this relationship between absolutely positioned elements within relatively positioned containers will serve as the basis for our work creating a flexible, three-column layout in the style of FastCompany.com.

Building Three Columns: Laying the Foundation

Just as when we converted the Harvard University home page to an all-CSS/XHTML layout (see Chapter 2), our three-column layout must be founded upon lightweight, well-meaning markup. To do so, we begin by taking a quick inventory of the content areas on the page (see Figure 7-8).

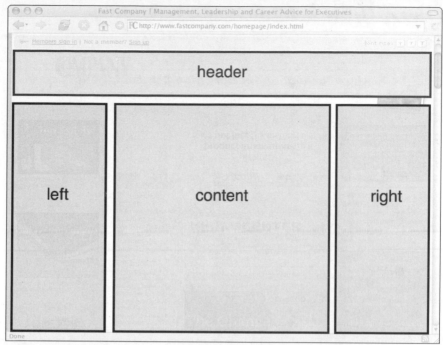

Figure 7-8: Identifying the areas of content we'll need to incorporate into our markup. (The footer's not shown because of the length of the page.)

For the purposes of this chapter, we'll focus on the primary areas of the home page's layout:

- ❑ The horizontal header that spans the top of the page

- ❑ The primary center column, which contains high-priority content and other features of interest

- ❑ The left- and right-hand columns, which house such auxiliary content as subnavigation, advertising banners, and the like

Think of each of these top-level blocks as a container for other content—which is, in fact, exactly how FastCompany.com uses them. Within each block, we can store other discrete chunks of content, and apply CSS rules to precisely control the presentation of each.

Establishing this flexible, three-column layout is the primary goal of this chapter. Once that has been established, we can style the finer points of the design to our heart's delight. Therefore, we'll focus on establishing this layout framework—of header, content, left- and right-hand columns—to prepare our page for a truly professional-looking design.

Writing the XHTML: From Mockup to Markup

With this in mind, let's create a basic markup document to reflect this framework, as shown in Listing 7-1.

Listing 7-1: The Markup Foundation for Our Three-Column Layout

```
<!DOCTYPE html PUBLIC "-//W3C//DTD XHTML 1.0 Transitional//EN"
    "http://www.w3.org/TR/xhtml1/DTD/xhtml1-transitional.dtd">
<html xmlns="http://www.w3.org/1999/xhtml">
<head>
<title>My 3-column layout</title>
<meta http-equiv="Content-Type" content="text/html; charset=utf-8" />
</head>
<body>
<div id="header">
  <p>How do you like them apples?</p>
  <hr />
</div>
<div id="left">
  <h2>This is the left column.</h2>
  <p>Some basic information goes here.</p>
  <!-- More content here -->
</div>
<div id="right">
  <h2>This is the right column.</h2>
  <ul>
    <li>Did you know that lists rock?</li>
    <li>They do.</li>
    <li>Quite a bit.</li>
  </ul>
  <!-- More content here -->
</div>
<div id="content">
  <h1>Welcome to my page layout.</h1>
  <p>Certe, inquam, pertinax non ero tibique, si mihi probabis ea...</p>
  <!-- More content here -->
</div>
<div id="footer">
  <hr />
  <p>Them apples were <em>tasty</em>.</p>
</div>
</body>
</html>
```

Reflecting the three areas of our content inventory in Figure 7-8, we've simply marked up the four divisions in our page as such—that is to say, by using the div element. Each of those divs has been given a unique id, which in turn corresponds to the section of the document it represents: the first div is "header," the next "left," and so on. We've also taken the liberty of including a "footer" block at the bottom of the page.

The ids used in our sample markup here (and throughout the rest of the chapter) are from the markup used on the Fast Company site. While their pages were built nearly two years ago, recent thinking suggests it's best to avoid "presentational names" such as these. By naming our elements according to how they might look, or where they might be positioned on-screen, we're effectively wedding our markup to one particular presentation. Should we ever redesign our site, what happens when our `#left div` suddenly is displayed on the right of the page? Or on the top?

Instead, we should consider the meaning of the content contained in our elements, and name those elements accordingly. Perhaps `#right` would be better described as `#advertising`, or `#left` as `#subnav`. There are no right answers here; instead, we should make our names as descriptive as possible, ensuring an even cleaner separation of structure from style.

Within each section of the page, we've settled on some simple (and admittedly, pretty arbitrary) content to serve as placeholders. However, even when coding gibberish, we try to keep our code well-meaning: the most important header on the page has been tagged with an `h1`, the titles of the left and right columns have been accorded a place next in line with `h2`, and the remainder of the page's text has been marked up with proper list and paragraph elements. Without any style rules, our markup looks pretty unimpressive indeed (see Figure 7-9).

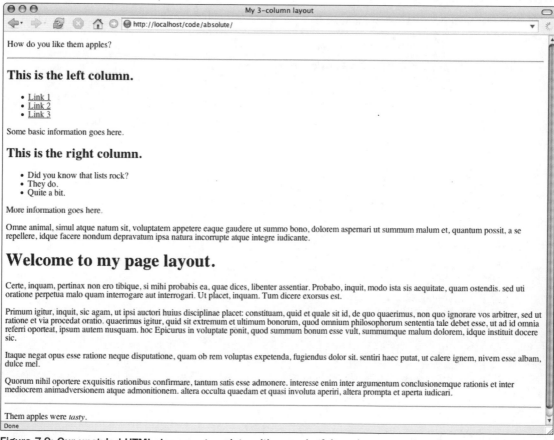

Figure 7-9: Our unstyled HTML document, replete with meaningful markup . . . and, well, meaningless text

It's at this stage that the need for well-meaning, semantically rich markup becomes a bit more evident. When using style sheets to control your site's presentation, it's important to consider exactly how users will access your content if they don't have a CSS-aware browser. When presented with a page that looks like the one in Figure 7-9, users might not be presented with your meticulously planned design. However, they will *still be able to access your site's content*; hence our use of horizontal rules (hr elements) in the header and footer divs. While we'll use CSS later to hide these elements in our design, these elements can provide a nice break in the content for users on legacy, CSS-blind browsers.

For a bit more detail, take the two levels of heading elements we've used in our markup. Sighted users surfing *sans* CSS will be able to quickly tell that "Welcome to my page layout" is weighted with more importance than the titles of our side columns. Screen readers will announce at what level the header has been marked up, which will enable non-sighted users to quickly orient themselves in the page's hierarchy. And, as accessibility advocates are quick to point out, the biggest blind user on the Web is Google — which is a trite way of saying that search engines don't care about presentation, but content. Applying this kind of intelligent markup to your content not only helps human users navigate your pages, but helps search engines better understand how they should weight and index them.

A Layer of Style

With that little digression out of the way, let's apply some basic presentational rules to our content, as shown in Listing 7-2.

Listing 7-2: Applying Basic CSS Rules to Our Document

```
body {
     color: #000;
     font: 76%/1.5em "Lucida Grande", Verdana, Geneva, Helvetica, sans-serif;
     margin: 0;
     padding: 0;
}

h1, h2 {
     font-family: "Trebuchet MS", Verdana, Geneva, Helvetica, sans-serif;
     font-weight: normal;
     line-height: 1em;
     margin-top: 0;
}

#header {
     background-color: #DFD;
     border: 2px solid #060;
}

#footer {
     background-color: #FDD;
     border: 1px solid #C00;
}

#left, #right {
     background-color: #DDF;
     border: 2px solid #00C;
}
```

```
#header hr, #footer hr {
    display: none;
}
```

The first rule applies some basic color and type information to the `body` element, information that is inherited from each of its descendant elements in the document tree — that is, until we override it in the second rule. By applying a different `font-family` value to the header elements in our document (`h1` and `h2`), we can override the inheritance and apply a different style than the default. This should, we hope, give them a bit more visual prominence in our rough-cut design.

The next three rules apply borders and background colors to the main sections of our document: a bright green for our header, an eye-catching red for the footer block, and a striking blue for the left- and right-hand columns. We're going for contrast here, not panache — and as you can see from Figure 7-10, that's exactly what we have.

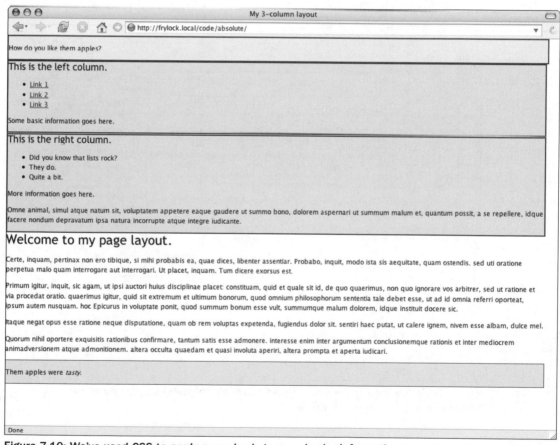

Figure 7-10: We've used CSS to apply some basic type and color information to our bare bones HTML document.

Get Our Offset On: Introducing Our Positioning Rules

With a clearer understanding of where the boundaries of our different content elements lie, let's now begin to flesh out the layout (see Figure 7-11):

```
#left {
    position: absolute;
    left: 0;
    top: 0;
    width: 175px;
}

#right {
    position: absolute;
    right: 0;
    top: 0;
    width: 175px;
}
```

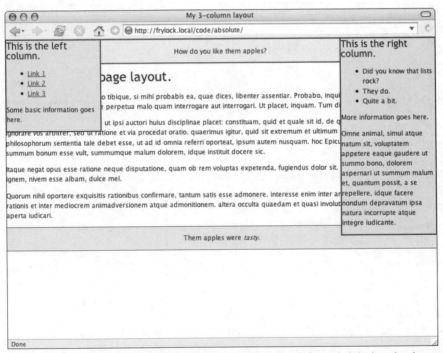

Figure 7-11: Absolute positioning allows us to place the left- and right-hand columns — however, we're not out of the woods yet.

These two selectors move the left and right blocks out of the normal document flow, and position them absolutely. Each `div` has been given an explicit width of 175 pixels, and is then catapulted to the top of the window (`top: 0;`). The horizontal offsets we've specified (`left: 0;` for #left, and `right: 0;` for

—you guessed it—#right) further complete the effect, and create the beginning of our three-column layout. The "left" and "right" blocks begin to live up to their names, and columns begin to take shape.

But, as you can see, the layout is far from complete. The left- and right-hand columns overlap the header, footer, and content divs. By applying absolute positioning to these two blocks, we've completely removed them from the normal document flow. This means that, while we've been able to place them with pixel-perfect precision, the other elements in the document flow no longer need to reserve space for them. To get our layout up and running, we'll need to take a few extra steps.

Remembering to Keep It Absolutely Relative

As we begin to puzzle through this issue, it's helpful to remember that the only reason the two blocks are positioned relative to the html element is that *they aren't descendants of a positioned element*. What happens if we change that?

In Listing 7-3, let's wrap the three non-header blocks in a div titled "container."

Listing 7-3: Applying a container to Our Markup

```
<div id="header">
  <p>How do you like them apples?</p>
  <hr />
</div>
<div id="container">
  <div id="left">
    <h2>This is the left column.</h2>
    <!-- More content here -->
  </div>
  <div id="right">
    <h2>This is the right column.</h2>
    <!-- More content here -->
  </div>
  <div id="content">
    <h1>Welcome to my page layout.</h1>
    <!-- More content here -->
  </div>
</div>
<div id="footer">
  <hr />
  <p>Them apples were <em>tasty</em>.</p>
</div>
```

Granted, this container doesn't add much to the document's overall semantic worth—it's what markup purists might term a *presentational hack*, an element added for the sole and simple reason of achieving some goal in our design. But with this container div in place, we can apply a three-line CSS selector upon it that will restore some measure of sanity to our site's layout (see Figure 7-12):

```
#container {
  position: relative;
}
```

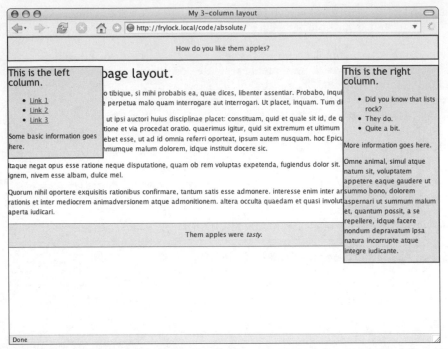

Figure 7-12: With position: relative; applied to our new container block, the left- and right-hand columns' top edges are now contained within their parent. But what about our page's content?

Because the container `div` can now be considered a positioned element, it establishes a new context for all of the positioned elements that descend from it—you guessed it, the left and right column blocks. The left, top, and right offsets are no longer relative to the dimensions of the `html` element, but of the container `div`. This means that as the container element expands and grows horizontally, the left and right blocks will reposition themselves to suit. If, say, the vertical size of the header block increases (see Figure 7-13), then the new horizontal position of the container `div` will be reflected in its absolutely positioned children.

But, while we've made the header visible once again, the bulk of our page is still unreadable. The content and footer still must be "saved" from their absolutely positioned brethren. Given that the content area needs to be flexible, how exactly do we do that?

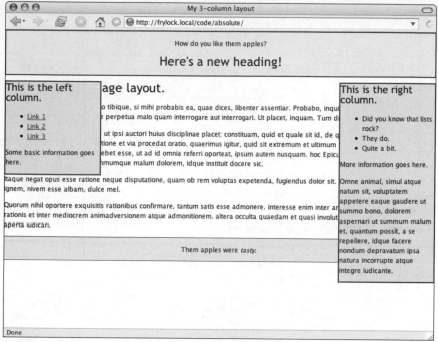

Figure 7-13: We can edit the content before the container without breaking our nascent layout.

Thankfully, we don't need to resort to any more fancy positioning footwork. Since we know the width of each of the side columns is a fixed 175 pixels, we can use the box model to escape our content block, like so:

```
#content {
    margin: 0 190px;
}
```

Here, we've settled upon 190 pixels for the two horizontal margin values: 175 pixels for the width of a side column, plus a healthy 15 pixels of white space. By applying these margins to the left- and right-hand sides of the inner block, the calculated width of the block is compressed and fits nicely within the visible space between the two sidebar columns (see Figure 7-14).

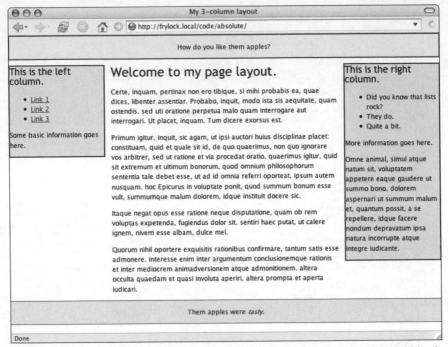

Figure 7-14: By adding padding to the content div that corresponds to the width of the flanking side columns, we can create the illusion of a middle column distinct from those on either side.

If we temporarily remove the columns from our markup (or hide them with CSS), we can better see what's at play here (see Figure 7-15). While the dimensions of the content block aren't affected by the two side divs (and vice versa), we've used CSS to create the illusion that it does. Any changes to the width of the window will cause the entire page's contents to reposition themselves.

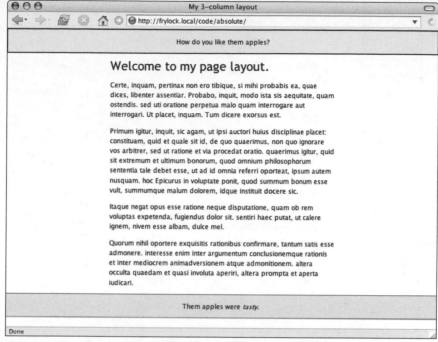

Figure 7-15: Let's temporarily delete the left- and right-hand columns from our markup to see how the margins affect the content div.

Sadly, we're not nearly as done as Figure 7-14 might lead us to believe. While we've gained quite a bit of mastery over the top-edge and horizontal positioning of our page's layout, the footer we've created is in a bit of a precarious spot. While our sidebar elements are *positioned* relative to the container div, they aren't *sized* relative to it. If their height exceeds that of their container, bad things can easily happen to elements that appear beneath them in the design. Figure 7-16 shows this in action. By adding a few additional paragraphs to the right-hand block, the footer quickly becomes obscured again.

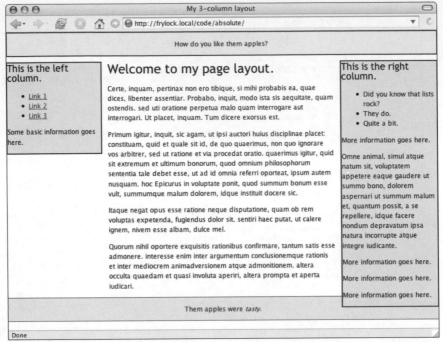

Figure 7-16: Adding a few additional paragraphs causes an overlap between the absolutely positioned column and the static element that succeeds it.

As we've seen before, elements in the regular document flow (such as the header, content, and footer blocks) obey a different positioning context than absolutely positioned elements, and vice versa. This is what causes the overlap we first saw in the header and content blocks, and that we're faced with again on the footer. Thankfully, we can apply the same logic used on the content block. With our understanding of the box model, we can define margins around the footer `div`, once again creating the illusion that the middle "column" exists independently of those on either side of it.

So, in some fashion, we must apply the same 190-pixel-wide margins to both horizontal sides of the footer `div`. With the rest of our layout in place, we have two options:

❑ Write a new CSS selector that applies margins to the footer element.

❑ In the markup, move the footer `div` into the content block. This will then effectively contain the footer within its own calculated width.

Either solution will have the same effect — whether the margins are applied to the footer `div` itself or a container, the effect will be the same (see Figure 7-17). The footer will always appear *between* the two sidebars, if not always below them. This is a problem that even Fast Company is forced to reckon with, as we can see from Figure 7-18.

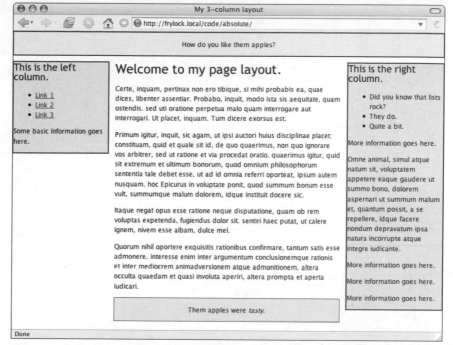

Figure 7-17: By applying the same margins to the footer div, we create the illusion of "escaping" it from the absolutely positioned elements that overlap it.

To prevent any overlap from the absolutely positioned sidebars, Fast Company opted to place the footer `div` within the main content block. However, when the height of the sidebar columns exceeds the height of the central column, the footer will appear significantly higher than the bottom of the page.

This is a serious shortcoming of the absolute positioning model. An absolutely positioned element can be removed from the document flow and placed with uncanny position on the page, true — but what severely limits absolute positioning as a design tool is its blindness to the context of elements surrounding each positioned element. Absolutely positioned elements can overlap not only non-positioned elements, but other `position: absolute;`–enabled blocks as well. This is why many CSS designers rely more heavily on the `float` model to control their layouts.

There are, in fact, non-CSS solutions to the "bottom blindness" of the absolute positioning model. Shaun Inman, a well-known Web designer and developer, wrote some rather elegant JavaScript (www.shauninman.com/mentary/past/absolutely_positive.php) to automatically clean up any overlap that resulted from absolute positioning.

Of course, any workarounds (CSS, markup, or otherwise) should be thoroughly tested before they're applied to our sites. While they may address the issue at hand, they add an additional layer of support and maintenance to which we should be prepared to commit.

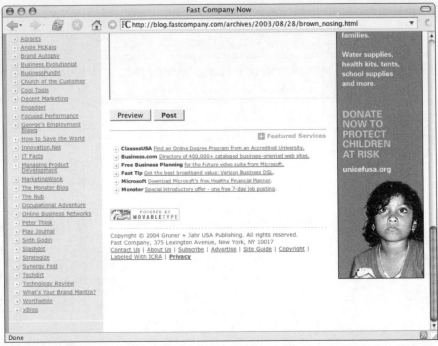

Figure 7-18: On this page, the height of the two sidebar columns is greater than that of the central content area. As a result, the "footer" no longer appears at the bottom of the page.

Battling Browser Bugs

Where are we now? Well, our layout's looking sharp in our browser of choice, the markup is valid, and our style sheet is selecting with ninja-like precision. So, naturally, our design is looking perfect in all browsers known to humanity, right? Right?

If we honestly believed that, we'd be riding the slow boat to Depressionville more than we care to think about. While contemporary browsers *do* enjoy rich support for cascading style sheets, the level of support between them varies quite drastically—as we like to say, all browsers are created unequal. Unfortunately, valid code does not equal a perfect display across today's browser landscape. Because of the small army of bugs each browser brings to the table, we must thoroughly test our code across the board. And, more often than not, we must introduce browser-specific hacks to ensure that our design displays as intended for all members of our audience.

Let's take a look at two bugs in our layout and investigate some workarounds.

Macintosh Internet Explorer 5

Upon opening our three-column layout in Internet Explorer 5 for the Macintosh, all seems to be displaying just fine — that is, until you notice the very bottom of the browser window (see Figure 7-19). To fix this little hiccup, let's see if we can't *isolate* the bug. Because we've validated our style sheet and our markup, we can eliminate invalid code as the issue. From there, we'll triage our troubleshooting approach: first, we'll try editing parts of the markup to see if we can restrict the issue to one particular section. From there, we'll see if editing style rules applied to that section of the document resolves the bug. Once we've established *what* is causing the bug, we can better create and apply a patch to fix it.

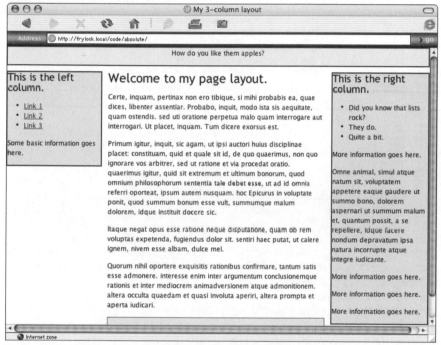

Figure 7-19: How'd that horizontal scroll bar get there?

Appendix D has some other great tips for working through browser-related issues.

With this process firmly in mind, let's see if we can't isolate the bug in the markup. Since the issue is occurring on the right-hand side of the page, perhaps that's a good place to start. If we temporarily remove the entire "right" `div` from the markup and reload the page, then our suspicions are confirmed: the horizontal scroll bar is gone! Removing the rightmost column establishes that it was at the heart of our scroll bar bug (see Figure 7-20). But now that we know the *where* of the bug, how do we determine exactly *what* is causing it? And more important, how do we fix it?

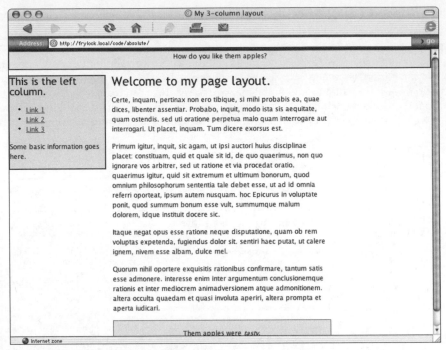

Figure 7-20: When in doubt, delete.

What follows is an occasionally frustrating goulash of coding, deleting, Web searching, and testing. Because each browser has its own set of idiosyncrasies, it can be frustrating to encounter each for the first time. Once you gain more experience with these bugs and how to work around them, the debugging process becomes much less time-intensive — and less frustrating as well. Until browsers have more uniform support for Web standards, however, such testing phases are going to be a fixture in any design project for some time to come. We're compelled to guess we'll be waiting for that until a certain place freezes over, but the eternal optimist must press on.

After a bit of experimentation, we hit on a small breakthrough. Changing the value of the `right` property can make the scroll bar disappear. Specifically, anything greater than or equal to 15 pixels will fix the bug; anything less, and we're scrolling until the cows come home. But applying this fix isn't an ideal one, as our layout doesn't exactly look perfect (see Figure 7-21).

So, while we've removed the scroll bar, the right-hand column is no longer flush against the edge of the window. If possible, we should fix this. Let's take a look at what we've established so far:

1. Even though we have no margin set on the right `div`, IE5/Mac seems compelled to supply a "hidden" margin of 15 pixels.

2. Therefore, IE5/Mac sees `margin-right: 0;` as `margin-right: 15px;`.

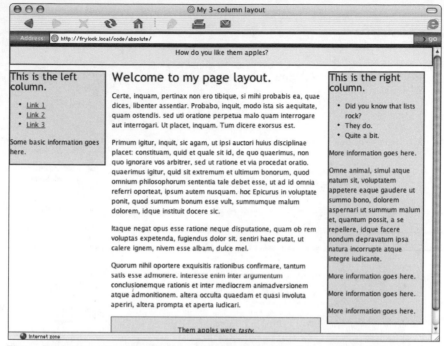

Figure 7-21: Changing the right property of our #right selector to 15 pixels removes the scroll bar, but the positioning is a bit off.

From this, wouldn't `margin-right: 15px;` translate to `margin-right: 0;` in IE5/Mac-speak? Let's try editing our #right selector:

```
#right {
    position: absolute;
    right: 0;
    top: 0;
    width: 175px;
}
```

Now, let's see if we can't apply some IE-friendly fuzzy math:

```
#right {
    position: absolute;
    margin-right: =15px;
    right: 15px;
    top: 0;
    width: 175px;
}
```

Let's reload and see what happens (see Figure 7-22).

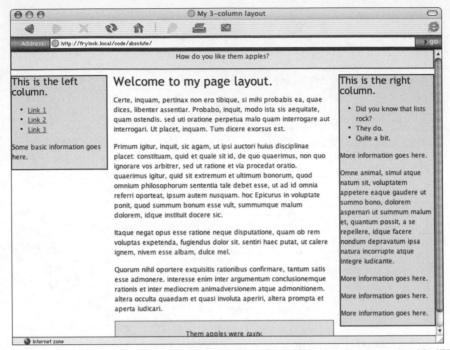

Figure 7-22: With our hack applied, the horizontal scroll bar has been removed in IE5/Mac.

Voilà! With our workaround in place, things are looking sexy once again. By catering to IE5/Mac's rendering quirk, we've restored order to that browser.

Furthermore, initial tests seem to indicate that these two new lines don't have any adverse effects on more well-behaved browsers. However, just to be safe, we can easily isolate the "hack" from the real rule:

```
#right {
    position: absolute;
    top: 0;
    right: 0;
    width: 175px;
}
```

```
/*\*//*/
#right {
    margin-right: =15px;
    right: 15px;
}
/**/
```

The first rule is our original `#right` selector that we've been using throughout the chapter; the second rule contains the one-two property values that iron out the display issue in IE5/Mac. Surrounding that second rule, however, is the IE5/Mac Band Pass Filter (see Chapter 2 for more information). This odd-looking sequence of characters makes the second rule invisible to all user agents *but* IE5/Mac, ensuring that all of the browsers that get the math right won't be affected by a browser-specific hack.

One bug down, one to go — let's move on.

As mentioned in Chapter 2, you can create separate browser-specific style sheets, each containing a host of hacks for that browser's idiosyncrasies. The benefit to (and details of) this approach is discussed in detail in that chapter, but suffice it to say that it leaves your core CSS files free of hacks — and as a result, easier to maintain.

Windows Internet Explorer 5.x+

As Figure 7-23 shows, opening our test page in any of the Windows versions of Internet Explorer — 5.0, 5.5, or 6.0 — left much to be desired.

Having just fixed a bug with the `#right` block, we're now faced with the exact opposite problem! Well, almost. Rather than being flush to the leftmost edge of the window, the left-hand column seems to be stuck inside the content block. After going through some of the steps outlined in our IE5/Mac debugging session — delete/revise the markup, tweak the CSS — nothing seems to work.

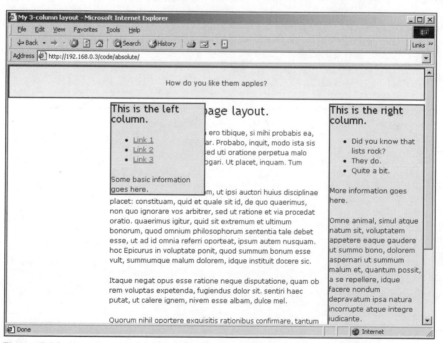

Figure 7-23: Now that ain't right — or more specifically, that ain't *left*.

Thankfully, a quick search online yields some information about a known IE/Win bug. When dealing with a box without stated dimension (as we are with the container `div`), IE/Win has some trouble initially drawing the box in such a way to sufficiently contain its descendant elements. To work around the issue, we must tell IE/Win that, "Yes, the box does indeed have a stated dimension—and if it isn't too much trouble, we'd like it to draw it *properly*."

To that end, an IE-specific workaround known as *The Holly Hack* (`http://positioniseverything .net/articles/hollyhack.html`) comes to the rescue:

```
/* hide from Mac IE5 \*/
* html #container {
    height: 1%;
}
/* END hide from Mac IE5 */
```

Named after its creator, Holly Bergevin, the Holly Hack is in fact two hacks in one. The backslash at the end of the first comment is a hack that causes IE5/Mac to ignore everything up to the second closing comment line. The selector in the second begins with a universal selector (*), followed by `html`, which is in turn followed by a selector for the problematic element—here, the container `div`. As it turns out, IE browsers on both the Windows and Macintosh operating systems recognize an invisible element wrapped around the `<html>` element. Known as the *Star HTML Hack*, the use of the universal selector before the `html` selector will work only in IE browsers. Therefore, because IE5/Mac isn't affected by this particular layout bug, we've used the comment hack in the first line to hide the rule from that browser.

With a height of 1 percent applied, let's see how our layout looks now (see Figure 7-24).

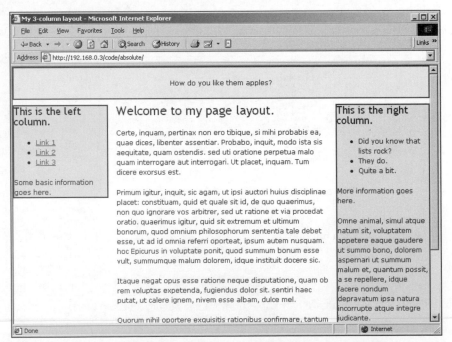

Figure 7-24: One quick hack later, and we're cooking with gas once more.

Our 1 percent height rule managed to kickstart IE's buggy rendering engine. By supplying it with an initial (if microscopic) height for the container block, IE knows to expand that block to surround its descendants (which, honestly, it should anyway — but let's not wait for that browser to make our lives easier).

After this bout of debugging, we've determined that our three-column framework is holding up admirably in all the browsers we've tested. However, what we've built so far is missing one crucial component. Let's turn to the last component needed to round out our imitation of the FastCompany.com layout, and put this three-column layout to bed.

Setting Some Boundaries:
The max-width Property

The final piece of the Fast Company puzzle is the flexible nature of the design. Currently, our layout expands to fill the entire width of the browser window, no matter how small (or wide) it may be. At larger window sizes, the lines of text in our fluid design can become almost unmanageably long, making it difficult to read. To mitigate this issue, Dan Cederholm and the Fast Company Web team decided to apply the max-width property to the container block on each page.

max-width is a handy CSS property that does exactly what it says: It establishes the *maximum width* for a given element. Let's apply this property to our own design and see what comes of it. As the Fast Company site settled upon a max-width of 1,000 pixels, we'll follow suit:

```
#header, #container {
    max-width: 1000px;
}
```

After refreshing, the difference might not be evident. However, once we begin to increase the width of our browser window, the property's effects are readily apparent (see Figure 7-25).

As the browser window expands or contracts, our design remains flexible enough to follow suit. However, once the width of the window exceeds 1,000 pixels (the value set in our max-width property), our page's layout stops scaling. With the max-width property, we've placed an implicit cap on the horizontal width of our page, ensuring a level of flexibility in our design that doesn't impede the ability of users to easily scan our content.

Unfortunately, max-width is a part of the style sheet specification that doesn't enjoy widespread browser support. Or, to be more specific, it enjoys incredibly robust support in your browser — unless, of course, your browser happens to be Internet Explorer. As of the writing of this book, the most prevalent browser on the planet turns a blind eye to this handy property, as well as other related properties such as min-width, min-height, and max-height. Given IE's inability to interpret them, each of these properties is relegated to the realm of the theoretical, of the best ideas we can't currently rely upon.

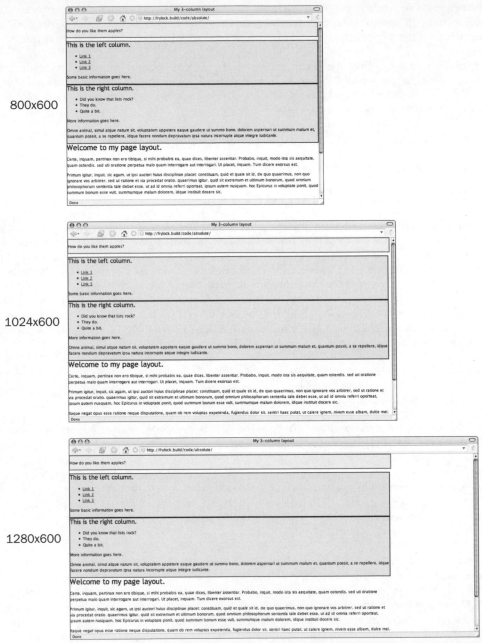

Figure 7-25: The max-width property places a cap on the width of the content area—do not pass "Go," do not collect $200.

Thankfully, this lack of support doesn't prevent us from *using* these techniques. Instead, our design will fill the entire horizontal space of browsers that don't support the `max-width` property (see Figure 7-26). In this respect, Dan's application of `max-width` to the Fast Company design was a bold move in support of *progressive enhancement*. By serving increasingly advanced layers of design functionality to more modern browsers while keeping their site accessible to all, Fast Company enables the widest audience possible to access its content—a move sure to keep users and business stakeholders alike very happy.

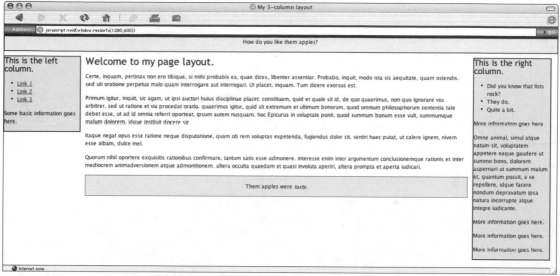

Figure 7-26: In browsers that don't respect the max-width CSS property (such as Internet Explorer on the Mac, shown here), the page layout will simply expand to the width of the window.

A number of workarounds are available online to force Internet Explorer to support useful CSS properties such as max-width (one example is `http://svendtofte.com/code/max_width_in_ie/`). However, many of these solutions involve introducing IE-only properties into your CSS—be wary of this, as proprietary code will invalidate your style sheet and could adversely affect other, more-compliant browsers.

Additionally, Dean Edwards has written "IE7" (`http://dean.edwards.name/IE7/`), a library of JavaScript modules that improve Internet Explorer 5+'s support for the CSS specification. As a JavaScript-only solution, Edwards' work has no chance of invalidating your style sheets. However, be sure to test and evaluate it fully before using it in a production environment.

Summary

Our whirlwind tour of the Fast Company layout began with a blank slate: the default, normal flow of an unstyled document. From there, we examined how CSS positioning could be used to override this default scheme, and allow us to remove elements from their normal place in the document flow. This understanding of absolute and relative positioning provided us with the building blocks for reconstructing the Fast Company layout. By using a combination of absolutely positioned blocks contained within a relatively positioned parent, we could create a flexible, three-column layout in the style of Fast Company. And with a minimal amount of CSS hacking, we've established a style foundation that's looking quite smart across all modern browsers, one that we can flesh out with additional content and information.

With this bulletproof framework in place, let's look ahead to the next chapter. In it, we'll discuss how we might allow our users to further customize our site's design, meeting their needs while simultaneously furthering the needs of our own site.

8

Stuff and Nonsense: Strategies for CSS Switching

We wish we had some *kung fu*–esque robes handy. This is the chapter where we tell our dear readers to forget all that we have taught them about CSS so far, to look beyond the surface of the pool and discover the truth within the truth . . . or something like that.

Honestly, we're more fun at parties than we might seem.

After seven chapters, it's worth remembering that as convenient as it is to site designers, cascading style sheets can also drastically improve the online experience for the users of our sites. In Chapter 2, you saw briefly how the cascade was written with our users' needs in mind, that user style sheets are ultimately given precedence over the author style sheets we write. The authors of the specification didn't do this to spite those that design for the Web, but rather to empower those who read it.

After all, the true wonder of the Web is its promise of universal access: an avenue through which a user can gain instant and complete entry to any topic, from anywhere in the world. In fact, much of the mantle we don as Web designers is to realize that promise — to make sites that are at once visually compelling *and* with an interface that presents no barrier to entry.

However, we've slowly come to realize that our understanding of our audience has been incomplete at best. While we focused on setting the type on our pages 9 pixels high in the early days of the Web, our development was focused on having sites "look right" on contemporary desktop browsers. But in recent years, our understanding of our users' needs has matured. People with physical, hearing, visual, or cognitive disabilities have always been using our sites; it's just taken us some time to realize it. So, it's only in recent years that our definition of "accessibility" has flowered, and our site-building techniques have followed suit.

While some designers may tell you that building an accessible site means building a boring site, we'd fling their *pooh-pooh* right back at them. Accessibility isn't about larger fonts and creating high-contrast guidelines. Some users of the Web can read only smaller texts, while others can see only yellow text on a black background. Rather, many of the design techniques explored throughout this book—semantic, well-structured markup, a separation between content and presentation—can and will afford us incredible leverage in building professional, inspiring designs *and simultaneously* improve the accessibility of our sites for all of our users, not just a select few. In short, we can better realize the Web's potential for universal access, and make some ultra-sexy sites to boot.

Ultimately, this chapter is not a manifesto on accessibility, space allotments and our meager skills being the largest impediments. Instead, we will explore different techniques for democratizing our design through the use of *style sheet switching*. By applying a different CSS file to a markup document, we can drastically change any or all aspects of its design—the layout, typography, or color palette. This technique may hold incredible appeal to designers because it exponentially decreases the amount of overhead required to redesign a site. But, as you'll see, this technique can wield incredible benefits to our site's users, allowing them fine-grained control over a page's presentation and, in turn, better access to the content therein. After all, it's about throwing the gates as wide open as possible.

Let's dive right in.

Laying the Foundation

As with other chapters, let's begin with a valid XHTML document. For the purposes of our style sheet switching experiments, the document in Listing 8-1 will do nicely.

Listing 8-1: The Markup Foundation for Our Style Switcher Experiments

```
<!DOCTYPE html PUBLIC "-//W3C//DTD XHTML 1.0 Transitional//EN"
"http://www.w3.org/TR/xhtml1/DTD/xhtml1-transitional.dtd">

<html xmlns="http://www.w3.org/1999/xhtml">
<head>

<title>Always offer an alternative.</title>

<meta http-equiv="Content-Type" content="text/html; charset=utf-8" />

</head>

<body>

<div id="container">
  <div id="content">
    <h1>Always offer an alternative.</h1>

    <p><span class="lead">Lorem ipsum dolor sit amet,</span> consectetuer
adipiscing elit. Nullam tortor. Integer eros...</p>
```

```
    <p id="blurb">This is, as they say, a &#8220;pull quote.&#8221;</p>

    <p>Donec id nisl...</p>

    <h2>Additionally, you might consider...</h2>

    <p><img src="portrait.png" alt="An author's handsome (if pixellated) mug"
class="portrait" />  Quisque sit amet justo. Cum sociis...</p>
  </div>
</div>

</body>
</html>
```

By now, this sort of markup should, we hope, feel rather old hat to you. The markup is simple, yet well meaning, with proper heading elements (h1 and h2) applied to suit their position in our (admittedly nonsensical) document's outline. Paragraphs have been marked up as such via the <p> element, with one earmarked with an id of "blurb" so that we might later style it differently than its siblings. And just to spice up the layout a bit, we've included a pixel illustration of one of our authors. Sorry, no door prizes are available for guessing which one it is.

Figure 8-1 shows you just how humble our beginnings are.

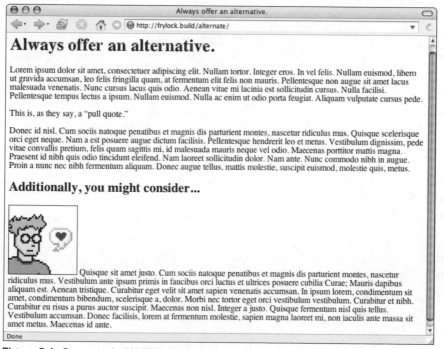

Figure 8-1: Our unstyled XHTML document, partying like it's 1994

And again, as always, we can apply a rough style sheet to this document, and slap a bit of mascara on that otherwise unimpressive wall of serifs. To begin, let's create a new style sheet called core.css, and include the rules in Listing 8-2.

Listing 8-2: The core.css Style Sheet

```css
/* default font and color information */
body {
  background: #FFF;
  color: #444;
  font: 62.5%/1.6em "Lucida Grande", Verdana, Geneva, Helvetica, Arial, sans-serif;
}
/* END default font and color information */

/* default link rules */
a {
  color: #C60;
}

a:hover {
  color: #F60;
  text-decoration: none;
}
/* END default link rules */

/* headings */
h1, h2 {
  color: #B61;
  line-height: 1em;
  font-weight: normal;
  font-family: Helvetica, Arial, Geneva, Verdana, sans-serif;
  margin: 1em 0;
  padding: 0;
}

h1 {
  font-size: 2.2em;
}
/* END headings */

/* container */
#container {
  margin: 0 auto;
  max-width: 60em;
}
/* END container */

/* content */
#content h2 {
  font-size: 1.2em;
  text-transform: uppercase;
}
```

```
#content p {
  font-size: 1.1em;
  line-height: 1.6em;
}

#content img.portrait {
  float: right;
  margin: 0 0 1em 1em;
}

#content span.lead {
  text-transform: uppercase;
}

#content #blurb {
  background: #FFC;
  border: 1px dotted #FC6;
  color: #000;
  font-size: 1.5em;
  line-height: 1.4em;
  padding: .5em;
  text-align: center;
}
/* END content */
```

Pardon us while we pause for breath — that was a bit of a rush, wasn't it? Rather than adding a few selectors at a time and discussing the visual result, we're taking a less Socratic approach in this chapter. The focus here is less upon the techniques the style sheet contains than upon the end result gained by switching them. After all, this CSS is merely a placeholder, one that could easily be replaced by your own efforts. With that, we won't bother to preen over this one. However, following are a few techniques worth briefly describing.

❑ #container { margin: 0 auto; }. While some in the audience might be *tut-tut*ing our use of a div with no real semantic worth, our #container establishes a handy means of controlling the width of the content within it. Setting left- and right-hand "auto" margins (0 auto;) allows us to horizontally center the div within its parent element — namely, the body of our markup.

The only issue with this approach is a slight one. Versions 5.*x* of Internet Explorer on Windows doesn't properly implement auto-margins, and will, therefore, not understand this rule. As a result, we need to apply text-align: center; to the body element. Granted, this is an incorrect interpretation of the text-align property (designed to control the inline content of a block, and *not* the block itself), but it nonetheless puts IE5/Windows back in its place. But, by applying body { text-align: center; }, IE5/Windows *also centers all of the text on the page*. Thankfully, once we set #container { text-align: left; }, our work is finally finished.

❑ #container { max-width: 60em; }. Setting the max-width property completes the effect, ensuring that the #container element never gets larger than 60ems. If the user reduces the size of his or her window below the width of #container, then the div will shrink accordingly. In short, it's a no-hassle way to gain a truly flexible layout.

The largest drawback to the `max-width` property is Internet Explorer's complete lack of support for it. Neither the Macintosh nor the Windows version of that browser will understand `max-width`. As a result, we have to serve up a defined width to IE. We've decided upon `width: 60em;`, but you might also opt to choose a more flexible percentage width. Serving this alternate value to IE and IE alone can be done through the judicious use of a CSS hack, or (our favorite method) by placing the "incorrect" value in a separate style sheet with browser-specific hacks. Chapter 2 discusses both of these concepts in more detail.

❑ `body { font: 62.5%/1.6em "Lucida Grande", Verdana, Geneva, Helvetica, Arial, sans-serif; }`. The font property we've set on the body element is actually a shorthand property. Here, we've declared the `font-size` (62.5%), `line-height` (1.6em) and `font-family` (Lucida Grande, Verdana, Geneva, Helvetica, Arial, sans-serif;) in one handy-dandy property/value pair. And furthermore, because these values are inherited by the body's descendant elements, we've immediately applied a basic type profile to the entire document with this one rule.

The 62.5 percent value for `font-size` is a technique first publicized by Web designer Richard Rutter ("How to Size Text Using ems," `http://clagnut.com/blog/348/`). Because the default text size for all modern browsers is 16 pixels, setting `font-size: 62.5%;` on the body nets us a default type height of 10 pixels ($16 \times 0.625 = 10$). From there, sizing descendant elements with ems (a relative unit of measurement) becomes much more logical: 1em is 10px, 1.6em is 16px, .9em is 9px, and so forth. Rather than using pixels throughout our document (which IE users cannot resize), this method gives us a near-pixel-perfect replacement for our typesetting, and one that allows users to resize text to a size that suits their needs.

❑ `#content img.portrait { float: right; }`. The oh-so-handsome pixel portrait is aligned flush with the rightmost edge of its containing paragraph. But rather than resorting to deprecated markup techniques such as `<img src="blah.gif" align="right" />`, we're using the powerful CSS `float` model to achieve the same effect. We recommend that you read CSS guru Eric Meyer's excellent article on "Containing Floats" (`http://complexspiral.com/publications/containing-floats/`).

With a better grip on some of the more clever points in our style sheet (as if that says much), we could easily paste this entire chunk of code into a `<style type="text/css">...</style>` block in the head of our document. Of course, that would muddy our markup with presentational information—and honestly, who wants to hunt down style information across a few hundred XHTML documents? That's right, some call it "adhering to a strict separation between structure and style." We call it "lazy."

In either event, let's create a second style sheet, and name it `main.css`; at the top of that new file, we'll use the `@import` command to invoke our `core.css` file, like so:

```
@import url("core.css");
```

We've effectively created a "wrapper" style sheet—a CSS file that acts as a gateway to other style sheets. With this `main.css` file in hand, we can now include it—and with it, `core.css`—in our XHTML with one simple `link` element, placed in the `head` of our document:

```
<link rel="stylesheet" href="main.css" type="text/css" />
```

And *voilà*! Our rather plain-looking document suddenly gets a bit of personality in Figure 8-2.

Figure 8-2: Applying some basic styles to our XHTML makes it a bit more readable.

After creating this seemingly superfluous `main.css` file, there might be some head-scratching in the audience. But rest assured, there are some very good reasons for putting this file in place. Although it wasn't designed as such, the `@import` rule is a kind of litmus test for a browser's support of advanced CSS techniques. Legacy browsers that have broken CSS implementations don't understand the `@import` rule, and will simply disregard it. This allows us to serve up high-octane style sheet rules to modern browsers, while such antiquated browsers as versions 4 and below of Netscape and Internet Explorer will simply ignore the style sheets that they wouldn't otherwise understand.

An added benefit to this intermediary style sheet is that we can place multiple `@import` rules therein. This could come in handy if we needed to break our site's presentation into multiple files (for example, one for layout, another for color, yet another for typography). Or even better, we can use this technique to manage our various CSS hacks, as we saw in Chapter 2. As you test the CSS in Listing 8-3, you may find that the different versions of Internet Explorer (both on the Macintosh and Windows platforms) break different aspects of the layout. While we could use a battery of style sheet hacks within our `core.css` file to serve up alternate property values to these browsers' broken CSS implementations, Listing 8-3 shows how we might use our wrapper style sheet to include browser-specific CSS hack files, which allow us to keep our `main.css` file clean and hack-free.

Listing 8-3: A Revised core.css File, with Intelligent Hack Management

```
@import url("core.css");

/* Import WinIEx-only bugs - hide from Mac IE5 \*/
@import url("hacks.win.iex.css");
/* END hide from Mac IE5 */

/* Import Win IE5x hacks */
@media tty {
    i{content:"\";/*" "*/}} @import 'hacks.win.ie5.css'; /*";}
}/* */

/* Import Mac IE5 hacks */
/*\*//*/
@import url("hacks.mac.ie5.css");
/**/
```

We've already discussed the CSS hacks needed to get our page looking good in less-than–CSS-savvy browsers, and triaging the different hacks into browser-specific files is an excellent way to keep our core.css file clean and hack-free. If we ever decide to drop support for a certain browser, we now need to remove only a few lines from main.css — definitely a more appealing thought than scouring our primary style sheet rules line by line, looking for CSS hacks. Again, it's equal parts "strategic" and "lazy" here at CSS Best Practices Headquarters.

Now that we've put our CSS and XHTML firmly in place, we can delve into the mechanics of style sheet switching.

CSS Switching

One fault of our page's current design is that legibility wasn't one of our guiding design goals. The contrast is a bit light, as we opted to use a near-black color for the text against the body's white background. And the default font size of 62.5 percent of the browser's default (or roughly 10 pixels) might be difficult to read for users suffering from visual impairments. (Even a reader with slight myopia might have to work at reading our content.) How can we improve the design to make it more legible, without sacrificing our original vision?

To begin, let's create a separate style sheet that addresses some of these possible pitfalls. In Listing 8-4, we've created a new CSS file named contrast.css.

Listing 8-4: The contrast.css Style Sheet

```
body {
  background: #000;
  color: #DDD;
}
```

```
h1, h2 {
  color: #FFF;
  font-weight: bold;
}

#content {
  font-size: 1.1em;
}

#content h2 {
  font-size: 1.6em;
  text-transform: none;
}

#content #blurb {
  background: #222;
  border-color: #444;
  color: #FF9;
}

span.lead {
  font-weight: bold;
}
```

Now let's simply add a `link` to our new `contrast.css` file in the head of our markup, like so:

```
<link rel="stylesheet" href="main.css" type="text/css" />
<link rel="stylesheet" href="contrast.css" type="text/css" />
```

When we reload the document in our browser, Figure 8-3 shows us that the landscape has changed pretty drastically.

First and foremost, it's worth mentioning that because the two CSS files are being included in tandem, we don't need to use `contrast.css` (Listing 8-4) to re-declare any of the layout or type rules established in `main.css`. Rather, we can simply selectively override individual rules and/or property values, and let the rules of specificity handle which rules cascade to the user.

From a purely aesthetic point, we've instantaneously changed the presentation of our markup — and all by including the new `contrast.css` file. The off-black text has been replaced with pure white, the text size has been increased *very* slightly (from 1em to 1.1em), and the colors on our pull quote have been changed to reflect the new palette. The completed effect feels much more nocturnal — but more important, we've created a style sheet that allows users to enjoy a higher level of contrast, as well as a slightly more legible type size.

But we've still not settled our original problem. How do we switch between the two style sheets? We grew pretty attached to that white, open design — it would be a real shame to lose it, wouldn't it?

Oh, at least *pretend* it's pretty. Please?

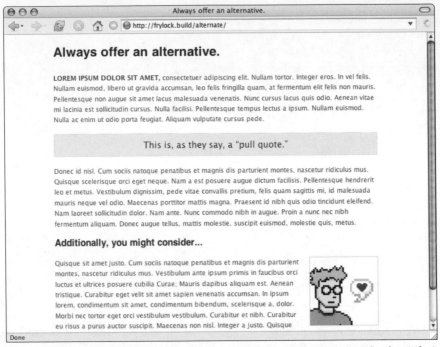

Figure 8-3: Now we're on our way, as we've added a supplementary style sheet that provides heightened contrast and an increased font size.

The Mechanics: How It's Supposed to Work

Thus far, we've associated two separate CSS files with one document. Currently, they're both being read and applied to the document with equal weight, with the rules of specificity resolving any conflicts that may arise between the two. However, to accommodate more complex scenarios than the one we currently have, the HTML and CSS specifications outline structured guidelines for how multiple style sheets interact. Web page authors are given a number of ways to prioritize the style sheets we include via the link element. Let's examine the three different classes of style sheets (no pun intended), and see how they might apply to our switching scenario.

Persistent Style Sheets

Persistent style sheets are always enabled. Think of them as CSS that is "turned on" by default. The persistent CSS file will be applied in addition to any other style sheets that are currently active, and acts as a set of shared style rules that every other style sheet in the document can draw upon.

Each `link` element with a `rel` attribute set to `"stylesheet"` is a persistent style sheet—and, in fact, we've created two already:

```
<link rel="stylesheet" href="main.css" type="text/css" />
<link rel="stylesheet" href="contrast.css" type="text/css" />
```

As we add additional kinds of style sheets, any `links` that we designate as persistent will act as the baseline, sharing their rules with all other included CSS files.

Preferred Style Sheets

By adding a title to a persistent style sheet, we can designate a style sheet as *preferred*, like so:

```
<link rel="stylesheet" href="main.css" type="text/css" />
<link rel="stylesheet" title="Higher Contrast" href="contrast.css" type="text/css"
/>
```

Additionally, we can specify multiple "groups" of preferred style sheets by giving them the same `title` attribute. This allows the user to activate (or deactivate) these groups of CSS files together. Should more than one group be present, the first group will take precedence.

Much as with persistent style sheets, preferred CSS files are enabled by default. So, in the previous example, our `contrast.css` file (refer to Listing 8-4) would be enabled when the user first visits our page (borrowing, as it did before, from our persistent `main.css` file). However, preferred style sheets are disabled if the user selects an alternate style sheet.

Alternate Style Sheets

An *alternate* style sheet can be selected by the user as, well, alternatives to a CSS file marked as preferred by the site's author. To designate a `link` as an alternate style sheet, it must be named with a `title` attribute, and its `rel` attribute set to `"alternate stylesheet"`. As with preferred style sheets, we can group `links` together by giving them identical `title` attributes. So, in short, this is what we've been looking for—a means through which we can allow users to select the design that best suits their needs. If we do, in fact, want `main.css` to be the default and `contrast.css` to be an optional, alternate CSS file, then we should update our two `link` elements to match:

```
<link rel="stylesheet" href="main.css" type="text/css" />
<link rel="alternate stylesheet" title="Higher Contrast" href="contrast.css"
type="text/css" />
```

Now, viewing the page in a browser that supports style sheet switching, the user can finally control the display of the page. Browsers such as Firefox or Opera include an option to select our new alternate style sheet, as shown in Figure 8-4.

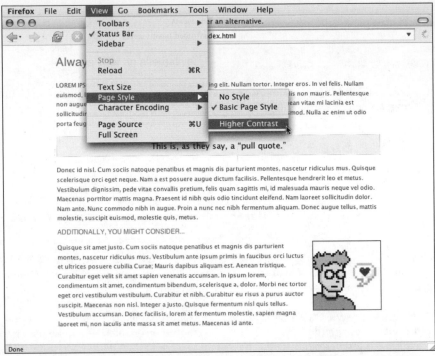

Figure 8-4: By changing the rel attribute of the second link element to "alternate stylesheet" and supplying a title, we've implemented some basic style switching.

Once the user selects Higher Contrast from the menu, the alternate style sheet with that title — namely, `contrast.css` — becomes active. So, we've finally settled on the solution we were looking for. Our original design is the active default, but we've created the means through which users can select another design altogether. Using this method, we can add even more alternate CSS options. Let's create a file named `hot.css` and use the rules in Listing 8-5.

Listing 8-5: The hot.css Style Sheet

```css
body {
  background: #000 url("bg-stylish.jpg") no-repeat 50% 0;
  color: #DDD;
}

h1, h2 {
  color: #FFF;
  font-weight: normal;
  text-align: center;
  text-transform: none;
}
```

```
#content {
  font-size: 1.1em;
}

#content h1 {
  font: 2.6em Zapfino, "Gill Sans", Gill, Palatino, "Times New Roman", Times,
serif;
  margin: 200px 0 70px;
}

#content h2 {
  font: 1.6em "Gill Sans", Gill, Palatino, "Times New Roman", Times, serif;
  margin: 1.4em 0;
  text-transform: uppercase;
}

#content #blurb {
  background: #222;
  border-color: #444;
  color: #FF9;
}

span.lead {
  font-weight: bold;
}
```

And now, by applying what we've learned about alternate style sheets thus far, we can easily present hot.css (refer to Listing 8-5) to our users as another user interface option:

```
<link rel="stylesheet" href="main.css" type="text/css" />
<link rel="alternate stylesheet" title="Higher Contrast" href="contrast.css"
type="text/css" />
<link rel="alternate stylesheet" title="Gratuitous CSS" href="hot.css"
type="text/css" />
```

If our users have the ability to select another alternate CSS file from their browsers, then they'll be able to see our new styles as shown in Figure 8-5. And, as before, the change is a fairly drastic one — but we've finally allowed the users to choose an appealing design and tailor our content to meet their needs.

Figure 8-5: With our understanding of how the cascade works, we can build even more complexity into our alternate CSS documents.

Another Solution We (Almost) Can't Quite Use

As with some of the most promising features of CSS, adoption of alternate style sheets would be more widespread if browser support were more robust. As of this writing, the number of browsers that natively allow users to select alternate style sheets is limited to Gecko-based browsers such as Mozilla or Firefox, and the Opera browser. For example, Apple's Safari has no way to select alternate or preferred style sheets. And, you guessed it, Internet Explorer (the browser known and loved the world over) won't allow users to select the alternate user interfaces we build for them. If the world's most popular browser keeps this feature out of the hands of our users, then we have a bit more work to do yet.

Furthermore, the browsers that *do* natively support alternate style sheet switching have only a limited switching functionality. While these browsers do allow the user to easily switch between the default CSS and any alternates provided by the author, they do not remember the user's selection. This means that, if a reader selects an alternate style sheet and then reloads the page or leaves and returns to it, the browser will forget the earlier choice and reinstate the default style.

Obviously, neither of these scenarios will work for our users. We're lucky that there are some additional steps we can take to bring the full benefits of CSS switching to them.

The Reality: How It Can Work Today

We've established that most of our audience won't be able to use in-browser CSS switching (and identified those who don't have much functionality available to them) so we must build an interface into our page that allows users to overcome these limitations. Now, you might realize that the two client-side technologies we've been studying up to this point aren't especially well equipped to handle this. While XHTML and CSS excel at describing and styling content, respectively, neither was designed to *interact* with the user. Sure, we can use XHTML to build a list of links on the page as follows:

```
<div id="switcher">
  <ul>
    <li id="style-default"><a href="styleswitch.html">Default style</a></li>
    <li id="style-contrast"><a href="styleswitch.html">Higher Contrast</a></li>
    <li id="style-hot"><a href="styleswitch.html">Gratuitous CSS</a></li>
  </ul>
</div>
```

And we can add some CSS to core.css (refer to Listing 8-2) to style them accordingly, as shown in Figure 8-6:

```
/* switcher styles */
#switcher ul {
  text-align: right;
  list-style: none;
}

#switcher ul li {
  border-left: 1px solid;
  list-style: none;
  display: inline;
  padding: 0 0 0 1em;
  margin: 0 1em 0 0;
}

#switcher #style-default {
  border-left: 0;
  padding-left: 0;
}

#switcher ul a.now {
  color: #000;
```

```
    font-weight: bold;
    text-decoration: none;
}
/* END switcher styles */
```

Figure 8-6: We've added the links for our switcher to the top of our page, but all they can do at the moment is look pretty—and we're about to change that.

However, what happens when the user clicks on those links? If your answer was something akin to "zilch," then you win the blue ribbon. XHTML and CSS can't really *do* anything when you're talking about responding to a user's actions. They can, in turn, affect the content and the presentation of the page, but when the user tries to click a link to change the active style sheet, that's where we need to turn to the third tool in the standards-savvy designer's toolkit: JavaScript.

Jumping on the JavaScript Bandwagon

To put it simply, JavaScript was created as a client-side scripting language. JavaScript (or JS, to use the parlance of lazy typists everywhere) is a language designed to add a layer of interactivity into our Web pages. When a user visits a Web page that has some JavaScript code in it, the browser reads the JS, and then follows any instructions that might be contained therein. Those instructions might tell the browser to display helpful messages to a user as he or she completes a form, or to perform basic validation on the data he or she enters there. We can even use JS to instruct the browser to perform a certain action when the user clicks a link. In short, JavaScript is the means through which we bridge the divide between our content and our users, allowing the latter to fully interact with the former.

Sounds intimidating (and more than a little stuffy), doesn't it? Perhaps it'd be best to just dive right in.

Gathering Requirements

Before we begin a lick of coding, we should make sure that we understand exactly what it is that we're building. Just as we discussed the benefits of requirements gathering to a client project in Chapter 1, the smallest development gig can benefit from some sort of needs analysis. With a better understanding of what we need to build and the goals that what we are building should achieve, we can code more quickly and efficiently—two qualities that will make our clients and us quite happy.

So let's take a quick inventory of what we're working with:

- ❏ We have three `link` elements in the `head` of our XHTML document that include screen-specific CSS files: a persistent style sheet (`main.css`), and two alternate style sheets (`contrast.css` in Listing 8-4 and the ultra-swank `hot.css` in Listing 8-5).

- ❏ Accordingly, at the top of our document we've created a list of three anchors, each corresponding to a different style sheets. Granted, these anchors are about as useful as a road map in the desert, but we're going to change that shortly.

With this in mind, what exactly should our function do? Ideally, when a user clicks a link:

1. The function should cycle through each of the `link` elements in the `head` of our XHTML, and inspect those that link to style sheets *and* have a title.

2. If the `link` matches the link that the user selected, then it should be set to be the "active" CSS.

3. Otherwise, the `link` should be set to "disabled," which will prevent the browser from loading the style sheet.

4. Once the function has finished setting the active link element, it should remember the user's choice. The style sheet the user selected will, therefore, remain "active" as the user browses through the site, and the choice will be remembered if the user returns to our site during a later browsing session.

How, you may ask, will we do all of this? Well, the solution ultimately involves a fair amount of pixie dust and happy thoughts—but we shouldn't get too far ahead of ourselves.

Building the Switching Function

With our goals firmly in mind, we can begin building our style sheet functions. Let's create a new file called `scripts.js`, and include the following markup in the head of our XHTML document:

```
<script type="text/javascript" src="scripts.js"></script>
```

Much as we're using the `link` element to include external CSS files for our site's presentation, we can use the `script` element to reference an external JavaScript file. And, in that file, we can write in the first lines that will power our CSS switcher. If JavaScript syntax looks a bit intimidating, don't worry. We'll simply touch on some of the highlights, and get back to that "Professional CSS" malarkey as quickly as possible.

```
// activeCSS: Set the active stylesheet
function activeCSS(title) {
  var i, oneLink;
  for (i = 0; (oneLink = document.getElementsByTagName("link")[i]); i++) {
    if (oneLink.getAttribute("title") && findWord("stylesheet",
oneLink.getAttribute("rel"))) {
```

```
      oneLink.disabled = true;
      if (oneLink.getAttribute("title") == title) {
        oneLink.disabled = false;
      }
    }
  }
}

// findWord: Used to find a full word (needle) in a string (haystack)
function findWord(needle, haystack) {
  return haystack.match(needle + "\\b");
}
```

In this code snippet, we have two JavaScript *functions*, which are basically discrete chunks of functionality. The two functions we're looking at here are `activeCSS()` and `findWord()`. Each function contains a series of instructions that are passed to the browser for processing. For example, when `activeCSS` is invoked, it performs the following tasks:

1. It assembles a list of all `link` elements in our document (`document .getElementsByTagName("link")`), and proceeds to loop through them.

2. For each `link` element found, it checks to see if there is a `title` available, and then evaluates the `rel` attribute to see if the word "stylesheet" is present. The `findWord()` function is used here to search the `rel` for a whole-word match only. This means that if someone accidentally types `rel="stylesheets"` or the like into their `link` element, our function ignores them.

3. Each link that meets the criteria in Step 2 will be disabled (`oneLink.disabled = true;`).

4. When the function is first invoked, an *argument* (or variable) is passed with the title of the desired "active" style sheet. So, as the function loops through each of the `link` elements, it checks to see if the title of the link matches the title of the function's argument. If so, the `link` element is reactivated.

Admittedly, this is a bit of a gloss of the functions' syntax. JavaScript is a robust and rewarding language, but we're nonetheless forced to breeze through some of its subtleties to get back on the CSS track. However, the preceding list demonstrates the high-level concepts at play in the code we've created, and should provide a fine starting point for those interested in further exploring JavaScript's elegant syntax.

While these two functions enable us to switch our CSS, they simply lie dormant until they are *invoked* (or called) by our markup. Because we want our switcher to fire when a user selects a link from our `#switcher` list, the easiest place to do so is within the anchors of our style switcher list:

```
<div id="switcher">
  <ul>
    <li id="style-default"><a href="styleswitch.html"
onclick="activeCSS('default'); return false">Default style</a></li>
    <li id="style-contrast"><a href="styleswitch.html" onclick="activeCSS('Higher
Contrast'); return false">Higher Contrast</a></li>
    <li id="style-hot"><a href="styleswitch.html" onclick="activeCSS('Gratuitous
CSS'); return false">Gratuitous CSS</a></li>
  </ul>
</div>
```

The onclick attribute we've introduced here is called an *event handler*. When the user performs a certain action or "event" (such as, in this case, a mouse click), the JavaScript contained in the attribute value is fired. So, in the preceding example, the onclick handler will detect when a user clicks on the anchor, and will in turn fire the activeCSS() function.

> *Strictly speaking, you could argue that use of these event handlers, such as* onclick, onblur, onmouseover, *and so on, is analogous to relying on the* style *attribute — that these inline attributes blur the separation of structure and behavior, and can easily increase the cost of maintenance and support. Rather than editing our XHTML to reflect any changes in the JavaScript, it would instead be possible to use more modern JS to automatically generate the event handlers our links will need, and, therefore, keep the necessary divide between our markup and our scripting. For more information, we recommend Peter-Paul Koch's "Separating behavior and structure"* (http://digital-web.com/articles/separating_behavior_and_structure_2/).

However, as we look closely at the three different event handlers, we can see that each reference to activeCSS() differs slightly. Between the parentheses, we've included the title of the style sheet the link should activate. This is the *argument* we mentioned earlier and is the string of text that the activeCSS() function compares to the title of each link element.

> *You may have noticed that after the call to the* activeCSS() *function, the* onclick *handler contains some additional text:* return false;. *This plays a very small (but integral) part in our switcher because it tells the handler not to follow the URL referenced in the anchor's* href *attribute. Otherwise, the user would end up deposited on* styleswitch.html *after clicking any of the links.*

So, let's do a bit of role-playing. Let's just run through the steps that occur when we click a link. For argument's sake (oh, aren't we clever), let's assume that our user selects the third anchor, the onclick handler that contains the activeCSS('Gratuitous CSS'); reference:

1. The three link elements are compiled into an array, and the function proceeds to loop over each of them. Remember that only those links that contain titles *and* that have a rel attribute that contains the word "stylesheet" will be examined. This leaves us with the links for contrast.css (refer to Listing 8-4) and hot.css (refer to Listing 8-5).

2. The first link element has a title of "Higher Contrast." The function disables the link element. Because its title doesn't match our function's argument ("Gratuitous CSS"), it *stays* disabled.

3. The second link element has a title of "Gratuitous CSS." The function disables the link element. Because the title *does* match our function's argument, the link is *immediately* reactivated.

And *voilà!* As you can see in Figure 8-7, we've completed the effect. Clicking each anchor activates the alternate style sheet whose title matches the one referenced in the activeCSS() function call.

However, even though we've successfully built a function to switch between the different CSS files, we're only halfway there. If the user refreshes the page or leaves the current one after selecting a new alternate style sheet, the choice is forgotten, and the default style sheet is restored. So, obviously, we've a bit more work to do. Let's see if we can't put a little memory into our JavaScript functions.

Figure 8-7: With our JavaScript-enabled style switcher in place, our users can now select a look that best suits their needs.

Baking a JavaScript Cookie

As you've seen with our not-quite-finished CSS switcher, our browsers don't seem to remember anything about a page once we've left or refreshed it. This is by design. The HTTP standard (which is the protocol over which the Web's pages are transferred from a server to your desktop) was designed to be "stateless." This means that each time you visit a page, the Web server considers it to be your first time, every time. Thankfully, we have a way to fill this memory gap. It's called a *cookie*, and it's less fattening than its baked namesake.

A cookie is a small text file that is sent by a Web server to a user's browser, and contains small bits of important information about that user's browsing session. Cookies may contain user preferences, registration information, or the items placed in an online shopping cart, and so on. Once it receives a cookie, the browser saves the information on the user's computer, and sends it back to the Web server whenever the user returns to that Web site.

We're not just flapping our gums here. We're mentioning cookies because we can use JavaScript to set and read them. So, armed with this knowledge, we can finally see our way to the finish line. By adding a few more JavaScript functions to those we've already written, we can build an improved style sheet switcher, and one that will respect our user's preferences across multiple pages, or visits to, our site.

From this, we need two tools in our cookie-baking toolkit (we can mix metaphors with the best of them). We need to be able to set a cookie containing our user's style preference, and to then later read the cookie. So, let's add a new cleverly named function to our `scripts.js` file, `setCookie()`:

```
// Set the cookie
function setCookie(name,value,days) {
  if (days) {
    var date = new Date();
    date.setTime(date.getTime()+(days*24*60*60*1000));
    var expires = ";expires="+date.toGMTString();
  } else {
    expires = "";
  }
  document.cookie = name+"="+value+expires+";";
}
```

And now, in our original `activeCSS()` function, we can add a single line to store our user's preferences in a cookie on the user's computer:

```
// Set the active stylesheet
function activeCSS(title) {
  var i, oneLink;
  for (i = 0; (oneLink = document.getElementsByTagName("link")[i]); i++) {
    if (oneLink.getAttribute("title") && findWord("stylesheet",
oneLink.getAttribute("rel"))) {
      oneLink.disabled = true;
      if (oneLink.getAttribute("title") == title) {
        oneLink.disabled = false;
      }
    }
  }
  setCookie("mystyle", title, 365);
}
```

With this one line, half of our work is finished! The `setCookie()` function accepts three arguments: a name for the cookie (so that we might later reference it), the value to be stored in the cookie, and the number of days until the cookie expires. So, in the previous code snippet, we've created a cookie named `"mystyle"`, the value of which is set to the value of the `title` argument of `activeCSS()`. This means that if a user selects a link that specifies `activeCSS('Higher Contrast')` in its `onclick` handler (that is, it invokes `activeCSS` with a title argument of Higher Contrast), then our `"mystyle"` cookie will, therefore, have a value of Higher Contrast.

In our `setCookie()` function, specifying the number of days until cookie expiration is optional. The latter argument is optional. In the preceding example, we've arbitrarily decided to set the `"mystyle"` cookie to expire in 365 days, or one calendar year. Because the argument is optional, we could leave it out entirely. However, omitting it will cause the `setCookie()` function to create a `"mystyle"` cookie that expires at the end of the user's session — causing the user's preference to be lost as soon as he or she closes the browser.

So, with this lone call to setCookie(), we've managed to store the user's selection from our list of style sheet anchors. But now that we've stored it, how do we read the cookie and honor the preference? Well, once we place the following lines in our scripts.js file, it would seem that the answer is, "simply enough":

```
window.onload = initCSS;

// initCSS: If there's a "mystyle" cookie, set the active stylesheet when the page
loads
function initCSS() {
  var style = readCookie("mystyle");
  if (style) {
    activeCSS(style);
  }
}

// Read the cookie
function readCookie(name) {
  var needle = name + "=";
  var cookieArray = document.cookie.split(';');
  for(var i=0;i < cookieArray.length;i++) {
    var pair = cookieArray[i];
    while (pair.charAt(0)==' ') {
      pair = pair.substring(1, pair.length);
    }
    if (pair.indexOf(needle) == 0) {
      return pair.substring(needle.length, pair.length);
    }
  }
  return null;
}
```

With these last lines of JavaScript in place, we're finally finished. Our new function, initCSS(), has two simple tasks. First, it checks to see if there is a "mystyle" cookie on the user's machine (var style = readCookie("mystyle");). If one is present (if (style)), then the activeCSS() function is invoked with the value of the user's cookie as its argument.

But it's the first line of this code snippet that does the heavy lifting, even though it looks rather innocuous. window.onload = initCSS; fires our initCSS() function when the document finishes loading in the user's browser. Now, as the user moves between the pages of our site (hypothetical though they may be), or when the user returns during a later session, we can immediately poll for the presence of a "mystyle" cookie as each of our pages comes up. As the user makes selections from our style switcher, our pages will honor them, allowing the user to tailor not only individual pages, but an entire *site* to his or her browsing needs.

Listing 8-6 shows the complete JavaScript file.

Listing 8-6: The Complete scripts.js File That Powers Our JavaScript-Enabled CSS Switcher

```javascript
/*
  Onload
*/
window.onload = initCSS;

// initCSS: If there's a "mystyle" cookie, set the active stylesheet when the page
loads
function initCSS() {
  var style = readCookie("mystyle");
  if (style) {
    activeCSS(style);
  }
}

/*
  Switcher functions
*/
// activeCSS: Set the active stylesheet
function activeCSS(title) {
  var i, oneLink;
  for (i = 0; (oneLink = document.getElementsByTagName("link")[i]); i++) {
    if (oneLink.getAttribute("title") && findWord("stylesheet",
oneLink.getAttribute("rel"))) {
      oneLink.disabled = true;
      if (oneLink.getAttribute("title") == title) {
        oneLink.disabled = false;
      }
    }
  }
  setCookie("mystyle", title, 365);
}

// findWord: Used to find a full word (needle) in a string (haystack)
function findWord(needle, haystack) {
  var init = needle + "\\b";
  return haystack.match(needle + "\\b");
}

/*
  Cookie functions
*/

// Set the cookie
function setCookie(name,value,days) {
  if (days) {
    var date = new Date();
    date.setTime(date.getTime()+(days*24*60*60*1000));
    var expires = ";expires="+date.toGMTString();
  } else {
    expires = "";
```

(continued)

Listing 8-6: *(continued)*

```
  }
  document.cookie = name+"="+value+expires+";";
}

// Read the cookie
function readCookie(name) {
  var needle = name + "=";
  var cookieArray = document.cookie.split(';');
  for(var i=0;i < cookieArray.length;i++) {
    var pair = cookieArray[i];
    while (pair.charAt(0)==' ') {
      pair = pair.substring(1, pair.length);
    }
    if (pair.indexOf(needle) == 0) {
      return pair.substring(needle.length, pair.length);
    }
  }
  return null;
}
```

Down with PHP

We hope we're not becoming incredibly predictable by now. But since we've completed our JavaScript solution, we feel compelled to point out some potential issues with it. Actually, we'll limit ourselves to one drawback because it's the largest: How do we know that the user has JavaScript on his or her machine? Okay, we can almost hear the snorts of derision from here — after all, JavaScript is the new black, right? What browser *doesn't* have this ultra-cool language available to it?

As it turns out, quite a few. Internet statistics repositories such as TheCounter.com (www.thecounter.com/) suggest that anywhere from 9 percent to 11 percent of all Web users are browsing without JavaScript. It's true; it does sound like betting odds — 1 in 10 isn't so bad, right? Well, once we remember that we're talking about millions of people in that group of "9 percent to 11 percent," then the demographic starts to look a little different. And, regardless of exactly how many people browse without JavaScript, why should we exclude any from accessing our site? Especially since (as you'll soon see) it's incredibly easy to replicate the same functionality with server-side programming.

Rather than relying on client-side code that may or may not be available to our users, we can instead build a script that resides on our Web server to handle the style switching. Because we'll be working in a server-side environment, we can stop worrying about whether or not JavaScript is active on our users' computers. As long as our users can accept cookies, our server-side script will be able to handle the style sheet switching logic with ease.

Of course, there are nearly as many server-side programming languages as there are authors on this book. For our purposes, we'll use PHP (www.php.net/). It's a wildly popular, open source (read: "free") programming language, and is available on a staggering number of today's Web servers. Because of its popularity, its speed, and its robust feature set, it makes a fine choice for this chapter's experiments.

And besides, it's free. Did we mention that? Free. We rather like that.

Of course, PHP isn't a magic bullet—if it's not installed on our Web server, we can't take advantage of it. So while we're no longer reliant on our readers' browser configuration , we've replaced it with a technical requirement on our server. Contact your server's administrator to see if it's installed on yours—otherwise, if you want some help getting PHP installed on your machine, there are plenty of resources available.

The official PHP documentation (www.php.net/docs.php) is possibly the best place to start—although in all honesty, we find their installation instructions (while very clearly written) a bit intimidating for those of us somewhat lacking in the 133t-ness category. If you find yourself a bit lost among the configuration instructions, we recommend resorting to your favorite search engine. A search for "install php windows" or "install php mac" will yield hundreds of (we hope) easy-to-read results, yet another testament to PHP's popularity as a powerful, robust programming language.

Additionally, Mac OS X users can avail themselves of easy-to-install packages. We personally recommend Server Logistics' feature-rich PHP installer (www.serverlogistics.com/php4.php), but other comparable packages are available. The drawback to such packages is that it limits the amount of control we can exercise over PHP's configuration. If an "as-is" installation isn't appealing to you, then the official documentation is the best resource out there.

Creating the Script

Once we have PHP up and running on our server, we can get to work. To begin, let's modify our XHMTL—specifically, the unordered list that contains the different style sheet options. Whereas we previously used `onclick` handlers to do the dirty work, the landscape has changed somewhat:

```
<ul>
    <li id="style-default"><a href="switch.php?style=">Default style</a></li>
    <li id="style-contrast"><a href="switch.php?style=contrast">Higher
Contrast</a></li>
    <li id="style-hot"><a href="switch.php?style=hot">Gratuitous CSS</a></li>
</ul>
```

Now, all of our links are currently pointing to a file named `switch.php`—but what's all of that `?style=` stuff in our link? The text that follows the question mark in the `href` is known as a *query string*, and allows us to pass parameters to our CSS switcher script. Query string parameters always come in name/value pairs, like so:

```
file.name?name=value
switch.php?style=contrast
```

If we want to pass multiple name/value pairs to our script, then we concatenate them with ampersands (&):

```
Switch.php?style=contrast&amp;font=serif&amp;css=cool
```

In HTML, ampersands have a special meaning. They are used to signal the start of character entities, codes that represent a special character in HTML. For example, © is the entity for ©, ™ will display ™ in our browser, and so forth. However, when we want a literal ampersand to appear, as we do in our query string, we need to use &, which is the proper entity reference. Otherwise, our HTML will be invalid, and our query string may break—and we don't know about our readers, but those two options aren't appealing to us.

You'll see shortly how these parameters play a part in our style switcher, but for now let's create this switch.php file, and paste in the following code:

```php
<?php
$domain = "my-site-here.com";

if (stristr($_SERVER['HTTP_REFERER'], $domain)) {
  $bounce_url = $_SERVER['HTTP_REFERER'];
} else {
  $bounce_url = "http://$domain/";
}

setcookie('mystyle', $_GET['style'], time() + 31536000);

header("Location: $bounce_url");
?>
```

And that's it. No, really — this won't be evolving into 80 lines of code over the next 50 pages, we promise. In JavaScript, we had to write custom functions to handle some of the basic tasks we needed our style switcher to tackle. But many of these common tasks (such as reading and writing cookies) are already a part of the language. By using these built-in functions, we can cut down drastically on code bloat, and get our style sheet switcher out the door as quickly as possible.

The meat of this code is the antepenultimate line:

```php
setcookie('mystyle', $_GET['style'], time() + 31536000);
```

Whereas we had to create a custom function to set a cookie in JavaScript, it seems that PHP has done the hard work for us. Its setcookie() function is readily available to us, and snaps in nicely to our script. But the one overlap with our JavaScript setCookie() function is that we're also passing three arguments to the function, the first two being the most critical. The first argument is, as before, simply the name for our cookie, and we're sticking with "mystyle".

The second argument ($_GET['style']) defines what's actually stored as the value of our "mystyle" cookie. The $_GET variable is actually a named list, or *associative array*, of all the parameters passed to the page in a query string. Let's assume that our switch.php page is called with the following URL:

```
http://my-site-here.com/switch.php?style=hot&css=cool
```

Given that query string, the value of $_GET['style'] is what follows the equal sign in the style=hot name/value pair, or "hot"; similarly, $_GET['css'] would return a value of cool. As a result, our setcookie() function will build a "mystyle" cookie with a value of hot, which is exactly what we (and our users) want.

The time() + 31536000 may look like we'd need a decoder ring to make sense of it, but it's not quite as intimidating as it might seem. The time() function simply returns the current time, measured in seconds from midnight on January 1, 1970 — also called "the Unix Epoch," a common point of reference for functions dealing with time-based tasks. Once we have the current time, we're adding a year's worth of seconds to it (60 seconds * 60 minutes * 24 hours * 365 days = 31536000). So, with all this, we're essentially getting the time that is exactly one year later than when the cookie was set, and using that to determine when the cookie expires.

Once the cookie's been set, we simply redirect the user back to $bounce_url, which was set at the beginning of the file. We've included some extra processing at the top of switch.php, examining the user's referrer (the URL of the page he or she was visiting before being sent to switch.php). If the user was referred from a page on our $domain (if (stristr($_SERVER['HTTP_REFERER'], $domain))), then we'll simply redirect the user to it. However, if another site decided to link directly to our style switcher, we'll set $bounce_url to our homepage ($bounce_url = $_SERVER['HTTP_REFERER'];).

So, we've successfully set the cookie in record time and redirected the user back to our site. What happens next? We need to set up some sort of logic for handling the cookie we've just baked. Let's dive right in and see what we can uncover.

Eating the Cookie

This second step requires inserting some PHP code directly into our XHTML—nothing onerous, but we first need to convert our markup document into one that our PHP server can read. To do so, we simply rename the file, and change its .html extension to .php—if our system administrator has done his or her job properly, then this should be all that's required to ready our XHTML for a little PHP-fu.

Once we've changed the file extension, we can insert the following code in the head of our document:

```
<link rel="stylesheet" href="main.css" type="text/css" />
<?php
if ($_COOKIE['mystyle']) {
?>
<link rel="stylesheet" href="<?= $_COOKIE['mystyle']; ?>.css" type="text/css"
media="screen" />
<?php
}
?>

<link rel="alternate stylesheet" title="Higher Contrast" href="contrast.css"
type="text/css" />
<link rel="alternate stylesheet" title="Gratuitous CSS" href="hot.css"
type="text/css" />
```

When our markup document is loaded in the browser, the snippet of PHP is inserted into the head. If no "mystyle" cookie has been set (or the value is just an empty string), then none of the code wrapped in the if { ... } statement gets run. However, if our cookie is present, then a new link element is printed into our markup. Let's expand on this.

According to the query strings we put in place in our #switcher unordered list, the two possible values for our "mystyle" cookie are either hot or contrast. As a result, if you click a link with an href of switch.php?style=hot, then the resulting link element will be:

```
<link rel="stylesheet" href="hot.css" type="text/css" />
```

And with that, we've successfully completed our PHP style sheet switcher. Building on the goals and concepts we outlined for our JavaScript switcher, we've now implemented a solution that allows our users to select a design at their leisure, with a much lower technical barrier for entry.

CSS Beyond the Browser

So, we've established that our document is looking quite fetching when viewed in a modern desktop browser. We've also explored a few different ways to allow users to change our sites' presentation layer. What happens when we take that document outside of the browser context? What happens when we try to print one of our hyper-stylized designs?

Well, we've selected the Gratuitous CSS skin, quite a bit — let's look at Figure 8-8.

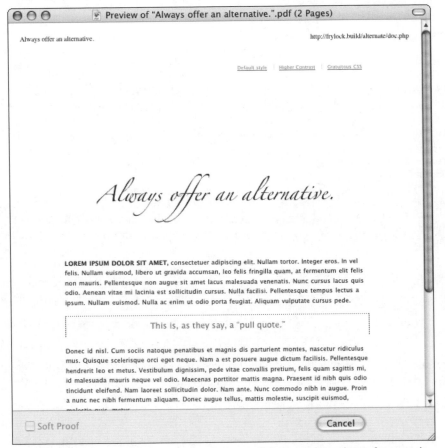

Figure 8-8: Here's the printed version of our page (or a preview thereof, anyway). We can definitely do better.

As you can see, a little too much of our design is showing through when it's printed, but not enough to be particularly effective. Gone are the page's background color and graphic, which printers won't render by default. Additionally, the rules that govern the page's layout are still fully intact. Our content appears to have been pushed down the page for no good reason. The white space at the top doesn't serve any purpose, and instead clips the amount of text visible on the page. Furthermore, the small sans-serif face we've settled on for the body copy might be fine on-screen (where the user can increase the size of the type as he or she sees fit), but it's less than ideal for paper. Serif faces are generally used to improve legibility when reading a page offline, and something a few points taller than our current type size might not hurt. In short, unless you're Emily Dickinson, this printed version isn't exactly appealing.

So, ultimately, we should create a separate design for the printed version of our page—one that emphasizes legibility over style, yet without sacrificing aesthetics altogether. Historically, this would require no small amount of overhead on our part. The days of separate, "print-only" versions of pages still loom largely in our memory. Keeping these "design-light" pages in sync with their "design-full" counterparts was an incredibly time- and resource-consuming affair that often required complicated scripts, grueling hours of manual editing, and occasionally more than a little late-night swearing at the computer monitor (not that the pain is still fresh in our minds or anything).

Media Types: Let the Healing Begin

The authors of the CSS specification anticipated this problem. They introduced the notion of *media types*, a means of classifying style sheets to deliver different designs to different devices such as printers, computer monitors, screen readers, handheld Internet-ready devices, and the like. Simply by earmarking our three link elements as containing "screen"-specific designs that should be delivered only to full graphic browsers (such as IE or Firefox), we can avoid some of the unpleasantness we saw earlier. To do so, we simply specify a value of "screen" in the link's media attribute:

```
<link rel="stylesheet" href="main.css" type="text/css" media="screen" />
<link rel="alternate stylesheet" title="Higher Contrast" href="contrast.css"
type="text/css" media="screen" />
<link rel="alternate stylesheet" title="Gratuitous CSS" href="hot.css"
type="text/css" media="screen" />
```

Now, when we preview our document in its printed view, Figure 8-9 shows us that things look quite a bit different.

It might not look like it, but this is, in fact, progress. By adding the media="screen" attribute to our links, we've wedded our designs to one context—the browser—and divorced them from all others. So, when viewing our document in a different media type (such as a printer), we're shown the raw, unstyled content.

We can also specify multiple media types for any given link element. For example, the Opera browser (www.opera.com/) respects the "projection" media type when browsing in its full-screen viewing mode. As a result, it disregards any CSS we reserve exclusively for the "screen" media. If we want to reuse our screen-specific style sheet in a projection environment, we can simply append it to the media attribute with a comma: <link rel="stylesheet" href="main.css" type="text/css" media="screen, projection" />.

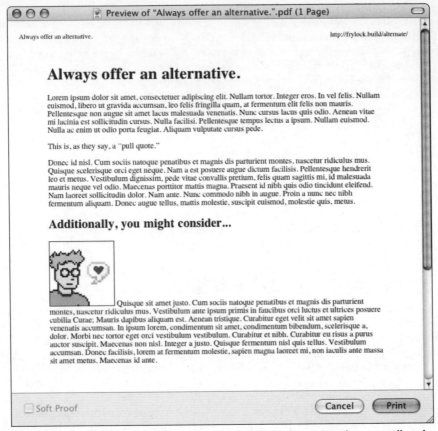

Figure 8-9: Once we add media="screen" to our link element, we've . . . well, we've messed up our printed document royally. Thankfully, we're only laying the foundation.

Of course, while we can deny styles to non-browser devices, we can also deliver styles exclusively to them as well. After all, there's no reason to suffer through an unstyled printout when our on-screen design is so robust. So, with that, let's create a style sheet called `print.css`, as shown in Listing 8-7.

Listing 8-7: Our print.css Style Sheet

```
body {
  background: #FFF;
  color: #000;
  font: 12pt/1.4em Georgia, Garamond, "Times New Roman", Times, serif;
}
```

```
h1, h2 {
  font-weight: normal;
  margin: 1em 0;
  padding: 0;
  text-transform: small-caps;
}

img.portrait, #switcher {
  display: none;
}

#blurb {
  background: #CCC;
  border: 1px solid #999;
  float: right;
  font: 16pt/1.5em Helvetica, Arial, Geneva, Verdana, sans-serif;
  margin: 0 0 1em 1em;
  padding: 1em;
  text-align: right;
  text-transform: small-caps;
  width: 10em;
}
```

Expecting something a bit more complex? As much as we enjoy throwing curveballs at our audience, there's no reason to do so here. When creating a print-specific style sheet, we can use the same syntax and tactics we've discussed throughout the book. Whether applied in the browser or on a piece of paper, it's still CSS — no curveballs required. Granted, there are a few things to consider when designing for print:

❑　Perhaps the most striking thing about our print-specific style rules is that we're using points to control the size of our type. While points are an absolute measure of font size, we opted to use them to show the only acceptable context for their use: print styles. When designing for the screen, we've avoided points like the plague because of browsers' inconsistent rendering of point sizes. For print, however, points are ideal. Of course, the other relative sizing tactics we've used in the past (that is, relying on ems or percentages to control the type relative to the user's settings) are perfectly acceptable, and will, in fact, be kinder to our users' browser preferences.

❑　We've decided that certain aspects of our markup don't need to be displayed in the printout. Perhaps we should spare users from printing out the photo of our ugly mug (and besides, we'd prefer it wasn't tacked up on office cube walls to be used as a dartboard). And of course, the links for our in-browser style sheet switcher are wholly pointless. With our print-specific style sheet, it's a simple matter of specifying img.portrait, #switcher { display: none; }. Through the magic of media types, these two elements will still be available on-screen, but removed from the printed version.

After creating our print-specific style sheet, let's include it in the `head` of our document. As always, we'll use a `link` to do so, but we'll take extra care to specify the correct media type: namely, `"print"`:

```
<link rel="stylesheet" href="main.css" type="text/css" media="screen" />

<link rel="stylesheet" href="print.css" type="text/css" media="print" />

<link rel="alternate stylesheet" title="Higher Contrast" href="contrast.css"
type="text/css" media="screen" />
<link rel="alternate stylesheet" title="Gratuitous CSS" href="hot.css"
type="text/css" media="screen" />
```

When we try printing again, the results should be a bit more pleasing to the eye. This time around, the screen-specific style sheets will be ignored, and our `print.css` will be allowed to control the presentation. As you can see from Figure 8-10, our assumptions seem to be pretty much spot-on.

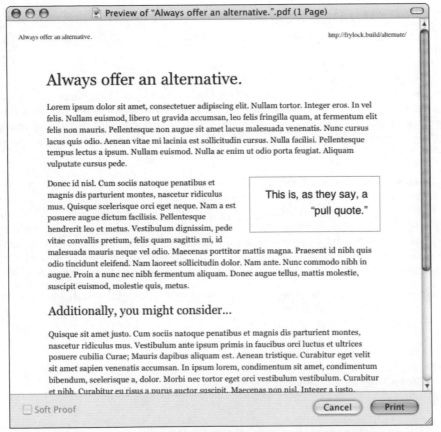

Figure 8-10: And here we are, with our print-specific style sheet in place.

Our minuscule, sans-serif typeface has been replaced with a much more attractive serif face. Of course, we're not ones to settle for the Model-T of fonts so we've opted to use the much more attractive Garamond or Georgia for our page's print version. And, whereas we previously styled our #blurb paragraph as a full-column block on its own row, we use the float model to pull it out of the document flow, and give our pull quote much more of an "in-content" feel.

All of this has happened independently of the progress we've made with our on-screen designs. Essentially, our use of media types has allowed us to create two separate and distinct "views" of our page: the on-screen (aesthetically rich) version of our on-screen design and the off-line (content-over-panache) printed view. One markup document is displayed on multiple devices. Style sheets allow us to realize the promise of device independence, all the while keeping us from those late-night sessions of yelling at our computer monitors.

The Problem with Choice

But now that we've implemented our media-specific designs, we are in some respects back at square one. Now that we've allowed our users the ability to choose an on-screen design that works most effectively for them, we've imposed a print-specific style sheet on them, with no option to change it. Do our users have to sacrifice choice in non-screen media?

We love asking leading questions. In short, the answer is, "No." We could go back to our JavaScript- and PHP-enabled style switchers and add in cases for print-specific styles. Of course, given the number of different media possibilities, our scripts (and the UI we present to our users) could become prohibitively large and difficult to maintain. What we need, then, is an elegant, scalable solution that allows us to easily and quickly manage our alternate styles for multiple media types—and all without sacrificing usability.

Stuff and Nonsense: Building a Better Switcher

We're lucky that certain innovative folks are already thinking along these lines. Enter Stuff and Nonsense, a design studio (www.malarkey.co.uk/) based in Wales, UK. (Figure 8-11 shows its home page.) A quick browse through the studio's portfolio (www.malarkey.co.uk/Our_work_and_our_clients.aspx) leads to two separate realizations: first, that the studio has done eye-catching, beautiful work for such globally recognized brands as Disney and the World Wildlife Fund; second, the design of each of their portfolio sites is driven by cascading style sheets, and built upon a foundation of valid XHTML.

Figure 8-11: The home page of Stuff and Nonsense (www.malarkey.co.uk/), a well-respected design boutique based in the UK

So, obviously, Web standards are a passion over at Stuff and Nonsense. But as you browse through its site, an obvious respect for its users' needs runs equally deep. Featured prominently on each page is a link inviting users to "Customise this site" (www.malarkey.co.uk/Customise_this_site.aspx), as shown in Figure 8-12. On the resulting page, users are able to select various style options for not only their in-browser experience, but different options for printing as well. Whether a user prefers reading printed documents in either a small sans-serif typeface or a larger serif, Stuff and Nonsense has given him or her the ability to decide. And furthermore, the user's preferences are stored in a cookie, so that the preferences persist throughout the time spent visiting the site. The user can browse to or print any page on the site, and will be presented with the design that best meets his or her needs throughout the stay.

This is the oddly named yet feature rich "Invasion of the Body Switchers" (IOTBS)–style switcher, its name derived from how its switching functionality is powered by switching the class attribute on the body element. It's quite possibly the perfect style switcher, and the authors of IOTBS have made it freely available for download at http://stuffandnonsense.co.uk/resources/iotbs.html. Remarkably easy to install and configure, IOTBS affords maximum convenience to site owners and users alike. It even generates its entire interface via JavaScript, ensuring that users unable to take advantage of CSS switching won't be presented with non-functional markup.

With a tool like IOTBS in our arsenal, we can avail ourselves more of the true power of media-specific style sheets. Its easy-to-install interface will have our users thanking us, as we've managed to democratize our design. They can now sand down the rough edges that don't meet their needs, and tailor our site into something truly usable.

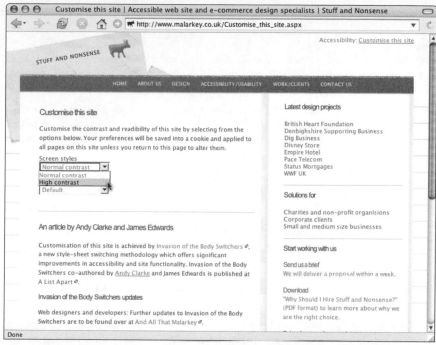

Figure 8-12: The "Invasion of the Body Switchers"–style switcher, seen here at the Stuff and Nonsense site, allows users to select style options for screen, print, or any other media type through one simple interface.

Meet the Designer: Andy Clarke

With our brief introduction to IOTBS behind us, let's meet one of the minds behind it. The creative director of Stuff and Nonsense, Andy Clarke is a rare breed of Web professional. A multitalented designer, developer, and writer, Andy has been the creative director of Stuff and Nonsense since founding it in 1998. As one-half of the team that brought the Web such an ingenious approach to style switching, Andy was gracious enough to answer a few brief questions about accessibility, high-caliber design, and how the two aren't mutually exclusive.

Q: *Andy, it's great to have you for this little chat. We've just had a browse through your personal Web site (www.stuffandnonsense.co.uk/), and can tell that, aside from some sort of odd scooter fixation, you're quite passionate about designing for the Web. Your professional biography (http://malarkey.co.uk/The_Stuff_and_Nonsense_team.aspx#clarke) tells us that you have a background in advertising. How is it, then, that you moved into Web design?*

A: Well, it's a long story, and I won't bore you with all of it. When I left college (having studied for a degree in Fine Art), I worked in various jobs, but was always involved in the arts and always with technology. I was one of the first people in the UK to work with professional digital cameras and before that, with electronic retouching, in the dark days before Photoshop!

My background in art always let me keep a creative eye on the job, and when I got the chance to move to a creative advertising agency in London, I jumped at the chance.

This was a time when the Web was beginning to "get commercial," and I saw very early that the Web done well is just like advertising: communicating messages and getting an audience to identify with a client. Then, in 1998, I moved away from London, and before long, people began asking, "Can you do . . .?" Seven years later, I'm very lucky in that they haven't stopped asking.

Q: *The client list of your studio, Stuff and Nonsense, features an impressive array of brand names, including (but not limited to) the Disney Store UK and World Wildlife Federation UK. Even more impressive is the fact that all of your portfolio work is both crisply designed and built with XHTML/CSS. Why Web standards?*

A: Why not? I don't see either Web standards or (for that matter) accessibility as issues. I believe that they are simply part of doing the job "right." One of the things that I have learned in working with clients at Stuff and Nonsense is that they rarely care "how" a job is done. What matters to them is successfully connecting with their target audience.

You mentioned Disney Store UK and I think that it is fair to say that like most clients, they did not ask for a standards-compliant site. But they were looking for reductions in download times, an altogether faster shopping experience, and easier ways for them to update their site. Implementing the design with Web Standards technologies fit the bill and achieved their goals perfectly.

The Disney Store UK site was developed using the Karova Store platform (www.karova.com/), which not only separates the presentation tier from the rest of site, but has an XML architecture rather than a database backend. XML is transformed into XHTML through XSLT, the end result being a site that is extremely flexible and will allow Disney Store UK new opportunities to deliver their content in the future, including through RSS feeds. At the end of the day, what matters to most clients is not the "tools," but the solutions offered to them. Web standards offers more solutions and that is why Stuff and Nonsense develops only with standards.

Q: *So, tell us a bit about this clever little thing you cooked up. Something about a style sheet switcher, we understand?*

A: You're referring to "Invasion of the Body Switchers" (IOTBS), the style sheet switcher that I wrote about on *A List Apart* magazine (www.alistapart.com/articles/bodyswitchers/)? Well, I can't take credit for the really clever stuff. The technical genius behind IOTBS was my good friend James Edwards (www.brothercake.com) who took my concept and made it work.

One of the important aspects of Web standards is the ability for designers to work on presentations through CSS without changing the underlying markup (HTML or XHTML) of a Web page. Nowhere is this demonstrated better than on Dave Shea's CSS Zen Garden (www.csszengarden.com/), where we see different designs of the same page made possible through using CSS style sheets.

"Switching" style sheets can be necessary for all sorts of reasons. Perhaps a client would like to offer visitors the ability to switch between a fixed-width or a "liquid" layout that fills the window — designer and author Dan Cederholm offers just such a choice on his site, SimpleBits (www.simplebits.com/). Alternatively, you may wish to offer visitors with low vision an "accessible" design. The possibilities are endless and sometimes the aims and results are serious, sometimes just geeky gimmicks.

Server-side and JavaScript style sheet switchers have been around for years. But what makes "Invasion of the Body Switchers" different is the ability to independently switch screen, printer, and other media styles. All with only one CSS and one JavaScript file. I'm very proud of IOTBS and I hope that it will help convince more designers that working with standards can expand their creative options.

Q: *We see that it's used heavily on the site of Stuff and Nonsense (www.malarkey.co.uk/). Have you used it on any professional projects? Is this something that's important to clients?*

A: What is becoming increasingly important to our clients is offering visitors choices. Style sheet switchers such "Invasion of the Body Switchers" can be used to offer separate design themes to different visitor groups. But by using CSS "display properties," we can also hide and reveal content.

This has been put to great effect in several recent projects that target young people. By using the possibilities opened up by CSS and IOTBS, we no longer have to code three or more versions of an XHTML document or even an entire Web site. This reduces development times, makes our business more efficient, and ultimately saves the client money. Everyone is happy.

Q: *Some designers might find it unsettling to allow users to, well, essentially revise their sites' design. What would you say to them? Why should we let our users have greater control over the design of our pages?*

As designers or developers of Web sites, we need to remember who we are working for. Of course it is our client who puts our food on the table, but our work is ultimately judged by site visitors. The happier they are, the happier our clients will be and the better the chance that they will come back.

The Web is unlike any other media. In television the picture stays pretty much the same no matter what size screen you are viewing on. CRT, LCD, or Plasma, 17-inch portable or 52-inch widescreen, things stay pretty much the same. On the Web, we do not simply "sit back and watch." We have more control over how the content is delivered and Web designers must remember that visitors' opinions matter more than their own.

Q: *After poking around a bit, it seems that there have been a number of style switchers published online. Some of them rely on client-side JavaScript (as yours does), whereas others rely on some back-end coding. Is there a clear benefit to either approach?*

A: Now you're getting all technical on me! I'm only a humble designer! Many different solutions are available to implement style sheet switching; some of them are "server side" (relying on back-end languages such as PHP) and others like "Invasion of the Body Switchers" are "client-side," using languages such as JavaScript. Which solution a developer chooses depends on the environment in which the site is running and the specific needs of the client.

It's only a personal preference, but as style sheet switching is a "client function," I prefer to use client-side solutions. That said, I can give you the exclusive news that there will be a server-side version of "Invasion of the Body Switchers" coming very soon.

So, I suppose that begs the question: What is it that makes your client-side switcher stand apart from the crowd?

"Invasion of the Body Switchers" takes a new approach to style sheet switching. Our approach does require abandoning conventional "stylesheet" and "alternate stylesheet" semantics, but this doesn't trouble me, because:

1. Many browsers do not implement native style sheet switching.

2. Those that do do not apply any persistence to a selected alternate style sheet.

Other solutions rely on multiple style sheets, using `<link />` elements and "stylesheet / alternate stylesheet" semantics. This adds extra server calls, but more important, it does not allow for different media styles to be selected independently of each other.

"Invasion of the Body Switchers" lets us target different media types independently, and gives site visitors a simple interface from which to select their preferences, all saved into a cookie until they change their mind.

IOTBS works by adding one or more unique class names to the page's `<body>` tag. Styles are then defined using descendant selectors. The end result gives users much greater control over the output of your Web pages.

Q: *Interesting, so what are these "media types" you speak of? Why should the CSS-savvy Web designer care about them?*

A: It's sometimes hard for designers who come to the Web from other media to understand that that not only is their work not viewed "pixel perfect" by everyone, but that people access Web content through different media. Sometimes that media is our good friend the computer monitor; sometimes it is an Internet kiosk at the airport; sometimes a handheld computer, a projected image, or even a mobile phone. Some people find it more difficult to read from a screen and like to print out pages.

In the past, preparing for all these different media types would have been cost-prohibitive, if not impossible, as it required making different versions for different viewing devices. But, with the advent of technologies that support common standards, we can create content that can be written once only, and then styled for different media output, all through the magic of CSS.

Q: *Stepping back a bit, we'd be interested to hear a bit more about your design process. How do you usually work?*

A: Our first job is to understand what the client is trying to communicate to his or her audience. We also get a feel for the "personality" of the company and look at their brand values (even if they haven't done so themselves) so that we can match the tone of the design to the personality and brand values. Effective design for the Web is about effective communication between a client and their audience. That is why we focus on what and how to communicate, before we think about technical or creative issues.

We start by developing paper prototype designs, from sketches to layouts made in either Photoshop or Macromedia Fireworks. These layouts begin as simple wireframes and from them we build markup guides, often on paper, which our developers use as their XHTML structure.

Some time ago, I developed a set of naming conventions for our site development, specific names for `<div>`s and classes that relate to content rather than presentation (`#branding` rather than `#header`, and so on). We stick tightly to these conventions so that the entire team understands what a particular CSS rule relates to. We also have conventions for the naming of images and this also speeds development.

Our graphic layouts then develop into production art for our design team and it is rare that our final Web pages do not match the graphic layout exactly. We also get approval from the client at each stage and always work within our internal convention framework to ensure that development is as efficient as possible.

Q: *And what about inspiration? When you're staring down a tight client deadline, from where do you get your ideas?*

A: I'm a real pop culture junkie. I love trashy pulp detective novels such as Mickey Spillane's Mike Hammer. I love comics even more and works by comic artists such as "Sin City's" Frank Miller and "Concrete" creator Paul Chadwick are a few of my passions.

You might find it unusual to hear that I am also passionate about political art from Soviet-era Russia, China, and Cuba. I find the cult of personality fascinating and across recent history there have been many terrific examples where political art in the form of posters or statues becomes almost "high" art. The most recent examples I have seen have come from pre-invasion Iraq.

I suppose that if I think about it, what these examples have in common is that they are both designed to engage an audience, drawing them into a different world. Again, it's about communicating messages . . . and so we get back on to the subject of the Web.

Q: *Are there any CSS issues that you face more regularly than others? How do you work through them?*

A: CSS issues are becoming rarer for me and when one does raise its ugly head, there is usually a solution to be found by doing a quick bit of Googling. Many people with far bigger brains than mine—Brothercake, Dave Shea (`http://mezzoblue.com`), Doug Bowman (`http://stopdesign .com/`), and John Gallant immediately spring to mind—have found solutions to browser bugs and behaviors I would never have dreamt existed. Of course, there are times when I curse one browser or another and yell "This would be soooo much easier with tables!" But those outbursts are getting rarer.

There are now ways to fix or work around almost every CSS issue and when one does appear unexpectedly, it is important to take a logical approach, as sometimes one element in combination with another will trigger a problem.

Validation is extremely important and ensuring that my code validates is always my first move before I even open a CSS file. If my code and CSS both validate and the problem still appears, I deconstruct the page, removing elements in turn so that I can see which element is straining my sanity.

Many browser bugs are now so well-known that entire sites such as John Gallant's Position Is Everything (`www.positioniseverything.net/`) are dedicated to them. If an answer can't be found on PIE or on many other sites, I recommend asking a question of the many experts who contribute to Eric Meyer's (`www.meyerweb.com/`) excellent CSS-D mailing list (`http:// css-discuss.org/`). Ask nicely and you're likely to find a helpful soul with a solution.

Q: *What exactly do you look for in a "successful" site design? Are there any design principles you hold especially dear?*

A: I suppose that I'm not the best person to judge whether or not a design is successful, but I do listen to feedback from clients and their customers. What matters to me is that the project has made good business for the client who pays my wages. That way, I hope that they will keep coming back.

When I look back on many of the designs I have made, it is always the clearer, simpler ones that I like the most. I take the approach that no amount of design "fairy dust" can transform a poor content site into a successful site. So, I work with clients on ensuring that content always come first.

Working from content outward is always better than trying to "shoehorn" content into a preconceived design or layout, and that is why I often spend more time on planning and wireframing a site before I contemplate the design look-and-feel.

Q: *Any last words you'd care to share with us?*

A: "When I didn't know what color to put down, I put down black. Black is a force: I depend on black to simplify the construction." Actually not my words, but those of artist Henri Matisse.

Summary

Well, that was something of a whirlwind, wasn't it? With a heightened understanding of media-specific CSS and three different style-switching strategies, we've covered no small amount of ground. Yet, as with much of this book, this is but a road map to some incredibly rich landscapes. As a result, it's going to feel like quite a gloss. We could cover an entire chapter on each of these topics, and would recommend further, deeper research on any of these CSS switching strategies. Our users will thank us if we do that, our sites will be available to a much wider audience, and we'll be able to tell our mother that we actually wrote something useful.

And to that end, it's time to stop seeing us walk the walk—in the next chapter, we talk all kinds of talk. By applying the techniques discussed throughout the book, it's time to finally put these strategies to practice in a real-world site design. Exciting, yes?

Bringing It All Together

"Good artists borrow, great artists steal." — *Picasso*

The first two chapters of this book discussed planning and best practices, and each subsequent chapter focused on a particular aspect of CSS-enabled design from some of today's most popular Web destinations.

From Blogger's use of rollovers to Stuff and Nonsense's style switcher, the methods in this book are just as crucial to online design success as they are relevant to the sites you build — whether you are building your company's site, a site for a client, or just building your own site.

In this chapter, the lead author, Christopher Schmitt, demonstrates the process that went into building his own home page design. He illustrates how the lessons in the previous chapters (as well as some new techniques) are helpful for your own professional projects.

Enter ChristopherSchmitt.com

I've been designing Web pages since 1993. While I had a couple versions of a home page, my own Web site came online around 1997, back when it was okay to have a tilde (~) character in the Web address.

That Web site was a glorified hodgepodge of nested HTML tables, single-pixel GIFs, and JavaScript-enabled rollovers, as shown in Figure 9-1. Updates to the site were difficult and rarely happened. Because JavaScript powered the menu navigation, a visitor using a text browser or screen reader wasn't able to get past the front page. Although that design wasn't too shabby for a site built in the mid-1990s, on many levels, my site was failing me.

Figure 9-1: An earlier version of ChristopherSchmitt.com (formerly known as Christopher.org)

To rectify the problem, I used a stopgap measure: taking that site design down and putting up a small site that was, in essence, a portfolio/resume site, as shown in Figure 9-2. I could have spent more time and energy making the site a blog or expanding the content, but I've been busy. My life the last couple of years has involved dealing with several moves, navigating a new relationship, working a part-time job, and attending graduate school. If you ever needed a reason why you didn't update your Web site, chances are I could have given you one. I've had plenty of excuses to spare.

Now my life has become more stable (knock on wood), and I have more time to devote to my spot on the World Wide Web. Before I crank open an HTML editor or even my cherished Photoshop application, I'm going to plan out what I'm going to do.

Figure 9-2: The bare-bones version

Planning Saves Time

My first hard lesson in planning as it relates to graphic design came when I was a journalism student in my high school. I was the graphics editor, and my responsibilities included creating the images for each edition of an eight-page newspaper. While today it's easy to surf over to a Web site and download a cheap royalty-free image at iStockPhoto.com, back in 1991 the process was a bit more laborious.

For the first couple of issues I worked on, I gathered the list of articles from my staff members to determine how many images were required for the next issue. With the list in hand, I then sat in front of the Macintosh computer with a blank Photoshop document open.

First I tinkered with the Photoshop settings and filters to see if something would just happen to appear. When that didn't work, I typed a couple of keywords related to the article in weird typefaces. Then I made another trip to the Photoshop settings and filters. After a few hours, I was lucky if I had a solid image or two to show for my effort.

By the time the third issue rolled around, I knew that I wasn't using the computer effectively. I had spent many hours listlessly trying to create graphics out of thin air instead of coming to the computer with an agenda or a goal. The solution was to change how I approached a computer and my work.

Instead of going straight to the computer to work on graphic designs, I took a few sheets of paper from the printer tray, walked past the computers, and headed over to a workbench. Once there, I came up with ideas for graphics for each story by doodling, sketching, or brainstorming and by using cluster diagrams. With the ideas for images in place, I then went to the computer.

The results were staggering. Instead of several days of working out only a couple of graphics, I spent one day coming up with the concepts for the images and then one to two days creating them. This immediate efficiency was also welcomed by my fellow staff members, who, having discovered that I had more free time, put me to work helping out with their tasks.

To effectively use the computer, I needed a plan on how to use it. Otherwise, the computer was a hindrance.

Defining the Site's Scope

With the lessons of planning firmly ingrained and underscored in Chapter 1, let's define the goals, deliverables, and assumptions for my new site:

❑ **Goals:**

   ❑ **Improve aesthetic design.** My current site is a simple, straightforward Web site built in CSS. One of the goals for the site is to be more visually appealing and push the CSS further.

   ❑ **Add a blog.** To ease when updating the site, I want to implement blogging software. My software of choice will be WordPress because it relies on open source software (PHP and MySQL). Also, I'm familiar with both technologies, so I should be able to make tweaks to the code or integrate other components of my site more easily than with another solution.

   ❑ **Provide usable navigation.** The design must make navigation simple and must be usable on text-only browsers as well as on screen readers.

   ❑ **Update photo headers.** To facilitate some updates, I want to include a photo in the header of the page and update it when I have an interesting photo I've taken with my trusty digital camera.

   ❑ **Increase traffic to the site.** With an improved design, generating heavier traffic to my domain name is still the major goal. While the blogging software will help to manage the content, site updates must happen on regular basis. That means, as the sole content producer, I have to publish on a regular basis.

❑ **Deliverables:**

   ❑ **Photoshop comps.** The design of the site will include a main page design that can be modified for other pages in the site.

   ❑ **HTML+CSS templates.** After the completion of the design in Photoshop, I will construct the design templates with valid HTML and CSS. Once the templates are finished, the next step is to integrate them into the blogging software.

❑ **Assumptions:**

   ❑ **Audience.** For the most part, the site's *audience is computer and Web savvy*. Because of the nature of my work with Web design, my primary audience has better-than-average computer systems, including up-to-date Web browsers and monitor resolutions.

   ❑ **Browsers.** With an advanced audience, the site design should *target certain browsers*. I will build the site for Internet Explorer for Windows 5.5+, Netscape Navigator 7+, Safari, and Firefox 1+.

Content and the Site Map

With the scope set, my attention turns to taking an inventory of the content. While it may sound like a difficult task, it's very easy. Only if the site is medium to large is the process time-intensive.

Considering all the material that was online (or material that I wanted to have online), I think the hardest part is really taking an honest look at what I have to work with.

When designing for someone other than yourself, you are warned that obtaining content from clients is the hardest part of the Web development process.

Where does the content come from? The choices fall into four categories:

❑ Gathered from internal sources (and, I hope, not strewn across databases, Microsoft Word files, and print collateral)

❑ Original content (previously unwritten) created by the client

❑ Content that you pay someone to write (preferably a professional copywriter or technical writer)

❑ A combination of the three

From my experience, clients will write their own content or reduce the number of sections to save costs. However, paying a professional copywriter or technical writer to create quality has more of a chance in improving the success of a project.

After an examination of my own content, I determined these were the main sections for my site, as shown in Figure 9-3:

- ❑ **Home (or Main).** Links back to the front page.
- ❑ **Journal.** The main page for the blog and the place that contains links to archived blog entries.
- ❑ **About.** A brief biography section.
- ❑ **Work.** The portfolio section for my print and work.
- ❑ **Shop.** A section for people to buy books and other items for sale.
- ❑ **Publications.** The listing of my writings and speaking engagements.
- ❑ **Contact.** A site's contact form should always be in easy reach of your audience.

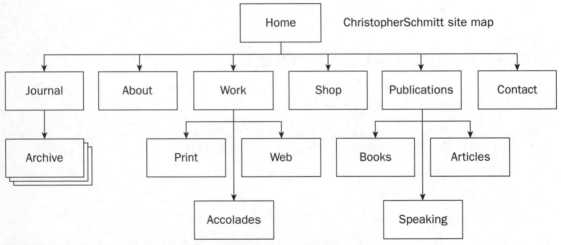

Figure 9-3: A site map representing the proposed site architecture

Framing the Layout

With the content inventory and site map in hand, I have the major building blocks in place. The next step is examining the structure of the Web pages themselves.

As mentioned in Chapter 2, a *wireframe* is a line drawing that illustrates the different areas of content on a page. It doesn't showcase any design-related information except for the composition of the elements within the page. Drawn in tools such as Adobe Illustrator or Omni Group's OmniGraffle, the wireframe is a simple schematic that showcases the placement of content areas within a page, as shown in Figure 9-4.

Figure 9-4: The wireframe for my page design

Designing the Site

With the preparation of scope, site map, content inventory, and wireframe done, it's time to start *designing* the site.

Based on the direction from Chapter 2, the next steps include deciding on the tone, looking for inspiration, determining the layout, and, you know, working on a design.

Emoting Is Designing

One of the key things you learn about design is that, at its core, it's about communicating *emotion*. All design elements that come into play with a design (whether it's print, television, or the Web) reflect how well the *design of the message* was aptly matched with *the message* itself.

A simple way to think about the separation of design and the message is to think about how you communicate with your voice. By placing emphasis on a different word in a sentence, you change the meaning of the sentence.

Read the following sentences aloud, placing the emphasis on the words in italics:

- ❑ *Why* did you sign the file?
- ❑ Why *did* you sign the file?
- ❑ Why did *you* sign the file?
- ❑ Why did you *sign* the file?
- ❑ Why did you sign the *file*?

As you go through the sentences, you should hear that the meaning of the sentence changes from one to the next, even though the words stay the same. With design, it's pretty much the same thing.

A designer has a toolbox of theories and techniques to apply the right emphasis to get a message the proper reception from the viewers. However, an uninformed designer can place the emphasis poorly in a design, minimizing the effect of the message and causing a communication problem with the audience.

Or, worse yet, the intended audience doesn't receive the message *at all*. With communication, it's the message that *is* received that's the most important message, no matter how good your intentions are. With any design, how you say it is as important as what you say.

Setting the Tone

As the designer, I must determine how to emphasize the message. There are elements of a design that a person can control to craft the right impression for a design, including typography, colors, imagery, and layout for the content. To set the right tone for my site, I must determine how to *best* use typography, colors, imagery, and layout for the content. I must choose these elements carefully, because when the elements I pick come together, they will set the tone of the site.

In my site design, the overall tone I want to set is friendly so that people respond to the site on an informal basis. However, at the same time, I do want to project a professional image. To achieve this, I want to have a mixture of organic characteristics (friendly) meshed with structured, conservative elements (professional).

To achieve the more structured, conservative approach to the site, the inherent nature of the CSS box model will help. Also, I will be using the SuperTiny SimCity style. If you have played games such as SimCity or visited sites that look like k10k (see www.k10k.net/), you will immediately recall the style of these images. This style is characterized by a heavy reliance on grid layout and a glorification of the pixelated imagery.

To provide some balance to the conservative nature of the site, I'm going to employ some organic artwork. I'm going to rely on the creative use of background images and a special typeface that is perfect with organic characteristics.

One problem with having an organic presentation on a Web page is that it's inherently chaotic at first glance. I'm not the first one to attempt to combine an organic approach with a more rigid framework — I just hope my design doesn't turn out to be another Frankenstein monster.

Typography

With the Web, I'm a bit in a bind because I must use typefaces that are installed on both Windows and Mac OS platforms. For areas of common text (such as blog posts), I will use common Web fonts, Georgia and Verdana, with font-matching substitutes for each font as shown in the following table.

Page Section	Typeface
Logo, special treatments	Not Caslon (see www.emigre.com/EF.php?fid=111)
Headings	Georgia, Times New Roman, Times (serif)
Content	Verdana, Arial, Helvetica (sans-serif)

However, for the logo (which will bear my name), I want to use Not Caslon from Émigré, as shown in Figure 9-5.

Figure 9-5: Not Caslon shown in the logo

Colors

For this Web site, I'm using a mixture of bold, modern colors. For the organic feel, the leaves around my hometown serve as inspiration. The colors I'm going to be using are bright greens and yellows, as well as brown and an orange for the highlight.

Feel free to visit ChristopherSchmitt.com for a look-see at the color choices and let me know what you think.

Imagery

The imagery comes from a variety of sources. For starters, I'm exploiting Émigré's typeface. It comes out of the box with great forms perfect for the organic style I desire, but it also begs for experimentation.

To complement the organic characteristics, I'm using circles balanced with horizontal rectangles, especially in the navigation, as shown in Figure 9-6.

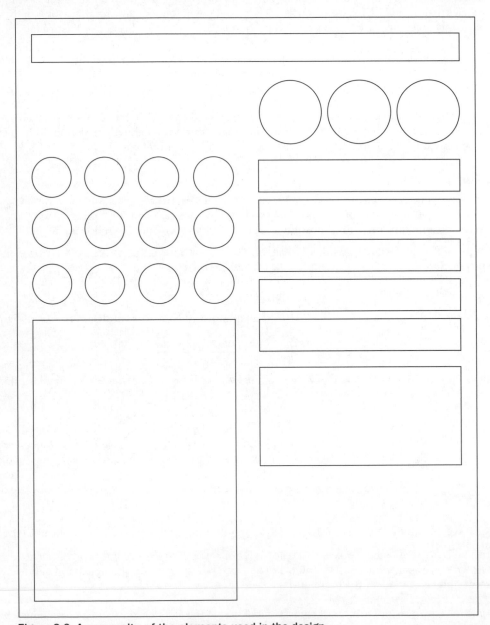

Figure 9-6: A composite of the elements used in the design

Layout

The layout is pretty much set in stone with the completion of the wireframe, but I want to take a moment to discuss the rationale behind some aspects of the layout:

- ❑ **Navigation.** Based on personal observation and preference, I placed the navigation on the right-hand side because most people position the cursor on the right-hand side of the browser window while they are skimming a Web page. As soon as the user wants to go to a different section, the amount of distance the cursor must cover to reach the navigation is less when the menu is on the right compared to the left. The less time to accomplish a task often means a better surfing experience for the visitor.

- ❑ **Search box.** I placed the search box on the top of the page because that's where Jakob Nielsen placed his on his site (see www.useit.com). Actually, I put the search feature there as a release valve for my readers. If they can't find what they are looking for through a couple clicks on the navigation, they can go to the search feature. But in these crazy search engine days of Google, I realize that people often "surf" through a site by hitting the search function first.

- ❑ **Fixed-width, 800 pixels wide.** As a designer, I like the control that having a fixed-width design affords me. Also, I'm in favor of making sure the design is large enough to fill the screen at 800 pixels wide. This width is slightly unusual in that Web pages monitor resolutions at 800 pixels wide. Resolutions that can expand only to 800 pixels wide mean that Web page designs must have a viewport of no more than 792 pixels to ensure that the entire page is visible. The rationale for having a larger page width is based on three things:

  - ❑ **Monitor resolutions are increasing.** Out of the box, new computers are coming with monitors that can handle higher resolutions. And the audience for my site is using the latest and greatest computer technologies and should be able to view the site just fine.

  - ❑ **Be bold, baby.** When I was first starting out as a designer, I was lucky enough to attend a talk given by Dr. Mario Garcia, who has redesigned newspapers for more than 30 years (see www.mariogarcia.com/Profile.asp?PageId=50). After he redesigned my local newspaper, he was asked by the publication to give a talk to the community about the redesign. One of the minor notes he made in his presentation that has stuck with me throughout my design career was that his clients always tended to be on the shy side with their logos. He makes it a point to make the logo a bold presence on the front page. In other words, don't hesitate to be bold.

  - ❑ **It's a nice even number.** I'm not going to lie. Although I don't think of myself as a slouch in the math department, there's a reason I'm a designer rather than an engineer. I'm not big on math and 800 is a nice easy number to work with, especially in light of Microsoft's box model (see Chapter 8) and the need to make use of workarounds because of it. So, making things easier on myself at the beginning will help me down the road.

Now that we've looked at the tone of the forthcoming design, I open Adobe Photoshop and start working on design versions.

Building It in Photoshop

With a direction and tone set, I can open up Photoshop and simply design our page, right? No. The work I have done so far only reduces the amount of time I stay on the computer, as well as making sure I stay on target with my original goals. The actual designing still takes time. Thankfully, through the magic of book publishing, I already have the design finished (as shown in Figure 9-7), so we don't have to waste any time.

Figure 9-7: Finished home page design

Developing the Site

Now it's time to turn our attention to building the page template with markup and a flash of style.

When building a page with CSS, it's best to code the content in semantic HTML, as demonstrated in the projects discussed in the previous chapters. That means using the appropriate markup to reflect the contents of the element. A heading should be placed in a heading tag; a paragraph should be placed in a p tag and so on.

Outside-In, Top-Down Approach to CSS

Once the markup is complete, I then work with the *outside-in, top-down* approach when applying CSS properties to the HTML properties.

So, first I look at the page as a whole by applying CSS rules to the body element. This is the outside-in approach. Then I work from the top of the page to the bottom by working on the header, followed by the navigation, content areas, and then the footer.

For this design, the first step is to look at centering the fixed-width layout.

Centering the Page (and Why It Matters)

Back in the mid 1990s, my solution to center the Web site design came from the use of HTML frames. Frames aren't very user-friendly and, if they aren't coded correctly, can lock out disabled users or text-browser users to your site. Keeping visitors away from a Web site is not a habit I want to keep for this new design.

Thankfully, in this new millennium, we can use CSS without resorting to dreaded frames. Let's take a look at the markup:

```
<body>
 <div id="frame">
  [ ...content goes here... ]
 </div>
</body>
```

For the div titled frame, we want to set the width as well as the margins:

```
#frame {
 width: 800px;
 margin: 0 auto;
}
```

The margin property values are written in shorthand and tell the browser to reduce the margins on top and bottom of the element to zero, while automatically adjusting the margin on the left and right side so that they are equal, as shown in Figure 9-8.

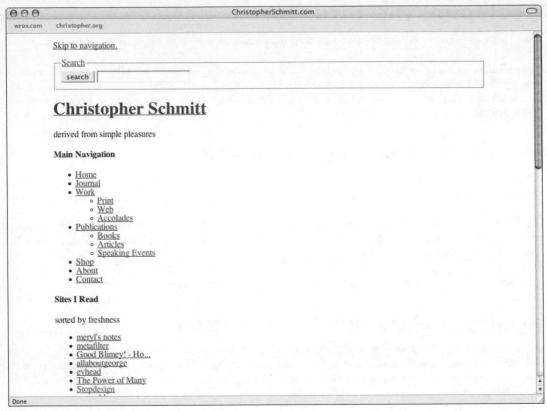

Figure 9-8: Centered content

In a world with only perfect CSS-compliant browsers, this little bit of CSS is all we would need to do. However, Internet Explorer for Windows doesn't understand the `auto` value for margins and thus won't center the layout in that browser, as shown in Figure 9-9.

To work around Internet Explorer, we apply the `text-align` property to the `body` element:

```
body {
  text-align: center;
}
```

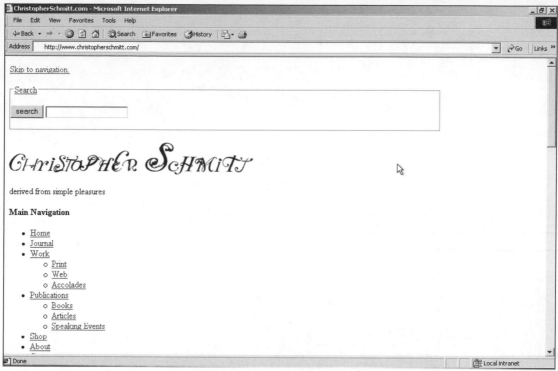

Figure 9-9: Internet Explorer for Windows 5.5 does not center the div element correctly.

The `text-align` property aligns the child element `frame` to the center. This means, too, that all the content within the `frame` container is aligned to the center as well. To counter that effect, I give the `frame` declaration block its own `text-align` property:

```
#frame {
 width: 800px;
 margin: 0 auto;
 text-align: left;
}
```

Now, the content within the frame container is centered for all the modern browsers, as shown in Figure 9-10.

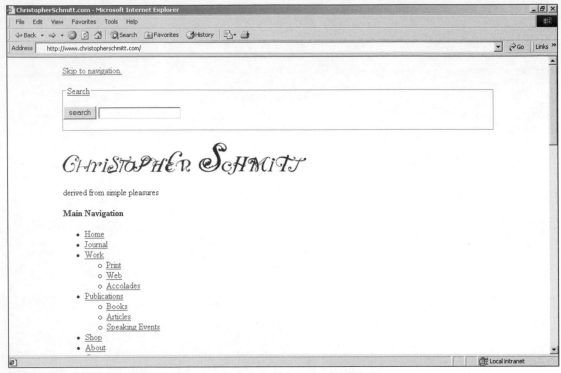

Figure 9-10: Frame container is centered for Internet Explorer for Windows.

With the body and frame of the page set, I then set some additional CSS declarations to every element in the page.

Font Sizing

Even though CSS provides greater control over the typography in a Web design, determining the best way to set the font sizes is not an easy thing to do. For designers who love typography (like myself), it's hard not to take browsers ruining the fonts in our designs personally.

Let's look at some of the common problems with Web typography:

❑ Fonts set in the value of pixels (for example, `font-size: 12px;`) are not resizable in Internet Explorer for Windows.

❑ Using the value of `font-size` keywords isn't an option without a workaround because Internet Explorer for Windows 4/5.5 sets the value of a keyword to the lower value. For example, a value of `x-small` is translated as `xx-small`.

❑ Even with an Internet Explorer for Windows workaround (set to deliver the appropriate keyword values), designers wanting more control over the fonts than seven keyword sizes are at a loss.

Without further losing our sanity, an ingenuous method to gain greater control over Web typography comes from the clever Richard Butter's excellent tutorial, "How to Size Text Using Ems" (see www.clagnut.com/blog/348/).

Butter's solution is to first set the value of the font-size in the body to a value of 62.5 percent:

```
body {
  text-align: center;
  font-size: 62.5%;
}
```

The rationale for this step is that current browsers apply the value of 16 pixels to the value of the medium keyword, which is the default size for HTML text. By setting the font-size for the body to 62.5%, that translates to a very manageable 10 pixels for the math-challenged:

```
16px * 62.5% = 10px
```

With the base value of 10 pixels set, I then adjust the size of the text elsewhere in the document using only em units. (One em unit is equal to the default size of the nearest font.)

For example, if I want a portion of text to be 12 pixels, I set the value of the font-size property to 1.2em.

```
(16px * 62.5%) * 1.2em = 12px
```

If I wanted to set text to the value of the rather large 25 pixels, what would the em value be?

```
(16px * 62.5%) * x = 25px
10px * x = 25px
x = 25/10px
x = 2.5em
```

There are a few curiosities with this solution that should be addressed. (You knew there was going to be a catch, right? This is *Web* typography after all.)

❏   The font-size property values for input, select, th, and td elements must be set to their appropriate size:

```
input, select, th, td {
  font-size: 1em;
}
```

❏   In browsers with the Gecko rendering engine (Mozilla and Firefox, to name two), the values in this method are set to the font-size of 12 pixels. To get a uniform size of the headers in Gecko and non-Gecko browsers, spell out the font sizes for the headings:

```
h1 {
  font-size: 2.5em;
}
h2 {
  font-size: 2em;
}
h3 {
```

```
  font-size: 1.75em;
}
h4 {
  font-size: 1.5em;
}
h5 {
  font-size: 1.25em;
}
h6 {
  font-size: 1em;
}
```

❑   When nesting elements such as list items, the sizes of fonts are going to be sized smaller and smaller. If the font size for a list item is .8em to get a value of 8 pixels, the value of a nested list item within that list will have a value of 6.4 pixels! Let's take a look at some examples and math:

```
<ul>
  <li>The Parent List Item: 10px * 8em = 8px
   <ul>
     <li>The Child List Item: 8px * 8em = 6.4px!</li>
   </ul>
  </li>
</ul>
```

To work around the problem, set the value of nested list items to 1em:

```
li li {
  font-size: 1em;
}
```

Other than that, it's easy. Okay, it's not exactly a walk in a park compared to using font-size keywords, but you do remember the talk about Web typography being tortuous? So, keeping an eye on the placement of HTML elements isn't that difficult a trade-off when there is more control over the Web typography.

With our font solution decided, and the framing of the Web page done (as shown in Listing 9-1), it's time to start working on the content from the top to the bottom starting with the header.

Listing 9-1: The Main CSS Rules for the Page Design

```
body {
  text-align: center;
  font-size: 62.5%;
  font-family: Verdana, Helvetica, Arial, sans-serif;
}
#frame {
  width: 800px;
  margin: 0 auto;
  text-align: left;
}
input, select, th, td {
  font-size: 1em;
}
```

Entering the Head

The first item in the header is a link for skipping the content portion of the Web page. This link allows visitors on a text browser (or people with visual disabilities) to skip past the repetition of hearing or seeing the logo and navigation sections on every page, as shown in Figure 9-11.

```
<body>
 <div id="frame">
  <p><a href="#content">Skip navigation.</a></p>
 </div>
</body>
```

Figure 9-11: The link is visible.

However, I want to hide this link from people seeing the visual design of the Web page. To do this, I create a new class selector in the style sheet with its sole purpose to keep certain elements of a page hidden from view:

```
.no {
 display: none;
}
```

Next, I apply the class selector to the markup so that the style sheet hides the link and the link is gone, as shown in Figure 9-12:

```
<body>
 <div id="frame">
  <p class="no"><a href="#content">Skip navigation.</a></p>
 </div>
</body>
```

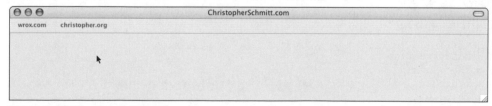

Figure 9-12: The link is invisible.

Finding the Search Box

With the link to the content dealt with, it's time to move to the search box. Listing 9-2 showcases the HTML for the search box (as shown in Figure 9-13).

Listing 9-2: The HTML for the Search Box

```
<body>
 <div id="frame">
  <p class="no"><a href="#content">Skip navigation.</a></p>
   <fieldset>
    <legend><a href="/search/">Search</a></legend>
    <form action="/search/" name="searchbox">
     <input type="submit" value="search" />
     <input type="text" name="q" />
    </form>
   </fieldset>
 </div>
</body>
```

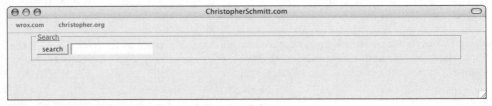

Figure 9-13: The default rendering of the search box

You'll notice that in Figure 9-13, the search box appears on the left, but I want it on the right of the page. To ensure that all the content within the fieldset is styled for this particular fieldset instead of another fieldset that might be placed in the content area of a Web page, the first step is to modify the fieldset property with an id attribute and an appropriate value:

```
<fieldset id="searchbox">
```

Again we are applying the outside-in approach to designing, so the next move is to apply styles to the fieldset itself. What I want to accomplish with the fieldset is to place the green bar at the top of the page, while also aligning the two elements of the form to the right. So, the first CSS rule is this one, as shown in Figure 9-14:

```
fieldset#searchbox {
 border: none;
 background: #d9ff00 url("/_assets/img/brandStripe_bkgd.gif") repeat-x;
 margin: 0;
 padding: 0;
 text-align: right;
}
```

Figure 9-14: Styling the fieldset element

With this CSS rule, I removed the border, the margins, and padding. Next, I added a green color (#d9ff00) to match the background image, which was repeated horizontally. The color was added so that, in case a user's default type size is larger than normal, at least the background color shows through. And the last declaration tells the browser to scoot the contents to the right.

The next step is to hide the legend value, which is easy to do:

```
fieldset#searchbox legend {
  display: none;
}
```

Instead of using a descendant selector, I could have re-used the class selector .no. *However, that would have required the additional markup of a class attribute and its value to the code. So, instead of adding more markup, I might as well be more specific in the CSS, rather than mess up the markup. (For more information on descendant selectors, see Chapters 2 and 6.)*

Now I want to adjust the margins, padding, and font size of the form itself, as shown in Figure 9-15:

```
fieldset#searchbox form {
  margin: 0 30px 0 0;
  padding: 4px 0;
  font-size: 0.8em;
}
```

Figure 9-15: Styling the form element

The next step is to adjust the width and colors of the input and submit buttons, respectively, as shown in Figure 9-16.

```
fieldset#searchbox form input[type="text"] {
 width: 152px;
}

fieldset#searchbox form input[type="submit"] {
 background-color: #FFFF00;
}
```

Figure 9-16: The stylized rendering of the buttons

If you notice, I'm using attribute selectors as mentioned in some detail in Chapters 2 and 6. This selector currently works in Netscape 6+ and Opera 5+ only. Also, browsers such as Safari use their own GUI elements for the form buttons, so styling those elements is out of the question.

A way around the problem of attribute selector support is to change to class selectors. Adding class attributes to both of the input elements changes the markup:

```
<input type="submit" value="search" class="submit" />
<input type="text" name="q" class="text" />
```

Then, all that is required is modifying the attribute selectors to class selectors like so:

```
fieldset#searchbox form input.text{
 width: 152px;
}

fieldset#searchbox form input.submit {
 background-color: #FFFF00;
}
```

Personally, I prefer to leave the attribute selectors in place. To borrow some language from the movie *Office Space*, "It's the browser that sucks, why do I have to change?" But then, that's not a positive attitude, so I should not digress and just move on.

Making Room for the Logo

The next part of the header deals with the logo and the site's tagline. I'm going to add a touch of magic with this approach, but I promise to explain why after it's all done. First, however, I provide the basic markup for the image of the logo as well as the text for the tagline (as shown in Figure 9-17):

```
<div id="header">
 <h1><a href="/" title="Christopher Schmitt, keeping it real
since 1975"><img src="/_assets/img/logo.gif" alt="Christopher Schmitt
logo" border="0" /></a></h1>
 <p>derived from simple pleasures</p>
</div><!-- END #header -->
```

Figure 9-17: The default rendering of the header pieces under the search box

Breaking Down the HTML

While the last two items (the skip to content link and the search box) could be considered part of the header, I've left them out of the div container called "header" because I want the div header to contain components that I feel are essentially part of the header, the logo, and the tagline.

If you recall from Chapter 5 regarding the UFL.edu site redesign, the navigation labels were set in h2 elements to give what Mark Trammell refers to as "the proper gravitas" — the labels played an essential part in the content of the page as well as for the whole site. People using assisted-browsers such as JAWS will get a benefit from the improved markup, but also search engines notice the extra weight a heading element gives to the content. In this same vein, I'm wrapping the image with an h1 element.

Last, at the end of the markup for the header and tagline, notice the HTML comment that reads END #header. This marker is placed at the end of closing div tags to help in the editing of the HTML. With CSS, there is a heavy reliance on the div elements to create the necessary hooks to stylize the content. The more div elements, the more there are closing div elements. After a while, keeping track of all those closing div elements can make a person go cross-eyed. To help reduce the eye strain, I place an HTML comment marker at the end of every div element.

Applying the Style

With the basic HTML set, I want to apply the styles to the header. First, I want to remove the default margins for an h1 element that the browser supplies:

```
#header h1 {
  margin: 0;
}
```

The next step is to apply the photobar at the top of the header. The photobar will be a revolving image placed right above the logo. The next CSS rule accomplishes two things needed to do that: placing the image and then setting enough padding (40 pixels) to keep the background image from obscuring the logo:

```
#header {
  background: transparent url("/_assets/img/photoChange001.jpg") 0 0;
  padding: 40px 0 0 0;
}
```

Remember when I talked about magic? Well, here's the trick: I want to make my logo *disappear*.

The reason for this trick is that I want to keep the logo as shown in Figure 9-17 when users only print out the Web page. The logo that is currently seen in the default rendering is absolutely perfect for printing. However, for my intended Web page design, it's not so perfect. For color monitor displays, I want another logo to take its place, one that takes advantages of those colors.

To pull this off, I'm going to employ an ingenious trick by applying a CSS rule to the anchor element within the h1 element:

```
#header h1 a {
  display: block;
  width: 800px;
  height: 89px;
  background-image: transparent url("/_assets/img/logo_screen.gif") no-repeat 0 0;
  text-indent: -1000em;
}
```

By default, anchor elements are inline elements that cannot accept a width declaration, no matter how nicely you ask them. By setting the display to block, we can then tell the anchor element to take on fixed dimensions. In this case, the anchor element will take on a width of 800 pixels and a height of 89 pixels — the very same dimensions for the new logo. The background-image then brings in the background image, which is the image consistent with the new logo.

The bit of magic that does the trick is the text-indent property. By placing a negative value of 1,000 em units we are pretty much assured that the default logo image possessing the width of 494 pixels won't ever be seen. *Voilà!* Check out the results in Figure 9-18.

Figure 9-18: The new logo set firmly in place

Next, we need to add a bit of insurance. Because of a problem with Internet Explorer for Windows, there might be a flickering problem if you roll over the image. There are two ways to counter this problem. A setting in the browser's options creates the flickers.

In Internet Explorer, select Tools ⇨ Internet Options to pull up the Internet Options dialog box. Within the Temporary Internet Files fieldset, click Settings.... At the top of the Settings dialog box (as shown in Figure 9-19), there is an option to set how often the browser should check for new files.

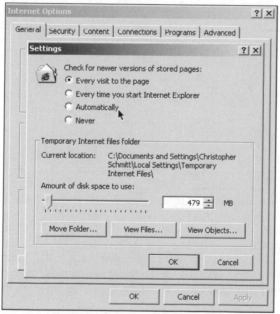

Figure 9-19: The Settings dialog box and the Temporary Internet files folder

Like the dedicated Web developer I am, I often have the option set to `Every Visit to the Web Page`. While this helps in troubleshooting problems with building Web page designs, I don't want the browser to cache and keep on displaying an old version of a Web page when I'm trying to solve another Web browser issue.

However, this setting also means that the browser is forced to reload the image every time the cursor rolls over the image, instead of relying on the cached version. So, to get the flickering to occur, I set the option to `Automatically`.

Another solution is a CSS rule addition that is also quite easy and doesn't rely on every visitor to my Web site to change his or her Internet Explorer settings. The CSS rule is set up to apply the very same background image in the anchor link to the parent element. So, as the browser goes to refresh the background image and the image vanishes, the same image will show up right behind it in the parent element's background:

```
#header h1.logo {
  background-image: transparent url("/_assets/img/logo_screen2.gif") no-repeat 0 0;
}
```

Moving to the Tagline

With the logo adequately addressed, I move to the tagline. The tagline is set an HTML text, so I can change it whenever it strikes my fancy without having to crack open a digital imaging software application or rack my brain trying to learn how to use PHP and the GD library to generate an image on the fly.

For the tagline, let's apply a few declarations:

```
#header p.tagline {
  font-family: Verdana, Arial, Helvetica, sans-serif;
  font-size: 1.2em;
  color: #6e2703;
  margin: -10px 0 35px 0;
  padding: 0 0 0 15px;
  letter-spacing: 0.3em;
}
```

First, I set the tagline to the Verdana font (with appropriate typeface backup measures), and then I set the typeface to `1.2em`.

Next, in the CSS rule is a setting for the color for the text (which is set to `#6e2703`). When picking colors for a design, a little trick I use is to pick colors from other areas in the design. For this color, I went to the circles in the logo design and used the Eye Dropper tool to pick the color. By doing this, I quickly and painlessly pick a color that works harmoniously with other colors in the design, as shown in Figure 9-20.

Figure 9-20: Selecting the extra color from elsewhere in the design

After the color selection, I want to move the tagline to be closer to the logo. I do this by applying a negative value to the margin property. Also, I want the tagline to be flush to the left of the logo, so I apply a left padding value of 15 pixels. Finally, I want to spread out the letters in the tagline by setting the value of letter-spacing to 0.3em, as shown in Figure 9-21.

With the logo all set up, it's time to move to the Web page columns.

Figure 9-21: The logo with the newly stylized tagline

Starting the Two-Column Layout

The elements of the header span the entire 800 pixels I allotted for the design. While that's good for branding purposes, it's not an efficient use of the space in terms of displaying information. Imagine if everything you read from newspapers to magazines had their articles and photos stacked on top of each other from top to bottom.

It would take a lot longer to scroll down the Web page, and it would probably look a lot like what the Web looked like in 1993. (I sure don't want to re-create that for my Web site.) Thus, I need columns — actually, two columns.

Columns in HTML

First, let's look at the HTML for that's what will be used to define the areas of the two columns in the Web page:

```
<body>
  <div id="frame">
   <fieldset id="searchbox">
     [ ...content goes here... ]
   </fieldset>
   <div id="header">
     [ ...content goes here... ]
   </div>
   <div id="sidecol">
     [ ...content goes here... ]
   </div>
   <div id="maincol">
     [ ...content goes here... ]
   </div>
  </body>
```

In this version, I decided to have the content for the side column (on the right-hand side) come first in the HTML, while the main content (on the left-hand side) comes later.

Side Column

What I want to do to get the side column is to bring the content out of the normal flow of the document. I do this by using the position property and setting the value to absolute.

Absolute positioning allows me to take a certain element and put it at a precise point in the Web page. I'm talking pixel-perfect positioning, which after the discussion on Web typography, seems as if it is an impossibility. However, it's the truth.

So, reviewing my design in Adobe Photoshop (as shown in Figure 9-22), I measure where I want the top-left corner of the side column to start and come up with the values 545 pixels from the left and 185 pixels from the top. Also, I double-check my column widths and make a note from the Info palette that the width of the side column in my design is 255 pixels.

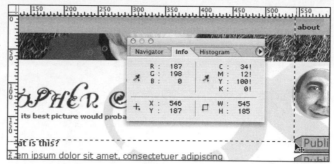

Figure 9-22: Using Photoshop to determine the placement for the side column

I will use these three new pieces of information to write the offset properties in the following CSS rule to help position the side column:

```
#sidecol {
  position: absolute;
  top: 185px;
  left: 545px;
  width: 255px;
  margin: 0;
  padding: 0 0 1.6em 0;
  background: transparent url("/_assets/img/sidecol_bkgd.gif") no-repeat top right;
}
```

I also place in properties for the margin (set to zero), the padding, and a background image as a flourish for the site design. But, looking at the column in my browser, I notice a problem.

When using absolute positioning, the column stays in place, no matter if the browser window is resized large or small, and, what's worse, it could obscure the other content in the Web page, as shown in Figure 9-23.

Unfortunately, this is the nature of the absolute positioning. It's impossible to set an element to be positioned and have it move with the content as the user resizes the window (that is, if we just use absolute positioning by itself).

To solve this problem, I use another magic trick. This time, I set the positioning to relative of the *parent* element of the side column container.

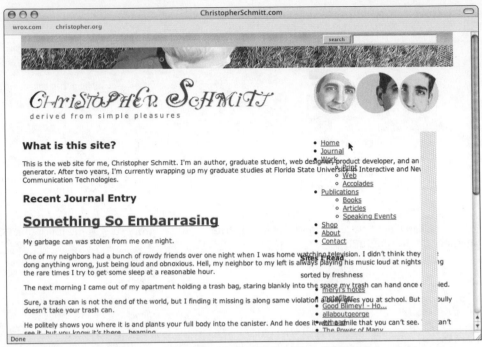

Figure 9-23: The side column not playing well with the other content

Elements that are positioned with relative positioning aren't taken out of the flow of a document rendering as they are for absolutely positioned elements. Those elements are placed as they would normally appear in a Web browser. However, the offset properties such as left and top apply only to the element's location in that document flow. So, an element that's relatively positioned with an offset property of top set to a value -2em appears to be moved up, as shown in Figure 9-24.

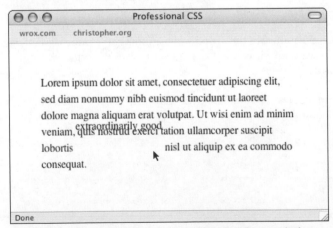

Figure 9-24: A couple of words levitating thanks to relative positioning

When combined with relative positioning on a parent element (such as the div frame container), absolute positioned elements can be placed precisely *and* still expand with the rest of the content as a user expands the browser. Why the frame container? Because that's the element that is setting the overall width of the design of the Web page. Recalling what I did earlier, I looked up the offset property values for top and left by the upper-left corner of the Photoshop document. The frame container acts as the representation of that document by, well, framing all the Web page design elements into the 800-pixel width.

> *Take note that you can use this setup on other elements in a Web page design in addition to side columns. This is truly a great technique that has so many applications. So, experiment and share with others what you find out.*

So, let's apply the position property to the frame container:

```
#frame {
 width: 800px;
 margin: 0 auto;
 position: relative;
}
```

Now, the side column should be placed exactly where I want it within the frame container. However, I still have the overlap issue, with the content in the left and right columns, as shown in Figure 9-25. Not to fear, though, for it's time to work on the main, left-hand column.

Figure 9-25: The side column positioned perfectly

Main Column

The positioning of the side column has left some work to be done. I need to remove the obfuscation of the content that's created by both columns. The solution is a very easy addition of applying padding to the right side of the main column so that there is enough room for the side column. In this design, the side column is 255 pixels.

So, I give the padding on the right side that much, plus 40 extra pixels, to make it a total of 295 pixels, as shown in Figure 9-26. The 40 pixels create a gutter (a space between the two columns so that they don't touch or run into each other).

```
#maincol {
 margin: 0;
 padding: 0 295px 1.6em 0;
 color: #030;
 background: transparent url("/_assets/img/journal_bkgd.gif") no-repeat 0 0;
}
```

Figure 9-26: Two columns of text

The other CSS properties for the main column container include the addition of design flourishes such as the color of the text, as well as a background image that starts at the top of the main column.

The color property is very important because any new HTML text that is written within this container gets set to this color by default. So, that frees my hands of setting the color for each element within the main column container to the same value. In the future, I need to worry about changing the color of an element only if it needs to be something other than the default value.

Now, my next step is to work on the content that goes into the main content column.

Main Column Content

With the two columns set up, it's time to take a look at the content within the two columns. First up is the content in the main column.

My Site Says, "Hi," Does Yours?

One of the most important things I tell my students and clients is to have an introductory paragraph on the main page of your site. It's important to let new visitors (and maybe some of the regulars) know what to expect when they come to a Web site.

When Web developers build their own sites, we sometimes get so caught up in the designing and developing that something as simple as a few quick lines describing what we are trying to accomplish seems foolish.

Not everyone can determine the purpose of a site by the domain name or title. For example, my new media design and publishing company name is Heatvision.com. What does it do? Sell comic books or sunglasses? Well, it does neither. So, to stop the confusion, I have a few lines that say what the company does:

> Heatvision.com consults on user interface design issues, builds brands, offers training in Web production and design techniques, and assists in Section 508 compliance.

> Whether the goal is to sell, promote, teach, enlighten, or entertain, we sidestep hype and fashion to focus on what really works in making a client's message compelling and useful to their audience.

It's simple and to the point. People thinking I sell comics or sunglasses are as quick as The Flash told otherwise, and they can search elsewhere for the issue where he races Superman.

For my personal site, I want to put in the following markup for the introductory text, as shown in Figure 9-27:

```
<div id="desc">
 <h2>What is this site?</h2>
 <p>This is the web site for me, Christopher Schmitt. I'm an author, graduate
student, web designer, product developer, and an idea generator. After two years,
I'm currently wrapping up my graduate studies at Florida State University in
Interactive and New Communication Technologies.</p>
</div><!-- END #desc -->
```

Figure 9-27: The default styling of the introductory text

I wrap the introductory paragraph in a div with an id attribute set to the value of "desc". This will be the containing block for the description. Within the div element are the question wrapping in an h2 elements and a paragraph containing the answer.

Now that we have the markup set up in place, I start again to style the content from the outside in, starting with the div element, as shown in Figure 9-28.

Figure 9-28: The styling of the description container

```
#desc {
  margin: 12px 0 0 0;
  padding: 0 0 0 111px;
  background: transparent url("/_assets/img/pageDesc/dots_4x3.gif") no-repeat
16px 0;
  color: #2D6734;
  line-height: 1.5;
  width: 350px;
}
```

The first declaration for the margin sets 12 pixels at the top of the introductory text. This move is made to create some white space.

The next rule is important when it comes to the introductory text. Since I want to have the graphic image of dots positioned in the upper-left corner, I need to position the text out of the way so that the dots don't interfere with the background image. So, in the same manner I moved the main column content by adjusting the padding on the right side, I adjust the padding on the left-hand side of the introductory text to make room for the background image.

The next three declarations set the background image, color of the text, and the line-height for the text.

The last property sets the width of the introductory text. I have set the width in my design for the main column to 505 pixels. Even with the left-side padding of 111 pixels, that still leaves 394 pixels. Why shrink the width of the paragraph by 44 pixels?

The answer is that I want to create that white space again because I want the visitor's eye to see the logo and not be hindered by a block of text. Although there is 40-pixel gutter between the two columns, enlarging the gutter at the very top of the main page acts as a sort of visual funnel. It diverts the eye from the header into the main content of the main page.

However, by setting the width on the sides of the desc container, I've run afoul of Microsoft's box model for Internet Explorer 5.5 for Windows. So, do get around this, I use the hack as described in Chapter 8:

```
#desc {
 margin: 12px 0 0 0;
 padding: 0 0 0 111px;
 background: transparent url("/_assets/img/pageDesc/dots_4x3.gif") no-repeat
16px 0;
 color: #2D6734;
 line-height: 1.5;
 width: 461px;
 voice-family: "\"}\"";
 voice-family: inherit;
 width: 350px;
}
```

The first width value is a false value slipped like a poison to WinIE 5.5 so that it correctly sizes the desc container. The other browsers are able to read the second width property value through the voice-family hack.

By "all the other browsers" I mean all except Opera, which requires an extra CSS rule by itself. But this isn't a problem. Extra CSS rules don't cost much:

```
html>#desc {
 width: 350px;
}
```

Then, the next two properties apply the styles for the heading and paragraph text to make it look more in tune with the way I designed, as shown in Figure 9-29:

```
#desc h2 {
 font-size: 1em;
 font-weight: bold;
 margin: 0;
 padding: 0;
}

#desc p {
 font-size: 0.9em;
 margin: 0 0 15px 0;
 padding: 0;
}
```

Figure 9-29: The stylized introductory text

Styling the Blog Posts

Much like the heading and paragraph in the introductory text, the styling of the text in the blog posts is a fairly straightforward exercise. Today, most blog posts are auto-generated by applications such as WordPress (see www.wordpress.org) or Movable Type (see www.movabletype.org).

If you are following along at home with a different blogging software package, your mileage will vary in how closely my markup matches up with yours because of the differences in each application. However, the markup from these tools should be somewhat similar, although you might need to make some adjustments if you want to re-create my design.

First, I take a look at the markup for a sample blog post, as shown in Figure 9-30:

```
<div class="post">
 <h2>Recent Journal Entry</h2>
 <h1 class="storytitle"><a href="/log/index.php?p=1" rel="bookmark"
title="Permanent Link: Something So Embarrasing">Something So Embarrasing</a></h1>
 <div class="storycontent">
  <p>My garbage can was stolen last night.</p>
  <p>[ ...content goes here ... ]</p>
```

```
    <p>That'll show &#8216;em. That'll show em, all! Bwahahahaha! </p>
  </div><!-- END #storycontent -->
  <div id="postfooter">
    <div class="meta"> filed under
      <ul class="post-categories">
        <li><a href="/log/index.php?cat=1" title="View all posts in
General">General</a></li>
        <li><a href="/log/index.php?cat=4" title="View all posts in
Life">Life</a></li>
        <li><a href="/log/index.php?cat=5" title="View all posts in
Miscellaneous">Miscellaneous</a></li>
      </ul>
        on <a href="http://www.christopherschmitt.com/log/index.php?p=1"
rel="bookmark" title="Posted at 9:24 pm">2/3/2005</a> </div>
    <!-- END .meta -->
    <div class="feedback"> <a
href="http://www.christopherschmitt.com/log/index.php?p=1#comments">Comments
(1)</a>
    </div><!-- END #feedback -->
  </div><!-- END #postfooter -->
</div><!-- END #post -->
```

It looks like a lot is going on and, for the most part, it is. But if we take it apart piece by piece, I can make a bit of sense out of it. Along the way, I will apply CSS rules to the markup to create the look I want.

The first bit of markup is the `div` element with the class value of `post`. Everything within this container is going to pertain to the blog post and, using a descendant selector in the following CSS rules, I can control the design of the elements only in the `post` container:

```
<div class="post">
 [ ...content goes here... ]
</div><!-- END #post -->
```

Now I set up the CSS rule for the `post` container:

```
.post {
 margin: 0 0 0 15px;
 font-size: 1.25em;
}
```

I set the left-side margin for 15 pixels. This is done to line up visually the 4 by 3 sets of dots, as well as the logo and tagline elements that are located in the introductory section and header. Then I set the size of the type to 1.25ems, which translates into 12.5 pixels based off our typography rundown earlier in this chapter.

The next item is the heading for the blog post:

```
<div class="post">
 <h2>Recent Journal Entry</h2>
 [ ...content goes here... ]
</div><!-- END #post -->
```

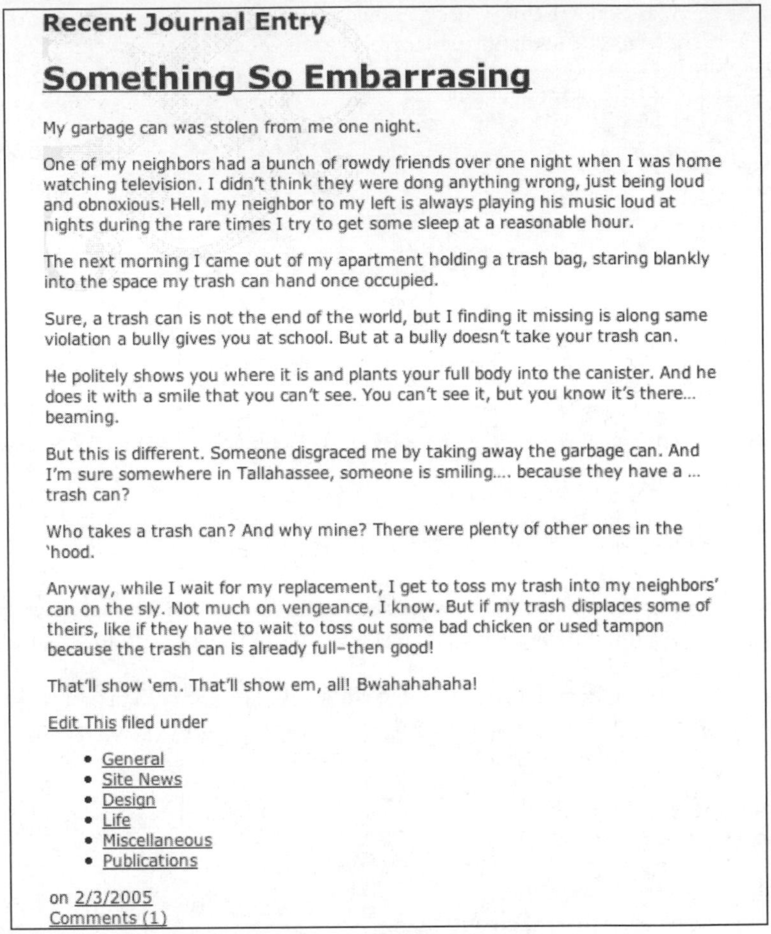

Recent Journal Entry

Something So Embarrasing

My garbage can was stolen from me one night.

One of my neighbors had a bunch of rowdy friends over one night when I was home watching television. I didn't think they were dong anything wrong, just being loud and obnoxious. Hell, my neighbor to my left is always playing his music loud at nights during the rare times I try to get some sleep at a reasonable hour.

The next morning I came out of my apartment holding a trash bag, staring blankly into the space my trash can hand once occupied.

Sure, a trash can is not the end of the world, but I finding it missing is along same violation a bully gives you at school. But at a bully doesn't take your trash can.

He politely shows you where it is and plants your full body into the canister. And he does it with a smile that you can't see. You can't see it, but you know it's there… beaming.

But this is different. Someone disgraced me by taking away the garbage can. And I'm sure somewhere in Tallahassee, someone is smiling…. because they have a … trash can?

Who takes a trash can? And why mine? There were plenty of other ones in the 'hood.

Anyway, while I wait for my replacement, I get to toss my trash into my neighbors' can on the sly. Not much on vengeance, I know. But if my trash displaces some of theirs, like if they have to wait to toss out some bad chicken or used tampon because the trash can is already full–then good!

That'll show 'em. That'll show em, all! Bwahahahaha!

Edit This filed under

- General
- Site News
- Design
- Life
- Miscellaneous
- Publications

on 2/3/2005
Comments (1)

Figure 9-30: The default rendering of the blog post

For the design, I want to have a background image placed behind the heading to make it stand out a little more, as well as tweak the margin, padding, color, and typography:

```
.post h2 {
background-image: url("/_assets/img/content_hdg_bkgd.gif");
margin: 0;
padding: 0;
color: #495301;
font-family: normal Geneva, Arial, Helvetica, sans-serif;;
letter-spacing: .1em;
}
```

However, I also want to add some brackets on either side of the heading. I could add them to the HTML text, but I feel that would not be semantically correct. After all, the brackets are a design element, not actually the heading. To add the brackets as shown in Figure 9-31, I use the pseudo-elements :after and :before to insert content into the heading:

```
.post h2:after {
 content: " ]";
}

.post h2:before {
 content: "[ ";
}
```

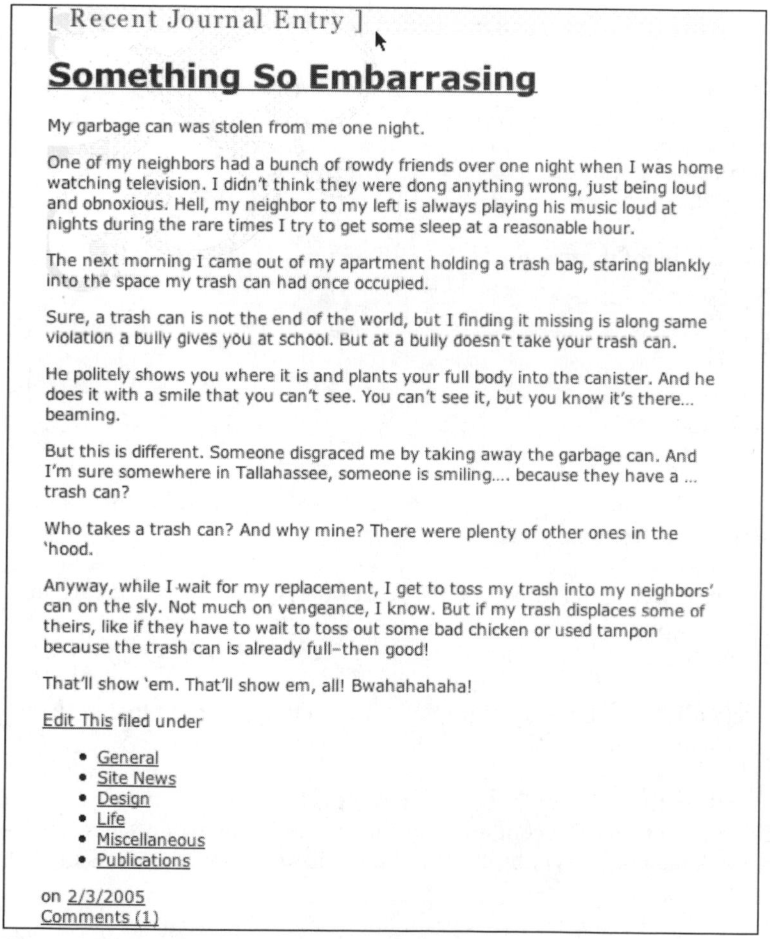

[Recent Journal Entry]

Something So Embarrasing

My garbage can was stolen from me one night.

One of my neighbors had a bunch of rowdy friends over one night when I was home watching television. I didn't think they were dong anything wrong, just being loud and obnoxious. Hell, my neighbor to my left is always playing his music loud at nights during the rare times I try to get some sleep at a reasonable hour.

The next morning I came out of my apartment holding a trash bag, staring blankly into the space my trash can had once occupied.

Sure, a trash can is not the end of the world, but I finding it missing is along same violation a bully gives you at school. But at a bully doesn't take your trash can.

He politely shows you where it is and plants your full body into the canister. And he does it with a smile that you can't see. You can't see it, but you know it's there… beaming.

But this is different. Someone disgraced me by taking away the garbage can. And I'm sure somewhere in Tallahassee, someone is smiling…. because they have a … trash can?

Who takes a trash can? And why mine? There were plenty of other ones in the 'hood.

Anyway, while I wait for my replacement, I get to toss my trash into my neighbors' can on the sly. Not much on vengeance, I know. But if my trash displaces some of theirs, like if they have to wait to toss out some bad chicken or used tampon because the trash can is already full—then good!

That'll show 'em. That'll show em, all! Bwahahahaha!

Edit This filed under

- General
- Site News
- Design
- Life
- Miscellaneous
- Publications

on 2/3/2005
Comments (1)

Figure 9-31: The heading with the brackets

The only warning about using the pseudo-elements is that they aren't supported by Internet Explorer for Windows. However, I'm not that concerned about it because the brackets are a rather small element in a larger design. Blame it on old age or too many scars, but I've learned to pick my battles instead of fighting every one.

> *However, one way of implementing the design would be to make an image out of each bracket. Then wrap the text in another level of markup like so:*
>
> ```
> <h2>Recent Journal Entry</h2>
> ```
>
> *Position the left bracket as a background image in the* h2 *element and then place the right bracket background image in the* em *element.*

Next is the h1 element reserved for each blog post:

```
<div class="post">
 <h2>Recent Journal Entry</h2>
 <h1 class="storytitle">Something So Embarrassing</h1>
 [ ...content goes here... ]
</div><!-- END #post -->
```

Then I apply a CSS rule for the design:

```
h1.storytitle {
 margin: 12px 0 0 0;
 padding: 0 33px 0 0;
 font-family: Georgia, "Times New Roman", Times, serif;
 font-weight: normal;
}
```

There's nothing too fancy here. I apply a margin of 12 pixels to the top of the heading to give it some space (or leading) away from the previous heading.

Then, I also apply a padding of 33 pixels to the right side. Again, this is to create some white space in case the heading runs long. I'd prefer to have a blog title run two lines rather than have the text be equal to the width of the blog content in order to create more contrast in the design.

The last two declarations deal with typography issues: setting the right font, as well as removing the bold weight associated with a heading element.

The next item deals with the footer for the blog post. Each blog post contains what's referred to as *meta information*. The meta information contains information regarding what categories are associated with the blog post, when the post was published, as well as links to any comments that a visitor might have left in regard to the post.

Let's take a look at the markup for the blog post footer:

```
<div class="post">
 <h2>Recent Journal Entry</h2>
 <h1 class="storytitle"><a href="/log/index.php?p=1" rel="bookmark"
title="Permanent Link: Something So Embarrasing">Something So Embarrasing</a></h1>
  <div class="storycontent">
   <p>My garbage can was stolen last night.</p>
   <p>[ ...content goes here ... ]</p>
    <p>That'll show &#8216;em. That'll show em, all! Bwahahahaha! </p>
   </div><!-- END #storycontent -->
    <div id="postfooter">
     <div class="meta"> filed under
       <ul class="post-categories">
         <li><a href="/log/index.php?cat=1" title="View all posts in
General">General</a></li>
         <li><a href="/log/index.php?cat=4" title="View all posts in
Life">Life</a></li>
         <li><a href="/log/index.php?cat=5" title="View all posts in
Miscellaneous">Miscellaneous</a></li>
       </ul>
        on <a href="http://www.christopherschmitt.com/log/index.php?p=1"
rel="bookmark" title="Posted at 9:24 pm">2/3/2005</a> </div>
     <!-- END .meta -->
    <div class="feedback"> <a
href="http://www.christopherschmitt.com/log/index.php?p=1#comments">Comments
(1)</a>
    </div><!-- END #feedback -->
   </div><!-- END #postfooter -->
  </div><!-- END #post -->
```

From the source code, there are two nested `div` element containers, `meta` and `feedback`, as shown in Figure 9-32.

Figure 9-32: The default rendering of the blog post footer

For the `postfooter` container, I'm going to apply the following CSS rule:

```
#postfooter {
  margin: -.5em 0 1em 0;
  text-transform: lowercase;
  letter-spacing: .1em;
  color: #cccc99;
  font-size: 1em;
}
```

The rule applies some minor design changes. It moves the footer up by `-.5em` and places a padding of `1em` at the bottom of the footer. Then, to differentiate the content in the footer from the blog post, the CSS rule also does the following:

❑   Changes the text in the footer to be all lowercase through the `text-transform` property

❑   Spaces out the letters by a tenth of an em unit

❑   Colors the text in the footer to a light brown color

❑   Reduces the size of the text in the footer

With the `postfooter` container examined, I move to the `meta` container. Keep in mind that I want to have the meta container and the `feedback` container on the same line, but on the left and right side of each other, respectively. To do this, I use the `float` property.

The `float` property lets content wrap around the floated element. I want to adjust the widths of each of the `meta` and `feedback` elements so that they don't overlap each other *and* I want to set the float value to left and right, respectively. I quickly achieve part of my goal by having the two containers side-by-side, as shown in Figure 9-33:

```
#postfooter .meta {
  width: 355px;
  float: left;
  text-align: left;
  padding: 0 0 1.66em 0;
}

#postfooter .feedback {
      float: right;
      text-align: right;
      padding: 0 0 1em 0;
}
```

Figure 9-33: The meta and feedback containers on the same line

The next step is to address the list item in the `meta` container. The unordered list displays all the categories related to the blog post. However, it takes a rather large amount of space. To fix this problem, I'm going to change the display of the unordered list from block-level elements to inline, as well as remove the bullet point for each list item:

```
ul.post-categories {
  display: inline;
  padding: 0;
  margin: 0;
}

ul.post-categories li {
  display: inline;
  list-style-type: none;
  padding: 0;
  margin: 0;
}
```

And to add a final touch, I want to separate each category listing by a simple comma so that the category names don't run into each other. To do this I re-use the pseudo-element `:after` for the `content` property, as shown in Figure 9-34:

```
#postfooter .meta li:after {
  content: ", ";
}
```

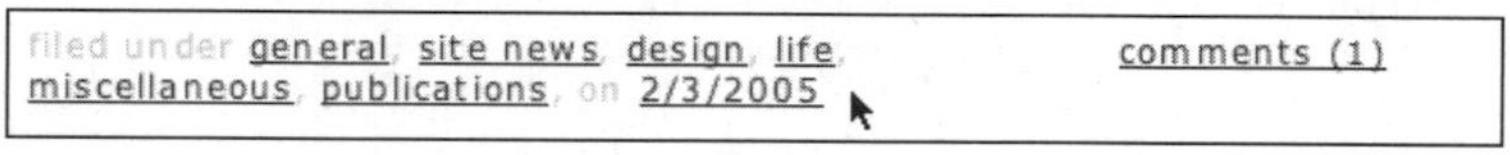

filed under general, site news, design, life, miscellaneous, publications, on 2/3/2005   comments (1)

Figure 9-34: The streamlined unordered list

Again, something to keep in mind is that Internet Explorer for Windows doesn't support this property. And, again, I'm not going to lose any sleep over the fact a handful of commas don't show up in a broken browser.

With the end of styling the post, I've reached the end of main column content. In the main column is the introduction describing the nature or author of the site, as well as a typical blog post and respective content such as the categories and comment link.

Side Column Content

Moving from the main column to the second column, the approach is the same, but the parameters are bit different. I'm going to be working in a smaller amount of space, letting blog posts gain a greater portion of the screen real estate. However, the content in the side column is still very important, with the most important being the site navigation, followed by the ubiquitous blog roll.

Again, I start to apply styles by working from top to bottom. The first item in the side column is the main navigation.

Start of Site Navigation

The spine for any site is the menu navigation. The Web is a loose collection of documents that are connected by links. The difference between any old link and a site's menu can be debated by people wiser than I, but links in a site menu need to do a few things:

❑ Stand out from the rest of the Web page design

❑ Be easy to find within a page design

❑ Let the user know where he or she is in the structure of a Web site

Because I'm going to focus a lot of attention in the design and execution of the navigation, I want to create a separate HTML page so that I won't interfere with the other elements on the Web page. When I'm done working on the navigation, I will move the HTML over to the original Web page design and graft the CSS rules for the navigation to the main CSS file.

So, with a new HTML page, I set up an unordered list structure to mirror the site map I worked out earlier in the chapter, as shown in Figure 9-35.

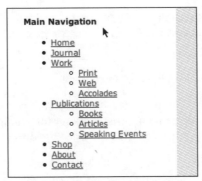

Figure 9-35: The default rendering of the main navigation

The look for menus needs to be similar to (yet stand out from) the rest of the design to facilitate quick reference by visitors.

In my design I conjured up in Photoshop, I believe that I have the successful look — but the interesting part is to see if I can get CSS to help me produce it.

First, let's take a look at the navigation markup, as shown in Figure 9-35:

```
<h4 class="no">Main Navigation</h4>
<ul>
  <li><a href="/">Home</a></li>
  <li><a href="/journal/">Journal</a></li>
  <li><a href="/work/">Work</a>
    <ul>
      <li><a href="/work/print/">Print</a></li>
    <li><a href="/work/web/">Web</a></li>
    <li><a href="/work/accolades/">Accolades</a></li>
    </ul>
  </li>
  <li><a href="/publications/">Publications</a>
    <ul>
      <li><a href="/publications/books/">Books</a></li>
      <li><a href="/publications/articles/">Articles</a></li>
      <li><a href="/publications/speaking/">Speaking Events</a></li>
    </ul>
  </li>
  <li><a href="/shop/">Shop</a></li>
  <li><a href="/about/">About</a></li>
  <li><a href="/contact/">Contact</a></li>
</ul><!-- END #mainnav -->
```

For the most part the markup is straightforward. It is your normal, everyday-looking heading and an unordered list. Let's break this apart piece by piece and see how CSS can help power our navigation. First up is the heading:

```
<h4 class="no">Main Navigation</h4>
```

I apply the `class` attribute in the heading with the value of `no`. The CSS rule associated with the `no` class selector removes the heading from browser. This removal is done because the menu links themselves will stand out from the rest of the page, so there is no need to have a visual label above the menu. However, the heading is left for those using screen readers or text-only browsers.

The first `ul` element is up first. To apply CSS rules only to the site menu, I apply an `id` attribute with the value of `mainnav` so that it will act as a container for my CSS rules:

```
<ul id="mainnav">
```

With the container marked, I can now add a few design touches. First, I want to zero-out the margin and padding. Also, I want to remove the list bullets that come by default with an ordered list. The CSS rule to do the changes I want (as shown in Figure 9-36) is a simple one:

```
ul#mainnav {
  margin: 0;
  padding: 0;
  list-style: none;
}
```

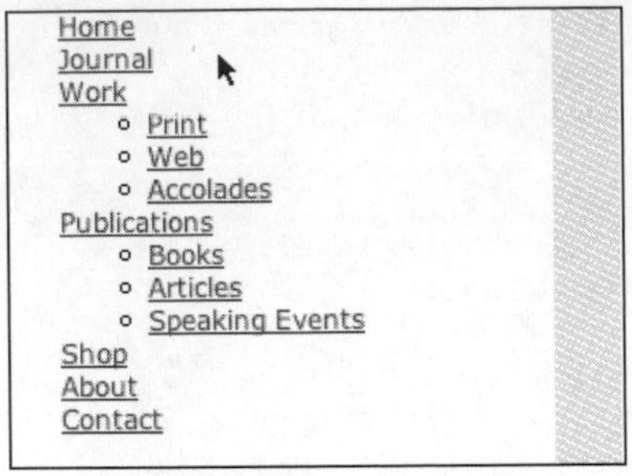

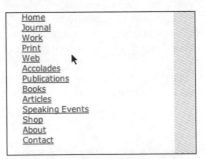

Figure 9-36: Removing the margin, padding, and bullets

As you can see, I've adjusted the main unordered list in the navigation, but not the nested unordered list. To do that, I add another CSS rule that addresses those lists with the same properties and values, as shown in Figure 9-37:

```
ul#mainnav {
  margin: 0;
  padding: 0;
  list-style: none;
}
```

```
/* Nested lists */
ul#mainnav li ul {
  padding: 0;
  margin: 0;
  list-style: none;
}
```

Figure 9-37: Removing the margin, padding, and bullets for the nested lists

While I'm in the process of removing items from the menu, I might as well not stop. The next rule removes the underlines associated with the links:

```
ul#mainnav a {
  text-decoration: none;
}
```

With the foundation set, I can now move forward and start working in the design for the navigation.

The design I've built for the navigation makes use of three-dimensional–looking graphics. The idea of the navigation is to make the menu links look like buttons. However, with typical buttons in Web design, the text of the label is "trapped" in the image. Designers write the name of the button in Photoshop and then export the image as a GIF or JPEG file.

This technique has worked throughout the history of Web design and is perfectly acceptable practice. But if I need to edit a label or add a new button, I need to make another stop in Photoshop and create new images to upload, as well as rework the HTML, if I need to add a new image to the menu. So, I want to be sure to use HTML text for the labels because, well, I'm lazy. I don't want to spend my *entire* life in Photoshop.

To re-create the buttons from Photoshop into the Web document, I want to use a variation of Douglas Bowman's excellent Sliding Doors technique (see www.alistapart.com/articles/slidingdoors/). Essentially, I want to separate the button graphic into two parts: a top and bottom part, as shown in Figure 9-38.

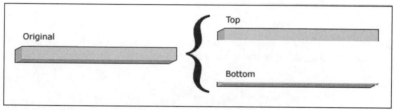

Figure 9-38: Splitting the button into two parts

Then, I'm going to extend the length of one of the images (as shown in Figure 9-39).

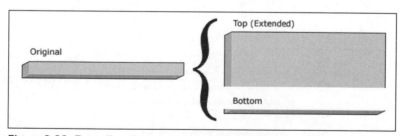

Figure 9-39: Extending the top portion of the button

Now that I have the button set, I want to create a set of similar-looking images to indicate that the page is currently being viewed. So, with my design for the buttons, I create two sets with two images each (as shown in Figure 9-40):

❑   **Off State.** Two images that indicate an "off" state

❑   **On State.** Two images that indicate an "on" state

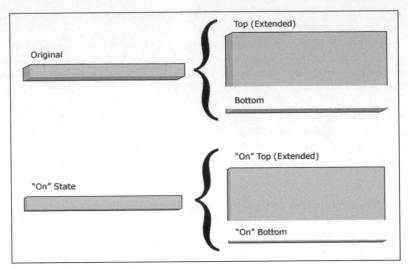

Figure 9-40: The button sets

With the images ready, it's time to focus on bringing the menu navigation into the browser. I start by revising the CSS rule for the links (as shown in Figure 9-41):

```
ul#mainnav li a {
  display: block;
  width: 240px;
  margin: 0;
  padding: 0 0 7px 0;
  background: transparent url("/_assets/img/mainNav/nav_button_full_bottom.gif") no-repeat
  bottom left;
  text-decoration: none;
}
```

Figure 9-41: The bottom graphic comes through.

In the CSS rule, I set the display to block. Again, this allows me to set the width of the anchor links to 240 pixels, a value I picked up by measuring the width of the graphics I created in Photoshop.

Next, I set the margin to zero, while setting the bottom padding to 7px. The reason I did that was to make room for the bottom portion of the button, which comes in as the next declaration.

With the bottom graphic in place, I need to quickly put the top graphic on the links. To do this, I'm going to insert a bit of extra markup in the menu by wrapping the span element around the text of each link, but *only* those links in the parent unordered list:

```
<h4 class="no">Main Navigation</h4>
<ul id="mainnav">
  <li><a href="/"><span>Home</span></a></li>
  <li><a href="/journal/"><span>Journal</span></a></li>
  <li><a href="/work/"><span>Work</span></a>
    <ul>
      <li><a href="/work/print/">Print</a></li>
      <li><a href="/work/web/">Web</a></li>
      <li><a href="/work/accolades/">Accolades</a></li>
    </ul>
  </li>
  <li><a href="/publications/"><span>Publications</span></a>
    <ul>
      <li><a href="/publications/books/">Books</a></li>
      <li><a href="/publications/articles/">Articles</a></li>
      <li><a href="/publications/speaking/">Speaking Events</a></li>
    </ul>
  </li>
  <li><a href="/shop/"><span>Shop</span></a></li>
  <li><a href="/about/"><span>About</span></a></li>
  <li><a href="/contact/"><span>Contact</span></a></li>
</ul><!-- END #mainnav -->
```

With the spans in place, I now have a hook where CSS can apply the top of the button background images, as shown in Figure 9-42:

```
ul#mainnav li a span {
    font-size: 1.25em;
    display: block;
    width: 240px;
    margin: 0;
    padding: 0 0 0 15px;
    background-image: transparent
url("/_assets/img/mainNav/nav_button_full_top.gif")
no-repeat0 0;
    color: #6E6F5E;
}
```

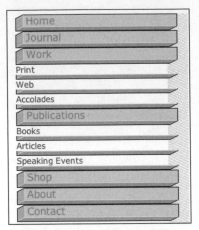

Figure 9-42: The top of the button is put in place.

With this CSS rule, I also apply other styles such as a padding on the left of the HTML text, as well as setting the color of the text. Looking at Figure 9-42, I can tell that the bottom image is showing in the nested lists. That's because the browser is told by the CSS rules to apply the bottom background image to any instance of li. So, in the next couple of CSS rules, I take care of that problem, as well as shore up some other design touches (as shown in Figure 9-43) to get the navigation closer to what I have envisioned:

```
ul#mainnav li li {
    font-family: Verdana, Arial, Helvetica, sans-serif;
    font-size: 1em;
    background-image: none;
    padding: 0 0 0 8px;
    margin: 0;
}

ul#mainnav li li a {
    background-image: none;
    margin: 0;              ,
    padding: 0 0 0 8px;
    color: #8d8d4d;
}
```

Now, with the menu navigation almost set, I want to work on spacing out the options a bit because the main options are running together. To do this, I apply a 2-pixel margin to the top of every list item, as shown in Figure 9-44.

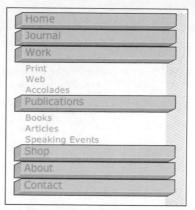

Figure 9-43: A spitting image of the menu navigation I want

```
ul#mainnav li {
    margin-top: 2px;
}
```

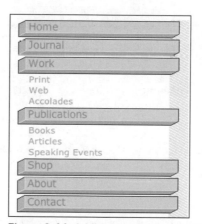

Figure 9-44: Additional space around the main menu items

Wayfinding with Navigation

Now that I have the menu designed the way I designed it, I need to adjust the menu to follow my third observation of menus: letting the user know where the he or she is in the structure of a Web site.

To do this, I want to show only the submenu links of the sections the user happens to be viewing. For example, I don't want the visitor to see options for Publications while they are looking at the Work section.

I go about accomplishing this by hiding all submenu links (as shown by Figure 9-45). To do this, I update the CSS rule that was previously used to remove the space around the nested lists:

```
ul#mainnav li ul {
  display: none; /* Hides Submenu */
  padding: 0;
  margin: 0;
  list-style: none;
}
```

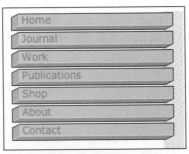

Figure 9-45: The submenus are gone.

Now that I've removed all the submenus, I need to devise a system that will bring back only the menus of pages the user is visiting. The solution involves a couple of tweaks to the markup. First, I need to add a marker to the page itself that identifies itself as belonging to a particular section of the site.

For example, if I want to mark a page as belonging to the Publications section, I add a `class` attribute to the body of the Web document like so:

```
<body class="pub-page">
```

Next, I need a marker for the Publications menu. I add this marker by using an `id` attribute in the `li` element that contains the Publications submenu:

```
<li id="pub-link"><a href="/publications/"><span>Publications</span></a>
  <ul>
    <li><a href="/publications/books/">Books</a></li>
    <li><a href="/publications/articles/">Articles</a></li>
    <li><a href="/publications/speaking/">Speaking Events</a></li>
  </ul>
</li>
```

And, because I might need a marker for all the sections of the menu at some point in the future, I include them in the other links for the main menu, as shown in Listing 9-3.

Listing 9-3: The Markup for the Navigation

```
<h4 class="no">Main Navigation</h4>
<ul id="mainnav">
  <li id="home-link"><a href="/"><span>Home</span></a></li>
  <li id="journal-link"><a href="/journal/"><span>Journal</span></a></li>
  <li id="work-link"><a href="/work/"><span>Work</span></a>
   <ul>
    <li><a href="/work/print/">Print</a></li>
    <li><a href="/work/web/">Web</a></li>
    <li><a href="/work/accolades/">Accolades</a></li>
   </ul>
  </li>
  <li id="pub-link"><a href="/publications/"><span>Publications</span></a>
   <ul>
    <li><a href="/publications/books/">Books</a></li>
    <li><a href="/publications/articles/">Articles</a></li>
    <li><a href="/publications/speaking/">Speaking Events</a></li>
   </ul>
  </li>
  <li id="shop-link"><a href="/shop/"><span>Shop</span></a></li>
  <li id="about-link"><a href="/about/"><span>About</span></a></li>
  <li id="contact-link"><a href="/contact/"><span>Contact</span></a></li>
</ul><!-- END #mainnav -->
```

Now that I've included the markers, I need to use CSS to bring the Publications menu back so that the user can see it (as shown in Figure 9-46) by using the display property with a value of block.

```
.pub-page ul#mainnav li#pub-link ul {
display: block;
margin: 0;
padding: 0 0 7px 0;
}
```

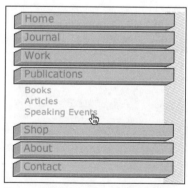

Figure 9-46: Only the Publications menu appears.

This menu reveal is done by using the specificity in the CSS. The CSS selector is instructed to "look" for our markers in the HTML and, if they exist, to apply the styles set in the CSS rule. If the markers aren't there in the HTML, then the submenu stays hidden.

Now, while I have the CSS rule working just for the Publications page at the moment, I want to apply other selectors for the other options in the main menu. Remember that I want to make this menu as trouble-free as possible. By planning now for the time I want to add more submenus, I can save myself some time in the future. Won't my future self be so grateful that my past self did all the work! (Well, he'd better be!)

So, the revised CSS rule looks like this:

```
.home-page ul#mainnav li#home-link ul,
.journal-page ul#mainnav li#journal-link ul,
.work-page ul#mainnav li#work-link ul,
.pub-page ul#mainnav li#pub-link ul,
.shop-page ul#mainnav li#shop-link ul,
.about-page ul#mainnav li#about-link ul,
.contact-page ul#mainnav li#contact-link ul {
display: block;
background-image: none;
margin: 0;
padding: 0 0 7px 0;
}
```

There's one more thing to add. I want to change the button on the menu option currently being displayed. By using the images that showcase the "on" stage, I give my users more visual feedback as to their location within my site.

To accomplish this visual reinforcement, I again use the markers to specifically tell CSS that I want the section currently being viewed to have different background images than the other list options (as shown in Figure 9-47):

```
.home-page ul#mainnav li#home-link a,
.journal-page ul#mainnav li#journal-link a,
.work-page ul#mainnav li#work-link a,
.pub-page ul#mainnav li#pub-link a,
.shop-page ul#mainnav li#shop-link a,
.about-page ul#mainnav li#about-link a,
.contact-page ul#mainav li#contact-link a {
background: transparent url("/_assets/img/mainNav/nav_button_on_bottom_1item.gif")
no-repeat left bottom;
margin: 0;
padding: 0 0 4px 0;


}
```

```
.home-page ul#mainnav li#home-link a span,
.journal-page ul#mainnav li#journal-link a span,
.work-page ul#mainnav li#work-link a span,
.pub-page ul#mainnav li#pub-link a span,
.shop-page ul#mainnav li#shop-link a span,
.about-page ul#mainnav li#about-link a span,
.contact-page ul#mainnav li#contact-link a span {
  background-image: transparent url("/_assets/img/mainNav/nav_button_on_top.gif")
no-repeat 0 0;
  padding: 0 0 0 8px;
  margin: 5px 0 0 0;
  color: #003300;
}
```

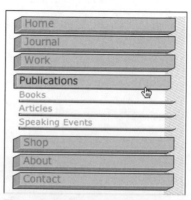

**Figure 9-47: The current option is
visibly different from the other links
in the menu.**

However, if you notice in Figure 9-47, the submenu links now have the bottom background images as
well. This is an easy fix. I explicitly tell the browser that if a page is being shown when both the page
and link markers exist, get rid of any background images (as shown in Figure 9-48):

```
.home-page ul#mainnav li#home-link ul li a,
.journal-page ul#mainnav li#journal-link ul li a,
.work-page ul#mainnav li#work-link ul li a,
.pub-page ul#mainnav li#pub-link ul li a,
.shop-page ul#mainnav li#shop-link ul li a,
.about-page ul#mainnav li#about-link ul li a,
.contact-page ul#mainnav li#contact-link ul li a {
 background-image: none;
}
```

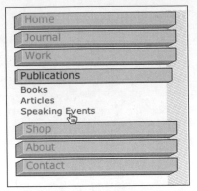

Figure 9-48: The finalized navigation

One of the reasons why I love this solution is how it handles type sizing. If a user increases or reduces the font size of the navigation, the buttons grow and shrink with it (as shown in Figure 9-49):

Figure 9-49: The menu as displayed when the user has a large font size

As of this moment, I never need to touch the markup that makes up the navigation, unless I want to make edits. And, if I make any revisions to the menu, I simply add some basic HTML and then the CSS instantly styles the menu.

BlogRoll

One of the common characteristics of a blog is the *blogroll*, which is a collection of links that the site owner likes to read often. With Internet technology, the links can be dynamically sorted by the last time they were updated. Like a few e-mails from friends and a nice cup of tea, a blogroll makes surfing in the mornings nicer.

While keeping tabs on a lot of interesting links, a blogroll can quickly get out of hand. A very long list of links can often overshadow the main site itself. One solution would be, of course, to keep a short list of links. But why subject myself and friends to the awkward social construct of being virtually "defriended" because I want to save some space on a Web page?

The right solution, then, is keeping the list, but shrinking the space allotted to the blogroll.

Let's first take a look at the markup for the blogroll, as shown in Figure 9-50. (In the spirit of saving trees, I'm going to use only a handful of links.)

```
<div id="blogroll">
 <h4>Sites I Read</h4>
 <p>sorted by freshness</p>
 <ul>
  <li><a href="http://www.meryl.net/blog">meryl's notes</a></li>
  <li><a href="http://www.metafilter.com/">metafilter</a></li>
  <li><a href="http://www.goodblimey.com/">Good Blimey! - Ho...</a></li>
  <li><a href="http://www.allaboutgeorge.com/">allaboutgeorge</a></li>
  <li><a href="http://www.evhead.com/">evhead</a></li>
  <li><a href="http://x-pollen.com/many/">The Power of Many</a></li>
  <li><a href="http://www.stopdesign.com/">Stopdesign</a></li>
  <li><a href="http://www.mezzoblue.com/">mezzoblue</a></li>
  <li><a href="http://www.nickfinck.com/journal.html">Nick Finck</a></li>
  <li><a href="http://www.bizstone.com/">Biz Stone, Genius</a></li>
  <li><a href="http://www.7nights.com/asterisk/">asterisk*</a></li>
  <li><a href="http://www.sidesh0w.com/">sidesh0w.com</a></li>
  <li><a href="http://www.veen.com/jeff/">Jeffrey Veen</a></li>
 </ul>
</div><!-- END #blogroll -->
```

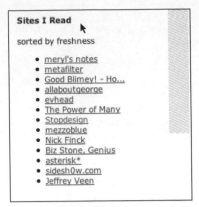

Figure 9-50: The default rendering of the blogroll

With the markup in place, I'm again going to work my way from the outside-in, starting with the `blogroll` container. First I want to create a bugger of space at the top as well as the bottom. Because I want the image to show at the bottom, I'm going to use the `padding` property to let the background image show through, as shown in Figure 9-51.

```
#blogroll {
  margin: 1.66em 0 0 0;
  padding: 0 0 45px 0;
  background: transparent url("../img/blogRoll_bkgd.gif") 0 0 repeat-y;
}
```

Figure 9-51: Styles applied to the blogroll container

The next step brings me to the header and the first paragraph. I want to place a white color in the background so that, as the background color stretches across the width of the column, it overlaps the background image in the parent container, `sidecol`.

Also, this CSS rule accomplishes two other items at the same time. It removes the background image placed in the `blogroll` container from showing through the headlines. It also adds padding to the left side of the text so that the heading and a paragraph are aligned left with the text in the main navigation, as shown in Figure 9-52.

```
#blogroll h4, #blogroll p {
 background-color: white;
 margin: 0 17px 0 0;
 padding: 0 0 0 13px;
}
```

Figure 9-52: Revised headings for the blogroll

The next CSS rule reduces the footprint of my blogroll, but also removes the bullets from the list items:

```
#blogroll ul {
 list-style-type: none;
 margin: 0;
 padding: 0;
 height: 100px;
 overflow: auto;
}
```

I've reduced the footprint of the blogroll, but I want to move the vertical scroll bar to the left a bit so that the right edge of the scroll bar is aligned with the right side of the navigation menu. I do this push by applying a margin of 17 pixels to the right side (as shown in Figure 9-53):

```
#blogroll ul {
 list-style-type: none;
 margin: 0 17px 0 0;
 padding: 0;
 height: 100px;
 overflow: auto;
}
```

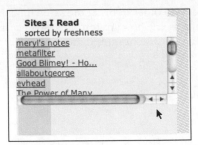

Figure 9-53: The shortened blogroll list

As you can tell from Figure 9-54, the space allotted on my Web page for the links is smaller, but there is an addition of a two scroll bars to the right and bottom of the list. The property overflow is the reason for both scroll bars.

Figure 9-54: The removal of the horizontal scroll bar

By default, the overflow property is set to auto. Typically when you have text that's a bit long (such as an article), the browser expands the containing box to make room for the content.

Yet, I want to make sure that *doesn't* happen. So, I put in the value of auto for the overflow property, which doesn't do much by itself. It's only with the addition of the height property set to 100 pixels that the browser creates the scroll bar that stops the text from visually running long.

While I want the smaller footprint for my blogroll, which I now have, the addition of two scroll bars is a bit too much. I want to keep the vertical scroll bar for the blogroll so that users can move up and down the list of links, but the horizontal scroll bar is fairly useless and should be removed.

The horizontal scroll bar is showing because of the vertical scroll bar. Because the vertical scroll bar takes away some of the 100 pixels allocated for the width of the blogroll, the browser displays the horizontal scroll bar so that users can scroll to the right and view the content that is behind the vertical scroll bar.

Even though there's absolutely nothing behind the scroll bar I want to see, the browser can't make that decision on its own. So, to stop the browser from showing the vertical scroll bar, I must reduce the size of the content area.

I apply a padding of 25 pixels to the right-hand side. This should be enough width for any browser's vertical scroll bar.

Also, when I removed the horizontal scroll bar, I added a margin of 13 pixels to the right side (Listing 9-4) and background color to the list items to create the L-shaped pattern, as shown in Figure 9-54.

Listing 9-4: CSS for the Blogroll List Items

```
#blogroll li {
 background-color: #ffffcc;
 margin: 0 0 0 13px;
 padding: 0 25px 0 0;
}
```

I took out the bullets for the list items earlier in the code, I need to place another marker to take their place; otherwise the links are going to appear to run together. I don't want to go back to a browser's default markers.

To add a custom list marker, I can use the `list-style-image` property, but I also need to replace the previous `list-style-type` declaration with a new one (as a backup, in case my image fails to load), as shown in Figure 9-55:

```
#blogroll ul {
 /* list-style-type: none; */
 list-style-type: disc;
 list-style-image: url("../img/bullet_green_dark.gif");
 margin: 0 17px 0 0;
 padding: 0;
 height: 100px;
 overflow: auto;
}
```

The main problem with this CSS rule (as Figure 9-55 shows) is that the marker is pushed off to the left of the screen and fairly invisible to the user. This is because of the left margin value of 13 pixels in Listing 9-4. Reducing the size of the margin isn't going to work because I need that space to move the list elements over.

Figure 9-55: The replacement of the list marker

One fix could introduce more elements (such as a span or div) into the unordered list to add more hooks. With those hooks, I can then associate styles to create finer control over the margin and padding. That process, however well-intentioned, would take us further away from semantic markup. To solve the problem, I find a different approach.

Instead of applying a custom marker image to the list via the list-style-image property, I apply padding to the left side of each link in the blogroll. Then I turn off the list markers altogether (like before) and apply a background image to each link in the blogroll, as shown in Figure 9-56:

```
#blogroll li a {
    padding-left: 20px;
    list-style-image: url("/_assets/img/bullet_green_dark.gif");
}
```

Figure 9-56: A better list marker solution

With that, the blogroll is done, with a smaller footprint and with a better-looking style.

The Footer

The footer (or content that is at the bottom of the page) is pretty straightforward. It usually contains some sort of copyright or common creative license information. Sometimes Web designers place links to validators or a listing of the tools that help them maintain the page. There is nothing fancy in terms of content:

```
<div id="footer">
 <p class="credit">Copyright &copy; 2005 Chrisopher Schmitt. All rights
reserved.<br />
 Powered by <cite><a href="http://wordpress.org" title="State-of-the-art semantic
personal publishing platform"><strong>WordPress</strong></a></cite>.
 </p>
</div><!-- END #footer -->
```

When styling the footer, it's good to think about what could happen in the content in the other sections. In this case I'm concerned about content in the main column and elements that might be floated. For example, the blog post footer uses floats to balance the meta and comment areas on the same line.

With the floats, however, the content in the footer also starts to flow around the meta information, as shown in Figure 9-57.

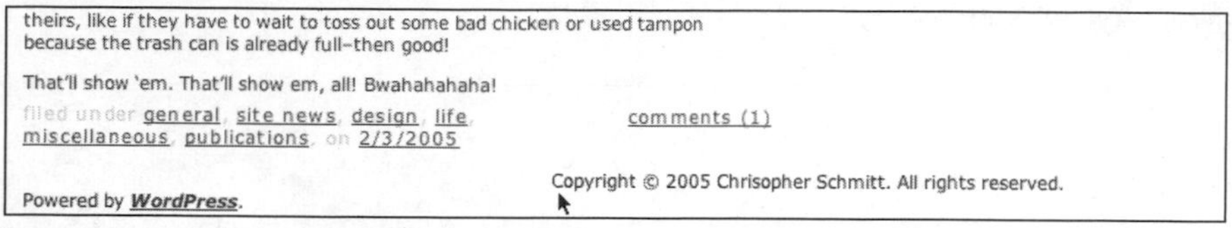

Figure 9-57: The footer is raised to the content in the main column container.

So, the workaround is to set a clear property for the footer container with the value of both, as shown in Figure 9-58:

```
#footer {
    text-align: left;
    clear: both;
    border-top: 1px solid #c2fa00;
    margin: 0;
    padding: 0.33em 15px 0.66em 15px;
    color: #acacac;
    font-size: bold 10px Verdana, Arial, Helvetica, sans-serif;
}

#footer p {
    margin: 0;
    padding: 13px 0;
}
```

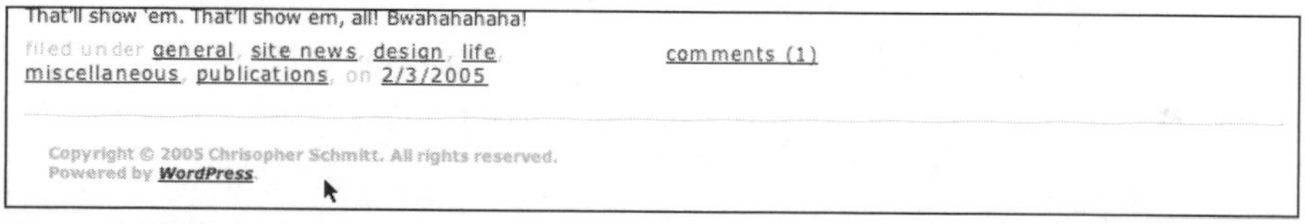

Figure 9-58: Fixing the footer

The clear property is used to design the control of elements that are floated. Elements with the clear property set to clear won't be wrapped around elements preceding it that are floating to the left or to the right.

Other values for the clear property are none, left, right, and inherit. The default value is none and that means the element will be wrapped around floated content. For clear values of left or right, content won't be wrapped if the content preceding it is floating to the left or right, respectively.

The value of inherit takes whatever the clear property value is for its parent element. If the parent element does not have a value, the child element goes with none (because it is the default value).

Page as a Whole

With the footer done, my page design is complete, as shown in Figure 9-59, and is ready to be incorporated into the blogging software!

Figure 9-59: The finished home page design

Summary

The development of the Web page has been a long road that began with some random thoughts in my head and led to the finished product.

Starting out with planning, I developed the site's scope. With the scope in place, the parameters for the project were set in place as well as determining the content and site map. Afterward, I focused on the design of site and creating emotion through typography, colors, and layout.

With the preparation finished, the process of development started. When designing with CSS, I followed my mantra of outside-in and top-down by applying styles to the body of the page, and then the header, the main column, the side column, and, finally, the footer.

While the development of the Web page may seem to have taken a long time, it would have taken longer without the proper planning and the methodical approach to the production.

Remember that when you work on your own projects, set the goal and work diligently. Good luck!

All of the source code used in this chapter is available for download at www.wrox.com. Once at the site, simply locate the book's title (either by using the Search box or by using one of the title lists) and click the Download Code link on the book's detail page to obtain all the source code for the book. Because many books have similar titles, you may find it easiest to search by ISBN; this book's ISBN is 0-7645-8833-8.

HTML 4.01 Elements

Before you design with CSS, the content in a Web document must be marked up with HTML elements. To efficiently make use of CSS, those HTML elements must be used correctly by placing the correct HTML element around the appropriate content.

The following table provides a listing of all the HTML elements in the 4.01 specification provided by the World Wide Web Consortium (W3C), the governing body that determines Web-related standards. The far-left column shows the name of the element. The next column indicates whether the element has a start tag. The next three columns describe the element in more detail. If the column has an "O," it means the part of the element is optional. "F" means forbidden, "E" means empty, and "D" means deprecated. The DTD column provides information on which Document Type Definition an element belongs in. If the element is found only in one kind of DTD, the key will either be "L" for Loose DTD or "F" for Frameset DTD. The final column provides a text description of the element.

Name	Start Tag	End Tag	Empty	Deprecated	DTD	Description
A						Anchor
ABBR						Abbreviated form (for example, WWW, HTTP, and so on)
ACRONYM						Indicates an acronym
ADDRESS						Information on author

Table continued on following page

Name	Start Tag	End Tag	Empty	Deprecated	DTD	Description
APPLET				D	L	Java applet
AREA		F	E			Client-side image map area
B						Bold text style
BASE		F	E			Document base URI
BASEFONT		F	E	D	L	Base font size
BDO						I18N BiDi override
BIG						Large text style
BLOCKQUOTE						Long quotation
BODY	O	O				Document body
BR		F	E			Forced line break
BUTTON						Push button
CAPTION						Table caption
CENTER				D	L	Centers content
CITE						Citation
CODE						Computer code fragment
COL		F	E			Table column
COLGROUP		O				Table column group
DD		O				Definition description
DEL						Deleted text
DFN						Instance definition
DIR				D	L	Directory list
DIV						A division
DL						Definition list
DT		O				Definition term
EM						Emphasis
FIELDSET						Form control group
FONT				D	L	Local change to font
FORM						Interactive form
FRAME		F	E		F	Subwindow

Name	Start Tag	End Tag	Empty	Deprecated	DTD	Description
FRAMESET					F	Frame container; replacement of body for frames
H1						Heading level 1
H2						Heading level 2
H3						Heading level 3
H4						Heading level 4
H5						Heading level 5
H6						Heading level 6
HEAD	O	O				Document head
HR	F	E				Horizontal rule
HTML	O	O				Document root element
I						Italic text style
IFRAME					L	Inline subwindow
IMG	F	E				Embedded image
INPUT	F	E				Form control
INS						Inserted text
ISINDEX	F	E	D		L	Single-line prompt
KBD						Text to be entered by the user
LABEL						Form field label text
LEGEND						Fieldset legend
LI	O					List item
LINK	F	E				A media-independent link
MAP						Client-side image map
MENU			D		L	Menu list
META	F	E				Generic meta-information
NOFRAMES					F	Alternate content container for nonframe-based rendering

Table continued on following page

Name	Start Tag	End Tag	Empty	Deprecated	DTD	Description
NOSCRIPT						Alternate content container for nonscript-based rendering
OBJECT						Generic embedded object
OL						Ordered list
OPTGROUP						Option group
OPTION		O				Selectable choice
P		O				Paragraph
PARAM	F		E			Named property value
PRE						Preformatted text
Q						Short inline quotation
S				D	L	Strikethrough text style
SAMP						Sample program output, scripts, and so on
SCRIPT						Script statements
SELECT						Option selector
SMALL						Small text style
SPAN						Generic language/an inline style container
STRIKE				D	L	Strikethrough text
STRONG						Strong emphasis
STYLE						Style info
SUB						Subscript
SUP						Superscript
TABLE						Container element for tables
TBODY	O	O				Table body
TD		O				Table data cell
TEXTAREA						Multiline text field
TFOOT		O				Table footer
TH		O				Table header cell

Name	Start Tag	End Tag	Empty	Deprecated	DTD	Description
THEAD		O				Table header
TITLE						Document title
TR		O				Table row
TT						Teletype or monospaced text style
U				D	L	Underlined text style
UL						Unordered list
VAR						Instance of a variable or program argument

The listing of HTML 4.01 elements (www.w3.org/TR/html4/index/elements.html) is copyright © December 24, 1999 World Wide Web Consortium, (Massachusetts Institute of Technology, European Research Consortium for Informatics and Mathematics, Keio University). All Rights Reserved. www.w3.org/Consortium/Legal/2002/copyright-documents-20021231

B

Rules for HTML-to-XHTML Conversion

Hypertext Markup Language (HTML) is a simple language that led to the boom of the Web in the 1990s. However, its simplicity was also a roadblock for progress. The early success of HTML attracted a larger Web developer audience and spawned a desire to push the medium. HTML outgrew its simple upbringing.

For example, while placing images in a Web page is easy to do with HTML, placing the images in a specific location on a Web page is impossible without violating the intent of the table tag. Another example is placing the multimedia content in a Web page, which usually results in the use of invalid, proprietary elements and attributes.

In addition, HTML contained a limited set of elements and attributes. Other industries such as engineering or chemical companies couldn't mark up their formulas. Instead of writing an all-encompassing version of HTML, the W3C worked on eXtensible Markup Language (XML), which is a flexible meta-language.

XML provides the framework for other markup languages to be created. Other industries can create their own markup languages rather than face a restrictive environment such as HTML.

However, for most Web developers who are familiar primarily with HTML, the major benefits of XML (creating new elements and specifying their treatment) are not important. Instead, the elements found in HTML will be of the most use.

The W3C reformulated HTML off of the XML standard to create backward-compatibility, while making the language embrace the structure found in XML. XHTML is the essence of HTML defined in the XML syntax.

In other words, XHTML is a set of rigid guidelines written to allow Web developers familiar with HTML to write valid XML documents without being completely lost.

Yet, reworking content from HTML into XHTML creates headaches when developers move into a stricter coding environment. The XHTML syntax (or rules for coding) is less forgiving of coding mistakes than old-school HTML and browsers.

To help you achieve more solid understanding of coding XHTML correctly, this appendix serves as a guide to transition the Web developer from an old-school HTML developer to a proper XHTML user.

The XML Declaration

No doubt, as a Web developer you know the importance of having the html element at the top of your Web document. With XHTML you may place the following line above the html element:

```
<?xml version="1.0" encoding="iso-8859-1"?>
```

That line simply states that you are using version 1.0 of XHML with the character set of iso-8859-1.

Note that XML declaration is recommended, but not required. Because it's a simple line that goes at the top of your Web document, why wouldn't you include it? Well, here are some potential problems when using the XTML declaration:

❑ Some browsers might render the markup as it appears when you "view source" a Web page instead of rendering the document.

❑ Other browsers might parse the Web document as an XML tree instead of rendering the document.

❑ In Internet Explorer for Windows 6.0, the browser will display the Web document in quirks mode, even if the Web document is valid.

❑ If you use PHP to create dynamic pages, you might notice that the start of that line with the left bracket and question mark is how you begin writing PHP code. This code, if left as-is in your PHP document, confuses your server and will not successfully parse your page. The workaround for this situation is to use the echo function in PHP at the start of the document to write out the first line:

```
<?php echo "<?xml version=\"1.0\" encoding=\"iso-8859-1\"?>\n"; ?>
```

Picking Your Comfort Level

XHTML comes in three different flavors: *strict, transitional,* and *frameset.* These varieties are based on three Document Type Definitions (DTDs). DTDs define XHTML, and determine which elements and attributes are allowed and how they should be used. Think of a DTD as a dictionary of allowable terms for a certain document.

To create a valid XHTML document, you must include a DOCTYPE Declaration, which makes up a line or two at the top of your document below the XML declaration (should you decide to use one). The line of code indicates what kind of DTD you are using, and sets the groundwork for how the browser and validators should handle your content.

To define your Web document in *strict* means that you will follow the letter of the law as well as the spirit. You are a true believer in XHTML and no longer want to use any HTML elements that were used for presentation. With the *strict* DTD, you are using XHTML elements to mark up content and not format the presentation of the page. Place the following line below the XML declaration, but before the html element:

```
<!DOCTYPE html
  PUBLIC "-//W3C//DTD XHTML 1.0 Transitional//EN"
  "http://www.w3.org/TR/xhtml1/DTD/xhtml1-transitional.dtd">
```

The *transitional* DTD is best if you want to dive into XHTML, but want some more freedom to use deprecated elements and attributes along the way, or to use certain classic HTML tags:

```
<!DOCTYPE html
  PUBLIC "-//W3C//DTD XHTML 1.0 Transitional//EN"
  "http://www.w3.org/TR/xhtml1/DTD/xhtml1-transitional.dtd">
```

The *frameset* DTD is for the Web documents that require you to use frames in your Web pages:

```
<!DOCTYPE html
  PUBLIC "-//W3C//DTD XHTML 1.0 Frameset//EN"
  "http://www.w3.org/TR/xhtml1/DTD/xhtml1-frameset.dtd">
```

Note that the frameset DTD is to be used in Web documents that contain the frameset only. You do not need to use the frameset DTD for each Web document that comprises a "frame" in a frameset. For those documents, you should use either a strict or transitional DTD.

Rules for XHTML

Now that you have set up the XML declaration and the DTD, the next step is to properly format your Web document. The following sections cover how to properly mark up your content and use XHTML correctly.

Don't Forget the Namespace Attribute

Stating what type of document type you're using at the top of the document indicates which elements and attributes are allowed in the document. Along with the DOCTYPE declaration, the namespace is an additional means of identifying your document's markup, in this case XHTML.

In order to identify the namespace, place what's called a *namespace attribute,* xmlns, in the html element, in the opening html tag:

```
<html xmlns="http://www.w3.org/1999/xhtml" lang="en">
```

Quoting Attribute Values

All values for attributes in an element are required to be wrapped in quotation marks. So, you would not use this example:

```
<img src=file.gif width=133 height=133 />
```

Instead, you should follow this correct example:

```
<img src="file.gif" width="133" height="133" />
```

No Attribute Minimization

For some elements in HTML (such as the horizontal rules tag, hr), attributes can be minimized, and simply listing the attribute name is valid:

```
<hr noshade />
```

In XHTML, however, there is no attribute minimization. When you are faced with an attribute that typically has never needed a value, set the value of the attribute to the name. In the case of this example using the hr element, the value for the attribute noshade is noshade:

```
<hr noshade="noshade" />
```

Terminating Empty Elements

Empty elements are elements that do not come in pairs (such as img, br, or hr).

Non-empty elements (such as p or h2) are fairly common in HTML. They are used for marking the starting and ending of content in a Web page, such as using the following p tag to indicate a paragraph:

```
<p>That's when I thought I should decline a second helping of her infamous
spaghetti and meatball salad.</p>
```

With XHTML, all elements must be terminated, including empty elements.

To keep on using empty elements in XHTML, empty elements must be modified slightly. Add a space and a forward slash at the end of the element:

```
<img src="file.gif" alt="Company logo" width="125" height="36" />
```

Note that including the space before the trailing slash isn't a requirement for the code to be valid, but a technique to keep older browsers such as Netscape Navigator 4 from failing to render the element.

Cleaning Nests

Nesting elements properly is simple and should already be a part of any Web developer's practices. In the following line, the ending tag for the strong element is outside of the closing p element.

```
<p>That's when I thought I should <strong>decline a second helping of her infamous
spaghetti and meatball salad.</p></strong>
```

Whereas, this is the correct method for marking up the content:

```
<p>That's when I thought I should <strong>decline</strong> a second helping of her
infamous spaghetti and meatball salad.</p>
```

XHTML with CSS and JavaScript Files

Associating CSS and JavaScript files is the preferred method by which you incorporate presentation and behaviors to your Web pages:

```
<script src="/js/validator.js" type="text/javascript"></script>
<link rel="stylesheet" href="/css/layout.css" type="text/css" />
```

If you must use internal JavaScript, wrap the code with the starting marker, <![CDATA[, and ending marker,]]>.

Keep It on the Downlow

From now on, all elements and attribute names in XHTML must be set in lowercase. This means you should not use all uppercase, or mix uppercase and lowercase. The following are examples of incorrect usage:

```
<HTML> </HTML>
<Strong></Strong>
```

Following is an example of correct usage:

```
<body></body>
```

Note that using a mixture of lowercase and uppercase for the values of attributes is still valid:

```
<a href="IWantToBelieve.html">Photos of Aliens</a>
```

Introduce ID When Using name

In XHTML the name attribute is deprecated and will be removed from the specification altogether in the future. In its place, you must use the id attribute. Until the name attribute is no longer a valid attribute, use id in addition to the name attribute:

```
<a name="admin" id="admin">Administration at CLC</a>
```

Encode Ampersands

When you are using an ampersand (&) for the value of an attribute, be sure to use the character entity, &.

When encoding ampersands, and when working with dynamic pages, pass parameters through the URL string in the browser like so:

```
<a href="add-cart.html?isbn=0764588338&amp;id=023">Add this
item to your cart</a>
```

When in Doubt, Validate

We all are human. We make mistakes with coding. To help point out troubles with XHTML, or just to make sure what has been created is coded correctly, take your page to a validator such as http://validator.w3.org/ and test often.

Also, most WYSIWYG and some non-WYSIWYG Web authoring tools have built-in validators. Read the documentation that came with the software to learn more about these validators.

CSS 2.1 Properties

When marking up content with HTML, you must be aware of the elements that are at your disposal. The same goes for designing with CSS: you must be fully aware of the properties and their values to effectively design for the Web.

In this vein, the following table lists all the CSS 2.1 properties that are at your disposal. In the far-left column is the name of the CSS property. Next are the values associated with that property and then the initial value. The next column states what HTML element that CSS property applies to. The Inherited column states whether the property can be inherited to other elements. The far-right column indicates the applicable media group.

Name	Values	Initial Value	Applies to (Default: All)	Inherited	Media Groups
'azimuth'	\<angle\> | [[left- side | far-left | left | center-left | center | center-right | right | far-right | right-side] || behind] | leftwards | rightwards | inherit	center	All	Yes	Aural
'background-attachment'	scroll | fixed | inherit	scroll	All	No	Visual

Table continued on following page

Name	Values	Initial Value	Applies to (Default: All)	Inherited	Media Groups
'background-color'	`<color>` | transparent | inherit	transparent	All	No	Visual
'background-image'	`<uri>` | none | inherit	none	All	No	Visual
'background-position'	[[`<percentage>` | `<length>` | left | center | right] [`<percentage>` | `<length>` | top | center | bottom]?] | [[left | center | right] || [top | center | bottom]] | inherit	0% 0%	All	No	Visual
'background-repeat'	repeat | repeat-x | repeat-y | no-repeat | inherit	repeat	All	No	Visual
'background'	['background-color' || 'background-image' || 'background-repeat' || 'background-attachment' || 'background-position'] | inherit	Shorthand property; see individual properties	All	No	Visual
'border-collapse'	collapse | separate | inherit	separate	'table' and 'inline-table' elements	Yes	Visual
'border-color'	[`<color>` | transparent] {1,4} | inherit	Shorthand property; see individual properties	All	No	Visual
'border-spacing'	`<length>` `<length>`? | inherit	0	'table' and 'inline-table' elements	Yes	Visual
'border-style'	`<border-style>`{1,4} | inherit	Shorthand property; see individual properties	All	No	Visual

Name	Values	Initial Value	Applies to (Default: All)	Inherited	Media Groups
`'border-top'` `'border-right'` `'border-bottom'` `'border-left'`	`[ <border-width> |` `| <border-style> |` `| 'border-top-color' ]` `| inherit`	Shorthand property; see individual properties	All	No	Visual
`'border-top-color' 'border-right-color' 'border-bottom-color' 'border-left-color'`	`<color>	transparent` `	inherit`	The value of the `'color'` property	All	No	Visual
`'border-top-style' 'border-right-style' 'border-bottom-style' 'border-left-style'`	`<border-style> |` `inherit`	none	All	No	Visual
`'border-top-width' 'border-right-width' 'border-bottom-width' 'border-left-width'`	`<border-width> |` `inherit`	medium	All	No	Visual
`'border-width'`	`<border-width>` `{1,4}	inherit`	Shorthand property; see individual properties	All	No	Visual
`'border'`	`[ <border-width> |` `| <border-style> |` `| 'border-top-color' ]` `| inherit`	Shorthand property; see individual properties	All	No	Visual
`'bottom'`	`<length>	` `<percentage>	` `auto	inherit`	auto	Positioned elements	No	Visual
`'caption-side'`	`top	bottom	` `inherit`	top	`'table-caption'` elements	Yes	Visual
`'clear'`	`none	left	right |` `both	inherit`	none	Block-level elements	No	Visual
`'clip'`	`<shape>	auto	` `inherit`	auto	Absolutely positioned elements	No	Visual

Table continued on following page

Name	Values	Initial Value	Applies to (Default: All)	Inherited	Media Groups
'color'	<color> | inherit	Depends on user agent	All	Yes	Visual
'content'	normal | [<string> | <uri> | <counter> | attr(<identifier>) | open-quote | close-quote | no-open-quote | no-close-quote]+ | inherit	normal	:before and :after pseudo-elements	No	All
'counter-increment'	[<identifier> <integer>?]+ | none | inherit	none	All	No	All
'counter-reset'	[<identifier> <integer>?]+ | none | inherit	none	All	No	All
'cue-after'	<uri> | none | inherit	none	All	No	Aural
'cue-before'	<uri> | none | inherit	none	All	No	Aural
'cue'	['cue-before' || 'cue-after'] | inherit	Shorthand property; see individual properties	All	No	Aural
'cursor'	[[<uri> ,]* [auto | crosshair | default | active pointer | move | e-resize | ne-resize | nw-resize | n-resize | se-resize | sw-resize | s-resize | w-resize | text | wait | help | progress]] | inherit	auto	All	Yes	Visual, Inter-
'direction'	ltr | rtl | inherit	ltr	All	Yes	Visual
'display'	inline | block | list-item | run-in | inline-block | table | inline-table | table-row-group | table-header-group | table-footer-group | table-row | table-column-group | table-column | table-cell | table-caption | none | inherit	inline	All	No	All

Name	Values	Initial Value	Applies to (Default: All)	Inherited	Media Groups
`'elevation'`	`<angle>` | `below` | `level` | `above` | `higher` | `lower` | `inherit`	`level`	All	Yes	Aural
`'empty-cells'`	`show` | `hide` | `inherit`	`show`	`'table-cell'` elements	Yes	Visual
`'float'`	`left` | `right` | `none` | `inherit`	`none`	All but positioned elements and generated content	No	Visual
`'font-family'`	`[[ <family-name>` | `<generic-family> ]` `[,<family-name>`|`<generic-family>]* ]` | `inherit`	Depends on user agent	All	Yes	Visual
`'font-size'`	`<absolute-size>` | `<relative-size>` | `<length>` | `<percentage>` | `inherit`	`medium`	All	Yes	Visual
`'font-style'`	`normal` | `italic` | `oblique` | `inherit`	`normal`	All	Yes	Visual
`'font-variant'`	`normal` | `small-caps` | `inherit`	`normal`	All	Yes	Visual
`'font-weight'`	`normal` | `bold` | `bolder` | `lighter` | `100` | `200` | `300` | `400` | `500` | `600` | `700` | `800` | `900` | `inherit`	`normal`	All	Yes	Visual
`'font'`	`[ [ 'font-style' ||` `'font-variant' ||` `'font-weight' ]?` `'font-size' [ / 'line-height' ]?'font-family' ] |` `caption	icon |` `menu	message-box |` `small-caption |` `status-bar	inherit`	Shorthand property; see individual properties	All	Yes	Visual

Table continued on following page

Name	Values	Initial Value	Applies to (Default: All)	Inherited	Media Groups
'height'	<length> | <percentage> | auto | inherit	auto	All elements but non-replaced inline elements, table columns, and column groups	No	Visual
'left'	<length> | <percentage> | auto | inherit	auto	Positioned elements	No	Visual
'letter-spacing'	normal | <length> | inherit	normal	All	Yes	Visual
'line-height'	normal | <number> | <length> | <percentage> | inherit	normal	All	Yes	Visual
'list-style-image'	<uri> | none | inherit	none	Elements with 'display: list-item'	Yes	Visual
'list-style-position'	inside | outside | inherit	outside	Elements with 'display: list-item'	Yes	Visual
'list-style-type'	disc | circle | square | decimal | decimal-leading-zero | lower-roman | upper-roman | lower-greek | lower-latin | upper-latin | armenian | georgian | none | inherit	disc	Elements with 'display: list-item'	Yes	Visual
'list-style'	['list-style-type' || 'list-style-position' || 'list-style-image'] | inherit	Shorthand property; see individual properties	Elements with 'display: list-item'	Yes	Visual
'margin-right' 'margin-left'	<margin-width> | inherit	0	All elements except elements with table display types other than table and inline-table	No	Visual

Name	Values	Initial Value	Applies to (Default: All)	Inherited	Media Groups
'margin-top' 'margin-bottom'	`<margin-width>` `| inherit`	0	All elements except elements with table display types other than `table` and `inline-table`	No	Visual
'margin'	`<margin-width>{1,4}` `| inherit`	Shorthand property; see individual properties	All elements except elements with table display types other than `table` and `inline-table`	No	Visual
'max-height'	`<length> |` `<percentage> |` `none	inherit`	none	All elements except non-replaced inline elements and table elements	No	Visual
'max-width'	`<length> |` `<percentage> |` `none	inherit`	none	All elements except non-replaced inline elements and table elements	No	Visual
'min-height'	`<length> |` `<percentage> |` `inherit`	0	All elements except non-replaced inline elements and table elements	No	Visual
'min-width'	`<length> |` `<percentage> |` `inherit`	0	All elements except non-replaced inline elements and table elements	No	Visual
'orphans'	`<integer>	inherit`	2	Block-level elements	Yes	Visual, Paged
'outline-color'	`<color>	invert |` `inherit`	invert	All	No	Visual, Inter-active
'outline-style'	`<border-style> |` `inherit`	none	All	No	Visual, Inter-active

Table continued on following page

Name	Values	Initial Value	Applies to (Default: All)	Inherited	Media Groups
'outline-width'	`<border-width>` | `inherit`	`medium`	All	No	Visual, Inter-active
'outline'	['outline-color' | | 'outline-style' | | 'outline-width'] | `inherit`	Shorthand property; see individual properties	All	No	Visual, Inter-active
'overflow'	`visible` | `hidden` | `scroll` | `auto` | `inherit`	`visible`	Block-level and replaced elements, table cells, inline blocks	No	Visual
'padding-top' 'padding-right' 'padding-bottom' 'padding-left'	`<padding-width>` | `inherit`	0	All elements except elements with table display types other than `table`, `inline-table`, and `table-cell`	No	Visual
'padding'	`<padding-width> {1,4}` | `inherit`	Shorthand property; see individual properties	All elements except elements with table display types other than `table`, `inline-table`, and `table-cell`	No	Visual
'page-break-after'	`auto` | `always` | `avoid` | `left` | `right` | `inherit`	`auto`	Block-level elements	No	Visual, Paged
'page-break-before'	`auto` | `always` | `avoid` | `left` | `right` | `inherit`	`auto`	Block-level elements	No	Visual, Paged
'page-break-inside'	`avoid` | `auto` | `inherit`	`auto`	Block-level elements	Yes	Visual, Paged
'pause-after'	`<time>` | `<percentage>` | `inherit`	0	All	All	Aural, No
'pause-before'	`<time>` | `<percentage>` | `inherit`	0	All	No	Aural

Name	Values	Initial Value	Applies to (Default: All)	Inherited	Media Groups
'pause'	[[<time> | <percentage>] {1,2}] | inherit	Shorthand property; see individual properties	All	No	Aural
'pitch-range'	<number> | inherit	50	All	Yes	Aural
'pitch'	<frequency> | x-low | low | medium | high | x-high | inherit	medium	All	Yes	Aural
'play-during'	<uri> [mix || repeat]? | auto | none | inherit	auto	All	No	Aural
'position'	static | relative | absolute | fixed | inherit	static	All	No	Visual
'quotes'	[<string> <string>]+ | none | inherit	Depends on user agent	All	Yes	Visual
'richness'	<number> | inherit	50	All	Yes	Aural
'right'	<length> | <percentage> | auto | inherit	auto	Positioned elements	No	Visual
'speak-header'	once | always | inherit	once	Elements that have table header information	Yes	Aural
'speak-numeral'	digits | continuous | inherit	continuous	All	Yes	Aural
'speak-punctuation'	code | none | inherit	none	All	Yes	Aural
'speak'	normal | none | spell-out | inherit	normal	All	Yes	Aural
'speech-rate'	<number> | x-slow | slow | medium | fast | x-fast | faster | slower | inherit	medium	All	Yes	Aural
'stress'	<number> | inherit	50	All	Yes	Aural
'table-layout'	auto | fixed | inherit	auto	'table' and 'inline-table' elements	No	Visual

Table continued on following page

Name	Values	Initial Value	Applies to (Default: All)	Inherited	Media Groups
'text-align'	left | right | center | justify | inherit	'left' if 'direction' is 'ltr'; 'right' if 'direction' is 'rtl'	Block-level elements, table cells, and inline blocks	Yes	Visual
'text-decoration'	none | [underline | | overline || line-through || blink] | inherit	none	All	No	Visual
'text-indent'	\<length> | \<percentage> | inherit	0	Block-level elements, table cells, and inline blocks	Yes	Visual
'text-transform'	capitalize | uppercase | lowercase | none | inherit	none	All	Yes	Visual
'top'	\<length> | \<percentage> | auto | inherit	auto	Positioned elements	No	Visual
'unicode-bidi'	normal | embed | bidi-override | inherit	normal	All elements, but see prose	No	Visual
'vertical-align'	baseline | sub | super | top | text-top | middle | bottom | text-bottom | \<percentage> | \<length> | inherit	baseline	Inline-level and 'table-cell' elements	No	Visual
'visibility'	visible | hidden | collapse | inherit	visible	All	Yes	Visual
'voice-family'	[[\<specific-voice> | \<generic-voice>],]* [\<specific-voice> | \<generic-voice>] | inherit	Depends on user agent	All	Yes	Aural
'volume'	\<number> | \<percentage> | silent | x-soft | soft | medium | loud | x-loud | inherit	medium	All	Yes	Aural

Name	Values	Initial Value	Applies to (Default: All)	Inherited	Media Groups
'white-space'	normal | pre | nowrap | pre-wrap | pre-line | inherit	normal	All	Yes	Visual
'widows'	<integer> | inherit	2	Block-level elements	Yes	Visual, Paged
'width'	<length> | <percentage> | auto | inherit	auto	All elements but non-replaced inline elements, table rows, and row groups	No	Visual
'word-spacing'	normal | <length> | inherit	normal	All	Yes	Visual
'z-index'	auto | <integer> | inherit	auto	Positioned elements	No	Visual

Troubleshooting CSS Guide

Does everything appear fine in the code, but not in the page design? Relax. CSS beginners and gurus alike have all been through this. This troubleshooting guide will save the frustrations and help determine the cause of your CSS crisis.

Validation

When you run into a problem, the first thing that must be done is to ensure that your HTML and CSS syntax are correct. Even if you use a product such as Macromedia Dreamweaver or Microsoft FrontPage that can hide the markup and code while you design, the syntax the software generates in the background still must be checked.

If your Web development software does not come with its own validators (check your software's documentation for details), be sure to set the preferences so the Web development software excludes proprietary elements, like `center`, so that the validator is checking the standard DTD.

Use the following Web sites.

HTML

For HTML validation service, see `http://validator.w3.org/`.

Once at this site, enter into the form the URL of the page that is causing your trouble. If you use the URL, make sure the Web address is actually visible on the Web, meaning that the file is not behind a firewall or a password-protected zone such as an intranet. If your HTML file falls into one of those categories, use the upload feature provided by the validation service.

For information about HTML elements, see Appendix A. If you need information on how to convert HTML to XHTML, see Appendix B.

CSS

For CSS validation service, see http://jigsaw.w3.org/css-validator/.

Like the HTML validator, validation can be conducted through the submission of a URL or uploading a style sheet file. Be sure not to submit a file that includes both CSS and HTML because that will confuse the validator and create grounds for automatic failure of validation.

Another option to test CSS syntax is to copy and paste the code in the direct input form located at the bottom of the page. This option might be best suited for your needs and might be a bit faster, too, if your CSS is not accessible on the Web, or if your file is actually an HTML file with some CSS code.

Manipulating the Elements

At this stage, the syntax is accurate, but that doesn't mean much. Even if your French is spot on, you could still find yourself *accurately* ordering your aunt's handbag for lunch to the bewilderment of your waiter at an outdoor café near the Louvre.

The next move is direct manipulation of the CSS itself. Use one or a combination of the following techniques to help isolate your CSS problems.

Zeroing Out the Padding and Margins

The default style sheet used by browsers places default values for margins and paddings on block-level elements. To ensure that those default values are not interfering with your design, set the margin and padding for the block-level elements to zero.

A fast way to zero out the padding and margins is to use the universal selector like so:

```
* {
margin: 0;
padding: 0;
}
```

Then, place that CSS rule at the start of the style sheet. By placing the CSS rule at the start of the CSS, other CSS rules that have values for padding, margin, or both in the style sheet can override the effects of zeroing out the padding or margins.

Look for any changes in your page design and make any required adjustments.

Applying Color to Borders and Backgrounds

The purpose of this method is to highlight the CSS rules you are working on and see if they are indeed the design elements of the Web page that are causing the problems. Once you have identified the right problematic element, you can move on to the next steps in fixing the problem.

Apply a color to the block-level element (or elements) in your CSS that is causing you grief. An example of this CSS rule might look something like this:

```
#content #navigation {
 border: 1px solid red;
}
```

This CSS rule creates a red border around the specified block-level element to better see it in the page design. If you already have too much red in the design to notice a red outline, try blue, or green, or simply change the background color instead, as shown here:

```
#content #navigation {
 background-color green;
}
```

Placing Variations in Property Values

After finding the CSS that is causing problems, the next step is to adjust the values of the properties. Is the problem that the padding is too much in one browser? Or, maybe the font size is too small in another browser?

When placing different values than the ones you are using, start with cartoonish large amounts. For example, change 25 px for padding to 2500px to see if the design breaks as you know it should.

Then the next moves should be small. Use tiny increments, for example, in adjusting font sizes from 0.8 em to .81 em.

Playing Hide and Seek

The way in which we write CSS rules can also cause problems. CSS is set up to allow certain properties and their values to become inherited by their children. For example, if you set the font properties for the body element, then child elements within that body will take up those characteristics as well.

While CSS has built-in conflict resolution with the cascade, inheritance, and specificity, CSS rules can still have unintended results in the design. If there's a problem with your design, you might have to check the CSS rules you have written. There's a possibility that the CSS rules are conflicting or are inheriting values you don't want.

If this is the case, simply comment out unnecessary property and value pairs from problematic CSS rules and refresh the page design to look for changes.

Validating Again

At this stage, the CSS might have been rewritten, revised, or completely mangled during the troubleshooting process. Double-check the validation again, just to be sure nothing was missed.

Looking Outside for Help

At this stage, if you haven't found the cause of the CSS problem, it's time to seek help. Use the following resources to investigate the problem or ask for help.

Web Site Resources

This section provides information on some key Web site resources.

positioniseverything.net

Maybe the problem isn't the CSS, but instead it is the browser. For a list and explanation of modern browser bugs, check out www.positioniseverything.net/.

Web Developer Toolbar

If you use Netscape 7+, Mozilla, or Firefox browsers for development, run (don't walk) to Chris Pederick's browser extension called Web Developer at www.chrispederick.com/work/firefox/webdeveloper/.

Offering numerous features that benefit the Web designer and CSS wrangler, this an indispensable tool when troubleshooting CSS. Some of the tips mentioned in this troubleshooting guide can be implemented with the click of the button on the Web Developer's toolbar, rather than editing code by hand.

Mailing Lists

This section provides information on some key mailing list resources.

css-discuss

If everything else has not worked to your satisfaction, then try the kind folks at css-discuss. This is a mailing list dedicated to practical discussions of CSS-enabled design. The people that occupy the mailing list range from professionals to beginners, so chances are they have seen every problem you might encounter.

For more information on the list and instructions on how to join, see www.css-discuss.org.

Babble List

Geared to advanced Web design issues, this community offers a lively exchange of information, resources, theories, and practices of designers and developers including CSS development. The overall goal is to hone skills and share visions of where this new medium is going.

For more information on the list and instructions on how to join, see www.babblelist.com.

Index

M